Multinational Enterprises, Sustainability and Innovation

Multinational Enterprises, Sustainability and Innovation

Editors

Jeoung Yul Lee
Dilek Zamantili Nayir
Charles Chen

MDPI • Basel • Beijing • Wuhan • Barcelona • Belgrade • Manchester • Tokyo • Cluj • Tianjin

Editors
Jeoung Yul Lee
School of Business Management
Hongik University
Sejong
Korea, South

Dilek Zamantili Nayir
Economic and Administrative Sciences
Turkish German University
Istanbul
Turkey

Charles Chen
College of General Studies
University of Phoenix
Kapolei, Hawaii
United States

Editorial Office
MDPI
St. Alban-Anlage 66
4052 Basel, Switzerland

This is a reprint of articles from the Special Issue published online in the open access journal *Sustainability* (ISSN 2071-1050) (available at: www.mdpi.com/journal/sustainability/special_issues/multinational_enterprises).

For citation purposes, cite each article independently as indicated on the article page online and as indicated below:

LastName, A.A.; LastName, B.B.; LastName, C.C. Article Title. *Journal Name* **Year**, *Volume Number*, Page Range.

ISBN 978-3-0365-6679-5 (Hbk)
ISBN 978-3-0365-6678-8 (PDF)

Contents

About the Editors

Jeoung Yul Lee

Dr. Lee is a Full Professor at Hongik University School of Business Management (South Korea). At present, he serves as the Deputy Editor of Asian Business and Management, Associate Editor of The International Journal of Human Resource Management and Journal of Business Research, editorial advisory board member of the International Business Review, and editorial review board member of the Journal of Management Studies, Management International Review, Asia Pacific Journal of Management, Management and Organization Review, Cross Cultural & Strategic Management, and International Journal of Consumer Studies, and European Journal of International Management. He has served as a leading/managing guest editor of 11 SSCI journal Special Issues of the Management International Review, Journal of Business Research, Management and Organization Review, Management Decision, Sustainability, etc. He was a postdoctoral fellow at the Wharton School (U.S.) and has published 59 papers in SSCI journals, such as the Journal of International Business Studies (2015, 2019, 2022, forthcoming), Human Resource Management (2019, 2022), British Journal of Management, Global Strategy Journal, Long Range Planning, Management International Review, International Business Review, Journal of International Management, Journal of Business Research, and International Journal of Human Resource Management, among many others.

Dilek Zamantili Nayir

Dr. Dilek Zamantili Nayir is well known as experienced professor with a demonstrated history of working in the higher education industry. Skilled in Analytical Skills, Lecturing, English, Management, and Data Analysis. Strong education professional graduated from Istanbul University.

Charles Chen

Dr. Charles Chen, received his BSEE, MSEE, MBA, and PhD (in International Management) from University of Hawaii at Manoa. He is an assistant professor at Hawaii Pacific University, a lecturer at University of Hawaii West Oahu, and an associate faculty at University of Phoenix (Hawaii campus). He served in editorial board for Journal of Eastern European and Central Asian Research (JEECAR) and an ad hoc reviewer for Journal Baltic Journal of Management, International Journal of Emerging Markets, Journal of Business and Economics, Management and Organization Review, and International Trade Journal. He has been practiced in electrical engineering over 30 years in Hawaii, mainland U.S. and Asia, specializing in electrical power, fossil/nuclear power generation plant, renewable power distribution, and transmission engineering design and project management, including selected projects such as: Los Alamos National Laboratory project for U.S. DOE, Florida Power & Light Company nuclear power generation plant and Northern State Power Company fossil power generation plant. He is a licensed Professional Engineer (PE) in Hawaii, California and Illinois States; Member of U.S. National Council of Examiners for Engineering and Surveying (NCEES); International Registry Membership for Asia-Pacific Economic Cooperation (APEC) Engineer Coordinating Committee and Engineers Mobility Forum (EMF) International Register Coordinating Committee Directed with 13 Countries (i.e., Australia, Canada, Chinese Taipei, Hong Kong China, Indonesia, Japan, Korea, Malaysia, New Zealand, Philippines, Singapore, Thailand, and USA).

sustainability MDPI

Editorial

Multinational Enterprises, Sustainability and Innovation

Jeoung-Yul Lee [1,*], Dilek Zamantili Nayir [2] and Charles Chen [3]

1 School of Business Management, Hongik University, Sejong 30016, Republic of Korea
2 Faculty of Economic and Administrative Sciences, Turkish German University, 34820 Istanbul, Turkey
3 College of Business, Hawaii Pacific University, Honolulu, HI 96813, USA
* Correspondence: jeoungyul@hongik.ac.kr

Citation: Lee, J.-Y.; Nayir, D.Z.; Chen, C. Multinational Enterprises, Sustainability and Innovation. *Sustainability* **2023**, *15*, 2524. https://doi.org/10.3390/su15032524

Received: 25 January 2023
Accepted: 30 January 2023
Published: 31 January 2023

In recent decades, multinational enterprises (MNEs) have increasingly endeavored to establish foreign direct investments (FDIs) across the globe. Consequently, they must face diverse and differential sustainability agendas, due to the homogeneous and heterogeneous sustainability issues and policies emerging from both home and host countries [1]. In this vein, MNEs must realize superior methods of establishing sustainable development and innovation-based solutions in both home and host countries [2]. Furthermore, the number of studies on sustainable international business and innovative practices by MNEs in developed markets has rapidly increased in recent years, providing knowledge on shareholder values, environmental agendas, and processes for managing macroeconomic instability. Indeed, there has been a stream of literature focusing on sustainability-oriented innovation, relating to both the environmental and social aspects of sustainability. Of these two, the environmental aspect has been particularly driven by the market demand for more sustainable products, and by strengthening environmental regulations and the desire for cost reductions. Nevertheless, unfortunately, there has been lack of studies focusing on sustainable international business and innovative practices by MNEs in emerging and frontier markets [1,2]; however, Brazil, Russia, India, China, and South Africa (BRICS) have undeniably progressed in terms of sustainable development and innovation-based solutions, by virtue of the operation of MNEs inside and outside of their home countries [1]. Additionally, innovation has assumed a rather different form in the case of emerging market MNEs (EMNEs) [3]. As research and development possibilities are limited, learning by doing and organizational capabilities possess greater weight in EMNEs [4,5]. Although the innovation of some EMNEs from advanced emerging markets, for example, South Korea, Singapore, Taiwan, etc., is scientifically savvy, even when compared to those of developed countries [4,5], the innovation of other EMNEs, especially from less-advanced emerging markets, is scientifically less refined than those of developed countries and has generally not involved frontier technologies [6]. The alternative type of innovation pursued by EMNEs, especially considering sustainability issues, thus requires a deeper investigation; this looks at the creation of technology more comprehensively than by simply considering the sphere of research and the patenting activity [6]. Thus, the objective of this Special Issue is to overcome the limitations of the existing studies, which have mostly focused on developed markets, and to expand our relevant themes for research into the realm of international business sustainability and the search for innovative solutions by emerging and frontier market MNEs.

For this Special Issue, we invited both conceptual and (qualitative and quantitative) empirical articles, as well as literature reviews and meta-analysis articles from a range of fields; these included not only business and management, but also sociology, political science, psychology, economics, and economic geography, among others. Our examples of the relevant topics included in this issue are as follows:

- How do EMNEs shape sustainable development and the related innovations in home and host countries via sustainable processes and innovative solutions? How are they similar to or distinct from advanced market MNEs?

- What are the challenges or opportunities that these EMNEs are presented with when considering the unique political, cultural, religious, and commercial environments of their home and host countries, in order to achieve their sustainability and innovation objectives?
- How does context affect these EMNEs' sustainable practices and innovative solutions, especially for the country of origin and considering the domicile pressures in home and host countries?
- How do recent environmental disruptions, such as the global financial crisis of 2008 and the current COVID-19 pandemic crisis, affect sustainable international business practices and innovative solutions, based on the social and environmental responsibility of corporate enterprises in emerging and advanced markets?
- How do developed versus emerging/frontier market MNEs enhance their sustainability and innovation based on their human resources, transnational, or virtual teams when they face challenges to the enhancement of their sustainable practices and innovative solutions?
- Can the high-level internationalization of EMNEs lead to superior corporate sustainability, which encompasses various social issues, including stakeholder wellbeing and environmental protection?
- The legal guarantee of the sustainable development of the green economy; MNEs, political stability, and the risk of emerging capital markets; foreign executives, R&D innovation, and corporate social responsibility; green innovation efficiency; and path innovation for labor security and flexible employment.

This Special Issue on MNEs, Sustainability and Innovation contains a collection of thirteen papers that address several subjects that are related to the themes discussed above. The authors of these contributions study the boundaries of the previous literature on these relevant topics by providing insightful findings and review, as well as proposals for future research ideas in various contexts. We will elaborate upon the summary of these thirteen contributions to our Special Issue below.

Using an organizational learning perspective, Kim, Lee, and Shim explore the corporate activities of exploitation versus exploration in regard to firm performance (Contribution 1). These two contrasting activities require differential corporate structures, strategies, and environments. Kim et al.'s investigation into "how implementing organizational ambidexterity affects managerial performance in small- and medium-sized enterprises (SMEs)" can expand the existing literature on this topic. Kim et al. explore the impact of the ambidexterity strategy of SMEs on corporate performance. Kim et al.'s observation of the positive relationship between ambidexterity in SMEs and their managerial performance conforms with the previous literature on ambidexterity in larger organizations [7].

Kim, Choi, and Zhang explore the principal *ex ante* determinants of the staff localization of MNE subsidiaries, and locate the collective effects of cultural distance, local subsidiary experience, and local competition intensity (Contribution 2). In their study, Kim et al. extend the existing "home–host country" perspective to the "home–intermediary–host country" association; they used 520 observations from survey data collected by the Export–Import Bank of Korea during 2006–2013. Kim et al.'s research theoretically contributes to the subject of MNE behavior by expanding the existing perspective of cultural distance to the "home–subsidiary–subsidiary structure".

Zhou, Lei, and Jiménez explore the potential determinants of the international competitiveness of state-owned enterprises (SOEs) and locate the influence of foreign shareholders' corporate social responsibility and the moderating effect of R&D, based on a sample of internationalized Chinese SOEs during 2011–2019 (Contribution 3). Zhou et al. find that R&D innovation strengthens the relationship between foreign shareholders' corporate social responsibility and international competitiveness. Zhou et al.'s study contributes to the current debate and provides insight into the role and performance of foreign shareholders in the "mixed-ownership-reform" process.

By applying the longitudinal data of 11 provinces and cities in the Yangtze River Economic Belt during 2005–2018, Wu, Fu, Zhang, Wu, and Sindakis employ the "SBM-DEA efficiency model", with an undesired output, in order to measure the green innovation efficiency of the economic zone in China (Contribution 4). Wu et al. find that, while the Chinese government's environmental laws/rules and subsidies for green innovation technology can enhance the efficiency of regional green innovation, government investment in environmental governance aggravates the efficiency of regional green innovation. In particular, Wu et al. observe that, when government investment exceeds a certain threshold, the negative impact turns into an opposite impact.

Polloni-Silva, Roiz, Mariano, Moralles, and Rebelatto utilize the panel data econometrics, alongside Data Envelopment Analysis (DEA), in order to examine the environmental impact in regions that can attract FDIs; this includes, for example, more well-developed regions with robust infrastructures, via an investigation into the environmental cost of attracting FDIs (Contribution 5). With the new perspectives on the FDI–environment debate, Polloni-Silva et al.'s observations suggest that the FDI is heterogeneous, with its presence in peripheral regions being more inclined to harm the environment.

Müller-Pérez, Acevedo-Duque, Llanos-Herrera, García-Salirrosas, Ovalles-Toledo, Barraza, and Álvarez-Becerra seek to determine which factors are likely to have a more substantial impact on Mexicans' intention to buy green products, ecological awareness, or moral obligation, and to determine the extent to which moral obligation is influenced by ecological awareness (Contribution 6). Müller-Pérez et al. find that moral obligation and ecological awareness can provide some explanation regarding the intention to purchase green products. Müller-Pérez et al.'s study contributes to the literature on consumer behavior, based on an insight that encourages firms to manufacture sustainable products, and to understand and promote a "green consumer behavior".

Utilizing A-shares, a dataset of non-financial and non-real estate listed firms in Shanghai and Shenzhen markets between 2015 and 2020, Gao and Jin investigate the impact of financial technology on firm innovation and examine the influence of organizational characteristics on the association between financial technology and innovation through a moderation model (Contribution 7). Gao and Jin reveal that financial technology enhances the feasibility of serving enterprises; this technology reshapes financial services, which, in turn, augments organizational innovation, while the mechanism is heterogeneous.

Based on a dataset representing the Chinese stock market between 2014 and 2020, Gao, Lin, and Zhai evaluate the effect of digital transformation on a firm's international strategy (Contribution 8). Gao et al. confirm that digital transformation has a positive relationship with the international strategy of Chinese firms. The firms that increasingly pursue digital transformation, increasingly implement international strategy; they possess a higher level of internationalization, along with the mediation effect of corporate innovation.

Iwaloye, Im, Olarewaju, Gbadamosi, Alves, and Trimarchi argue that the Chinese firms' strategic choice is preferable, in order to avoid direct confrontation with established large firms from developed countries who possess superior ownership advantages on their own (Contribution 9). Iwaloye et al. examine the ownership advantages of resources seeking Chinese firms in the overseas markets and by applying the OLI theory; they contribute to explaining the specific advantages of Chinese MNEs when they enter emerging markets, with a focus on resources seeking Chinese MNEs operating in Nigeria.

Lin, Zhai, and Zhao empirically examine the effect of industrial poverty alleviation on the sustainable economic growth of the region, considering the regulatory effect of digital innovation (Contribution 10). Lin et al. observe that digital innovation produces a regulatory effect; if firms seek digital innovation and conduct a higher degree of digital innovation, their industrial poverty alleviation behavior is likely to have a more significant role in promoting regional economic growth.

Du, Shao, Jiménez, and Lee conduct a systematic review of the literature focusing on the corporate social responsibility of Chinese MNEs and extract six key constructs: "(1) the relationship between corporate governance and CSR practice, (2) the relationship between institutional environments and CSR practice, (3) the relationship between resources and capabilities and CSR practice, (4) the relationship between strategy/activity and CSR practice, and (5) the relationship between corporate performance and CSR practice" (Contribution 11).

Using the provincial data of China between 2005 and 2019, Li, Zhang, Jin, and Huang empirically investigate the influence and moderation mechanism of the reverse technology spillovers of outward FDIs on domestic-manufacturing Green Total Factor Productivity (GTFP) (Contribution 12). Li et al. find that absorptive capacity, characterized by human capital, economic development and financial development, can adjust the influence of the reverse technology spillover of outward FDIs on manufacturing GTFP; of these, financial development has the most significant positive moderation effect.

Lastly, Shin and Choi pursue empirical evidence regarding the way in which digital competency contributes to the innovativeness of medical research and the institutional environment; this has been a research gap (Contribution 13). Based on the data of 63 nations, Shin and Choi investigate how national-level digital competency influences the innovation of medical research and how it tests the moderation of the government and the economic environment.

Conflicts of Interest: The authors declare no conflict of interest.

List of Contributions

1. Kim, G.; Lee, W.J.; Shim, H. Managerial Dilemmas and Entrepreneurial Challenges in the Ambidexterity of SMEs: A Systematic Review for Execution System. *Sustainability* **2022**, *14*, 16550. https://doi.org/10.3390/su142416550.
2. Kim, C.B.; Choi, S.-J.; Zhang, L. Determinants of Staff Localization in Headquarters-Subsidiary-Subsidiary Relationships. *Sustainability* **2022**, *14*, 249. https://doi.org/10.3390/su14010249.
3. Zhou, Y.; Lei, C.; Jiménez, A. Foreign Shareholders' Social Responsibility, R&D Innovation, and International Competitiveness of Chinese SOEs. *Sustainability* **2022**, *14*, 1746. https://doi.org/10.3390/su14031746.
4. Wu, F.; Fu, X.; Zhang, T.; Wu, D.; Sindakis, S. Examining Whether Government Environmental Regulation Promotes Green Innovation Efficiency—Evidence from China's Yangtze River Economic Belt. *Sustainability* **2022**, *14*, 1827. https://doi.org/10.3390/su14031827.
5. Polloni-Silva, E.; Roiz, G.A.; Mariano, E.B.; Moralles, H.F.; Rebelatto, D.A.N. The Environmental Cost of Attracting FDI: An Empirical Investigation in Brazil. *Sustainability* **2022**, *14*, 4490. https://doi.org/10.3390/su14084490.
6. Müller-Pérez, J.; Acevedo-Duque, Á.; Llanos-Herrera, G.R.; García-Salirrosas, E.E.; Ovalles-Toledo, L.V.; Barraza, L.A.S.; Álvarez-Becerra, R. The Mexican Ecological Conscience: A Predictive Model. *Sustainability* **2022**, *14*, 7050. https://doi.org/10.3390/su14127050.
7. Gao, Y.; Jin, S. Corporate Nature, Financial Technology, and Corporate Innovation in China. *Sustainability* **2022**, *14*, 7162. https://doi.org/10.3390/su14127162.
8. Gao, F.; Lin, C.; Zhai, H. Digital Transformation, Corporate Innovation, and International Strategy: Empirical Evidence from Listed Companies in China. *Sustainability* **2022**, *14*, 8137. https://doi.org/10.3390/su14138137.
9. Iwaloye, O.O.; Im, H.K.; Olarewaju, A.D.; Gbadamosi, A.; Alves, J.; Trimarchi, M. The Emergence of Resources Seeking Chinese Firms' Specific Advantages in Emerging Market. *Sustainability* **2022**, *14*, 8345. https://doi.org/10.3390/su14148345.
10. Lin, C.; Zhai, H.; Zhao, Y. Industrial Poverty Alleviation, Digital Innovation and Regional Economically Sustainable Growth: Empirical Evidence Based on Local State-Owned Enterprises in China. *Sustainability* **2022**, *14*, 15571. https://doi.org/10.3390/su142315571.
11. Du, S.Y.; Shao, X.; Jiménez, A.; Lee, J.Y. Corporate Social Responsibility of Chinese Multinational Enterprises: A Review and Future Research Agenda. *Sustainability* **2022**, *14*, 16199. https://doi.org/10.3390/su142316199.
12. Li, Y.; Zhang, X.; Jin, C.; Huang, Q. The Influence of Reverse Technology Spillover of Outward Foreign Direct Investment on Green Total Factor Productivity in China's Manufacturing Industry. *Sustainability* **2022**, *14*, 16496. https://doi.org/10.3390/su142416496.

13. Shin, W.; Choi, B. Digital Competency, Innovative Medical Research, and Institutional Environment: A Global Context. *Sustainability* **2022**, *14*, 16887. https://doi.org/10.3390/su142416887.

References

1. Lee, J.Y.; Choi, J.; Xiao, S.S.; Lew, Y.K.; Park, B.I. How do the institutions matter for MNE subsidiaries' CSR in host countries? Evidence from Chinese overseas subsidiaries. *Bus. Res. Q.* 2023; *in press*. [CrossRef]
2. Lee, J.Y.; Ma, Y. The impact of the exchange of sustainable technological HR innovation knowledge within Chaebols on the performance of global subsidiaries. *J. Korea Trade* **2021**, *25*, 108–127. [CrossRef]
3. Lee, J.Y.; Choi, B.C.; Xiao, S.S. Unpacking the drivers of emerging market firms' international joint venture formation: The interplay between technological innovation strategies and home- and host-institutional pressures. *J. Bus. Res.* **2021**, *134*, 378–392. [CrossRef]
4. Lee, J.Y.; Yang, Y.S.; Park, B.I. Interplay between dual dimensions of knowledge sharing within globalized chaebols: The moderating effects of organization size and global environmental munificence. *Int. Bus. Rev.* **2020**, *29*, 101637.
5. Zeng, Y.; Song, S.; Lee, J.Y.; Choe, S. Investment attributes and learning from failure in foreign direct investments. *Long Range Plan.* **2022**, *55*, 102109.
6. Lee, J.Y.; Taras, V.; Jiménez, A.; Choi, B.C.; Pattnaik, C. Ambidextrous knowledge sharing within international R&D teams and MNE performance: The moderating effects of cultural gaps between teams and subnational regions in China. *Manag. Int. Rev.* **2020**, *60*, 387–425.
7. Lee, J.Y.; MacMillan, I.C. Managerial knowledge-sharing in chaebols and its impact on the performance of their foreign subsidiaries. *Int. Bus. Rev.* **2008**, *17*, 533–545. [CrossRef]

sustainability

Article

Examining Whether Government Environmental Regulation Promotes Green Innovation Efficiency—Evidence from China's Yangtze River Economic Belt

Feng Wu [1], Xiaopeng Fu [2,*], Ting Zhang [2], Dan Wu [3] and Stavros Sindakis [4]

1 Criminal Justice School, Zhongnan University of Economics and Law, Wuhan 430073, China; wufeng1988@stu.zuel.edu.cn
2 Chongqing Intellectual Property School, Chongqing University of Technology, Chongqing 400054, China; zscqxyzt@cqut.edu.cn
3 School of Public Affairs, Chongqing University, Chongqing 400044, China; wudan@cqu.edu.cn
4 School of Social Sciences, Hellenic Open University, 26335 Patras, Greece; sindakis.stavros@ac.eap.gr
* Correspondence: fupengonline@cqut.edu.cn

Abstract: Based on the panel data of 11 provinces and cities in the Yangtze River Economic Belt from 2005 to 2018, this paper uses the SBM-DEA efficiency model with undesired output to measure the green innovation efficiency of the Yangtze River Economic Belt. The panel Tobit empirical analysis model was used to quantitatively analyze the impact of three different forms of government environmental regulations on the efficiency of green innovation. The research results show that the government's mandatory environmental regulations and government financial subsidies for green innovation technology are two regulatory methods that positively promote the efficiency of regional green innovation, but government investment in environmental governance has a negative impact on the efficiency of regional green innovation. Then the study found that this negative impact has a significant inflection point effect: when it exceeds a certain threshold, the negative impact turns into a positive effect. At the same time, the impact of environmental regulations on the efficiency of green innovation has significant regional heterogeneity, and the three environmental regulations have a greater impact on downstream provinces and cities.

Keywords: environmental regulation; green innovation efficiency; SBM-DEA efficiency model

Citation: Wu, F.; Fu, X.; Zhang, T.; Wu, D.; Sindakis, S. Examining Whether Government Environmental Regulation Promotes Green Innovation Efficiency—Evidence from China's Yangtze River Economic Belt. *Sustainability* **2022**, *14*, 1827. https://doi.org/10.3390/su14031827

Academic Editors: Jeoung Yul Lee, Dilek Zamantili Nayir, Charles Chen and Luigi Aldieri

Received: 9 December 2021
Accepted: 31 January 2022
Published: 5 February 2022

1. Introduction

Since the reform and opening up of China's economy, it has experienced a long period of rapid development and achieved remarkable economic development, but behind the rapid economic growth is huge resource consumption and environmental pollution. Domestic and international experience shows that the development path of high energy consumption and high pollution leading to high growth is not sustainable. In this context, the Chinese government has been committed to properly handling the relationship between economic development and environmental protection and enhancing the capacity of sustainable economic development. In 2018, Xi Jinping emphasized the need to build a resource-saving and environment-friendly green development system. Then, as one of the regions with the strongest comprehensive strength and the largest strategic support role in China, the Yangtze River Economic Belt, as a super basin spanning 11 provinces and cities in the east and west of China, had a GDP in 2020 that accounted for nearly half of the national GDP. However, due to the development of heavy industry, the region has seen rapid growth in energy and resource consumption, environmental pollution, and water and soil erosion.

For this reason, the 19th Report of the Communist Party of China and the Outline of the Yangtze River Economic Belt Development Plan clearly put forward the construction plan of "grasping big protection and not big development" to strengthen environmental regulations and thus promote the green development of the Yangtze River Economic Belt. Technological innovation is a prerequisite for green development [1]. Compared with the traditional production efficiency, green innovation efficiency, which is similar to eco-efficiency, can better reflect the quality of economic development and the impact of resources on the environment. The concept of green innovation efficiency involves reducing the use of natural resources, reducing the emissions of pollutants into the environment, and reducing the amount of waste generated [2,3]. Compared with eco-efficiency, green innovation efficiency emphasizes the importance of R&D investment and the application of green technology on the input side. However, can environmental regulation lead to increased green innovation efficiency? How are the two related, and through what channels can this influence be exerted? An accurate answer to this question is of crucial relevance and theoretical value for the green development of the Yangtze River Economic Belt and for the choice of China's future economic development model.

Scholars have done a lot of research around this research topic, and based on different perspectives, scholars obtain different research conclusions or even diametrically opposed views. The current research can be divided into two main directions. The first is the one-way relationship, in which environmental regulations enhance or reduce the efficiency of green innovation efficiency. Jeffe argues that although environmental regulation has an incentive effect on green innovation efficiency, it brings benefits to firms, but the direction is unclear [4]. Thomas et al. argued that environmental regulation policies have increased the need for firms to enhance environmental management behaviors, such as treating sewage and cleaning polluted wastewater [5]. This increases the cost expenditure of following environmental policies and squeezes out the investment in productivity-enhancing R&D. The empirical results show that environmental regulations significantly inhibit the improvement of green production efficiency. The second, the non-linear relationship, the impact of environmental regulation on green innovation efficiency, is not a unidirectional linear relationship. Deng Feng et al., Zang Chunqiu, Jiang Fuxin et al., Li Ling et al., and others confirmed that the impact of environmental regulation on the green total factor productivity of enterprises has an inverted "U" relationship [6–9].

Furthermore, when the intensity of environmental regulation reaches a certain threshold value, environmental regulation helps enterprises green the relationship between environmental regulation, and the green total factor productivity is inverted. However, the relationship becomes negative after a certain threshold value is exceeded. In the study of the relationship, Li Yang et al. found that the impact of environmental regulations on green innovation efficiency has a coexistence of short-term inhibition and long-term promotion [10]. Furthermore, Lanjouwjo et al., found no significant correlation between the increased emission reduction expenditure of environmental regulations and green technology innovation [11]. There was no evidence of a correlation between green technology innovation productivity and environmental regulation.

The above studies have enriched the research content and direction of environmental regulation and green innovation efficiency. However, there are also certain shortcomings. First, there is the green innovation efficiency measurement method. At present, there are controversies in the measurement methods; in particular, some important non-expected output indicators have not been included in the measurement index system, so there is some space for improvement. Second, the definition of environmental regulation is controversial. The vast majority of researchers define environmental regulation as the introduction of environmental policies by government departments and the more frequent use of environmental pollution fines, environmental taxes, and other measures. Environmental regulation laws are not simply defined as a single punishment by the government in the market but can only be used as a means of environmental regulation. At present, government agencies are also beginning to use indirect environmental regulation methods, such as financial subsidies for enterprises to develop advanced green technologies. The logic mechanism of the two impacts on green total factor productivity is not consistent.

Therefore, conflating them may not accurately describe the logical relationship between environmental regulation and green innovation efficiency, which is obviously not conducive to the rational use of environmental regulation policies by the government. Based on these arguments, this paper measures the green total factor production efficiency with the help of the SBM-DEA modeling method. Additionally, the study explores the relationship between environmental regulation and green innovation efficiency from two dimensions of environmental governance inputs and environmental market penalties, respectively, starting from the differences of environmental regulation tools and expecting to provide some reference for choosing a reasonable and effective regulation organization and policy dynamic adjustment.

2. Theoretical Analysis

Environmental regulation is a general term for the environmental protection policies and implementation tools enacted by government and related departments to solve the environmental problems associated with economic growth. In the early days, the Chinese government used more direct means, such as fines for environmental pollution, and direct financial investment in environmental pollution control to achieve the goal of reducing environmental pollution. At present, the Chinese government has also begun to pay attention to indirect means, such as green subsidy policies and environmentally friendly technology R&D subsidy policies. According to the standard of government participation in environmental pollution governance, we divide environmental regulation into two parts: direct environmental regulation and indirect environmental regulation. The content of the theoretical analysis is also carried out in accordance with this classification.

2.1. Government Directly Intervenes in Environmental Governance

The government directly intervenes in environmental governance by introducing environmental regulations and policies and directly undertaking environmental pollution control and restoration.

First, the government enforces environmental regulation measures directly. This measure includes pollutant emission standards, environmental audits, and emission tax collection. The public goods attribute of environmental resources determines the typical externality characteristic of environmental pollution. The existing insurmountable limitations of the market mechanism to address environmental pollution through property rights definition and integration provide room for governmental environmental regulation. Environmental regulation is ensured through public power and thus has a strong binding capacity. However, it has a different impact on the efficiency of firms' green production.

On the one hand, such regulation is conducive to the improvement of green production efficiency. Based on Michael Porter's hypothesis, which is that strict environmental regulations can induce efficiency and encourage innovations that help improve commercial competitiveness [12], Scherer et al., Han Jing, and Han Xianfeng et al. argue that the introduction of these environmental regulation policies is conducive to forcing enterprises to improve their existing production processes, optimize management procedures, and invest more R&D funds to promote the development of innovative green technologies, thus enhancing overall green production efficiency [13–15]. However, on the other hand, Collop and Roberts and Cary argue that harsh environmental regulations increase the cost of environmental pollution control, which reduces the scale of green innovation investment and is not conducive to the improvement of overall green production efficiency [16,17].

Second, the government directly undertakes environmental pollution controls and restoration. The government's sharing of responsibility for corporate environmental pollution management also has two different directions of influence on the impact of corporate green production efficiency. On the one hand, the government's increased investment in pollution management can make up for the lack of pollution management investment at the enterprise end, so enterprises can shift more resources to the research and development of green production technology, which helps to improve the overall green production efficiency. On the other hand, the government's commitment to pollution control investment may also cause enterprises to reduce pollution control investment. Enterprises will expand their own production scale and bring more pollution, which is ultimately not conducive to the improvement of green innovation efficiency.

2.2. Government Indirectly Intervenes in Environmental Governance

In this case, the government does not directly participate in environmental governance activities but guides enterprises to develop and adopt environmentally friendly technologies through targeted financial subsidies. The government's indirect environmental regulation through financial subsidies may have two effects on the production efficiency of green innovation. On the one hand, the government's green subsidy policy is conducive to improving the efficiency of green innovation. Government financial subsidies reduce the cost and risk of R&D of environmentally friendly technologies, thus motivating enterprises to increase their confidence in innovation investment, which is conducive to enhancing green innovation capacity and green innovation efficiency [18]. On the other hand, the government's green subsidy policy may also be detrimental to the improvement of green innovation efficiency of enterprises. Excessive reliance on government financial subsidies to carry out technology research and development activities may reduce the scale of investment in research and development funds for the purpose of enterprise development, which reduces the competitiveness of enterprises and will eventually be eliminated by the market [19–21].

Overall, the relationship between environmental regulation and green innovation efficiency is shown in Figure 1.

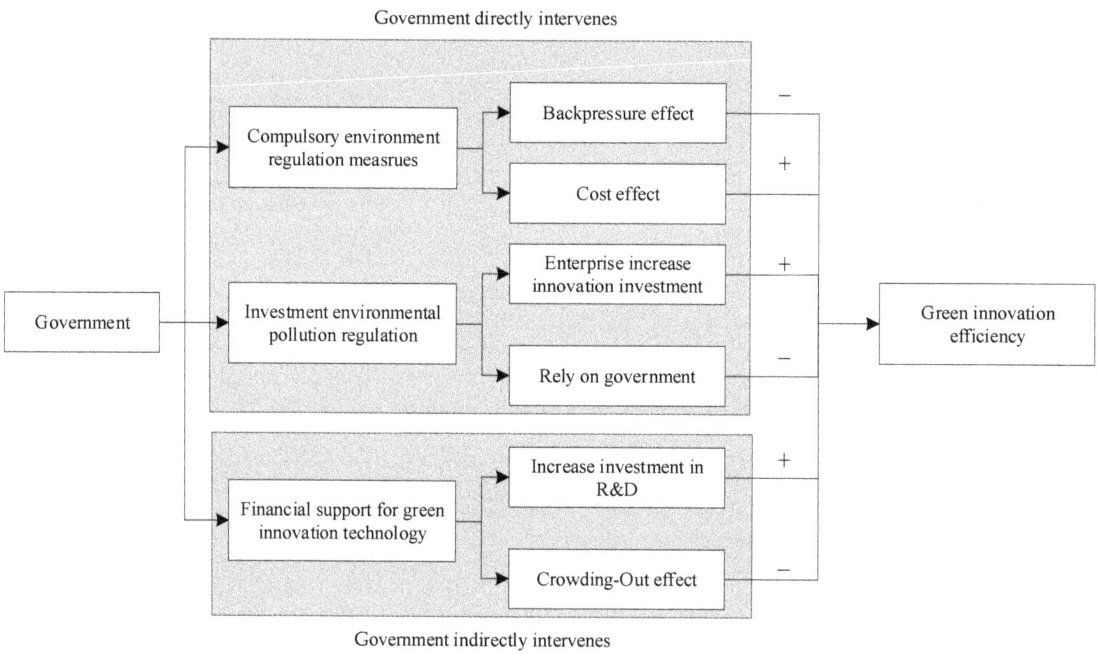

Figure 1. The relationship between government environmental regulations and green innovation efficiency.

3. Research Design and Empirical Model

3.1. Research Method

3.1.1. SBM-DEA Efficiency Model

The basic principle of data envelopment analysis (DEA) is to construct a nonparametric envelope frontier from the spatial data of decision units, and all the points on the frontier are valid, while those placed outside the frontier are invalid. The non-radial and non-angular SBM model overcomes the influence of traditional CCR and BCC models that do not consider input–output slack variables on the reliability of model estimation [22,23]. Adding the slack variables to the objective function can effectively solve the problem of efficiency measures that contain pollution variables. The basic idea is as follows.

Suppose the number of decision units in a system is n, and each decision unit contains three variables: input (X), desired output (Y^g), and undesired decision output (Y^b). Define the matrix of X, Y^g, and Y^b as follows:

$$X = [x_1, x_2, x_3, \ldots, x_n] \in R_{m\times n}$$

$$Y^g = \left[y_1^g, y_2^g, y_3^g, \ldots, y_n^g\right] \in R_{s1\times n}$$

$$Y^b = \left[y_1^b, y_2^b, y_3^b, \ldots, y_n^b\right] \in R_{s2\times n}$$

Among them, $X > 0$, $Y^g \geq 0$, $Y^b \geq 0$ define the production possible set as

$$p = \{(x, y^g, y^b) \mid x \geq X\lambda, y^g \leq Y^g\lambda, y^b \geq Y^b\lambda, \lambda \geq 0\}$$

The linear programming form of the SBM model is as follows:

$$\rho* = \min \frac{1 - \frac{1}{m}\sum_{i=1}^{m}\frac{s_i^{-1}}{x_{i0}}}{1 + \frac{1}{s_1+s_2}\sum_{s_2}^{s_1}\frac{s_r^g}{y_{r0}^g} + \left(\sum_{r=1}^{s_2}\frac{s_r^b}{y_{r0}^b}\right)}$$

$$s.t.\begin{cases} x_0 = X\lambda + s^{-1} \\ y_0^g = Y^g\lambda - s^g \\ y_0^b = Y^b\lambda + s^b \\ \lambda, s^{-1}, s^g, s^b \geq 0 \end{cases}$$

In the above formula, $0 \leq \rho^* \leq 1$ and for s^{-1}, s^g, s^b are strictly decreasing. The s represents the slack variable. The s^{-1}, s^g, s^b represent excessive input, insufficient expected output, and excessive undesired output, respectively; λ represents the weight of each variable. Objective function (ρ^*) expresses the deviation of input and output from the optimal state. The decision-making unit is the most effective only when there is no redundancy or deficiency in input and output.

3.1.2. The Data of Green Innovation Efficiency

According to the suggestion of Yang Shuwang et al., this paper selects R&D talent full-time equivalent and R&D internal funding expenditure as input variables [24]. Scientific researchers and funding are the most direct guarantee of innovation input and output. In terms of innovation output, the number of patent applications granted is more indicative of the quality of innovation output than the number of patent applications accepted. The three industrial wastes (industrial waste gas, wastewater emissions, and industrial solid waste output) are important sources of environmental pollution. With the entropy method used by Yi Ming et al., the three industrial wastes are synthesized into an environmental pollution index to serve as non-desired outputs [1]. As a result, the input variables become two, and the output variables are two, which meets the limitation of the number of indicators by DEA method when the number of decision units is 11. The overall data were obtained from the China Statistical Yearbook (2005–2019), the China Statistical Yearbook of Science and Technology (2005–2019), and the China Statistical Yearbook of Environment (2015–2019).

3.2. Empirical Model

The Tobit regression model is a restricted dependent variable regression model, first proposed by James Tobin, and the Undesirable-SBM measures green innovation efficiency at 0–1, which is truncated data. Tobit regression is more efficient and unbiased. The basic model setup is as follows.

$$Y = \begin{cases} Y* & = \beta X + \mu(Y* > 0) \\ 0 & (Y* < 0) \end{cases}$$

In the above formula, Y^* is the truncated dependent variable. Y is the value of green innovation efficiency tendency. X is a vector of independent variables, β a vector of parameters, and μ is a random interference term.

When $Y^* > 0$, the Tobit model based on the impact of environmental regulation on the productivity of green innovation is as follows.

$$GTFP_{i,t} = \beta_i + \beta_2 ERE_{i,t} + \beta_3 X_{i,t} + \varepsilon_{i,t}$$

The $GTFP_{i,t}$ represents the green innovation efficiency of each province of the Yangtze River economy in different years, as measured by Undesirable-SBM. The *ERE* represents government environmental regulation measures, and based on the previous analysis, this paper selects government-mandatory environmental regulation (*ERE1*); government financial subsidies for innovation (*ERE2*); and government environmental governance (*ERE3*), respectively. The *X* represents other control variables that affect the efficiency of green innovation, representing the random disturbance term.

3.3. Variable Selection and Source

Green innovation is a complex process in which multiple subjects and factors act together [24]. With the help of previous scholars' studies, this paper defines the following important independent variables as a way to discover the impact of government regulation on green production efficiency.

3.3.1. Government Regulation Variables (*ERE*)

Three main dimensions are chosen to measure the level of government environmental regulation. The first is the level of government compulsory environmental regulation (*ERE1*). In this paper, we choose to use the amount of emission fees collection as a proxy variable for the level of compulsory government regulation as a percentage of government revenue. The second is government innovation financial subsidies (*ERE2*) This paper chooses the ratio of local government innovation subsidies to the scale of local fiscal expenditures to measure this indicator. The third is government environmental governance (*ERE3*). Drawing on the idea of Yang Shuwang et al., this paper selects government pollution control investment as a percentage of the scale of local government fiscal expenditure to measure the intensity of government environmental governance investment [24].

3.3.2. Industrial Structure (Str)

In a general sense, regional green development relies on the tertiary industry rather than the secondary industry. Ruiji Pun et al. and Weiqi Tang argue that the service industry in China is ineffective in influencing green development, and the degree of ineffectiveness is deepening [25,26]. This paper chooses the share of the value added from the tertiary industry to the GDP as a proxy scalar of industrial structure so as to examine how exactly the industrial structure affects the green production efficiency.

3.3.3. The Degree of Market Openness (Open)

The opening to the outside world introduces advanced foreign technology and undertakes international industrial transfer, and the relatively low strength of environmental controls can also lead to the entry of international pollution, which brings a heavy environmental burden while enhancing the level of innovation and development, especially for the middle and upper reaches of the Yangtze River Economic Belt provinces [27]. Brunnermeier, however, argues that the demand for green products and fierce competition in the international market is conducive to the improvement of green production efficiency [28]. In this section, FDI to regional GDP ratio is chosen as an alternative indicator.

3.3.4. Maturity of Technology Market (Tech)

The more mature the technology market is, the more it is conducive to accelerating the transformation of innovation results, activating the regional innovation atmosphere and improving the overall regional innovation capacity [29]. The maturity of the technology market is expressed using the turnover of the regional technology market.

3.3.5. Regional Factor Endowment (RFE)

Regional factor endowment lays the foundation for local green innovation development, and Xiao Quan et al. (2021) argue that the richer the regional factor endowment, the higher the level of local innovation development and the higher the level of green production efficiency. This paper mainly uses the ratio of local fixed asset investment stock to regional employees as a proxy variable for regional factor endowment.

The descriptive statistics for the variables and data are shown in Table 1.

Table 1. Descriptive statistics of variables.

Variables Name	Variables	Obs	Mean	Std
Green innovation efficiency	*GTFP*	165	0.7112	0.228
	ERE1	165	0.0121	0.039
Government regualtion	*ERE2*	165	0.0281	0.011
	ERE3	165	0.0131	0.024
Industrial structure	*Str*	165	0.5019	0.1395
The degree of market openness	*open*	165	0.0651	0.046
Maturity of the technology market	*Tech*	165	12.0981	4.099
Regional factor endowment	*RFE*	165	89.0761	12.701

The data were mainly obtained from the overall data from the China Statistical Yearbook (2005–2019), the China Statistical Yearbook of Science and Technology (2005–2019), and the China Statistical Yearbook of Environment (2005–2019). The data of 11 provinces and cities in the Yangtze River Economic Zone from 2005 to 2019 were selected to verify the impact of environmental regulation on the efficiency of green innovation. The results of the analysis were obtained from Stata 14.0.

4. Empirical Results and Discussion

4.1. Basic Regression Results

The results of the Tobit regression analysis with green innovation efficiency as the dependent variable, using the panel Tobit mixed-effects model, the panel Tobit fixed-effects model, and the panel Tobit random-effects model, are shown in Table 2. The results of the F-test significantly reject the assumption that the mixed-effects model is not different from the fixed-effects model, and the empirical evidence of the panel Tobit fixed-effects model should be accepted. The results of the Hausman test also significantly reject the panel Tobit random-effects model. Therefore, the panel Tobit fixed-effects model is selected in the empirical analysis section to analyze the effect of environmental regulation on the green innovation effect in the Yangtze River Economic Belt.

Table 2. Baseline regression results of environmental regulation and green innovation efficiency.

Explanation Variables	Panel Tobit Fixed-Effects Model		
ERE1	0.0169 *** (4.098)		
ERE2		0.0189 ** (2.402)	
ERE3			−0.0207 *** (−3.098)
Str	0.0197 (1.201)	0.0201 (1.191)	0.0196 (1.313)
open	2.911 ** (2.402)	2.981 *** (3.107)	3.092 *** (3.215)
Tech	0.0012 *** (3.091)	0.0009 *** (3.129)	0.0015 *** (2.764)
RFE	0.0233 *** (5.019)	0.0216 *** (3.201)	0.0219 *** (4.019)

Note: (1) The numbers in brackets are the t statistics corresponding to the regression coefficient; ***, ** indicate they have passed the significance test at the 1%, 5% confidence levels, respectively, with the same interpretations below. (2) The empirical results of the panel Tobit random-effects model and panel Tobit mixed effects model are not reported due to space limitation.

According to the above table, firstly, there is a positive relationship between the cost of emissions (*ERE1*) and green innovation, which also indicates that the government's use of sewage charges to regulate the environment is conducive to improving the efficiency of local green production. This is because the government's sewage charges raise the production costs of polluting firms and reduce their production profits. In this context, enterprises are more willing to change their innovative activities to reduce the amount of emissions, reduce the scale of pollution emissions, and reduce pollution costs, thereby gaining a competitive advantage in the market and thus improving green production efficiency. Second, the government's science and technology innovation input-based (*ERE2*) environmental regulation is also conducive to enhancing green production efficiency. This shows that, at this stage, the positive impact of government innovation investment on enterprises' green production efficiency is greater than the negative impact. Additionally, government investment in environmental science and technology R&D helps alleviate enterprises' shortage of R&D funds, reduce R&D risks, and thus improve green production efficiency. The scale of the crowding-out effect of enterprises' own innovation input brought by the government's science and technology innovation input is not yet large enough to affect the overall green production efficiency enhancement. Finally, government environmental governance inputs (*ERE3*), on the contrary, are not conducive to the improvement of green production efficiency. This is because government environmental governance inputs lead to higher environmental governance costs, which inhibit other government inputs, especially government investments in R&D, which is not conducive to the improvement of green production efficiency. This partly proves the existence of Porter's hypothesis.

For the other control variables, the direction and sign of the effects of all control variables are as expected, except that there is no significant correlation between industrial structure (*Str*) and green production efficiency. First, the degree of openness to the outside world (open) contributes to green production efficiency. This is also consistent with Brunnermeier's study, where the introduction of regional foreign investment helps to enhance local innovation competition and improve the level of local science and technology innovation [28]. Second, the maturity of the technology market (*Tech*) helps to enhance local green production efficiency. A well-developed technology transfer market helps establish a good innovation R&D atmosphere, which in turn helps accelerate the innovation results into the practical application process, thus promoting green innovation efficiency. Third, regional factor endowment (*RFE*) helps to enhance local green production efficiency. This is the same as the findings of Xiao Quan et al., mainly because the higher the regional factor endowment and the richer the resources held by enterprises, the higher the green production efficiency improvement brought by innovation [30]. Finally, there is no significant correlation between industrial structure and green production efficiency. The possible reason for this is that there is currently a non-green development trend in the tertiary industry in the Yangtze River Economic Zone, which means that even if the tertiary industry accounts for a higher share, it does not translate into green production efficiency improvement [25].

4.2. Inflection Point Effect of Environmental Regulation on Green Production Efficiency

The current research literature has found that the impact of environmental regulation on green innovation efficiency is not a unidirectional impact, but there is an obvious inflection point when certain conditions are reached [24]; that is, the impact of environmental regulation on green production efficiency can vary significantly with the degree of regulation, and the direction of its impact changes. In order to verify the existence of this influence mechanism, this section introduces three different quadratic terms of environmental regulation variables and continues to use the panel Tobit fixed-effects model to estimate the Tobit model based on the impact of environmental regulation on green innovation productivity as follows (when truncating the dependent variable *GTFP* > 0).

$$GTFP_{i,t} = \beta_i + \beta_2 ERE_{i,t} + \beta_3 ERE^2{}_{i,t} + \beta_4 X_{i,t} + \varepsilon_{i,t}$$

The specific results are shown in Table 3. It can be found that the sign before the quadratic term of *ERE3* changes. The sign of the first term is negative, but the sign before the second term is positive. The result shows that environmental regulation by means of environmental fines may have an inverted U-shaped impact on green innovation efficiency, which also confirms the Porter hypothesis. This also proves that the Porter Hypothesis exists in the Yangtze River Economic Belt. In the short-term environmental pollution control is not conducive to the improvement of green production efficiency of enterprises; this is because short-term environmental pollution control raises the cost of environmental management and increases the tax burden on enterprises, which is not conducive to the competitive advantage of enterprises in the market. However, in the long run, this means it is still conducive to the improvement of green production efficiency, probably because the "compensation effect" brought by the improvement of the environment and the increase in innovation output covers the "cost effect", allowing enterprises to obtain additional economic benefits. This is conducive to the improvement of green innovation efficiency. In contrast, no change is found in the sign of the quadratic terms of *ERE1* and *ERE2*, which indicates no inflection point of green innovation subsidies and environmental management inputs on green innovation productivity in the region during the sample period.

4.3. The Impact of Environmental Regulation on the Heterogeneity of Green Innovation Production Efficiency

Are there heterogeneous effects of inter-regional differences? In order to verify whether heterogeneity exists, this study divides the Yangtze River economic belt into three categories according to the criteria of "upstream, midstream and downstream": upstream provinces include Chongqing, Sichuan, Guizhou, and Yunnan; midstream provinces are Jiangxi, Hubei, and Hunan; downstream provinces are Shanghai, Jiangsu, Zhejiang, and Anhui. The panel Tobit fixed-effects model continues to be used for the empirical estimation of the existence of the effect of environmental regulation on the heterogeneity of green innovation production efficiency. The specific results are shown in Table 4.

According to the results shown in Table 4, the impact of environmental regulations on green innovation productivity in the upstream, midstream, and downstream provinces remains similar to the overall empirical results, controlling for other variables. First, the positive relationship between emission costs (*ERE1*) and green innovation is still present. Still, significant differences in intensity emerge, with downstream provinces having the largest situation of emission costs on green innovation efficiency, followed by midstream provinces and the smallest in the west. Secondly, government science and technology innovation input-based (*ERE2*) environmental regulation is also beneficial to enhance green production efficiency. Moreover, the intensity of the impact appears to be significantly different, with government science and technology support in upstream provinces producing the largest effect on green innovation efficiency, followed by midstream provinces and the smallest in the west. Finally, there is still a negative correlation between government environmental governance inputs (*ERE3*) and green innovation efficiency. Additionally, there are significant differences in the degree of impact, with the upstream provinces having the greatest impact and the downstream provinces having the least.

Table 3. Inflection point effect of environmental regulation on green production efficiency.

Explanation Variables	Panel Tobit Fixed-Effects Model		
ERE1	0.0138 *** (4.098)		
ERE2		0.0215 ** (2.116)	
ERE3			−0.0214 *** (−3.401)
$ERE1^2$	0.0141 *** (3.701)		
$ERE2^2$		0.0191 *** (3.064)	
$ERE3^2$			0.0221 *** (3.081)
Other variables	YES	YES	YES
Constant	0.0871 * (2.169)	0.7601 (1.6319)	−0.193 * (−1.703)

Note:(1) The numbers in brackets are the t statistics corresponding to the regression coefficient; ***, ** and * indicate that they have passed the significance test at the 1%, 5% and 10% confidence levels, respectively, with the same interpretations below. (2) $ERE1^2$, $ERE2^2$, $ERE3^2$ represent the squares of *ERE1*, *ERE2*, *ERE3* respectively.

Table 4. Inflection point effect of environmental regulation on green production efficiency.

Explanation Variables	Panel Tobit Fixed-Effects Model		
	Upstream	Midstream	Downstream
ERE1	0.0106 *** (3.112)	0.0127 ** (2.237)	0.0203 *** (4.103)
ERE2	0.0112 ** (2.039)	0.0176 *** (3.149)	0.0204 *** (2.971)
ERE3	−0.0304 *** (−2.411)	−0.0181 ** (−2.364)	−0.0135 *** (−3.429)
Other variables	YES	YES	YES

Note: (1) The numbers in brackets are the t statistics corresponding to the regression coefficient; *** and ** indicate that they have passed the significance test at the 1% and 5% confidence levels, respectively, with the same interpretations below. (2) Regression equation variables for all variables were not included in the table due to space limitations. The three different environmental regulation variables were included in Equation (3) separately for the panel Tobit fixed-effects model, and the results are summarized in the table.

There are two possible reasons for the heterogeneous impact results: first, there are differences in the degree of perfection of relevant systems in different provinces. Compared with upstream and midstream provinces, the degree of economic development, green innovation resources, and market mechanisms is sounder in downstream provinces, so it is easier for enterprises in downstream provinces to obtain more advanced green production technologies. Moreover, due to the sound market and public management mechanisms, enterprises in downstream provinces have higher pollution costs and stronger regulation. This leads enterprises to choose cleaner but more efficient green production technologies, obtaining higher economic returns. Second, different provinces are at different stages of economic development. Compared with the middle and upper reaches of the provinces, the downstream provinces have already moved past the stage of extensive pollution treatment, and there is not much pressure on pollution management. In contrast, the middle and upstream provinces are under very high pressure for pollution treatment and environmental protection, which requires a lot of investment in environmental pollution treatment, which crowds out other government funds for improving green production efficiency.

5. Discussion

Research on the relationship between environmental regulation and green innovation efficiency has become an important research topic. However, the current related research also has two certain shortcomings. In particular, there are research limitations in how to accurately measure green innovation efficiency and the impact of different environmental regulations on green innovation efficiency.

5.1. Research Implications

This study addresses these issues in an attempt to understand the relationship between the different environmental regulations and green innovation efficiency. To this end, two main contributions are made in terms of research implications.

First, this study addresses the measurement problem of green innovation efficiency by using the SBM-DEA method. The concept of green innovation efficiency involves reducing the use of natural resources, reducing the emissions of pollutants into the environment and reducing the amount of waste generated. Traditional DEA methods cannot solve the slackness problem caused by the unintended output. This study addresses the slackness problem by using the SBM-DEA method. The data using the SBM-DEA method show that the higher the level of production technology, the higher the efficiency of green innovation, which is also in line with the connotation of high-quality development in the general sense.

Second, this study expands the conceptual scope of environmental regulation, and empirical research methods are used to verify the impact of different environmental regulations on the efficiency of green innovation, as well as the heterogeneity of this impact. Environmental regulations cannot be simply defined as direct government enforcement of environmental regulation laws. More and more indirect environmental regulatory measures, such as financial subsidies to companies that adopt clean technologies, are also being adopted by the government. Direct or indirect environmental regulations have different logical mechanisms for the impact of green innovation efficiency. When environmental compulsory and government financial subsidies are used as proxy indicators of environmental regulation, government environmental regulation is conducive to improving green innovation efficiency. Conversely, the relationship between government regulation and green innovation efficiency becomes negative when the government environmental investment variable is used. The subsequent empirical results show that the impact of environmental regulation on the efficiency of green innovation is not linearly related but presents an obvious "U" shape. Further empirical results show that the relationship has obvious spatial heterogeneity, which shows that environmental regulation in downstream provinces and cities has a greater positive impact on green production efficiency. Relatively, the degree of positive impact in the middle and upper reaches of the province is small. Previous studies have focused more on analyzing the impact of a single environmental regulation, which may not be conducive to grasping the overall impact of environmental regulation on green innovation efficiency. This research extends the literature on the relationship between environmental regulation and green innovation efficiency in empirical insights.

5.2. Practical Implications

In terms of practical relevance, the province and city governments, which lie in the Yangtze River Economic Belt, may find this research useful in two parts. First, in the short term, governments could adopt compulsory environmental regulation and financial subsidies to improve local green innovation efficiency. First, it can reduce the R&D risks associated with enterprises' green innovation development and enhance their innovation enthusiasm. Second, the government's financial subsidies can also play the role of leading relevant enterprises to adopt more green innovation technologies, which will help to improve local green innovation efficiency. Third, this can expand the intensity and quality of government investment in environmental governance to enhance the efficiency of green innovation in the long term. It can increase the intensity of environmental governance investment, strive to cross the influence inflection point, and put the government's environmental governance investment into enhancing the efficiency of green innovation. It can also improve the government's environmental governance input towards quality. The quality of the government's environmental governance investment can be adjusted to ensure that each project, especially major projects, has a reasonable proportion of ex-ante protection, ex-post control, and governance subjects to improve the efficiency of energy-saving and environmental protection spending. It also needs to strengthen supervision to enhance the efficiency of using environmental protection funds.

5.3. Limitations and Future Research

As with any research, the present study is constrained by certain limitations [31,32]. This research also has some limitations. First, this research only discusses the mechanism of the impact of different environmental regulations on green production efficiency through theoretical deduction, but it does not verify these mechanisms through empirical methods. In future studies, we will introduce micro-panel data at the enterprise level located in the Yangtze River Economic Belt to empirically verify the internal mechanism of the impact of environmental regulations on the efficiency of green innovation. Second, we found evidence that the impact of environmental regulations on the efficiency of green innovation has significant regional heterogeneity. However, we have only given possible reasons for the heterogeneous impact of environmental regulations on green innovation efficiency. The above reasons have not been confirmed by empirical work. In future studies, we will combine micro-enterprise data and macro-provincial data and use the panel fixed-effect empirical model to find the reasons for the heterogeneity of the impact of environmental regulations on green innovation efficiency.

6. Conclusions

Based on the panel data of 11 provinces and cities in the Yangtze River Economic Belt from 2005 to 2018, this paper uses the SBM-DEA efficiency model with undesired output to measure the green innovation efficiency of the Yangtze River Economic Belt. It used the panel Tobit empirical analysis model to quantitatively analyze the impact of three different forms of government environmental regulations on the efficiency of green innovation. The research results are as follows. (1) The overall results show that the impact of different environmental regulation instruments on the green innovation productivity of the study sample is not consistent, and the government compulsory environmental regulation measures and government financial subsidies for technological innovation are conducive to the improvement of its green innovation productivity, but the government environmental pollution input is not conducive to the improvement of this indicator. (2) There is an inflection point for the impact of environmental pollution control measures on green innovation productivity, and when this inflection point is exceeded, environmental pollution control measures will improve green innovation efficiency. (3) There is significant regional heterogeneity in the impact of environmental regulation on green innovation efficiency. This heterogeneity is mainly manifested by the fact that different environmental regulation instruments have a greater impact on downstream provinces, and the different degrees of institutional perfection and different economic development stages may be the reasons for this heterogeneity.

Author Contributions: Conceptualization, F.W., X.F.; Data curation X.F. and T.Z.; Formal analysis, X.F.; Investigation, D.W.; Methodology, X.F.; Project administration, F.W. and S.S.; Resources, F.W. and X.F; Software, X.F.; Supervision, S.S.; Writing—original draft, X.F.; Writing—review & editing, S.S., F.W., T.Z. and D.W. All authors have read and agree to be published version of the manuscript.

Funding: This Research was funded by the Youth project of the National Social Science Fund of China, grant number 17CGJ003, Project of Humanities and Social Sciences, Ministry of Education in China, grant number 15YJC820079, and Doctoral Project of Chongqing Social Science Fund, grant number 2020BS39.

Institutional Review Board Statement: Not applicable.

Informed Consent Statement: Not applicable.

Data Availability Statement: The data presented in this study are available on request from the corresponding author. The data are not publicly available due to privacy.

Conflicts of Interest: The authors declare no conflict of interest.

References

1. Yi, M.; Cheng, X.M. Spatial and Temporal Divergence in Green Innovation Efficiency of Cities in the Yangtze River Economic Belt and Its Influencing Factors. *Urban Issues* **2018**, *8*, 31–39.
2. Kristoffersen, E.; Mikalef, P.; Blomsma, F.; Li, J. Towards a business analytics capability for the circular economy. *Technol. Forecast. Soc. Change* **2021**, *171*, 120957. [CrossRef]
3. Wojdalski, J.; Krajnik, M.; Borowski, P.F.; Dróżdż, B.; Kupczyk, A. Energy and water efficiency in the gelatine production plant. *AIMS Geosci.* **2020**, *6*, 491–503. [CrossRef]
4. Jaffe, A.B.; Palmer, K. Environmental regulation and innovation: A panel data study. *Rev. Econ. Stat.* **1997**, *79*, 610–619. [CrossRef]
5. Dean, T.J.; Brown, R.L. Pollution regulation as a barrier to new firm entry: Initial evidence and implications for future research. *Acad. Manag. J.* **1995**, *38.1*, 288–303.
6. Deng, F.; Chen, C. R&D Investment Intensity and Green Innovation Efficiency in China—A Threshold Study Based on Environmental Regulation. *Ind. Technol. Econ.* **2020**, *39*, 30–36.
7. Zang, C.; Zhang, H. Spatial differences in the technological innovation effects of environmental regulations—An empirical analysis based on panel data in China from 2000 to 2013. *Macroeconomics* **2015**, *204*, 72–83.
8. Jiang, F.; Ji, Y.; Bai, J. The relationship between the intensity of environmental regulations and the technological progress of industrial production—An empirical study based on threshold regression. *Mod. Econ. Res.* **2014**, *11*, 39–43.
9. Li, L.; Tao, F. Selection of the optimal environmental regulation intensity for China's manufacturing industry—Based on the perspective of green innovation efficiency. *China Ind. Econ.* **2012**, *5*, 70–82.
10. Li, Y.; Dang, X.; Han, X.; Song, W.F. Heterogeneous effects of environmental regulations on the long- and short-term effects of technological innovation: A two-stage analysis based on a value chain perspective. *Stud. Sci. Sci.* **2014**, *32*, 937–949.
11. Lanjouw, J.O.; Mody, A. Innovation and the international diffusion of environmentally responsive technology. *Res. Policy* **1996**, *25*, 549–571. [CrossRef]
12. Porter, M. America's Green Strategy. *Sci. Am.* **1991**, *264*, 168. [CrossRef]
13. Scherer, F.M.; Harhoff, D. Technology policy for a world of skew-distributed outcomes. *Res. Policy* **2000**, *29*, 559–566. [CrossRef]
14. Han, J. Study on the efficiency of regional green innovation in China. *Res. Financ. Econ.* **2012**, *11*, 130–137.
15. Han, X.F.; Hui, N.; Song, W.F. Can informatization improve the efficiency of technological innovation in China's industrial sector. *China Ind. Econ.* **2014**, 70–82.
16. Gollop, F.M.; Roberts, M.J. Environmental regulations and productivity growth: The case of fossil-fueled electric power generation. *J. Political Econ.* **1983**, *91*, 654–674. [CrossRef]
17. Gray, W.B. The cost of regulation: OSHA, EPA and the productivity slowdown. *Am. Econ. Rev.* **1987**, *77*, 998–1006.
18. Li, D.Q.; Zhong, C.L.; Hu, J.W. Environmental regulation, government support and efficiency of green technology innovation—An empirical study based on industrial enterprises above the scale from 2009–2017. *J. Jianghan Univ. (Soc. Sci. Ed.)* **2020**, *206*, 39–50+126.
19. Sun, X.; Guo, X.; Wang, Y. Government subsidies, ownership nature and firms' R&D decisions. *J. Manag. Sci.* **2017**, *20*, 18–31.
20. Yi, M.; Li, G.; Peng, J.C.; Chen, W.L.; Man, X. Study on the Temporal and Spatial Differentiation Characteristics of Green Total Factor Productivity in the Yangtze River Economic Belt. *J. Manag. World* **2018**, *6*, 178–179.
21. Borowski, P.F. Adaptation strategy on regulated markets of power companies in Poland. *Energy Environ.* **2019**, *30*, 3–26. [CrossRef]
22. Tone, K.; Tsutsui, M. Network DEA: A slacks-based measure approach. *Eur. J. Oper. Res.* **2009**, *197*, 243–252. [CrossRef]
23. Tone, K. A slacks-based measure of efficiency in data envelopment analysis. *Eur. J. Oper. Res.* **2001**, *103*, 498–509. [CrossRef]
24. Yang, S.; Wu, T.; Li, Z. Study on the spatial and temporal variation of green innovation efficiency in Yangtze River Economic Zone and the influencing factors. *Macroeconomics* **2018**, *6*, 107–117.
25. Pang, R.-C.; Wang, L. Is service industry development green?—Based on Total Factor Efficiency Analysis of Service Industry Environment. *Ind. Econ. Res.* **2016**, 18–28.
26. Tang, W.; Wu, L.; Qian, H. From "pollution paradise" to green growth—A study on the regulation and control mechanism of inter-regional energy-consuming industry transfer. *Econ. Res. J.* **2016**, *51*, 58–70.
27. Sun, J.; Liu, W.G.; Zhou, Y.D. China's openness to the outside world, industrial structure and green economic growth: An empirical test based on inter-provincial panel data. *J. Manag. World* **2014**, 172–173.

28. Brunnermeier, S.B.; Cohen, M.A. Determinants of environmental innovation in US manufacturing industries. *J. Environ. Econ. Manag.* **2003**, *45*, 278–293. [CrossRef]
29. Cao, X.; Yu, J. A study on regional innovation efficiency in China from a green and low-carbon perspective. *China Popul. Resour. Environ.* **2015**, *25*, 10–19.
30. Xiao, Q.; Zhao, L. Heterogeneous environmental regulations, FDI and the efficiency of green technology innovation in China. *Mod. Econ. Res.* **2020**, *4*, 29–40.
31. Kristoffersen, E.; Mikalef, P.; Blomsma, F.; Li, J. The Effects of Business Analytics Capability on Circular Economy Implementation, Resource Orchestration, Capability and Firm Performance. *Int. J. Prod. Econ.* **2021**, *12*, 108–205. [CrossRef]
32. Borowski, P.F. Innovation strategy on the example of companies using bamboo. *J. Innov. Entrep.* **2020**, *10*, 1–17. [CrossRef] [PubMed]

sustainability

Article

Industrial Poverty Alleviation, Digital Innovation and Regional Economically Sustainable Growth: Empirical Evidence Based on Local State-Owned Enterprises in China

Chuan Lin, Haomiao Zhai * and Yanqiu Zhao

Research Center for International Business and Economy, Sichuan International Studies University, Chongqing 400013, China
* Correspondence: zhaihaomiao@sisu.edu.cn

Abstract: This paper takes the industrial poverty alleviation of local state-owned enterprises in China as the research object, and takes the local state-owned enterprises listed in Shanghai and Shenzhen A shares in China from 2016 to 2020 as the sample to empirically test the impact of industrial poverty alleviation on the sustainable economic growth of the region and consider the regulatory effect of digital innovation. This study found that China's local industrial poverty reduction behavior in state-owned enterprises can effectively promote regional economic growth. Moreover, the digital innovation produced a regulating effect; that is, if enterprises carry out digital innovation and have a higher degree of digital innovation, their industrial poverty alleviation behavior will have a stronger role in promoting regional economic growth. This conclusion still holds even after controlling for factors of robustness and endogeneity. In addition, the study of influence mechanisms found that the proportion of primary industry in GDP was the mediating effect of industrial poverty alleviation on regional economic growth, and the proportion of primary industry in GDP had a partial mediating effect. Further heterogeneous group testing shows that the impact of industrial poverty alleviation on regional economically sustainable growth is more obvious in agriculture-related, local state-owned enterprises; non-high-tech, local state-owned enterprises; and local state-owned enterprises with subsequent poverty alleviation plans. The empirical evidence in this paper verifies the role of local state-owned enterprises' participation in industrial poverty alleviation in promoting regional economic growth. It is a useful supplement to the research literature on the economic consequences of Chinese enterprises' participation in targeted poverty alleviation, which helps to better understand such a phenomenon and also provides a powerful explanation for China's poverty alleviation achievements.

Keywords: industrial poverty alleviation; regional economic sustainable growth; digital innovation; local state-owned enterprises in China

Citation: Lin, C.; Zhai, H.; Zhao, Y. Industrial Poverty Alleviation, Digital Innovation and Regional Economically Sustainable Growth: Empirical Evidence Based on Local State-Owned Enterprises in China. *Sustainability* **2022**, *14*, 15571. https://doi.org/10.3390/su142315571

Academic Editors: Jeoung Yul Lee, Dilek Zamantili Nayir and Charles Chen

Received: 16 October 2022
Accepted: 19 November 2022
Published: 23 November 2022

1. Introduction

Poverty alleviation is a great practice carried out by the Chinese government to target poor areas and poor people in the long term. It is an organic embodiment of China's 'common prosperity' ideal, and an important component of China's high-quality economic development [1,2]. On 13 November 2013, General Secretary Xi put forward the idea of 'targeted poverty alleviation' for the first time, pointing out that poverty alleviation work should be 'practical and realistic, tailored to local conditions, guided by categories, and targeted'. On 23 November 2015, the Central Committee of the Communist Party of China (CPC) and the Central People's Government of the People's Republic of China jointly issued the Decision on Winning the Battle against Poverty, which further clarified China's policy measures for implementing targeted poverty alleviation and accelerating poverty alleviation in the coming period of time. Subsequently, various parts of China, its provinces and cities have also issued policy documents and implementation plans for poverty alleviation, so as to cement poverty alleviation as important work from top to bottom and from inside to outside. With interaction and coordination in poverty alleviation policies from governments at all levels, China has gradually formed a poverty alleviation and development policy system with socialist characteristics, presenting an overall pattern of large-scale poverty alleviation, and making remarkable achievements in poverty reduction [3]. According to the World Bank's international poverty standard of $1.90 per person per day, more than 800 million poor people in China have been lifted out of poverty, accounting for about two thirds of the world's total population benefiting from poverty reduction [4]. By the end of 2015, there were 55.75 million poor people in 832 poverty-stricken counties in China. The number of people living in poverty and the incidence of poverty in China have been reduced year by year (see Figure 1). By 2020, all the rural poor living under the current standards will be lifted out of poverty, and the poverty reduction target set by the United Nations 2030 Agenda for Sustainable Development will be fulfilled 10 years ahead of schedule. This is also an organic reflection of the effect of the poverty alleviation policies of the Chinese government [5].

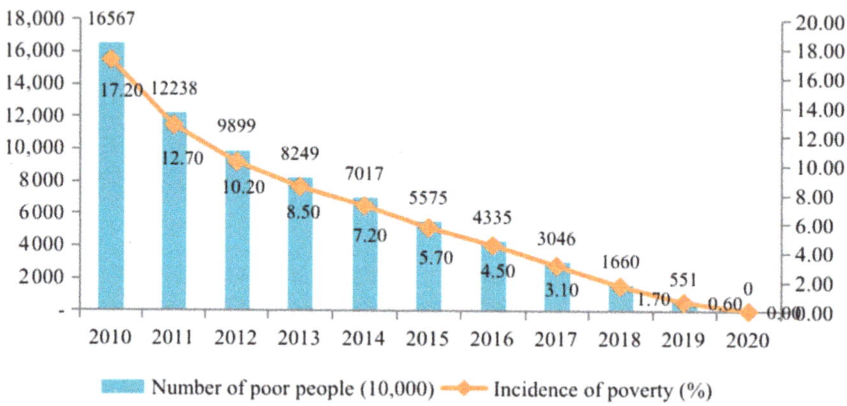

Figure 1. China's rural poverty under the poverty standard in 2010.

In the first stage of the Chinese government's poverty alleviation, the income of poor residents is mainly increased through transfer payments, expenditure reduction, etc., such as increasing financial support for poor households, increasing the reimbursement rate of rural medical insurance, and exempting various insurance premiums. In the second stage, the Chinese government carried out targeted poverty alleviation mainly by improving the endogenous power of poor areas, via methods such as relocation, employment poverty alleviation, industrial poverty alleviation, photovoltaic poverty alleviation, tourism poverty alleviation, and e-commerce poverty alleviation, among which industrial poverty alleviation not only promoted the transformation of economic and industrial structures of poor areas in China, but also brought more employment opportunities for residents in poor areas; it also improved infrastructure construction in poor areas [6]. Enterprises are important participants in industrial poverty alleviation, helping poor areas realize the transformation from resource advantages to industrial advantages and economic advantages, as well as being the most active subjects to strengthen the awareness of poverty and stimulate the endogenous power of poverty alleviation in poor areas. They can also make up for the lack of financial funds invested by the government to fight poverty, so as to promote the sustainable development of the economy in poor areas [7]. Among Chinese enterprises involved in industrial poverty alleviation, Chinese state-owned enterprises have always been the main force in the fight against poverty because of their economic, political and social responsibilities for China' economic and social development. By virtue of their advantages in capital, talent, technology, market, etc., SOEs fully tap the resource endowments of poor areas and regard the poor as an important link in the enterprise value chain, thus effectively promoting the benign development of industries and economies in poor areas [8]. During 2016–2020, China's central state-owned enterprises helped 221 poverty-stricken counties lift themselves out of poverty, invested more than 98 billion yuan in total, and built more than 8000 industrial poverty alleviation projects in poverty-stricken areas, driving investment totaling 14.7 billion yuan, and helping 104,400 laborers in poverty-stricken areas achieve transfer employment. Compared with China's central state-owned enterprises, China's local state-owned enterprises have more initiative and enthusiasm to participate in poverty alleviation. On the one hand, local state-owned enterprises have a better understanding of the economic situation, industrial situation and the situations of poor areas, and can rely on their own resource advantages and professional expertise to develop targeted poverty alleviation strategies more 'according to local conditions'. On the other hand, by participating in targeted poverty alleviation, local state-owned enterprises can drive their regions to overcome poverty and improve regional economic development, which is not only an important responsibility by which local state-owned enterprises fulfill their social responsibilities, but also can feed back the sustainable development of local state-owned enterprises. Therefore, it has important theoretical and practical significance to study the participation of local state-owned enterprises in poverty alleviation, effectively explore the mechanism and path of local state-owned enterprises in China to promote regional economic growth through industrial poverty alleviation, and provide empirical evidence for industrial poverty alleviation of local state-owned enterprises in China. China has actively promoted anti-poverty measures in recent years, and its achievements in anti-poverty action also provide a good realistic scenario for this study.

Numerous studies have explored the relationship between poverty reduction and economic growth. Some of them have found a negative correlation between poverty reduction and economic growth, and this negative relationship originates from numerous channels. For example, poor individuals have limited access to financial markets, which seals them off from potentially profitable investment opportunities, and they often suffer from poor health which affects their productivity; in turn, poor regions and countries have fewer individuals capable of adopting, managing and generating new technologies, they lack infrastructure and face much higher transaction costs [9–11]. In contrast, applying macroeconomic analysis to the linkages between poverty reduction and growth, some recent studies have provided evidence that interventions directly tackling the initial level of poverty could be beneficial in accelerating subsequent growth and making growth more effective in reducing poverty [12–14]. With international evidence, it is proven that faster poverty reduction is linked to faster growth in the entire developing world during 1981–2018 [15]. It can be seen that current literature ignores the important role of local state-owned enterprises, which are vital in the Chinese economy. Thus, this paper attempts to investigate the behavior of poverty reduction in local state-owned enterprises and its impact on economic growth. Meanwhile, as the world is entering a new era of digital economy, the impact of digital technology has also been ignored.

Digital economy has become a new driving force and engine for current global economic development [16,17]. In recent years, the Chinese government has actively promoted the development of the digital economy. By promoting the application of the Internet, big data, blockchain, artificial intelligence and other technologies in the real economy, enterprises are encouraged to actively start digital innovation, so as to realize the digital dividend of the development of the real economy and enterprises [18]. Through digital innovation, enterprises apply digital technology to product updates and iteration, marketing strategy innovation, production mode upgrade and business scope remodeling, management system change and organizational structure innovation, so as to realize leapfrog development and sustainable development of the enterprises. Similarly, digital innovation has also changed the original ecological chain and value chain of the industry in which the enterprise is located. It has not only changed the original boundary of the industry, but also brought new industrial participants to raise the level of competition within the industry, thus breaking the original industrial balance, continuing to drive the innovation and evolution of the business model within the industry, and promoting advancements in the industrial value chain. According to the survey data conducted by China Ai Media Consulting Company, in 2021, more than 80% of Chinese enterprise users used digital systems in their production, operation and management (see Figure 2).

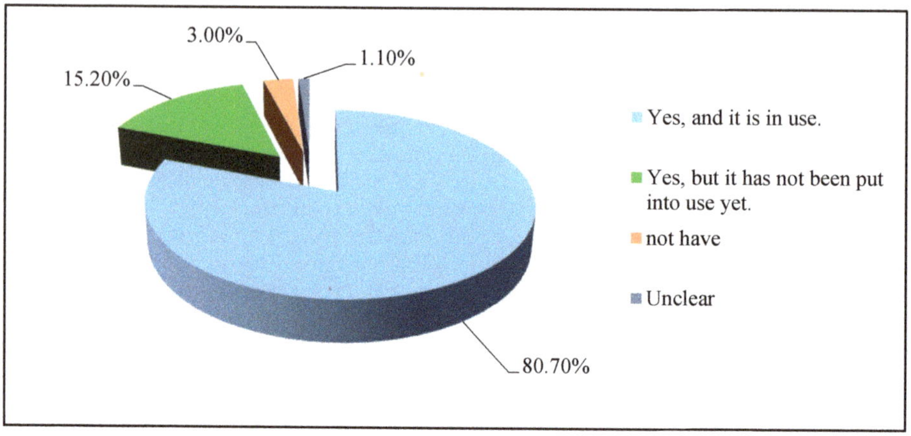

Figure 2. Usage of digital system for Chinese enterprise users in 2021.

Digital innovation is also widely used in the poverty alleviation work of the Chinese government. On the one hand, the digital village is an important path for the continuous integration and development of digital innovation and China's agricultural and rural areas, as well as an important means for China to achieve rural modernization and win the battle against poverty. Since 2018, the Chinese government has vigorously promoted digital agriculture (see Figure 3) through a number of policies, increased the application of digital technology in the primary industry, determined the ideas, requirements and tasks of digital rural construction, and strengthened the construction of rural digital infrastructure. In 2020, China will build 13,700 4G base stations in poverty-stricken areas, with an optical fiber coverage of more than 95%. The total amount of network retail in poverty-stricken areas will exceed 300 billion yuan. Furthermore, 5G technology and the Internet of Things have also begun to spread in poverty-stricken areas, and the penetration rate of digital economy in the primary industry will reach 8.9% [19]. On the other hand, digital innovation is also an important starting point for Chinese enterprises to participate in industrial poverty alleviation. Through digital innovation, enterprises use satellite remote sensing, the Internet of Things, artificial intelligence and other digital technologies to promote agricultural standardized production, improve the allocation of industrial resources in poverty relief areas, and effectively open up the agricultural production and operation systems in poor areas, so as to reshape the industrial ecosystem in such areas and promote the high-quality development of industries in them [20]. In addition, digital innovation can also reduce the degree of information asymmetry between farmers in poor areas and the market, and provide more market opportunities for industries in poor areas by promoting rural e-commerce, live broadcast e-commerce and other digital marketing models [14].

Therefore, this paper takes Chinese local state-owned enterprises' participation in industrial poverty alleviation as the research object, empirically tests the impact of enterprises' industrial poverty alleviation behavior on the sustainable economic development of poverty-stricken areas, and considers the mediating effect of digital innovation. Compared with the existing literature, the marginal contribution of this paper is reflected as follows: first, this paper expands the research object of the effect of different targeted poverty alleviation models on Chinese enterprises. The existing studies on Chinese enterprises' participation in targeted poverty alleviation mostly focus on their behavior in targeted poverty alleviation, and rarely distinguish the differences in participation modes in the process of targeted poverty alleviation. In addition, international evidence shows that subsidiaries of multinational companies (MNC) pay, on average, higher wages than local companies [21]; in developing countries, MNC subsidiaries have strong links backwards and forwards with domestic companies, including small and medium-sized ones, which favors employment and poverty reduction [22]. More specifically, the Multinational Enterprises of the United States (US-MNE) have a significant effect on poverty reduction of in a group of 18 developing countries [23]. This paper focuses on the industrial poverty alleviation behavior of Chinese enterprises and focuses on different models of targeted poverty alleviation, which is conducive to a clearer understanding of the effects of targeted poverty alleviation among Chinese enterprises. In addition, this paper discusses the impact of industrial poverty alleviation by Chinese enterprises on regional economic sustainable growth, which is also a useful supplement to the research on the economic consequences of targeted poverty alleviation by Chinese enterprises. Second, this paper complements the research on the mechanism of digital innovation in the targeted poverty alleviation process of Chinese enterprises. Although the existing literature has analyzed the promoting role of the development of the digital economy in China's rural economy, it has not paid attention to the mechanism and path of promoting the sustainable development of the regional economy by enterprises using their own digital innovation in the process of targeted poverty alleviation. Therefore, the study of this paper is conducive to a clearer explanation of how Chinese enterprises can effectively promote regional economic growth in the process of industrial poverty alleviation. Thirdly, this paper enriches the research literature on the participation of local state-owned enterprises in targeted poverty alleviation in China. The existing literature discusses the targeted poverty alleviation behavior of China's state-owned enterprises, but ignores the reality that local state-owned enterprises should become the main force of targeted poverty alleviation of China's state-owned enterprises due to their better understanding of the regional economic development, industrial development and the actual situation of poor areas. Therefore, this paper, taking Chinese local state-owned enterprises as samples, not only enriches the literature on targeted poverty alleviation in Chinese state-owned enterprises, but also has important practical guiding significance for Chinese local state-owned enterprises to further actively participate in rural revitalization.

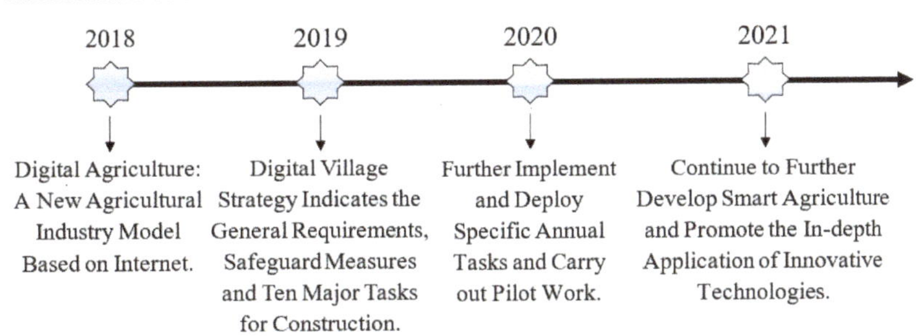

Figure 3. Development course of digital rural construction in China.

2. Theoretical Analysis and Research Hypothesis

2.1. Industrial Poverty Alleviation and Regional Economic Sustainable Growth

The participation of Chinese local state-owned enterprises in industrial poverty alleviation originates from the policy promotion and policy coordination of the Chinese government and local governments. The government has effectively stimulated the enthusiasm and initiative of local state-owned enterprises to participate in poverty alleviation through the supply, regulations, subsidies, support, etc. of relevant policies, and has also established a policy system for enterprises to participate in industrial poverty alleviation through systematic design, so as to provide support for industrial poverty alleviation and sustainable development in China's poor areas in the form of policy supply [24]. As one of the multiple kinds of entities involved in poverty alleviation, local state-owned enterprises can effectively marshal the elemental resources of local economic development, achieve the integration of different resources, promote market competition in poverty alleviation areas, and promote the upgrading of industries in these areas, such as by promoting the 'complementary chain' of the industrial chain, strengthening the brand construction of regional industries, and improving the service system of the whole industrial chain to promote the construction of the industrialization joint system [25]. This means that the participation of local state-owned enterprises in industrial poverty alleviation can help local poor households gain benefits by participating in industries, so as to improve the self-development ability of poor households. Furthermore, local state-owned enterprises can also help local governments achieve the goals of economic development planning by meeting the needs of local governments, so as to promote the social and economic development of the region. Following current literature [26], this paper describes the impact mechanism of industrial poverty alleviation by local state-owned enterprises on regional economic growth as Figure 4.

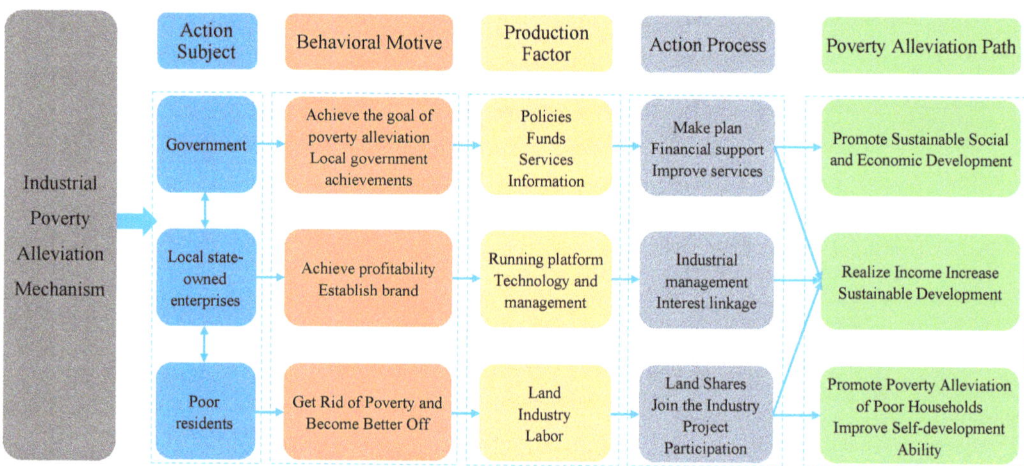

Figure 4. Industrial poverty alleviation mechanism of local state-owned enterprises in China.

From Figure 4, industrial poverty alleviation is a process in which local state-owned enterprises, by combining different actors (Government and Poor residents), allocate production factors according to the motives of these actors, so as to work together to build a poverty alleviation path. This is a process in which the links are complementary and integrated.

Directly speaking, the participation of local state-owned enterprises in industrial poverty alleviation can increase the income of poor residents, thus driving the economic growth of the region [15,27,28]. In the process of industrial poverty alleviation, local state-owned enterprises will formulate appropriate industrial poverty alleviation strategies for poor residents according to their poverty characteristics, development characteristics and industrial characteristics of agricultural production, so as to not only enable poor residents to obtain direct income, but also to drive and help them build corresponding industrial bases, and ensure the sustainability of poverty alleviation [22,23]. In addition, local state-owned enterprises will send staff to poor areas to help poor residents obtain more external resources, help them choose appropriate industrial projects and development forms based on their understanding of the actual situation of the poor, and mobilize the people in poor areas to actively participate in the work of industrial poverty alleviation and development, so as to drive the sustainable economic development of poor areas [29].

Indirectly, local state-owned enterprises have driven the industrial development of the regions through industrial poverty alleviation, meeting the industrial development needs of the local government, and can also drive the economic development level of the region. Local governments in China have a strong demand for industrial development, especially in the context of rapid changes in the current international economic form. Active industrial transformation and industrial upgrading can effectively drive the sustainable development of the local economy. However, being subject to practical problems such as financial pressure, industrial planning and infrastructure, many local governments are also faced with the dilemma of industrial upgrading. In particular, local governments in prefecture-level cities or county-level cities in western China are under great pressure in the process of industrial upgrading. Therefore, the industrial projects brought by local state-owned enterprises in the process of poverty alleviation can not only help the local government to complete the task of poverty alleviation, achieving the performance of the local government, but also help to drive the development of the regional economy [30] by cooperating with the industrial planning of the local government.

Therefore, we propose the following research hypothesis:

Hypothesis 1 (H1). *There is a positive relationship between industrial poverty alleviation and regional economic sustainable growth.*

2.2. Industrial Poverty Alleviation, Digital Innovation and Regional Economically Sustainable Growth

As a result of the integration of modern information technology with global economic development, human production and lifestyle in recent years, the digital economy has been driven by digital innovation based on big data, cloud computing, blockchain, artificial intelligence and other technologies. It has become the commanding heights for all countries in the world to improve the quality of economic development and compete for the right to speak in the international economy [31]. The digital innovation of enterprises can strongly promote the economic development of the region. First, digital innovation itself can drive the development of regional economies. Enterprises, through digital innovation, improve the ability to handle non-standardized and unstructured data, impel the transformation of enterprise management modes and management systems, and promote production efficiency and industrial upgrading. To enhance the degree of specialization, enterprises in the same industry have brought about innovation and development in other enterprises, so as to promote performance in the enterprise itself. In this way, the economic growth of the region is promoted [32,33]. Second, there is integration between enterprise digital innovation and the high-quality growth of the real economy. Digital innovation can also promote the sustainable development of regional economies and society. Digital innovation plays an important role in demand, supply and market transactions matching supply and demand. It also improves the fairness of regional economic development, improves economic efficiency, and promotes regional economic efficiency [34]. Third, digital innovation promotes the development of the industrial factor market, which also allows the ownership of data to flow from manufacturers to consumers, maximizing the value of data, and becoming a powerful driver of economic development in the current digital economy era [35].

Digital innovation has also played a boosting role in the process of industrial poverty alleviation of local state-owned enterprises in China. On the one hand, digital innovation has promoted the flow of information and data in poor areas of China, creating more opportunities for industrial remodeling and upgrading. The development of the digital economy has been continuously penetrating into the development of Chinese agriculture and rural areas, and has also played a role in promoting the development of such areas. For example, the penetration rate of the digital economy in China's primary industry was 8.2 percent in 2019 and had risen to 8.9 percent in 2020. The development and penetration of digital innovation in poverty-stricken areas in China improves the information transmission ability of poverty-stricken areas, reduces the information barrier in these areas, accelerates the transmission speed of data and information, and thus optimizes the flow channel of digital factor resources in urban and rural areas [36]. On the other hand, digital innovation also brings the application of digital technology into the poor areas of China, and expands the path of industrial development in these poor areas. Relying on the implementation of digital innovation, enterprises can apply more digital technologies to the process of industrial poverty alleviation, such as using big data technology to identify the industrial characteristics of poor areas, providing more industrial data, and using big data and cloud computing technology to expand the marketing path of industrial products in poor areas. In particular, when local state-owned enterprises in China participate in industrial poverty alleviation, many enterprises help poor areas to build on the model of 'digital technology + e-commerce + industry'. By combining digital technology with e-commerce, they sell products from poor areas, or build the model of 'digital technology + tourism + industry'. Digital leisure agriculture and other ways are used to drive the industrial transformation of poor areas so as to optimize the allocation of resources in these areas [37].

Digital innovation and industrial poverty alleviation have 'three integrations' of value, rule and mode in promoting local economic development (see Figure 5). In terms of value integration, industrial poverty alleviation recognizes the values of market orientation and profit creation, while digital innovation recognizes the values of innovation orientation and value reproduction in economic development and industrial reform [38]. In terms of law integration, industrial poverty alleviation proposes the law of poverty alleviation, while digital innovation proposes the law of new economic development [39]; In terms of mode integration, industrial poverty alleviation promotes the sustainable development of industries in poor areas, while digital innovation promotes the transformation and development of economy, industry and commerce in poor areas [40,41]. Therefore, under the effect of 'three integrations' and through the promotion of digital innovation, industrial poverty alleviation will play a stronger role in regional economic growth. This means that digital innovation will play a corresponding role between industrial poverty alleviation and regional economic growth. On the one hand, digital innovation reduces the cost of industrial poverty alleviation to promote regional economic growth, which will further increase the efforts of enterprises to strengthen industrial poverty alleviation [42]. Digital innovation reduces the degree of information asymmetry between local state-owned enterprises, local governments and poor residents involved in industrial poverty alleviation, which is conducive to better playing the role of market mechanism in poor areas, and also conducive to the formation of network effect and agglomeration effect in such areas, thus effectively boosting local economic development [43,44]. On the other hand, new industrial models and technologies brought about by digital innovation effectively boost regional economic growth by promoting industrial upgrading. By bringing digital technology to poverty-stricken areas, local state-owned enterprises have promoted e-commerce poverty alleviation, tourism poverty alleviation and other models, accelerated the formation of characteristic industries, and laid a good foundation for the development of these industries, which not only achieved the effect of poverty alleviation, but also provided opportunities for subsequent economic development in poverty-stricken areas [40,45].

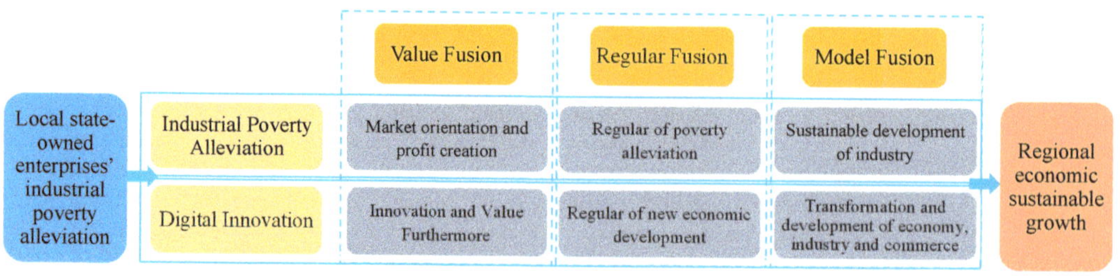

Figure 5. The integration of industry poverty alleviation and digital innovation.

Therefore, we propose the following research hypothesis:

Hypothesis 2 (H2). *Digital innovation has a moderating effect between industrial poverty alleviation and sustainable regional economic growth.*

3. Study Design

3.1. Variable Design

3.1.1. Dependent Variable: Regional Economic Sustainable Growth

This paper measures the annual GDP growth rate (*RESG*) of the poverty alleviation regions where the sample companies are located.

3.1.2. Independent Variable: Industrial Poverty Alleviation

This paper measures the dummy variables and degree variables of sample companies' participation in industrial poverty alleviation (*IPA*).

Participation in industrial poverty alleviation (*WIPA*): measured by whether the sample company participates in industrial poverty alleviation, that is, if the sample company participates in industrial poverty alleviation, *WIPA* = 1, otherwise *WIPA* = 0.

Industrial poverty alleviation degree (*DIPA*): measured by the natural logarithm of the industrial poverty alleviation investment amount of the sample company, namely *DIPA* = ln (amount of industrial poverty alleviation investment + 1).

3.1.3. Intervening Variable: Digital Innovation

This paper measures the dummy variable and degree variable of digital innovation (*DI*) of sample companies. For the definition of digital innovation, this paper refers to current measurement methods which measure the term frequency of digital innovation disclosed in the periodic financial reports of sample companies [46–48].

The first step is to define the dimensions of digital innovation words in this paper, including 'artificial intelligence technology', 'blockchain technology', 'cloud computing technology', 'big data technology' and 'digital technology application', and define relevant keywords under each word (see Figure 6). The second step is to use python to capture information from the regular financial reports of sample companies.

Digital innovation (*WDI*): measured by the digital innovation of the sample company, that is, if the frequency of digital innovation words appears in the annual financial report of the sample company, *WDI* = 1, otherwise *WDI* = 0.

Digital innovation degree (*DDI*): measured by the digital innovation degree of sample companies, namely *DDI* = ln (number of word frequency of 'digital innovation' keywords + 1).

3.1.4. Controlled Variables

The following control variables are added in this paper:

Total Assets (*Size*): measured by the natural logarithm of the total assets at the end of the year;

Asset-liability Ratio (*Debt*): measured by the ratio of the total liabilities at the end of the year to the total assets;

Return on Assets (*Roa*): measured by the ratio of year-end net profit to total assets;

Growth Rate (*Growth*): Measured by the growth rate of year-end operating income of sample enterprises;

Ownership Concentration (*H*10): measured by the squared sum of the shareholding proportion of the top 10 shareholders at the end of the year;

Management Shareholding (*MS*): measured by the enterprise shares held by the management of the sample enterprise;

Enterprise Area (*Area*): if the sample enterprise is located in western China, then *Area* = 1, otherwise *Area* = 0;

Institutional Environment (*IET*): measured by the index of marketization process in the region where the sample enterprises are located.

Figure 6. Innovative keyword composition.

3.2. Empirical Model Design

3.2.1. Benchmark Regression Test Model Design

In order to test the impact of industrial poverty alleviation by local state-owned enterprises on sustainable regional economic growth, this paper constructs the following benchmark regression model:

$$RESG_{i,t} = \alpha_0 + \alpha_1 IPA_{i,t} + \alpha_i Controls_{i,t} + Year + Industry + \varepsilon_{i,t} \tag{1}$$

To further test the moderating effect of digital innovation, this paper constructs the following regression model:

$$RESG_{i,t} = \alpha_0 + \alpha_1 IPA_{i,t} + \alpha_2 (IPA_{i,t} \times DI_{i,t}) + \alpha_3 DI_{i,t} + \alpha_i Controls_{i,t} + Year + Industry + \varepsilon_{i,t} \tag{2}$$

In Equations (1) and (2), the Year and Industry factors of the sample company are simultaneously controlled.

3.2.2. Endogeneity Test Model Design

Although control variables have been added to Equations (1) and (2) in this paper, the endogeneity problem may still exist in the empirical model. One possibility is that a local state-owned enterprise's own industry attribute determines its poverty reduction efforts involved in industry, such as compared to the public class of state-owned enterprises, state-owned business enterprises with stronger industry attributes can bring about more possible ways to alleviate poverty through industry, and thus may accomplish industrial poverty alleviation with regional economic growth. Therefore, the two-stage least-squares method is used for the endogeneity test in this paper. In the first stage, instrumental variables are used to estimate the explanatory variable *IPA*, namely:

$$IPA_{i,t} = \alpha_0 + \alpha_1 CSE_{i,t} + \alpha_i Controls_{i,t} + Year + Industry + \varepsilon_{i,t} \tag{3}$$

In Equation (3), the variable *CSE* is a tool variable; that is, if the sample state-owned enterprises belong to commercial state-owned enterprises, *CSE* = 1, otherwise *CSE* = 0.

According to the Guiding Opinions on the Definition and Classification of State-owned Enterprises (SOES) Functions jointly issued by the State-owned Assets Supervision and Administration Commission of the State Council, the Ministry of Finance and the National Development and Reform Commission of China in 2015, China's SOES are classified into public welfare SOES and commercial SOES. Among them, the main objectives of commercial state-owned enterprises are to enhance the vitality of the state-owned economy, enlarge the functions of state capital, maintain and increase the value of state assets, and carry out commercial operations in accordance with market requirements, while the main objectives of public welfare state-owned enterprises are to ensure people's livelihoods, serve society, and provide public goods and services. Referring to current studies [49], sample companies belonging to A01–05, B10–12, C13–15, C17–24, C26–30, C33, C35, C39–43, E47, E49–50, F, H, K, L, O and R88–89 in the industry classification of the China Securities Regulatory Commission are defined as commercial state-owned enterprises. The reason why this variable is selected as an instrumental variable is that, on the one hand, commercial state-owned enterprises have a better industrial foundation and are more likely to carry out industrial poverty alleviation, which meets the requirement of the correlation of instrumental variables. On the other hand, the industry attributes of local state-owned enterprises do not affect the level of regional economic growth, which also meets the requirement of exogeneity of instrumental variables. Therefore, on the basis of fitting variable IPA through Equation (3), Equations (1) and (2) are further tested.

3.2.3. Intermediary Effect Test Model Design

Local state-owned enterprises promote regional economic growth through industrial poverty alleviation. In this process, the industries built by local state-owned enterprises are basically primary industries. In other words, the poverty alleviation of local state-owned industries promotes the sustainable growth of regional economy by promoting the growth of local primary industries. Therefore, this paper takes the ratio of primary industry to *GDP* in the region where sample enterprises are located as the mediating variable (*PGDP*) to construct the mediating effect model test, namely:

$$PGDP_{\mathrm{i},t} = a_0 + a_1 IPA_{\mathrm{i},t} + a_{\mathrm{i}} Controls_{\mathrm{i},t} + Year + Industry + \varepsilon_{\mathrm{i},t} \tag{4}$$

$$RESG_{\mathrm{i},t} = b_0 + b_1 IPA_{\mathrm{i},t} + b_2 PGDP_{\mathrm{i},t} + b_{\mathrm{i}} Controls_{\mathrm{i},t} + Year + Industry + \varepsilon_{\mathrm{i},t} \tag{5}$$

In Equations (4) and (5), if there is a mediation effect, the coefficient value a_1 in Equation (4) and the coefficient value b_2 in Equation (5) are significant. If the coefficient value b_1 is not significant, it means that there is a complete intermediary effect, while if the coefficient value b_1 is significant, it means that there is a partial intermediary effect. However, if at least one of a_1 and b_2 is not significant, the Sobel test is required.

3.3. Data Selection and Description

The data are extracted from the China Stock Market and Accounting Research database (CSMAR). Starting from 2016, China's Shenzhen Stock Exchange and Shanghai Stock Exchange have required listed companies to disclose information on targeted poverty alleviation. Therefore, our sample period is from 2016 to 2020, and local state-owned enterprises listed on China's A-share stock market are selected in our sample. Based on the original samples, this paper conducts data deletion. The principles of deletion are as follows: first, the samples of enterprises in the financial, insurance and securities industries are removed; second, the sample of enterprises with special treatment is eliminated; third, the sample of enterprises with IPO is excluded; fourth, the enterprise samples with missing data which cannot be supplemented are removed. Finally, this paper obtains 2935 samples of 799 local state-owned enterprises in China from 2016 to 2020.

4. Results and Analysis of Empirical Tests

4.1. Descriptive Statistical Results and Analysis

Table 1 shows the descriptive statistical results of the full sample in this paper. The mean value of *RESG* is 0.063. On average, in recent years, China's overall economic growth level has been maintained at about 6%. The mean value of *WIPA* of the variable is 0.269, indicating that 26.9% of the local state-owned enterprises in the sample have carried out industrial poverty alleviation. The mean value of variable *DIPA* is 3.006, indicating that the average investment in industrial poverty alleviation of local state-owned enterprises in the sample is about 200,000 yuan. However, from the perspective of sample companies participating in industrial poverty alleviation, the average investment in industrial poverty alleviation is about 707.21 million Yuan. The mean value of *WDI* is 0.701, indicating that about 70% of local state-owned enterprises in the sample have carried out digital innovation. The mean value of the variable *DDI* is 1.316, indicating that on average, there are three instances of words related to digital innovation in the annual financial reports of local state-owned enterprises, but from the perspective of the sample companies carrying out digital innovation, the number of words related to digital innovation in the financial reports is six instances on average.

Table 1. Descriptive statistical results of full sample.

Variable	Mean	Median	Standard Deviation	Maximum	Minimum	5%	25%	75%	95%
RESG	0.063	0.068	0.022	0.118	−0.231	0.019	0.050	0.078	0.088
WIPA	0.269	0.000	0.444	1.000	0.000	0.000	0.000	1.000	1.000
DIPA	3.006	0.000	5.589	20.832	0.000	0.000	0.000	0.000	14.235
WDI	0.701	1.000	0.458	1.000	0.000	0.000	0.000	1.000	1.000
DDI	1.316	1.099	1.197	5.684	0.000	0.000	0.000	2.079	3.611
Size	22.987	22.896	1.330	28.636	17.954	20.991	22.056	23.801	25.297
Debt	0.496	0.501	0.207	2.123	0.027	0.163	0.336	0.646	0.832
Roa	0.048	0.046	0.076	0.745	−1.495	−0.027	0.027	0.070	0.139
Growth	0.004	0.001	0.083	4.290	−0.010	−0.004	0.000	0.002	0.006
H10	0.185	0.153	0.130	0.753	0.000	0.035	0.086	0.261	0.453
MS	0.004	0.000	0.025	0.474	0.000	0.000	0.000	0.000	0.012
Area	0.173	0.000	0.378	1.000	0.000	0.000	0.000	0.000	1.000
IET	7.473	7.047	1.790	11.109	0.969	4.557	6.393	9.054	10.290

Table 2 shows the statistical results based on the description of variable *WIPA* grouping. Compared with the group with variable *WIPA* value of 0, the average value and median value of *RESG* in the group with variable *WIPA* value of 1 are larger, and both can pass the significance test of the conventional confidence level, which indicates that compared with the local state-owned enterprises that do not carry out industrial poverty alleviation, the economic growth of the regions where the local state-owned enterprises carry out industrial poverty alleviation is faster.

Table 2. Descriptive Statistical Results of Groups.

Variable	*WIPA* = 1			*WIPA* = 0			*t* Test	Wilcoxon Z
	N	Mean	Median	N	Mean	Median		
RESG	790	0.066	0.070	2145	0.061	0.068	5.160 ***	4.674 ***

Note: *** indicates that they have passed the significance test at the 1% confidence level.

4.2. Correlation Test Results and Analysis

Table 3 shows the correlation values of the main variables in this paper. The correlation values of *WIPA*, *DIPA* and *RESG* are all significantly positive, indicating that there is a positive correlation between industrial poverty alleviation of local state-owned enterprises and regional economic growth. The correlation values of variables *WDI*, *DDI* and variable *RESG* are significantly positive, indicating that the digital transformation behavior of local state-owned enterprises is also positively correlated with the economic growth of their regions. The correlation values between variables *WIPA* and *DIPA* and variables *WDI* and *DDI* are also significantly positive, indicating that poverty alleviation in local state-owned industries will also have a positive correlation with digital innovation. In addition, the correlation value between variables in Table 3 is not high, indicating that there is no multicollinearity problem.

Table 3. Correlation Test Results.

Variable	*RESG*	*WIPA*	*DIPA*	*WDI*	*DDI*	*Size*	*Debt*	*Roa*	*Growth*	*H10*	*MS*	*Area*	*IET*
RESG	1												
WIPA	0.095 ***	1											
DIPA	0.083 ***	0.886 ***	1										
WDI	0.057 ***	0.071 ***	0.063 ***	1									
DDI	0.052 ***	0.035 **	0.019 ***	0.718 ***	1								
Size	−0.017	0.172 ***	0.169 ***	0.148 ***	0.140 ***	1							
Debt	−0.012	−0.012	−0.007	0.029 *	−0.006	0.394 ***	1						
Roa	−0.008	0.003	−0.002	0.009	0.005	0.042 **	−0.021	1					
Growth	0.016	0.023	0.028	0.010	0.027	0.021	0.023	−0.003	1				
H10	−0.025	0.131 ***	0.131 ***	0.062 ***	0.007	0.243 ***	−0.089 ***	0.026	0.040 **	1			
MS	−0.037 **	−0.073 ***	−0.062 ***	0.011	0.057 ***	−0.098 ***	−0.066 ***	−0.010	−0.005	−0.110 ***	1		
Area	0.081 ***	0.163 ***	0.144 ***	0.019	−0.008	−0.060 ***	0.031 *	−0.010	−0.004	0.006	−0.052 ***	1	
IET	−0.008	−0.176 ***	−0.168 ***	0.039 **	0.065 ***	0.014	−0.056 ***	0.019	−0.007	0.005	0.023	−0.433 ***	1

Note: ***, **, and * indicate that they have passed the significance test at the 1%, 5%, and 10% confidence levels, respectively.

4.3. Empirical Results and Analysis

4.3.1. Benchmark Regression Test Results

Table 4 shows the test results of the impact of industrial poverty alleviation of local state-owned enterprises on regional economic growth. Before the control variables are added, the regression results (1) and (2) have significantly positive *WIPA* and *DIPA* coefficients, indicating that compared with the regions where the local state-owned enterprises do not participate in industrial poverty alleviation, the local state-owned enterprises that participate in industrial poverty alleviation and the regions where the local state-owned enterprises with higher industrial poverty alleviation efforts are located have faster economic growth. After adding the control variables, the coefficients of *WIPA* and *DIPA* in the regression results (3) and (4) are still significantly positive, which also shows that the industrial poverty alleviation behavior of local state-owned enterprises can effectively promote the economic growth of the region. It can be seen that the industrial poverty alleviation behavior of local state-owned enterprises can bring more industrial development and industrial investment to poor areas, thus driving the local industrial reform and upgrading, and effectively promoting the local economic growth, which verifies the H1 above.

Table 5 shows the test results of industrial poverty alleviation and regional economic growth considering the moderating effect of digital innovation. In regression results (1) and (2), before adding control variables, the coefficient values of variables *WDI* and *DDI* are significantly positive, indicating that compared with local state-owned enterprises without digital innovation, local state-owned enterprises with digital innovation and higher degrees of digital innovation have faster economic growth in their regions. However, in the regression results (3) and (4), after adding the control variables, the coefficient values of variables *WDI* and *DDI* are still significantly positive, which also indicates that the digital innovation behavior of local state-owned enterprises can also promote the economic growth of their regions. Considering the moderating effect of digital innovation, in regression results (5) and (6), after adding the interaction term, the *WIPA* coefficient value of the variable is still significantly positive, and the interaction terms *WIPA* × *WDI* and *WIPA* × *DDI* are also significantly positive, indicating that under the conditions of considering the influence of digital innovation, the industrial poverty alleviation behavior of local state-owned enterprises plays a stronger role in promoting regional economic growth. The regression results (7) and (8) show a similar situation. The variable *DIPA* and the interaction terms *DIPA* × *WDI* and *DIPA* × *DDI* are all significantly positive, which also verifies that digital innovation has a moderating effect between industrial poverty alleviation and regional economic growth. It can be seen that local state-owned enterprises improve their digital capability through digital innovation, and also provide technical support for their participation in industrial poverty alleviation through digital technology, ensuring the full effect of industrial poverty alleviation, so as to be more conducive to promoting regional economic development, which verifies H2 above.

Table 4. Benchmark Regression Test Results (1).

	(1)	(2)	(3)	(4)
WIPA	0.0048 *** (0.0009)		0.0048 *** (0.0010)	
DIPA		0.0003 *** (0.0001)		0.0003 *** (0.0001)
Size			−0.0003	−0.0003
Debt			−0.0011	−0.0013
Roa			−0.0022	−0.0021
Growth			0.0045	0.0044
H10			−0.0067 **	−0.0066 **
MS			−0.0302 *	−0.0314 *
Area			0.0049 ***	0.0051 ***
IET			0.0006 **	0.0005 **
Year	Yes	Yes	Yes	Yes
Industry	Yes	Yes	Yes	Yes
Constant	0.0614 ***	0.0617 ***	0.0654 ***	0.0648 ***
Adj R^2	0.0087	0.0065	0.0153	0.013
F-statistics	26.6286 ***	20.1893 ***	60.7888 ***	54.458 ***

Note: ***, **, and * indicate that they have passed the significance test at the 1%, 5%, and 10% confidence levels, respectively.

Table 5. Benchmark Regression Test Results (2).

	(1)	(2)	(3)	(4)	(5)	(6)	(7)	(8)
WIPA					0.0055 *** (0.0018)	0.0047 *** (0.0014)		
DIPA							0.0003 ** (0.0001)	0.0002 ** (0.0001)
WIPA × *WDI*					0.0076 *** (0.0021)			
WIPA × *DDI*						0.0011 *** (0.0001)		
DIPA × *WDI*							0.0075 *** (0.0001)	
DIPA × *DDI*								0.0071 *** (0.0006)
WDI	0.0028 *** (0.0009)		0.0029 *** (0.009)		0.0029 *** (0.0010)		0.0032 *** (0.0010)	
DDI		0.0010 *** (0.003)		0.0010 *** (0.003)		0.0011 *** (0.0004)		0.0012 *** (0.0004)
Size			0.0002	0.0002	−0.0001	−0.0001	−0.0001	−0.0001
Debt			−0.0022	−0.0025	−0.0012	−0.0015	−0.0014	−0.0017
Roa			−0.0023	−0.0024	−0.0021	−0.0023	−0.0021	−0.0022
Growth			0.0051	0.0053	0.0046	0.0049	0.0045	0.0045
H10			−0.0054 *	−0.0060 *	−0.0064 *	−0.0072 **	−0.0065 **	−0.0072 **
MS			−0.0324 *	−0.0307 *	−0.0285 *	−0.0268 *	−0.0298 *	−0.0283 *
Area			0.0058 ***	0.0057 ***	0.0051 ***	0.0050 ***	0.0053 ***	0.0051 ***
IET			0.0005 *	0.0005 *	0.0006 **	0.0006 **	0.0006 **	0.0006 **
Year	Yes	Yes	Yes	Yes	Yes	Yes	Yes	Yes
Industry	Yes	Yes	Yes	Yes	Yes	Yes	Yes	Yes
Constant	0.0646 ***	0.0640 ***	0.0589 ***	0.0581 ***	0.0634 ***	0.0627 ***	0.0630 ***	0.0623 ***
Adj R^2	0.0029	0.0024	0.0106	0.0100	0.0186	0.0177	0.0166	0.0160
F-statistics	3.5479 ***	3.0220 ***	4.4774 ***	4.2841 ***	16.0552 ***	17.949 ***	15.5010 ***	15.3338 ***

Note: ***, **, and * indicate that they have passed the significance test at the 1%, 5%, and 10% confidence levels, respectively.

In order to verify the robustness of benchmark regression results, this paper conducts corresponding robustness tests. First, this paper tests the investment of local state-owned enterprises in industrial poverty alleviation as an explanatory variable. Furthermore, we use the number of projects of local state-owned enterprises in industrial poverty alleviation as an explanatory variable to conduct a new empirical test. Second, considering the lagging effect of industrial poverty alleviation on local economic growth, the next economic growth variable of the region where the sample local state-owned enterprises are located as the explained variable is taken to conduct an empirical test again. Third, considering the differences between administrative divisions and administrative levels in China, the sample of local state-owned enterprises located in municipalities directly under the Central Government (Beijing, Shanghai, Tianjin, Chongqing) is removed and a new empirical test is conducted. There is no substantial difference between the robustness test results and the benchmark regression test results above, which verifies the robustness of the regression results in this paper.

4.3.2. Endogeneity Test Results

Table 6 shows the results of the endogenous test. In the 1st Stage regression results (1) and (2), the coefficient values of variable *CSE* are significantly positive, indicating that compared with public welfare local state-owned enterprises, competitive state-owned enterprises are more likely to carry out industrial poverty alleviation, and the industrial poverty alleviation efforts are also higher, which verifies the correlation of tool variables. In the 2nd Stage regression results (3) and (4), the *WIPA* and *DIPA* coefficients of the variables are also significantly positive, which indicates that after considering endogenous factors, the industrial poverty alleviation behavior of local state-owned enterprises can still promote local economic growth. In addition, the J statistic of the 2nd Stage regression results failed to pass the significance test of the conventional confidence level, which also verified the rationality of the selection of tool variables.

Table 6. Endogeneity Test Results.

	1st Stage		2nd Stage	
	(1)	(2)	(3)	(4)
	WIPA	*DIPA*	*RESG*	*RESG*
CSE	0.0144 *** (0.0016)	0.2736 *** (0.0205)		
WIPA			0.0048 *** (0.0010)	
DIPA				0.0003 *** (0.0001)
Controls	Yes	Yes	Yes	Yes
Year	Yes	Yes	Yes	Yes
Industry	Yes	Yes	Yes	Yes
Constant	−0.9842 ***	−12.2941 ***	0.0661 ***	0.0655 ***
Adj R^2	0.0879	0.0792	0.0151	0.0132
F-statistics	32.4016 ***	29.0375 ***	55.0501 ***	49.3849 ***
J-statistics	—	—	0.2970	0.8240

Note: *** indicates that they have passed the significance test at the 1% confidence level.

4.3.3. Intermediary Effect Test Results

Table 7 shows the results of the intermediary effect test. The regression results (1) and (2) are the benchmark test results mentioned above. In the regression results (3) and (4), the *WIPA* and *DIPA* coefficients of variables are significantly positive, indicating that the greater the participation of local state-owned enterprises in industrial poverty alleviation and industrial poverty alleviation, the higher the proportion of primary industry in the GDP of the region. In the regression results (5) and (6), the *PGDP* coefficient of the variable is significantly positive, which verifies the existence of the intermediary effect, indicating that the increase in the proportion of primary industry in GDP effectively drives the sustainable economic growth of China's poor areas. However, in the regression results (5) and (6), the *WIPA* and *DIPA* coefficients of the variables are also significantly positive, which indicates that the influence of the proportion of the primary industry in GDP only has a partial intermediary effect.

Table 7. Intermediary Effect Test Results.

	(1)	(2)	(3)	(4)	(5)	(6)
	RESG	*RESG*	*PGDP*	*PGDP*	*RESG*	*RESG*
WIPA	0.0048 *** (0.0010)		0.0095 *** (0.0014)		0.0042 *** (0.0010)	
DIPA		0.0003 *** (0.0001)		0.0006 *** (0.0001)		0.0003 *** (0.0001)
PGDP					0.0571 *** (0.0123)	0.0589 *** (0.0123)
Controls	Yes	Yes	Yes	Yes	Yes	Yes
Year	Yes	Yes	Yes	Yes	Yes	Yes
Industry	Yes	Yes	Yes	Yes	Yes	Yes
Constant	0.0654 ***	0.0648 ***	0.2241 ***	0.2221 ***	0.0526 ***	0.0517 ***
Adj R^2	0.0153	0.013	0.4922	0.4896	0.0222	0.0208
F-statistics	60.7888 ***	54.458 ***	317.0343	313.7072 ***	76.6030 ***	72.4093 ***

Note: *** indicates that they have passed the significance test at the 1% confidence level.

4.4. Heterogeneity Grouping Regression Test Results and Analysis

4.4.1. Grouping Test between Agriculture-Related Enterprises and Non-Agriculture-Related Enterprises

Whether in China or other countries, the main targets of poverty alleviation are poor rural areas, and the industrial base driven by industrial poverty alleviation is mostly agriculture and agriculture-related processing and manufacturing industries. This means that local state-owned enterprises engaged in agricultural production or related to agricultural production (such as rural tourism developed in rural China in recent years, processing and manufacturing industries based on rural expertise, etc.) may form a better driving force for industrial poverty alleviation in poor areas due to their own technological base, product base, market base, etc. Therefore, this paper further tests the samples belonging to agriculture related enterprises and non-agriculture related enterprises in groups. According to the industry classification standards of the CSRC, this paper classifies enterprises that belong to A, C13–16, C20, H, N as agriculture related enterprises, and others as non-agriculture related enterprises.

Table 8 shows the grouping test results of agricultural enterprises and non-agricultural enterprises. In the regression results (1) and (2), the *WIPA* and *DIPA* coefficient values of the variables are significantly positive, indicating that industrial poverty alleviation can effectively promote the economic growth of the regions where agricultural local state-owned enterprises are located. In the regression results (3) and (4), the *WIPA* and *DIPA* coefficient values of the variables are also significantly positive, indicating that industrial poverty alleviation can also promote the economic growth of the regions where non-agricultural local state-owned enterprises are located. However, comparing the test results of different types of enterprises, the regression results (1) and (2) have larger *WIPA* and *DIPA* coefficients and higher significance, which indicates that compared with non-agriculture related enterprises, the industry poverty alleviation of agriculture related enterprises has a stronger role in promoting economic growth in the region. It can be seen that the agricultural enterprises themselves have a better understanding of agriculture, rural areas and farmers, which is more conducive to linking their own business with the development of poor areas, and more convenient for enterprises to establish good industrial planning for the local area so as to effectively implement industrial poverty alleviation.

Table 8. Grouping test results for agricultural and non-agricultural enterprises.

	Sample of Agriculture-Related Enterprises		Sample of Non-Agriculture-Related Enterprises	
	(1)	(2)	(3)	(4)
WIPA	0.0045 *** (0.0010)		0.038 ** (0.0017)	
DIPA		0.0003 *** (0.0001)		0.0002 * (0.0001)
Controls	Yes	Yes	Yes	Yes
Year	Yes	Yes	Yes	Yes
Industry	Yes	Yes	Yes	Yes
Constant	0.0671 ***	0.0066 ***	0.0747 ***	0.0759 ***
Adj R^2	0.0141	0.0126	0.0044	0.0410
F-statistics	15.1199 ***	14.6862 ***	12.717 ***	12.5814 ***

Note: ***, **, and * indicate that they have passed the significance test at the 1%, 5%, and 10% confidence levels, respectively.

4.4.2. Grouping Test between High-Tech Enterprises and Non-High-Tech Enterprises

Enterprises with different scientific and technological attributes have differences in digital innovation ideas, tendencies, degrees, etc., which will make different local state-owned enterprises have different efforts in industrial poverty alleviation through digital innovation, and may also make the economic consequences of industrial poverty alleviation different. For example, high-tech enterprises contain more technology in their own industrial development, but non-high-tech enterprises also attach importance to the application of technology in recent years, and technology plays a stronger role in promoting their industrial development. Therefore, this paper further conducts a grouping test on the samples of high-tech enterprises and non-high-tech enterprises [50].

Table 9 shows the grouping test results for high-tech enterprises and non-high-tech enterprises. In regression results (1) and (2), the values of variables *WIPA* and *DIPA* coefficients are significantly positive, indicating that in the regions where high-tech local state-owned enterprises are located, the poverty alleviation behavior of enterprises can significantly promote regional economic growth, while in regression results (3) and (4), the values of variables *WIPA* and *DIPA* coefficients are also significantly positive, indicating that in regions where non-high-tech local state-owned enterprises are located, the poverty alleviation behavior of enterprises can also significantly promote economic growth. Comparing the regression results of different samples, the values of *WIPA* and *DIPA* coefficients in regression results (3) and (4) are higher and more significant. It can be seen that because non-high-tech local state-owned enterprises use less technology, technological innovation can play a stronger role in the primary stage, which is more conducive to industrial poverty alleviation, and thus plays a stronger role in regional economic growth.

Table 9. Grouping test results for high-tech enterprises and non-high-tech enterprises.

	Sample of High-Tech Enterprises		Sample of Non-High-Tech Enterprises	
	(1)	(2)	(3)	(4)
WIPA	0.0041 ** (0.0018)		0.0049 *** (0.0011)	
DIPA		0.0002 * (0.0001)		0.0004 *** (0.0001)
Controls	Yes	Yes	Yes	Yes
Year	Yes	Yes	Yes	Yes
Industry	Yes	Yes	Yes	Yes
Constant	0.0712 ***	0.0698 ***	0.0629 ***	0.0626 ***
Adj R^2	0.0103	0.0077	0.0140	0.0126
F-statistics	12.0060 ***	11.7447 ***	14.2689 ***	13.9315 ***

Note: ***, **, and * indicate that they have passed the significance test at the 1%, 5%, and 10% confidence levels, respectively.

4.4.3. Grouping Test between Follow-Up Poverty Alleviation Plan Enterprises and No-Follow-Up Poverty Alleviation Plan Enterprises

When enterprises publicly participate in poverty alleviation, they will simultaneously publish whether there is a follow-up poverty alleviation plan. On the one hand, the existence of follow-up poverty alleviation plans means that enterprises will continue to participate in poverty alleviation in addition to participating at present, which shows the sustainability of enterprises' participation in poverty alleviation. On the other hand, releasing the follow-up poverty alleviation plan is also an effective means for enterprises to disclose information to market investors. Therefore, this paper further tests the samples of enterprises that have issued follow-up poverty alleviation plans and enterprises that have not issued follow-up poverty alleviation plans.

Table 10 shows the group test results of enterprises with and without follow-up poverty alleviation plan. In the regression results (1) and (2), the coefficient values of variables *WIPA* and *DIPA* are significantly positive, indicating that in the regions where enterprises with subsequent poverty alleviation plans are located, the industrial poverty alleviation behavior of enterprises can significantly promote regional economic growth. In regression results (3) and (4), the coefficient values of variables *WIPA* and *DIPA* are also significantly positive. It shows that in the regions where the enterprises have no follow-up poverty alleviation plan, the poverty alleviation behavior of enterprises can also promote the economic growth of the regions. However, compared with the test results of different samples, the coefficient values of variables *WIPA* and *DIPA* in the sample of enterprises with subsequent poverty alleviation plan are significantly larger, indicating that the industrial poverty alleviation of enterprises with a subsequent poverty alleviation plan has a stronger role in promoting the economic growth of their regions. It can be seen that the release of follow-up poverty alleviation plans by enterprises is not only an attitude of their continuous participation in poverty alleviation, but also a reflection of their own real investment in industrial poverty alleviation, so as to exert a stronger role in promoting regional economic growth.

Table 10. Grouping test results for follow-up poverty alleviation plan enterprises and no-follow-up poverty alleviation plan enterprises.

	Sample of Follow-Up Poverty Alleviation Plan Enterprises		**Sample of No-Follow-Up Poverty Alleviation Plan Enterprises**	
	(1)	**(2)**	**(3)**	**(4)**
WIPA	0.0062 *** (0.0024)		0.0057 *** (0.0013)	
DIPA		0.0006 *** (0.0002)		0.0003 *** (0.0001)
Controls				
Year				
Industry				
Constant	0.0686 ***	0.0687 ***	0.0574 ***	0.0585 ***
Adj R^2	0.0113	0.0122	0.0182	0.0110
F-statistics	13.2046 ***	13.3708 ***	13.4711 ***	12.4831 ***

Note: *** indicates that they have passed the significance test at the 1% confidence level.

5. Conclusions

Chinese enterprises, especially the local state-owned enterprises, not only build a good industrial development plan for poor areas and solve the problems of poor regions in terms of public poverty, but also contribute to the sustainable development of the regional economy. Especially in the era of the digital economy, digital innovation not only provides good technical means for enterprises, but also helps enterprises to apply digital technology for industrial poverty alleviation. Therefore, taking the industrial poverty alleviation of local state-owned enterprises in China as the research object with a sample of the local state-owned enterprises listed in Shanghai and Shenzhen stock exchanges from 2016 to 2020, this paper empirically tests the impact of industrial poverty alleviation on the sustainable economic growth of the local region and the moderating effect of digital innovation. Our findings show that China's local industrial poverty reduction behavior in state-owned enterprises can effectively promote regional economic growth. Moreover, if enterprises carry out digital innovation and have a higher degree of digital innovation, their industrial poverty alleviation behavior will have a stronger role in promoting regional economic growth. This conclusion still holds even after controlling for robustness and endogeneity factors. In addition, the study also finds that the mediation effect of the proportion of primary industry in GDP is statistically significant, and constitutes partial mediation. Heterogeneous analysis shows that the impact of industrial poverty alleviation on regional economic sustainable growth is more pronounced in agriculture-related local state-owned enterprises, non-high-tech local state-owned enterprises, and local state-owned enterprises with subsequent poverty alleviation plans

This study contributes to the current literature in the following aspects. Firstly, this paper focuses on the research of the behavior of Chinese enterprises participating in industrial poverty alleviation and the effect of different targeted poverty alleviation models on Chinese enterprises. Current studies have only focused on whether Chinese enterprises participate in poverty alleviation or how strongly they participate in poverty alleviation. Second, we further investigate the moderating effect of digital innovation. The existing literature only studied the digital economy in China's rural economy; this paper explores the impact mechanism of digital innovation on sustainable regional growth in the process of targeted poverty alleviation. Third, this paper investigates the role of local state-owned enterprises on targeted poverty alleviation, which has been ignored in current literature. Local state-owned enterprises should become the main force to promote regional economic development because they are more familiar with their regions.

6. Discussion

In recent years, the Chinese government has actively promoted poverty alleviation, giving poverty alleviation a prominent position in its governance, and promoting common prosperity by eliminating poverty and improving people's livelihood. This is not only the baseline task of the Chinese government, to build a moderately prosperous society in all respects, but also an essential requirement of the socialist political and economic system. According to the empirical evidence in this paper, as local state-owned enterprises are familiar with and make important contributions to regional economic development, their active participation in industrial poverty alleviation can effectively promote the economic growth of their regions. Therefore, combined with the research content and conclusion of this paper, this paper puts forward the following countermeasures and suggestions. First, we will give full importance to the role of local SOES in the follow-up work of poverty alleviation. Although the Chinese government has solved the problem of absolute poverty in China's poor areas, it still faces the problem of relative poverty after absolute poverty, the problem of preventing the return to poverty after solving poverty, and the problem of effectively connecting poverty alleviation with rural revitalization. Therefore, local state-owned enterprises should continue to go into districts, counties and rural areas where poverty has been eliminated, and maintain continuous attention and support to these areas, so as to ensure sustainable economic development in these areas. For example, the model of resident village cadres already implemented by local state-owned enterprises can be sustained in the post-poverty period and the period of rural revitalization, so as to ensure sustained support for the regional economy. Second, it is necessary to strengthen local state-owned enterprises to participate in rural industrial construction. Since local state-owned enterprises are more familiar with their regions and have the ability and strength to participate in rural industrial construction, they should play a more prominent role in the process of rural revitalization by the Chinese government, so that local state-owned enterprises can participate more in rural construction. In the process of participating in industrial construction, local state-owned enterprises should give full importance to the cultivation of farmers' abilities for self-development. Through the encouragement of local government, the management of local state-owned enterprises, and the participation of farmers and rural departments, they should promote the transformation of the concept of industrial development and industrial transformation in rural areas, so as to better promote regional economic development. Third, it is necessary to strengthen the application of digital technology in rural areas. The digital economy is the mainstream trend of economic development of all countries in the world. Digital technology is widely used not only in urban areas, but also in rural areas of China. On the one hand, in the process of agricultural mechanization production, the application of digital technology is beneficial to more efficient agricultural production; on the other hand, the development of digital technology can also be leveraged for the rural industry to provide a broader market space. For example, many rural areas in China are now actively promote the "e-commerce + industry" model, and have obtained very good results. Therefore, digital innovation and digital transformation in rural China should be actively promoted, and more digital technologies, such as big data and blockchain, should be used to provide new driving forces for the development of agricultural industry and rural economic growth.

Author Contributions: Conceptualization, C.L.; Methodology, C.L. and Y.Z.; Formal analysis, H.Z.; Data curation, H.Z.; Writing—original draft, Y.Z. All authors have read and agreed to the published version of the manuscript.

Funding: This research was funded by the National Social Science Fund Youth Project (20cgl013).

Data Availability Statement: Data will be made available on request.

Conflicts of Interest: The authors declare no conflict of interest.

References

1. Wang, L.; Xu, M. Research on Poverty Reduction Effect of China's Precision Poverty Alleviation Policy: Empirical Evidence from Quasi-natural Experiment. *Stat. Res.* **2019**, *36*, 15–26.
2. Wang, X.; Yan, H.; Huang, X.; Wen, H.; Chen, Y. The Impact of Foreign Trade and Urbanization on Poverty Reduction: Empirical Evidence from China. *Sustainability* **2022**, *14*, 735620. [CrossRef]
3. Luo, L.; Ping, W.; Shan, Q.; Wang, J. Summary from China's Poverty Alleviation Experience: Can Poverty Alleviation Policies Achieve Effective Income Increase. *J. Manag. World* **2022**, *38*, 70–83.
4. Chen, S.; Ravallion, M. The Developing World Is Poorer than We Thought, but No Less Successful in the Fight Against Poverty. *Q. J. Econ.* **2010**, *125*, 1577–1625. [CrossRef]
5. Li, X.; Li, L. Evaluation of China's Targeted Poverty Alleviation Policies: A Decomposition Analysis Based on the Poverty Reduction Effects. *Sustainability* **2021**, *13*, 662543. [CrossRef]
6. Li, G.; Li, J. China's Poverty Reduction through Industrial Development: Progress and Prospects. *Contemp. Econ. Manag.* **2020**, *42*, 9–16.
7. Morris, M.H.; Santos, S.C.; Neumeyer, X. Entrepreneurship as a Solution to Poverty in Developed Economies. *Bus. Horiz.* **2020**, *63*, 377–390. [CrossRef]
8. Tang, M.; Yang, H.; Liao, F. Determinants of the Disclosure Tone of Poverty Alleviation Information: The Case of A-share Listed Companies in China's Shanghai and Shenzhen Stock Exchange. *Appl. Econ. Lett.* **2022**, *29*, 988–992. [CrossRef]
9. Perry, G.E.; López, J.H.; Maloney, W.F.; Arias, O.; Luis Servén, L. *Poverty Reduction and Growth: Virtuous and Vicious Circles*; World Bank: Washington, DC, USA, 2006.
10. Thorbecke, E. Multidimensional poverty: Conceptual and measurement issues. In *The Many Dimensions of Poverty*; Palgrave Macmillan: London, UK, 2013; pp. 3–19.
11. Thorbecke, E. The interrelationship linking growth, inequality and poverty in sub-Saharan Africa. *J. Afr. Econ.* **2013**, *22* (Suppl. 1), i15–i48. [CrossRef]
12. Ravallion, M. Why don't we see poverty convergence? *Am. Econ. Rev.* **2012**, *102*, 504–523. [CrossRef]
13. Marrero, G.A.; Servén, L. *Growth, Inequality, and Poverty: A Robust Relationship?* Policy Research Working Paper (WPS); The World Bank: Washington, DC, USA, 2018.
14. Ouyang, Y.; Shimeles, A.; Thorbecke, E. Revisiting cross-country poverty convergence in the developing world with a special focus on Sub-Saharan Africa. *World Dev.* **2019**, *117*, 13–28. [CrossRef]
15. Thorbecke, E.; Ouyang, Y. Towards A Virtuous Spiral Between Poverty Reduction And Growth: Comparing Sub Saharan Africa With The Developing World. *World Dev.* **2022**, *152*, 105776. [CrossRef]
16. Singhal, K.; Feng, Q.; Ganeshan, R.; Sanders, N.R.; Shanthikumar, J.G. Introduction to the Special Issue on Perspectives on Big Data. *Prod. Oper. Manag.* **2018**, *27*, 1639–1641. [CrossRef]

17. Goldfarb, A.; Tucker, C. Digital Economics. *J. Econ. Lit.* **2019**, *57*, 3–43. [CrossRef]
18. Zhang, W. The Endogenous Attributes and Industrial Organization of Digital Economy. *J. Manag. World* **2022**, *38*, 79–90.
19. Wei, B.; Qu, A.; Li, A.; Chen, X. Research on Construction Methods of Digital Village. *Hubei Agric. Sci.* **2022**, *61*, 183–187.
20. Tang, H.; Xie, T. On the Effective Linkage Mechanism and Effect Between Industrial Poverty Alleviation and Industrial Revitalization from the Perspective of Digital Economy. *J. Guangdong Univ. Financ. Econ.* **2022**, *37*, 30–43.
21. Torky, M.; Hassanein, A.E. Integrating Blockchain and the Internet of Things in Precision Agriculture: Analysis, Opportunities, and Challenges. *Comput. Electron. Agric.* **2020**, *178*, 105476. [CrossRef]
22. Van Tulder, R. *The Role of Business in Poverty Reduction towards a Sustainable Corporate Story?* United Nations Research Institute for Social Development: Geneva, Switzerland, 2008.
23. De Backer, K.; Miroudot, S.; Rigo, D. Multinational Enterprises in the Global economy: Heavily Discussed, Hardly Measured. 2019. Available online: www.oecd.org/industry/ind/MNEs-in-the-global-economy-policy-note.pdf (accessed on 18 November 2022).
24. Castillo, O.N.; Chiatchoua, C. US multinational enterprises: Effects on poverty in developing countries. *Res. Glob.* **2022**, *5*, 100090. [CrossRef]
25. Gao, Q. Discussion on the Effective Connection Between Poverty Alleviation and Rural Revitalization: Based on the Perspective of Policy Transfer and Continuity. *J. Nanjing Agric. Univ. (Soc. Sci. Ed.)* **2020**, *20*, 49–57.
26. Tu, S. The Organic Integration of Poverty Alleviation and Rural Revitalization Strategies: Goal Orientation, Key Areas and Measures. *Chin. Rural Econ.* **2020**, *36*, 2–12.
27. Liu, J.; Chen, X.; Cao, J. The Mechanism of the Industrialization of Precise Poverty Alleviation. *China Popul. Resour. Environ.* **2017**, *27*, 127–135.
28. Wan, G.; Hu, X.; Liu, W. China's poverty reduction miracle and relative poverty: Focusing on the roles of growth and inequality. *China Econ. Rev.* **2021**, *68*, 101643. [CrossRef]
29. Ivanic, M.; Martin, W. Sectoral Productivity Growth and Poverty Reduction: National and Global Impacts. *World Dev.* **2018**, *209*, 429–439. [CrossRef]
30. Wang, C.; Yang, Y.; Gu, J. Can Resident Village Assistance of the First Secretary Enhance the Social Capital in Village: A Field Experiment Study. *J. Financ. Econ.* **2021**, *47*, 110–124.
31. Gao, F. China's Poverty Alleviation 'Miracle' from the Perspective of the Structural Transformation of the Urban–rural Dual Economy. *China Political Econ.* **2021**, *4*, 86–109. [CrossRef]
32. Lin, J.; Yu, Z.; Wei, Y.D.; Wang, M. Internet Access, Spillover and Regional Development in China. *Sustainability* **2017**, *9*, 9060946. [CrossRef]
33. Ostmeier, E.; Strobel, M. Building Skills in the Context of Digital Transformation: How Industry Digital Maturity Drives Proactive Skill Development. *J. Bus. Res.* **2022**, *139*, 718–730. [CrossRef]
34. Du, Y.; Lou, J. The Impact and Spillover Effect of Digital Transformation on Enterprise Upgrading. *J. Zhongnan Univ. Econ. Law* **2022**, *66*, 119–133.
35. Li, S.; Huang, Z. Digital Economy and High-quality Development: Mechanisms and Evidence. *China Econ. Q.* **2022**, *22*, 1–18.
36. Jones, C.I.; Tonetti., C. Nonrivalry and Economics of Data. *Am. Econ. Rev.* **2020**, *110*, 2819–2858. [CrossRef]
37. Yen, T.F. Leisure Agriculture in the Era of Targeted Poverty Alleviation. *Asian J. Educ. Soc. Stud.* **2020**, *9*, 1–6. [CrossRef]
38. Qiu, P.; Zhou, Z.; Kim, D.J. A New Path of Sustainable Development in Traditional Agricultural Areas from the Perspective of Open Innovation: A Coupling and Coordination Study on the Agricultural Industry and the Tourism Industry. *J. Open Innov. Technol. Mark. Complex.* **2021**, *7*, 1–15. [CrossRef]
39. Hao, X.; Li, Y.; Ren, S.; Wu, H.; Hao, Y. The role of digitalization on green economic growth: Does industrial structure optimization and green innovation matter? *J. Environ. Manag.* **2023**, *325*, 116504. [CrossRef]
40. Lv, C.; Song, J.; Lee, C.-C. Can digital finance narrow the regional disparities in the quality of economic growth? Evidence from China. *Econ. Anal. Policy* **2022**, *76*, 502–521. [CrossRef]
41. Mora-Rivera, J.; García-Mora, F. Internet access and poverty reduction: Evidence from rural and urban Mexico. *Telecommun. Policy* **2021**, *45*, 102076. [CrossRef]
42. Ye, Y.; Chen, S.; Li, C. Financial technology as a driver of poverty alleviation in China: Evidence from an innovative regression approach. *J. Innov. Knowl.* **2022**, *7*, 100164. [CrossRef]
43. Zhu, X.; Li, X.; Gong, J.; Xu, J. Technology empowerment: A path to poverty alleviation for Chinese women from the perspective of development communication. *Telecommun. Policy* **2022**, *46*, 102328. [CrossRef]
44. Holmes, H.; Burgess, G. Digital exclusion and poverty in the UK: How structural inequality shapes experiences of getting online. *Digit. Geogr. Soc.* **2022**, *3*, 100041. [CrossRef]
45. Lechman, E.; Popowska, M. Harnessing digital technologies for poverty reduction. Evidence for low-income and lower-middle income countries. *Telecommun. Policy* **2022**, *46*, 102313. [CrossRef]
46. Li, F. The Digital Transformation of Business Models in the Creative Industries: A Holistic Framework and Emerging Trends. *Technovation* **2020**, *92*, 102012. [CrossRef]
47. Huang, D.; Xie, H.; Meng, X.; Zhang, Q. Digital Transformation and Enterprise Value: Empirical Evidence based on Text Analysis Methods. *Economist* **2021**, *33*, 41–51.
48. Gao, F.; Lin, C.; Zhai, H. Digital Transformation, Corporate Innovation, and International Strategy: Empirical Evidence from Listed Companies in China. *Sustainability* **2022**, *14*, 8137. [CrossRef]

49. Wei, M., Cai, G., Liu, J. Research on Classified Governance of State-owned Listed Companies in China. *J. Sun Yat-Sen Univ. (Soc. Sci. Ed.)* **2017**, *57*, 175–192.
50. Guo, L.; Xiao, S.F.; Li, X.J.; Li, W.W. Non-executive Employee Equity Incentive and Innovation Outputs: Empirical Evidence from High-tech Listed Companies in China. *Account. Res.* **2019**, *40*, 59–67.

sustainability

MDPI

Article

Digital Transformation, Corporate Innovation, and International Strategy: Empirical Evidence from Listed Companies in China

Fuxia Gao, Chuan Lin and Haomiao Zhai *

Research Center for International Business and Economy, Sichuan International Studies University, Chongqing 400013, China; gaofuxia@sisu.edu.cn (F.G.); sisulc@sisu.edu.cn (C.L.)
* Correspondence: zhaihaomiao@sisu.edu.cn

Abstract: This paper empirically investigates the impact of digital transformation on corporate international strategy. With a dataset of the Chinese stock market from 2014 to 2020, our empirical results reveal that digital transformation has a positive impact on the international strategy of Chinese enterprises. More specifically, firms with digital transformation are more likely to implement international strategy, and firms with a higher degree of digital transformation are associated with a higher level of internationalization. In addition, our empirical results reveal that corporate innovation exhibits the mediation effect. Moreover, our findings show that the impact of digital transformation is more pronounced for private firms and non-high-tech enterprises, and this impact is also moderated by high institutional development in eastern China. Our findings survive numerous robustness checks.

Keywords: digital transformation; international strategy; corporate innovation

Citation: Gao, F.; Lin, C.; Zhai, H. Digital Transformation, Corporate Innovation, and International Strategy: Empirical Evidence from Listed Companies in China. *Sustainability* **2022**, *14*, 8137. https://doi.org/10.3390/su14138137

Academic Editors: Jeoung Yul Lee, Dilek Zamantili Nayir and Charles Chen

Received: 4 June 2022
Accepted: 28 June 2022
Published: 4 July 2022

Publisher's Note: MDPI stays neutral with regard to jurisdictional claims in published maps and institutional affiliations.

1. Introduction

As the main body of the national and industrial innovation system, enterprises build the dual-core of enterprise innovation through the innovation of technical elements such as technology investment and R & D and the use of new technologies, as well as the change and innovation of non-technical elements, such as their own organizational and institutional systems, which also promote innovation to become the driving force of enterprise progress and development [1]. Because it requires enterprises to invest a lot of money to obtain benefits through innovation, many enterprises will pay attention to the uncertainty and risk in the process of R & D and innovation [2]. However, innovation will eventually bring higher benefits to enterprises, enhance enterprise value, and bring enterprises stronger international competitiveness, better social responsibility, more government subsidies, smoother financing channels, etc. [3–5]. Thus, most firms are still willing to actively participate in innovation activities. In recent years, the Chinese government and enterprises have continued to increase their investment in innovation. Since 2001, the total R & D expenditure in China increased more than 20 times in the past 20 years (see Figure 1). In 2019, 507 Chinese firms were shortlisted as the top 2500 global R & D investments recognized by international organizations, and the number of high-tech enterprises reached 225,000, which represents an increase of 1.8 times over 2015. Even though COVID-19 had a great impact on social and economic development, the innovation investment of Chinese enterprises has still increased significantly. In 2021, China's R & D investment in the whole society was CNY 2.79 trillion, a year-on-year increase of 14.2%, and the R & D investment intensity increased by 2.44% (the data are collected from the China Stock Market and Accounting Research database (CSMAR).

In recent years, with the development of a new round of scientific and technological revolution and industrial transformation, the digital economy, driven by a new generation of information technologies such as the internet, big data, cloud computing, artificial intelligence, blockchain, and financial technology, is promoting profound changes in the production mode, lifestyle, organization form, governance model, and business model of human society. These digital economic elements have also become the basis for reorganizing global factor resources and reshaping the global economic structure. Therefore, Chinese President Xi Jinping clearly pointed out in his signed article "Continue to Grow Stronger, Better and Bigger China's Digital Economy" that we should "promote the deep integration of digital technology and the real economy, enable the transformation and upgrading of traditional industries, foster new industries, new forms and models of business, and continue to grow stronger, better and bigger China's digital economy". As an important participant in the digital economy, through the introduction of digital technology, firms build digital industrial chains, supply chains, and ecological chains in many ways, such as business digitization, operation digitization, management digitization, and industry digitization, so as to promote the digital transformation of all-round reform and system evolution. It is not only an effective path for enterprises to meet the digital economy and drive high-quality development but also an important manifestation of corporate innovation [6,7].

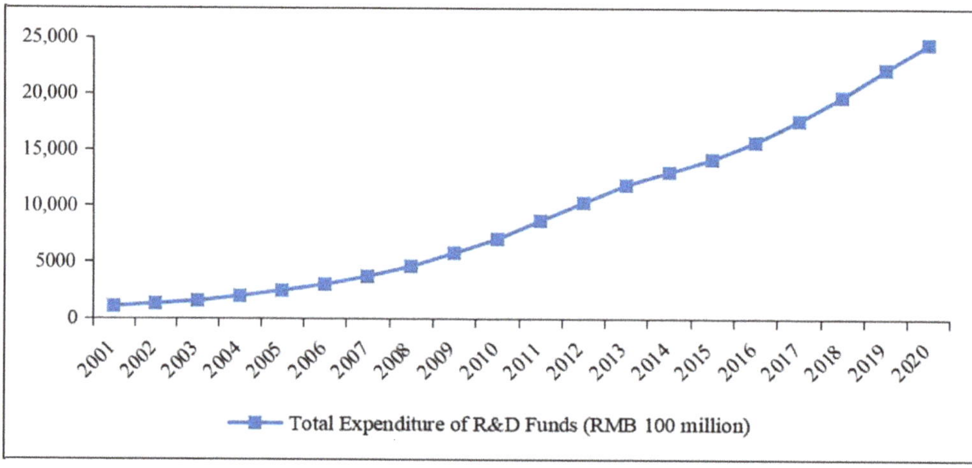

Figure 1. Total expenditure of R & D funds in China from 2001 to 2020.

Digital technology is fast growing and widely applied in China, which helps firms exerting international trade realize strategic transformation and reshape their international competitiveness. In recent years, a lot of cross-border digital platforms have emerged, and numerous Chinese firms achieved internationalization through these digital platforms. With the data from the ministry of commerce, in 2019, the total value of exports and imports for cross-border e-commerce was CNY 186 billion, with a growth rate of 38.3%. More specifically, exports achieved CNY 94.4 billion, with a growth rate of 68.2%. With these platforms, some traditional companies can identify and contact customers; for example, Safewell Group Holdings (China) can sell products directly to their international clients, which increases their profits. In addition, digital platforms help firms engaging in the domestic market explore the international market, such as Ningbo Meike Cultural Development Company and Ruian Aorui Electronic Commerce Company. They use these platforms to identify international opportunities, and they can modify their products to meet the requirements of overseas customers.

What can digital transformation bring to enterprises? Some findings show that digital transformation has improved the total factor productivity of enterprises by driving enterprise innovation, human capital structure, deep integration of the manufacturing industry and modern service industry, and enterprise operation levels [8]. And in the process of digital transformation, firms have improved their management efficiency and technical level so as to improve their productivity [9]. Moreover, digital transformation reduces the external transaction costs faced by firms, effectively promotes the level of the professional division of labor, and improves the productivity of enterprises [10]. Digital transformation can also promote firms to converge towards the goal of sustainable development, enable firms to better meet the expectations of relevant stakeholders, and promote better sustainable development by improving their business performance [11]. The digital economy reduces the labor share through the productivity improvement effect, factor bias effect, and scale return change effect [12]. They show that digital transformation can bring substantial changes to firms, promote firms to reduce their operating costs by introducing digital technology in the business process, enable firms to improve the efficiency and accuracy of enterprise decision-making by integrating digital thinking and mode, and improve the internal governance system and governance level so that enterprises can obtain a better operating income.

However, when the existing literature pays attention to the impact of digital transformation on enterprise decision-making, it rarely pays attention to whether digital transformation affects the international strategy of firms. As an important strategic decision of enterprises, international strategy will undoubtedly be affected by digital transformation [13]. With the promotion of enterprise digital transformation, enterprises can break the path of dependence on traditional operations at a lower cost, expand their own business boundaries more widely, and make it easy for enterprises to go deep into the international market [14]. With the implementation of various measures such as developing an open economy and improving the level of opening to the outside world, more and more Chinese firms gain market share by opening up the international market to enhance their international competitiveness. In 2012, China entered the world's three largest foreign investors. In 2014, China's foreign investment flow exceeded the absorption of foreign capital and became a net capital exporter. From 2002 to 2018, China's foreign direct investment soared from USD 2.7 billion to USD 143.04 billion, with an average annual growth rate of 33.8%. In 2017, China's total foreign trade in goods reached USD 4.10 trillion, accounting for 11.5% of the total global foreign trade, ranking first in the world [15,16]. It can be seen that the reality of Chinese enterprises actively exploring overseas markets provides a good realistic background for this study. Based on the background of the new scientific and technological revolution, exploring whether digital transformation can affect enterprise internationalization decision-making can not only reveal how Chinese enterprises affect enterprise decision-making through business model transformation and governance system upgrading in the process of digital transformation, but it also has important theoretical and practical significance for fully understanding the problem of Chinese enterprises' continuous development of overseas markets under the background of global economic integration.

Therefore, this paper takes Chinese A-share listed companies as samples to theoretically and empirically test the influence of digital transformation on the international strategy of enterprises. Compared with the existing literature, the marginal contribution of this paper is as follows: First, existing studies on the economic consequences of enterprises' digital transformation mostly focus on the impact of digital transformation on firms' business performance and production efficiency, while few pieces of literature focus on the impact of digital transformation on enterprises' international strategy decisions even though international strategy is the first choice for Chinese enterprises to expand markets in recent years. Therefore, the research of this paper can not only expand the research on the economic consequences of digital transformation but also be more in line with the reality of Chinese enterprises. Second, although much literature has studied the international strategy of Chinese enterprises, there is no literature discussing the international strategy decisions of Chinese enterprises from the perspective of digital transformation under the background of a new scientific and technological revolution. Therefore, this study not only expands the research perspective on the international strategy decisions of

Chinese enterprises. It is also helpful for exploring more influential factors that influence Chinese enterprises' international strategy decisions. Third, by analyzing the influence mechanism and heterogeneity of digital transformation on international business decisions, the research conclusion can provide more accurate suggestions for Chinese enterprises to further implement digital transformation decisions.

2. Theoretical Analysis and Research Hypothesis

2.1. Digital Transformation and International Strategy

As an adaptation to the current era of the digital economy, digital transformation is the first choice for the strategic transformation of many Chinese enterprises. Starting from their own needs, firms look for transformation schemes suitable for their own maturity and development strategy by introducing digital technology and actively promoting digital construction and enterprise reform and reconstruction. In the process of digital transformation, on the one hand, due to the application of digital technologies such as big data and artificial intelligence, firms can reallocate resources and capabilities, make them easier to enter the new business ecosystem, obtain more market opportunities, and face more market investors and consumers [17]. On the other hand, due to the digital transformation of enterprise in the mode of production, organization form, marketing mode, management mode, management strategy, and so on, firms operate in a more sophisticated way so that they can function in the face of the new business model of uncertainty and risk, obtain a better business performance, and enhance their own value [18]. Moreover, digital transformation will also affect the internal management model and governance system of firms while affecting the production and operation of enterprises. Through the digital management transformation and reform of core management links and management positions, the enterprise can promote the data sharing and opening within the enterprise, release the data application value, promote the circulation of data elements of enterprise management, and enable the enterprise to obtain sustainable competitive advantages [19,20]. This means that digital transformation will also affect the cost of enterprises' international market development, the economic basis for international strategy, and the market boundary they face, which will affect the decision of international strategy.

Firstly, digital transformation reduces the cost for enterprises to explore the international market [10,12]. The application of digital technology promotes opportunities for enterprises in new markets, reduces the cost of developing new markets, and enables enterprises to find market customers more accurately by relying on new marketing technology and new marketing models [21]. In the process of developing the international market, firms explore more market customers and market space at a lower cost based on the mining, processing, and analysis of big data. Without digital technology, enterprises need more labor force to expand the international market. The application of big data can not only enable enterprises to know the market situation through data analysis and reduce the cost of labor to expand the market, but also improve the timeliness and accuracy of enterprises to judge market opportunities. For example, in 2015, China instructed enterprises in the Linyi City of Shandong Province to use the cloud computing technology composed of the ORACLE database and distributed server to realize the real-time tracking and analysis of the trade environment, competitors, and international buyers through the calculation of import and export trade data of various countries around the world, so as to formulate marketing strategies for enterprises to explore the international market. It can be seen that in the process of digital transformation, enterprises have reduced the cost of exploring the international market, including the cost of obtaining international market information, developing the international market, international marketing, and international market maintenance, etc., and the international market information that enterprises can obtain is more objective, real, and reliable than when they do not use digital technology, It also makes enterprises more dynamic when facing international decision-making [22].

Secondly, digital transformation provides enterprise performance and a good economic foundation for enterprises to explore the international market. Digital transformation drives the reform of traditional production, operation mechanisms, and the management mode of enterprises, promotes the optimization of resource allocation efficiency and innovation of the management mode of enterprises, improves the efficiency of production and operation, and makes enterprises have better business performance and value [23]. Then, under the support of good business performance, enterprises' use of digital technology will improve and they can also effectively use digital technology to improve information processing abilities, enhance the understanding of foreign markets, and further improve the enterprise's ability to evaluate and predict the local market demand [24]. This also means the enterprise can rely on effective information decision systems analysis for information, calibration, and to grasp market opportunities. Moreover, digital transformation can also reduce the financing cost of enterprises so that enterprises not only have more capital and cash flow that can expand the international market but also have a better financial environment, so as to ensure that enterprises do not need to put more energy in the financial field and can allocate more resources to international business, so as to achieve the desired effect of developing the international market [25].

Finally, digital transformation breaks the traditional path dependence in the process of enterprise production and operation. It also expands the enterprise market boundary. The use of digital technology provides enterprises with the opportunity to cross the original market boundary so that they can move the original market boundary or blur their own established market boundary and take advantage of the possible cross-border market opportunity by constantly designing digital value propositions [26]. Therefore, digital transformation can make it easier for enterprises to break the inherent dependence on the internationalization path so that they are no longer limited to the established international or domestic market boundary, can re-establish the exclusive operation process adapted to the international market, and improve the success rate of enterprises operating in multiple countries to expand the market. For example, by introducing digital platform technology and using a digital platform operating system, e-commerce platform, and intelligent manufacturing system in digital technology infrastructure, enterprises can actively expand internationalization channels, improve internationalization efficiency and competitiveness in the international market, and make enterprises more flexible and changeable in the international market [27]. At the same time, the integration of digital technology and production technology improves the production technology level of enterprises, promotes intelligent, mechanized, and automated products, improves the value and added value of products, and enables enterprises' products to better integrate into the overseas market environment [28,29].

We, therefore, propose the following research hypothesis:

Hypothesis 1 (H1). *There is a positive relationship between digital transformation and the international strategy of enterprises.*

2.2. Digital Transformation, Innovation, and International Strategy

As the core driving force and important means of competition for high-quality development of enterprises, innovation behavior can help enterprises establish core competitiveness, improve production efficiency, and boost enterprises to obtain better profits in a long period of time, which is conducive to change the way of economic growth of enterprises, so as to achieve sustainable value creation. Although innovation is a resource-consuming activity of enterprises, with uncertain output factors and financing constraints, more enterprises are still willing to actively innovate and change their current operation mode, management mode, and market mode through innovation so as to ensure that enterprises have the power of sustainable development [30]. As the development of globalization expands the market scope faced by enterprises and intensifies the degree of market competition, enterprises can accumulate more knowledge reserves, technology reserves, and resource reserves in the international market through the R & D effect and learning effect of innovative behavior, so as to improve their production efficiency and enter the international market with lower cost and higher quality [31,32].

Digital transformation is an important form of enterprise innovation behavior. Enterprises in the process of digital transformation to restore the original production of the physical form of the product can assign a new attribute, change the enterprise's value creation logic, and even reshape the ecological system to form the unique path of enterprise value [33]. It can also lead to a sustainable competitive advantage for the companies, improved traditional innovation modes, and ensure that enterprises receive an "innovation bonus" in the process of digital innovation [34].

It can be seen that, as the process of digital transformation deepens, firms will pay more attention to the success of digital transformation through innovative behavior and realize the effect of digital transformation. Entrepreneurship will also stimulate enterprises to better release the power of digital transformation by entering the international market [35]. Innovation behavior will form a mediation effect between digital transformation and the enterprise's international strategy decision. On the one hand, the improvement of the degree of innovation will strengthen the degree of digital transformation of enterprises, which will improve the influence of digital transformation on international decision-making. The enhancement of innovation dynamics ensures the success of digital transformation, improves the efficiency of the application of digital transformation in firms [36], and encourages enterprises to make better use of data mining in the information resources with the international market, which makes firms more convenient to enter the international market. On the other hand, innovation is also an effective way for firms to expand their business boundaries. Driven by innovation, firms can not only enter new forms of business but also actively expand the boundaries of original forms of business by means of regional expansion. In other words, in the process of digital transformation, through the increase in innovation investment, firms can strengthen the ability and power basis of breaking through the original production and operation boundary, profoundly change the ability value, resource value and information value of firms, stimulate the awareness and power of enterprises to actively enter the international market, and reduce the risk for enterprises entering the international market.

We, therefore, propose the following research hypothesis:

Hypothesis 2 (H2). *There is an influence mechanism of digital transformation on the international strategy of enterprises, that is, corporate innovation plays a mediation effect between digital transformation and the international strategy of firms.*

3. Study Design

3.1. Data Selection and Description

Since 2013, Chinese firms have gradually begun to use digital technology to create corporate value. In 2014, the Chinese Government Work Report mentioned the concept of "big data" for the first time. Therefore, this paper takes Chinese A-share listed companies from 2014 to 2020 as a sample to empirically test the impact of digital transformation on the international strategy of Chinese enterprises. Firms in the financial industry and firms with special treatment are excluded from our sample. In addition, firms with their main business engaged in the digital industry are also eliminated. Finally, our sample contains 15,199 observations of 2635 listed companies from 2014 to 2020.

3.2. Variable Design

3.2.1. Dependent Variable: International Strategy

This paper measures the international strategy (IS) of enterprises by whether the sample companies adopt international strategy (ISW) and the degree of international strategy (ISD).

Firstly, this paper constructs the dummy variable of whether the sample company operates internationally. If there is international business income disclosed in the annual financial report of the sample company, then ISW = 1, otherwise, ISW = 0.

Secondly, this paper constructs the variable of the international strategy degree of firms using the proportion of the international business income in the total operating income.

3.2.2. Independent Variable: Digital Transformation

The digital transformation (DT) in this paper is also measured by whether the firm is digitally transformed (DTW) and the degree of digital transformation (DTD).

First, referring to the research methods of current studies [37,38], this paper extracts the word frequency involved in "digitization" in the disclosure contents of a firm's regular financial reports by Python. Among them, the dimensions of "digitalization" are defined as "artificial intelligence technology", "blockchain technology", "cloud computing technology", "big data", and "digital technology application", and specific keywords are captured again based on each dimension (see Figure 2).

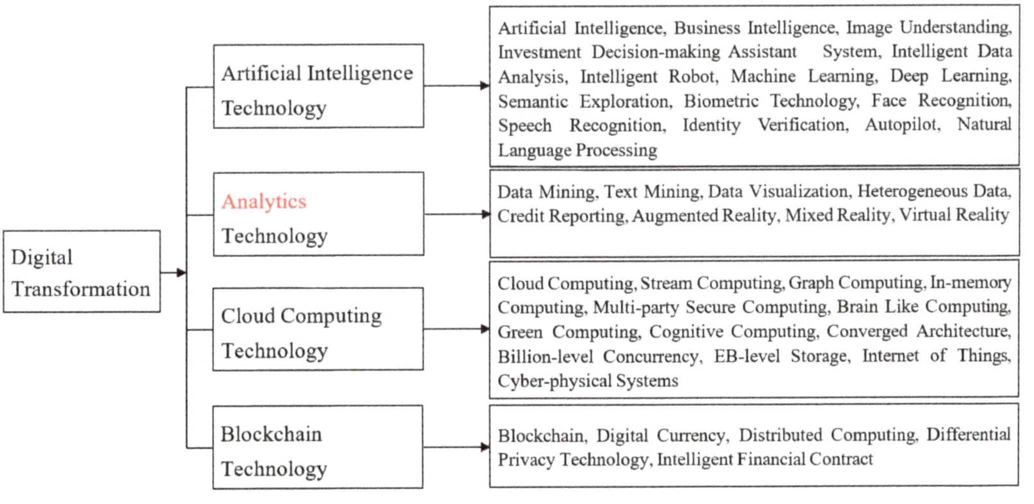

Figure 2. Lexical composition of digital transformation.

Secondly, this paper constructs the dummy variable of whether the sample company has digital transformation, that is, if the content disclosed in the annual financial report involves the word frequency of digital transformation, DTW = 1, otherwise DTW = 0.

Furthermore, this paper constructs the variable of the digital transformation degree of firms, which is defined as follows, DTD = ln (number of word frequency of 'digital' keywords + 1).

3.2.3. Intervening Variable: Innovation

In this paper, the annual R & D investment of sample companies is used to measure innovation behavior (Inn), namely Inn = ln (Annual R & D investment +1).

3.2.4. Controlled Variables

The following control variables are added in this paper:

Total Assets (Size): measured by the natural logarithm of the total assets at the end of the year;
Asset-liability Ratio (Debt): measured by the ratio of the total liabilities at the end of the year to the total assets;
Return on Assets (Roa): measured by the ratio of year-end net profit to total assets;
Stock Ownership (SO): measured by whether the sample company belongs to Chinese state-owned enterprises (SOEs) or Chinese non-state-owned enterprises (Non-SOEs). If it belongs to SOEs, then it is equal to 1, otherwise, it is 0;
Ownership Concentration (H10): measured by the squared sum of the shareholding proportion of the top 10 shareholders at the end of the year;
Team size of executives (TSE): measured by the natural logarithm of the total number of senior management teams at the end of the year.

3.3. *Empirical Model Design*

3.3.1. Benchmark Regression Test Model Design

To test the impact of digital transformation on the international strategy of Chinese enterprises, this paper constructs the following multiple regression model:

$$IO_{i,t} = \alpha_1 DT_{i,t} + \alpha_i Control_{i,t} + Year + Industry + C + \varepsilon_{i,t} \quad (1)$$

In Equation (1), the Year and Industry factors of the sample company are simultaneously controlled. In addition, all variables are winsorized at 1% and 99%.

3.3.2. Mediation Effect Test Model Design

From the previous analysis, innovation will have a mediation effect. Therefore, this paper constructs a mediation effect model to test. Based on Equation (1), this paper constructs a mediation effect model, that is:

$$Inn_{i,t} = a_1 DT_{i,t} + a_i Control_{i,t} + Year + Industry + C + \varepsilon_{i,t} \quad (2)$$

$$IO_{i,t} = b_1 DT_{i,t} + b_2 Inn_{i,t} + b_i Control_{i,t} + Year + Industry + C + \varepsilon_{i,t} \quad (3)$$

In Equations (2) and (3), if there is a mediating effect, the coefficient value a_1 in Equation (2) and coefficient value b_2 in Equation (3) are significant. If the coefficient value b_1 is not significant, it means that there is a complete mediation effect, while if the coefficient value b_1 is significant, it means that there is a partial mediation effect. However, if at least one of a_1 and b_2 is not significant, a further Sobel test is required.

3.3.3. Endogeneity Test Model Design

Although this paper has added control variables to Equations (1) and (2), there may still be endogenous problems in the empirical model. One possibility is that the location of the enterprise has a good foundation in the digital economy, which makes the enterprise more likely to carry out digital transformation so that there is a false relationship between digital transformation and international strategy. Therefore, this paper uses the two-stage least squares method for the endogenous test. In the first stage, the instrumental variable estimates the explanatory variable *DT*, that is:

$$DT_{i,t} = \alpha_1 Mobile_{i,t} + \alpha_i Control_{i,t} + Year + Industry + C + \varepsilon_{i,t} \quad (4)$$

In Equation (4), the variable *Mobile* is an instrumental variable which is measured by the natural logarithm of the total number of mobile phone users in the location of the sample company with reference to the method of previous literature [8]. The reason why this variable is selected as an instrumental variable is that, on the one hand, the greater the number of local mobile phone users, the better the digital economy infrastructure in the region and the greater the probability of digital transformation of firms, which meets the correlation requirements of instrumental variables. On the other hand, the number of local mobile phone users will not affect the international strategy decision-making of enterprises, so the instrumental variables also meet the exogenous requirements. After fitting the variable *DT* through Equation (4), we test it through Equations (1) and (2).

4. Results and Analysis of Empirical Tests

4.1. Descriptive Statistical Results and Analysis

Table 1 gives the descriptive statistical results of the main variables of the whole sample. Among the explained variables, the average value of the variable *ISW* is 0.543, indicating that about 54.3% of Chinese enterprises will choose the decision of international strategy, which suggests that more than half of Chinese enterprises will expand the international market. The average *ISD* is 0.109, indicating that about 10.9% of the operating income of Chinese enterprises comes from the international market, while about 20.2% of the operating income of enterprises with international business comes from the international market. Among the explanatory variables, the mean value of variable *DTW* is 0.568, indicating that about 56.8% of Chinese enterprises have carried out digital transformation, and more than half of Chinese enterprises will recognize digital transformation. The mean value of variable *DTD* is 1.117, which indicates that the digital word frequency appears twice in the annual financial report of Chinese enterprises, while the digital word frequency appears 6 times in the annual financial report of enterprises with digital transformation. It can be seen that there are some differences in the degree of digital transformation of different enterprises. The mean of the mediation variable *Inn* is 14.829, indicating that the average annual R & D investment of Chinese firms is about CNY 2.75 million, but there are great differences in R & D investment among different firms.

Table 1. Descriptive statistical results of full sample.

Variable	Mean	Median	Standard Deviation	Maximum	Minimum	25%	75%
ISW	0.543	1.000	0.498	1.000	0.000	0.000	1.000
ISD	0.109	0.004	0.189	1.000	0.000	0.000	0.141
DTW	0.568	1.000	0.495	1.000	0.000	0.000	1.000
DTD	1.117	0.693	1.253	6.071	0.000	0.000	1.946
Inn	14.829	17.683	7.049	24.104	0.000	15.959	18.777
Size	22.540	22.364	1.346	28.636	14.942	21.632	23.300
Debt	0.450	0.442	0.206	4.026	0.008	0.293	0.598
Roa	0.054	0.050	0.089	1.305	−3.978	0.028	0.081
SO	0.418	0.000	0.493	1.000	0.000	0.000	1.000
H10	0.164	0.135	0.119	0.810	0.000	0.075	0.225
TSE	2.841	2.833	0.232	3.912	2.079	2.708	2.996

Table 2 reports the descriptive statistical results grouped by variables *DTW*, *DTD*, and *Inn*. In the grouping test according to the variable *DTW*, the value of the variable *DTW* is 1. The mean and median values of the variables *ISW* and *ISD* in the group are higher, and the significance test of the conventional confidence level is confirmed, which shows that compared with the firms without digital transformation, the enterprises with digital transformation have higher international strategy probability and degree of international strategy. In the grouping test according to the variable *DTD*, the mean and median values of the variables *ISW* and *ISD* in the high *DTD* group are higher, which shows that compared with the enterprises with lower digital transformation degrees, the enterprises with higher digital transformation degrees also have higher probability and degree of international strategy. In the grouping test according to the variable Inn, the mean and median of the variables *ISW* and *ISD* in the high Inn group are higher, which can also pass the significance test of the conventional confidence level, which shows that compared with the firms with lower innovation investment, the enterprises with higher innovation investment will have higher probability and degree of international strategy.

Table 2. Descriptive statistical results of groups.

Variable	*DTW* = 1			*DTW* = 0			*T* Test	Wilcoxon Z
	N	Mean	Median	N	Mean	Median		
ISW	8634	0.566	1.000	6565	0.513	1.000	6.472 ***	5.577 ***
ISD	8634	0.115	0.007	6565	0.102	0.001	4.380 ***	4.901 ***
Variable	**High *DTD***			**Low *DTD***			***T* Test**	**Wilcoxon Z**
	N	Mean	Median	N	Mean	Median		
ISW	7063	0.569	1.000	8136	0.521	1.000	5.978 ***	5.152 ***
ISD	7063	0.115	0.007	8136	0.105	0.002	3.460 ***	4.246 ***
Variable	**High *Inn***			**Low *Inn***			***T* Test**	**Wilcoxon Z**
	N	Mean	Median	N	Mean	Median		
ISW	7600	0.711	1.000	7599	0.376	0.000	44.027 ***	35.775 ***
ISD	7600	0.144	0.048	7599	0.075	0.000	22.626 ***	36.066 ***

Note: *** indicates that they have passed the significance test at the 1% confidence level.

4.2. Correlation Test Results and Analysis

Table 3 shows the correlation coefficient values between the main variables. Firstly, the correlation coefficients between variables *DTW* and *DTD* and variables *ISW* and *ISD* are significantly positive, indicating that there is a positive correlation between digital transformation variables and enterprise international strategy variables. Secondly, the correlation coefficient between explanatory variables and control variables is not high, indicating that there is no problem of multicollinearity between variables.

Table 3. Correlation test results.

Variable	ISW	ISD	DTW	DTD	Inn	Size	Debt	Roa	SO	H10	TSE
ISW	1										
ISD	0.530 ***	1									
DTW	0.052 ***	0.036 ***	1								
DTD	0.060 ***	0.031 ***	0.778 ***	1							
Inn	0.387 ***	0.193 ***	0.151 ***	0.126 ***	1						
Size	0.024 ***	−0.026 ***	0.071 ***	0.050 ***	0.057 ***	1					
Debt	−0.027 ***	−0.020 **	−0.017 **	−0.020 **	−0.131 ***	0.462 ***	1				
Roa	−0.003	−0.031 ***	0.036 ***	0.026 ***	0.073 ***	0.063 ***	−0.228 ***	1			
SO	−0.122 ***	−0.132 ***	−0.108 ***	−0.092 ***	−0.155 ***	0.303 ***	0.225 ***	−0.066 ***	1		
H10	−0.060 ***	−0.050 ***	−0.030 ***	−0.025 ***	−0.041 ***	0.234 ***	0.024 ***	0.101 ***	0.190 ***	1	
TSE	0.012	−0.004	−0.012	−0.005	0.007	0.064 ***	0.042 ***	−0.007	0.117 ***	0.024 ***	1

Note: *** and ** indicate that they have passed the significance test at the 1% and 5% confidence levels, respectively.

4.3. Empirical Results and Analysis

4.3.1. Benchmark Regression Test Results

Table 4 shows the benchmark regression test results in this paper. In the regression results (1) and (2), when the control variables are not added, there is a significant positive correlation between the explanatory variable *DTW* and the explained variables *ISW* and *ISD*, which indicates that compared with the enterprises without digital transformation, the enterprises with digital transformation are more inclined to carry out international strategy, and the degree of international strategy is also higher. In the regression results (3) and (4), after the control variables are added, the explanatory variable *DTW* is still related to the explained variables *ISW*, which reveals a significant positive correlation. In the regression results (5) and (6), when the control variables are not added, there is also a significant positive correlation between the explanatory variable *DTD* and the explained variables *ISW* and *ISD*, which indicates that the stronger the degree of enterprise digital transformation, the greater the probability of the enterprise choosing international strategy and the higher the degree of international strategy. Similarly, in the regression results (7) and (8), after the control variables are added, the explanatory variable *DTD* and the explained variables *ISW* are still positively correlated with *ISD*. From the benchmark regression results, there is a positive correlation between digital transformation and international strategy. With more and more Chinese enterprises carrying out digital transformation, these digital transformation firms are also more inclined to use the international market to develop their own business. The benchmark regression results verify the previous research hypothesis 1.

Table 4. Benchmark regression test results.

	ISW	ISD	ISW	ISD	ISW	ISD	ISW	ISD
	(1)	(2)	(3)	(4)	(5)	(6)	(7)	(8)
DTW	0.212 *** (0.033)	0.014 *** (0.003)	0.125 *** (0.034)	0.008 ** (0.003)				
DTD					0.097 *** (0.013)	0.005 *** (0.001)	0.069 *** (0.013)	0.003 ** (0.001)
Size			0.147 ***	0.004 ***			0.146 ***	0.004 ***
Debt			−0.472 ***	−0.010			−0.468 ***	−0.011
Roa			−0.586 ***	−0.088 ***			−0.583 ***	−0.088 ***
SO			−0.543 ***	−0.052 ***			−0.540 ***	−0.052 ***
H10			−0.915 ***	−0.042 ***			−0.914 ***	−0.042 ***
TSE			0.220 ***	0.009			0.218 ***	0.009
Year	Yes	Yes	Yes	Yes	Yes	Yes	Yes	Yes
Industry	Yes	Yes	Yes	Yes	Yes	Yes	Yes	Yes
Constant	0.053 **	0.102 ***	−3.201 ***	0.032 ***	0.065 ***	0.104 ***	−3.195 ***	0.031 ***
Adj R^2	0.003	0.001	0.024	0.020	0.004	0.001	0.025	0.020
F-statistics	41.892 ***	19.187 ***	55.044 ***	45.741 ***	55.218 ***	14.883 ***	56.944 ***	45.583 ***

Note: *** and ** indicate that they have passed the significance test at the 1% and 5% confidence levels, respectively.

4.3.2. Intermediary Effect Test Results

Table 5 shows the results of the mediation effect in this paper. Based on the empirical results in Table 4 above, the regression results (1) and (2) show that the values of variable *DTW* and *DTD* coefficients are significantly positive, indicating that the innovation investment of enterprises undergoing digital transformation is also higher. In the regression results (3) and (4), the value of the variable Inn coefficient is significantly positive, which verifies the mediation effect of innovation between enterprise digital transformation and international strategy and the existence of the influence mechanism of corporate innovation, which verifies the previous research hypothesis 2. At the same time, in the regression results (3) to (6), the variables *DTW* and *DTD* are significantly positive, which proves that after considering the impact of the innovation intermediary mechanism, digital transformation still has a positive impact on international strategy, and innovation has a mediation effect.

4.3.3. Endogeneity Test Results

Table 6 shows the endogeneity test results in this paper. In the 1st Stage regression results (1) and (2), the *Mobile* coefficient of the variable is significantly positive, which indicates that the more mobile phone users in the region where the sample company is located, the higher the probability of digital transformation and the stronger the degree of digital transformation, which verifies the correlation of the instrumental variables. In the 2nd Stage regression results (3) and (4), the variable *DTW* coefficient is significantly positive, while in the 2nd Stage regression results (5) and (6), the variable *DTD* coefficient is also significantly positive, which shows that after considering endogenous factors, digital transformation can still promote the international strategy of enterprises. At the same time, the J statistics of the 2nd Stage regression results failed to pass the significance test of the conventional confidence level, which shows that the instrumental variables selected by the endogenous test are reasonable.

Table 5. Intermediary effect test results.

	Inn	Inn	ISW	ISD	ISW	ISD
	(1)	(2)	(3)	(4)	(5)	(6)
DTW	1.662 *** (0.112)		0.071 ** (0.037)	0.059 *** (0.003)		
DTD		0.543 *** (0.044)			0.091 *** (0.014)	0.026 *** (0.001)
Inn			0.130 *** (0.003)	0.005 *** (0.001)	0.129 *** (0.003)	0.005 *** (0.001)
Size	0.982 ***	1.013 ***	0.038 ***	−0.001 ***	0.035 ***	−0.001 ***
Debt	−6.153 ***	−6.203 ***	0.270 **	0.020 **	0.275 **	0.020 **
Roa	0.865	0.926	−0.856 **	−0.093 **	−0.858 ***	−0.093 **
SO	−2.166 ***	−2.234 ***	−0.360 ***	−0.041 ***	−0.350 ***	−0.041 ***
H10	−2.970 ***	−3.067 ***	−0.676 ***	−0.027 **	−0.665 ***	−0.027 **
TSE	0.698 ***	0.681 ***	0.162 **	0.006	0.163 **	0.006
Year	Yes	Yes	Yes	Yes	Yes	Yes
Industry	Yes	Yes	Yes	Yes	Yes	Yes
Constant	−6.110 ***	−6.359 ***	−2.902 ***	0.062 *	−2.864 ***	0.062 *
Adj R^2	0.078	0.074	0.157	0.051	0.157	0.051
F-statistics	184.970 ***	174.467 ***	354.810 ***	102.330 ***	354.375 ***	102.325 ***

Note: ***, **, and * indicate that they have passed the significance test at the 1%, 5%, and 10% confidence levels, respectively.

Table 6. Endogeneity test results.

	1st Stage		2nd Stage			
	DTW	DTD	ISW	ISD	ISW	ISD
	(1)	(2)	(3)	(4)	(5)	(6)
Mobile	0.263 *** (0.026)	0.115 *** (0.016)				
DTW			0.014 * (0.008)	0.059 *** (0.003)		
DTD					0.022 *** (0.003)	0.026 *** (0.001)
Control	Yes	Yes	Yes	Yes	Yes	Yes
Year	Yes	Yes	Yes	Yes	Yes	Yes
Industry	Yes	Yes	Yes	Yes	Yes	Yes
Constant	−6.230 ***	−1.860 ***	−0.109	0.062 *	−0.102	0.062 *
Adj R^2	0.046	0.030	0.157	0.051	0.157	0.051
F-statistics	93.377 ***	59.694 ***	354.810 ***	102.330 ***	354.375 ***	102.325 ***
J-statistics	—	—	1.099	1.405	1.056	1.396

Note: *** and * indicate that they have passed the significance test at the 1% and 10% confidence levels, respectively.

4.3.4. Robustness Check

(1) Robustness test 1: Lag phase I inspection. In the benchmark regression, this paper takes the current international strategy as the explained variable. Considering the lag of the impact of digital transformation on a firm's decision-making, in the robustness test, this paper further takes the lagging international strategy variable as the explained variable for the empirical test;
(2) Robustness test 2: International strategy sample test. The original samples in this paper include international business samples and non-international business samples. In the robustness test, this paper conducts an empirical test on the explained variable *ISD* for the international business samples;
(3) Robustness test 3: Reject sample inspection. The difference in the administrative level of the enterprise location will lead to the difference in the degree of enterprise digital transformation. In China, Beijing, Shanghai, Tianjin, and Chongqing are municipalities directly under the central government. The administrative level of these four cities is higher than that of other cities. Therefore, this paper makes an empirical test after excluding the sample enterprises located in these four cities.
(4) Table 7 shows the results of the robustness check. The three groups of robustness test results all proved that the explanatory variables *DTW* and *DTD* coefficient values are significantly positive, indicating that there was still a positive correlation between digital transformation and international strategy even after controlling the robustness factors, which verified the correctness of the empirical results mentioned above.

Table 7. Robustness test results.

	Robustness Test 1				Robustness Test 2		Robustness Test 3			
	ISW	ISD	ISW	ISD	ISD	ISD	ISW	ISD	ISW	ISD
	(1)	(2)	(3)	(4)	(5)	(6)	(7)	(8)	(9)	(10)
DTW	0.118 *** (0.037)	0.005 * (0.003)			0.020 *** (0.005)		0.099 *** (0.038)	0.009 *** (0.004)		
DTD			0.075 *** (0.015)	0.002 * (0.001)		0.012 *** (0.002)			0.064 *** (0.015)	0.003 ** (0.001)
Control	Yes	Yes	Yes	Yes	Yes	Yes	Yes	Yes	Yes	Yes
Year	Yes	Yes	Yes	Yes	Yes	Yes	Yes	Yes	Yes	Yes
Industry	Yes	Yes	Yes	Yes	Yes	Yes	Yes	Yes	Yes	Yes
Constant	−3.073 ***	0.043	−3.061 ***	0.043	0.363 ***	0.362 ***	−2.843 ***	0.100 **	−2.826 ***	0.098 **
Adj R^2	0.026	0.021	0.027	0.021	0.016	0.016	0.024	0.023	0.025	0.023
F-statistics	48.325 ***	38.712 ***	50.544 ***	38.922 ***	19.929 ***	19.968 ***	44.188 ***	42.560 ***	45.892 ***	42.328 ***

Note: ***, **, and * indicate that they have passed the significance test at the 1%, 5%, and 10% confidence levels, respectively.

4.4. Heterogeneity Grouping Regression Test Results and Analysis

4.4.1. Grouping Test between SOEs and Non-SOEs

Chinese SOEs and Chinese Non-SOEs have great differences in government resources, management style, and governance awareness, so different enterprises are also different in development goals, incentive goals, and pursuit goals. Compared with Chinese Non-SOEs, Chinese SOEs not only need to achieve the basic profit goal of the enterprise but also need to undertake the government goal and social responsibility goal of promoting local economic and social development. Then, in SOEs and Non-SOEs, this paper will test whether there are differences in the impact of digital transformation on international business decisions.

Table 8 reports the grouping test results of Chinese SOEs and Chinese Non-SOEs. It can be seen that in the test results of SOEs, although the correlation coefficient values between variable *DTW*, *DTD*, and explained variable *ISW* are significantly positive, the correlation coefficient values between variable *DTW*, *DTD*, and explained variable *ISW* cannot pass the significance test of conventional confidence level. In the test results of Non-SOEs, the values of variable *DTW* and *DTD* coefficients are significantly positive, which shows that the digital transformation of Chinese SOEs can significantly promote international business decisions. Compared with Chinese SOEs, Chinese Non-SOEs tend to be small in scale and have shorter enterprise management and decision-making chains. It is more convenient to make digital transformation decisions and international decisions, especially with more power and lower cost, so it is easier to play the role of digital transformation.

Table 8. Grouping test results for SOEs and Non-SOEs.

	Sample of SOEs				Sample of Non-SOEs			
	ISW	ISD	ISW	ISD	ISW	ISD	ISW	ISD
	(1)	(2)	(3)	(4)	(5)	(6)	(7)	(8)
DTW	0.107 ** (0.051)	0.002 (0.004)			0.147 *** (0.045)	0.012 ** (0.005)		
DTD			0.080 *** (0.021)	0.002 (0.002)			0.064 *** (0.017)	0.004 ** (0.002)
Control	Yes	Yes	Yes	Yes	Yes	Yes	Yes	Yes
Year	Yes	Yes	Yes	Yes	Yes	Yes	Yes	Yes
Industry	Yes	Yes	Yes	Yes	Yes	Yes	Yes	Yes
Constant	−4.463 ***	−0.019	−4.452 ***	−0.012	−3.113 ***	−0.006	−3.126 ***	−0.017
Adj R^2	0.021	0.012	0.022	0.002	0.009	0.002	0.009	0.012
F-statistics	23.542 ***	13.438 ***	25.287 ***	3.558 ***	14.175 ***	4.393 ***	14.677 ***	14.188 ***

Note: *** and ** indicate that they have passed the significance test at the 1% and 5% confidence levels, respectively.

4.4.2. Grouping Test between High-Tech Enterprise and Non-High-Tech Enterprise

Scientific and technological attributes will affect enterprise decision-making. Due to its high degree of digitization and its relatively special business model, the degree of digital transformation reflected by high-tech enterprises will be weaker than that of non-high-tech enterprises. Although the cost of non-high-tech enterprises in the process of digital transformation will be higher, the impact of digital transformation on enterprises, especially in promoting the transformation of enterprise organization systems and reducing enterprise risks, will be higher. Therefore, this paper tests the samples of high-tech enterprises and non-high-tech enterprises, respectively.

Table 9 reports the grouping test results of high-tech enterprises and non-high-tech enterprises. It can be seen that in the test results of high-tech enterprise samples, the values of variable *DTW* and *DTD* coefficients are not significant, which indicates that the impact of digital transformation on enterprise internationalization decision-making is not obvious in high-tech enterprises. In the test results of non-high-tech enterprises, the values of variable *DTW* and *DTD* coefficients are significantly positive, which proves that the digital transformation of non-high-tech enterprises has an obvious positive effect on internationalization decision-making. Because the business of high-tech enterprises is more closely related to digital technology, the application of digital technology in the process of digital transformation of non-high-tech enterprises can more effectively promote the obvious transformation of enterprises, and the digital transformation of non-high-tech enterprises is a more effective strategic transformation of enterprises. The management of non-high-tech enterprises will also cherish and pay more attention to the digital transformation behavior of enterprises, which will make the digital transformation play a stronger role in enterprise decision-making.

Table 9. Grouping test results for high-tech enterprise and non-high-tech enterprise.

	Sample of High-Tech Enterprise				Sample of Non-High-Tech Enterprise			
	ISW	ISD	ISW	ISD	ISW	ISD	ISW	ISD
	(1)	(2)	(3)	(4)	(5)	(6)	(7)	(8)
DTW	0.075 (0.054)	0.001 (0.005)			0.087 ** (0.046)	0.025 *** (0.004)		
DTD			0.009 (0.021)	0.001 (0.002)			0.062 *** (0.019)	0.021 *** (0.002)
Control	Yes	Yes	Yes	Yes	Yes	Yes	Yes	Yes
Year	Yes	Yes	Yes	Yes	Yes	Yes	Yes	Yes
Industry	Yes	Yes	Yes	Yes	Yes	Yes	Yes	Yes
Constant	−6.662 ***	−0.164 ***	−6.561 ***	−0.165 ***	−4.146 ***	0.037	−4.151 ***	0.038
Adj R^2	0.034	0.025	0.034	0.025	0.026	0.014	0.027	0.014
F-statistics	37.405 ***	27.500 ***	37.176 ***	27.528 ***	31.991 ***	17.281 ***	33.125 ***	17.512 ***

Note: *** and ** indicate that they have passed the significance test at the 1% and 5% confidence levels, respectively.

4.4.3. Grouping Test between High Institutional Development and Low Institutional Development

Institutional development is an important part of enterprise external governance. Good institutional development can not only create a fair relationship between government and enterprises and a good business environment for enterprises in the region, but it can also build good technical and trading conditions for enterprises to carry out digital transformation [39]. This means that the advantages and disadvantages of the regional institutional development where the enterprise is located will have different external effects on the enterprise so that the impact of digital transformation on international business decisions is different. Therefore, this paper will test the samples of enterprises in high institutional development and low institutional development, respectively.

Table 10 reports the grouping test results of areas with high institutional development and areas with low institutional development. It can be seen that in the test results of high institutional areas, the values of variable *DTW* and *DTD* coefficients are significantly positive, which shows that in the test results of high institutional areas, digital transformation can have an obvious positive effect on enterprise internationalization decision-making. In the low institutional development, the variables *DTW* and *DTD* can only have a significant positive effect on the explained variable *ISW*, but the test results with the explained variable *ISD* are not significant. Compared with areas with low institutional development, areas with high institutional development can form more institutional support and institutional supplement for enterprises, which is conducive to enterprises obtaining more external resources in the process of digital transformation, and enable enterprises to better control the costs and risks in the process of digital transformation, which is conducive to releasing the "dividend" of digital transformation.

4.4.4. Grouping Test between Eastern China and Non-Eastern China

Although China's overall economic development has been very fast in recent years, the phenomenon of unbalanced regional development still exists, so there are differences in the degree of digital transformation of enterprises in different regions. The degree of digitization of enterprises in eastern China is generally higher than that in central and western China [40]. Therefore, this paper will test the samples of enterprises in eastern China and non-eastern China, respectively.

Table 10. Grouping test results for high institutional development and low institutional development.

	Sample of High Institutional Development				Sample of Low Institutional Development			
	ISW	ISD	ISW	ISD	ISW	ISD	ISW	ISD
	(1)	(2)	(3)	(4)	(5)	(6)	(7)	(8)
DTW	0.121 *** (0.048)	0.009 ** (0.005)			0.099 ** (0.047)	0.001 (0.004)		
DTD			0.062 *** (0.019)	0.022 *** (0.002)			0.066 *** (0.019)	0.001 (0.001)
Control	Yes	Yes	Yes	Yes	Yes	Yes	Yes	Yes
Year	Yes	Yes	Yes	Yes	Yes	Yes	Yes	Yes
Industry	Yes	Yes	Yes	Yes	Yes	Yes	Yes	Yes
Constant	−1.934 ***	0.004	−1.921 ***	0.003	−4.650 ***	0.034	−4.645 ***	0.036
Adj R^2	0.027	0.018	0.028	0.018	0.023	0.016	0.024	0.016
F-statistics	31.264 ***	20.826 ***	31.968 ***	20.507 ***	26.569 ***	18.945 ***	27.671 ***	18.978 ***

Note: *** and ** indicate that they have passed the significance test at the 1% and 5% confidence levels, respectively.

Table 11 reports the results of grouping tests for eastern and non-eastern China. It can be seen that in the test results of the samples in eastern China, the variables *DTW* and *DTD* coefficient values are significantly positive, which indicates that digital transformation can have a significant positive effect on enterprise internationalization decisions in eastern China. However, in the test results of samples from non-eastern regions, the variable *DTW* and *DTD* coefficient values did not all pass the significance test. Compared with the central and western regions, the eastern region of China has a better digital economy foundation, which is not only conducive to the digital transformation of enterprises but also promotes the digital transformation to play a better role.

Table 11. Grouping test results for eastern China and non-eastern China.

	Sample of Eastern China				Sample of Non-Eastern China			
	ISW	ISD	ISW	ISD	ISW	ISD	ISW	ISD
	(1)	(2)	(3)	(4)	(5)	(6)	(7)	(8)
DTW	0.109 *** (0.041)	0.008 ** (0.004)			0.076 (0.061)	0.006 (0.004)		
DTD			0.064 *** (0.016)	0.028 *** (0.002)			0.054 ** (0.025)	0.001 (0.002)
Control	Yes	Yes	Yes	Yes	Yes	Yes	Yes	Yes
Year	Yes	Yes	Yes	Yes	Yes	Yes	Yes	Yes
Industry	Yes	Yes	Yes	Yes	Yes	Yes	Yes	Yes
Constant	−2.336 ***	0.062 ***	−2.332 ***	0.061 ***	−5.605 ***	−0.037	−5.574 ***	−0.034
Adj R^2	0.023	0.018	0.024	0.018	0.025	0.015	0.025	0.015
F-statistics	37.293 ***	28.436 ***	38.604 ***	28.276 ***	17.433 ***	10.858 ***	17.920 ***	10.659 ***

Note: *** and ** indicate that they have passed the significance test at the 1% and 5% confidence levels, respectively.

5. Conclusions

Digital technologies, such as big data, cloud computing, blockchain, and artificial intelligence, have become an important force driving China's economic development by changing the factors of production in the traditional economic system. In recent years, more and more Chinese enterprises have carried out digital transformation, trying to seize the trend of digital economy transformation and obtain opportunities for future development. Therefore, this paper empirically examines the impact of digital transformation on enterprises' internationalization decisions by taking listed companies on the main boards of Shanghai and Shenzhen A-share markets during 2014–2020 as samples and considers the impact mechanism of innovation. It is found that digital transformation has a positive impact on the internationalization operation decisions of Chinese enterprises, that is, compared with the enterprises without digital transformation, the probability and degree of internationalization operations of digital transformation enterprises are higher, and the probability and degree of internationalization operations of enterprises with a higher degree of digital transformation are also higher. At the same time, innovation is the influencing mechanism of digital transformation on international strategy, that is, innovation has a mediating effect between digital transformation and international strategy. This conclusion still holds after controlling for endogenous and robust factors. The heterogeneity grouping test found that the impact of digital transformation on the international strategy of Chinese enterprises is more obvious in Chinese Non-SOEs, non-high-tech enterprises, areas with high institutional development, and eastern China. Empirical evidence in this paper verifies that digital transformation can effectively promote Chinese enterprises' international strategy decisions, expands the research on the economic consequences of Chinese enterprises' digital transformation, and helps to better understand the behavior of Chinese enterprises' digital transformation.

Our research contributes to current studies in the following aspects: first, this paper employs the text mining method to construct indices to reflect a firm's digital transformation. Most current studies apply provincial or city-level indices of digital transformation, but they cannot perfectly reflect the digital level of each firm. Second, this paper investigates the impact of digital transformation on international strategy. Whereas previous literature focuses on the exports of firms, our study concentrates on a firm's strategy, which is extremely crucial for firms. Third, we investigate the mechanism of how international strategy is impacted by digital transformation. We show that innovation channels can explain the relationship between digital transformation and international strategy. Finally, heterogeneity is considered. We test whether the impact of digital transformation differs across different features of firms.

The empirical evidence of this paper shows that the digital transformation of Chinese enterprises can promote international business decision-making. Combined with the research conclusions of the existing literature, although there are some risks and uncertainties in the digital transformation, on the whole, the advantages outweigh the disadvantages for Chinese enterprises. First, China's national and local governments should actively guide Chinese enterprises in digital transformation. Through the formulation and implementation of supporting policies, such as financial support, fiscal and tax support, policy support, and technical support for digital transformation enterprises, they should encourage enterprises to actively carry out digital transformation and encourage universities and R & D institutions to cooperate with enterprises to assist them in R & D and innovation from the technical level, so as to reduce the worries of digital transformation enterprises. Second, for enterprises, they should establish the confidence and determination of digital transformation. Enterprises should seize the development opportunities of the digital economy era, relying on a good external environment, first to solve their own "dare not transformation" and "do not want to transition" point of view and take the initiative to contact, identify, and adapt the digital transformation to build their own digital transformation plan. Through technological innovation, management innovation, and operation innovation, the problem of "no transformation" can be solved to enhance the core competitiveness of enterprises and provide sustainable development paths. Third, for market investors, they should pay more attention to digital transformation enterprises and obtain the "dividend" of enterprise digital transformation in time. Digital transformation can not only bring benefits to enterprises themselves but also ensure the benefits of market investors. Therefore, market investors should strengthen their investment in digital transformation enterprises, which can not only ensure that market investors obtain sufficient income but also provide a stable source of funds for digital transformation enterprises to form a "win-win" between digital transformation enterprises and market investors.

From the perspective of future research, first, the current research on enterprise digital transformation focuses on testing the economic consequences of digital transformation, while there is less research on the influencing factors of digital transformation. Is why enterprises choose digital transformation due to the guidance of external policies, the decision of enterprises' own operation and development, or the factors of enterprise management? Exploring the influencing factors of digital transformation is also of great significance to understand the digital transformation of enterprises and its economic consequences. Second, the current research on the economic consequences of enterprise digital transformation mostly focuses on the enterprise level, such as the impact on corporate performance, the influence of total factor productivity on the enterprise, the fulfilment of the social responsibility of the enterprise, and the influence of the impact on enterprise information disclosure, etc., but does not pay attention to the impact of digital transformation on other levels. For example, whether digital transformation will have an impact on the performance of enterprises in the stock market is also a matter of concern for further research. Third, the current research on the digital transformation of Chinese enterprises is an empirical test for China's main board-listed companies. However, in China's capital market, in addition to the main board-listed companies, there are also many types of enterprises, such as GEM-listed companies and science and innovation board-listed companies. These enterprises are very different from the main board-listed companies due to their own scale differences and industry attribute differences. It is worth further studying the impact of digital transformation on enterprises. In particular, the high risk and high return of Chinese GEM-listed companies have attracted the attention of many market investors, so the digital transformation of GEM-listed companies is more worthy of attention.

Author Contributions: Conceptualization, F.G.; Formal analysis, F.G. and C.L.; Methodology, C.L. and H.Z.; Writing—original draft, H.Z. All authors have read and agreed to the published version of the manuscript.

Funding: This research was funded by the General Project of Humanities and Social Sciences Research of Chongqing Municipal Education Commission, grant number 21SKGH141, and the General Project of Science and Technology Research of Chongqing Municipal Education Commission, grant number KJQN202100903, KJQN202100904.

Institutional Review Board Statement: Not applicable.

Informed Consent Statement: Not applicable.

Data Availability Statement: The data used to support the findings of this study are available from the corresponding author upon reasonable request.

Conflicts of Interest: The authors declare no conflict of interest.

References

1. Damanpour, F.; Evan, W.M. Organizational Innovation and Performance: The Problem of Organizational Lag. *Adm. Sci. Q.* **1984**, *29*, 392–409. [CrossRef]
2. Yap, C.M. R&D Investment and Systematic Risk. *Account. Financ.* **2004**, *44*, 393–418.
3. Chan, L.; Lakonishok, J.; Sougiannis, T. The Stock Market Valuation of Research and Development Expenditures. *J. Financ.* **2001**, *56*, 2431–2456. [CrossRef]
4. Eberhart, A.; Maxwell, W.; Siddique, A. An Examination of Long Term Abnormal Stock Returns and Operating Performance Following R&D Increases. *J. Financ.* **2004**, *59*, 623–650.
5. Dangelico, R.M.; Pontrandolfo, P. Being Green and Competitive: The Impact of Environmental Actions and Collaborations on Firm Performance. *Bus. Strategy Environ.* **2015**, *24*, 413–430. [CrossRef]
6. Elbert, C.; Duarte, H.C. Digital Transformation. *IEEE Softw.* **2018**, *35*, 16–21. [CrossRef]
7. Hanelt, A.; Bohnsack, R.; Marz, D.; Antunes, M.C. A Systematic Review of the Literature on Digital Transformation: Insights and Implications for Strategy and Organizational Change. *J. Manag. Stud.* **2020**, *58*, 1159–1197. [CrossRef]
8. Zhao, H.; Wang, W.; Li, X. How Does Digital Transformation Affect the Total Factor Productivity of Enterprises. *Financ. Trade Econ.* **2021**, *42*, 114–129. (In Chinese)
9. Zeng, G.; Lei, L. Digital Transformation and Corporate Total Factor Productivity: Empirical Evidence Based on Listed Enterprises. Discret. *Dyn. Nat. Soc.* **2021**, *2021*, 9155861. [CrossRef]
10. Yuan, C.; Xiao, T.; Geng, C.; Sheng, Y. Digital Transformation and Division of Labor between Enterprises: Vertical Specialization or Vertical Integration. *China Ind. Econ.* **2021**, *9*, 137–155.

11. Renato, C.; Alex, A. Digital Transformation and Convergence toward the 2030 Agenda's Sustainability Development Goals: Evidence from Italian Listed Firms. *Sustainability* **2021**, *13*, 11831.
12. Chen, N.; Sun, D.; Chen, J. Digital Transformation, Labour Share, and Industrial Heterogeneity. *J. Innov. Knowl.* **2022**, *7*, 100173. [CrossRef]
13. Banalieva, E.R.; Dhanaraj, C. Internalization Theory for the Digital Economy. *J. Int. Bus. Stud.* **2019**, *50*, 1372–1387. [CrossRef]
14. Adomako, S.; Amankwah-Amoah, J.; Tarba, S.Y.; Khan, Z. Perceived Corruption, Business Process Digitization, and SMEs' Degree of Internationalization in Sub-Saharan Africa. *J. Bus. Res.* **2021**, *123*, 196–207. [CrossRef]
15. Yu, M. The Miracle of China's Foreign Trade in the Forty Years of Reform and Opening-up: Achievements and Paths. *Intertrade* **2018**, *37*, 4–9.
16. Tai, P.; Li, J. China's Foreign Direct Investment: Experience Summary, Problem Examination and Promotion Path. *Intertrade* **2019**, *38*, 50–57.
17. Atluri, V.; Dietz, M.; Henke, N. Competing in a World of Sectors without Borders. *McKinsey Q.* **2017**, *54*, 33–47.
18. Brillinger, A.S.; Els, C.; Schäfer, B.; Bender, B. Business Model Risk and Uncertainty Factors: Toward Building and Maintaining Profitable and Sustainable Business Models. *Bus. Horiz.* **2020**, *63*, 121–130. [CrossRef]
19. Mikalef, P.; Pateli, A. Information Technology-enabled Dynamic Capabilities and Their Indirect Effect on Competitive Performance: Findings from PIS-SEM and fsQCA. *J. Bus. Res.* **2017**, *70*, 1–16. [CrossRef]
20. Liu, S.; Yan, J.; Zhng, S.; Lin, H. Can Corporate Digital Transformation Promote Input-Output Efficiency. *Manag. World* **2021**, *37*, 170–190.
21. Li, W.; Xia, J. Business Model Innovation Based on 'Big Data'. *China Ind. Econ.* **2013**, *27*, 83–95.
22. Zhang, G.; Wang, Z.; Zhao, H. The Marketing Innovation Mode under 'Internet Plus': The Perspective of Value Network Reconstruction. *Manag. Rev.* **2019**, *31*, 94–101.
23. Frynas, J.G.; Mol, M.J.; Mellahi, K. Management Innovation Made in China: Haier's Rendanheyi. *Calif. Manag. Rev.* **2018**, *61*, 71–93. [CrossRef]
24. Elia, S.; Giuffrida, M.; Mariani, M.M.; Bresciani, S. Resources and Digital Export: An RBV Perspective on the Role of Digital Technologies and Capabilities in Cross-border E-commerce. *J. Bus. Res.* **2021**, *132*, 158–169. [CrossRef]
25. Yi, L.; Wu, F.; Xu, S. Research on Performance-driven Effect of Digital Transformation of Enterprises. *Secur. Mark. Her.* **2021**, *31*, 15–25.
26. Ojala, A. Business Models and Opportunity Creation: How IT Entrepreneurs Create and Develop Business Models under Uncertainty. *Inf. Syst. J.* **2016**, *26*, 451–476. [CrossRef]
27. Nambisan, S. Digital Entrepreneurship: Toward a Digital Technology Perspective of Entrepreneurship. *Entrep. Theory Pract.* **2017**, *41*, 1029–1055. [CrossRef]
28. Abramova, N.; Grishchenko, N. ICTs, Labour Productivity and Employment: Sustainability in Industries in Russia. *Procedia Manuf.* **2020**, *43*, 299–305. [CrossRef]
29. Hong, J.; Jiang, M.; Zhang, C. Digital Transformation, Innovation and the Improvement of Enterprises' Export Quality. *J. Int. Trade* **2022**, *48*, 1–15.
30. Hart, O.; Moore, J. Contracts as Reference Points. *Q. J. Econ.* **2008**, *123*, 1–48. [CrossRef]
31. Tseng, C.H.; Tansuhaj, P.; Hallagan, W.; McCullough, J. Effects of Firm Resources on Growth in Multinationality. *J. Int. Bus. Stud.* **2007**, *38*, 961–974. [CrossRef]
32. Zhou, L.; Barnes, B.R.; Lu, Y. Entrepreneurial Proclivity, Capability Upgrading and Performance Advantage of Newness among International New Ventures. *J. Int. Bus. Stud.* **2010**, *41*, 882–905. [CrossRef]
33. Yoo, Y. Computing in Everyday Life: A Call for Research on Experiential Computing. *MIS Q.* **2010**, *34*, 213–231. [CrossRef]
34. Abrell, T.; Pihlajamaa, M.; Kanto, L.; Jan, V.B.; Uebernickel, F. The Role of Users and Customers in Digital Innovation: Insights from B2B Manufacturing Firms. *Inf. Manag.* **2016**, *53*, 324–335. [CrossRef]
35. Carboni, O.A.; Medda, G. Linkages between R&D, Innovation, Investment and Export Performance: Evidence from European Manufacturing Firms. *Technol. Anal. Strateg. Manag.* **2020**, *32*, 1379–1392.
36. Tan, K.H.; Zhan, Y.Z.; Ji, G.; Ye, F.; Chang, C. Harvesting Big Data to Enhance Supply Chain Innovation Capabilities: An Analytic Infrastructure Based on Deduction Graph. *Int. J. Prod. Econ.* **2015**, *165*, 223–233. [CrossRef]
37. Huang, D.; Xie, H.; Meng, X.; Zhang, Y. Digital Transformation and Enterprise Value: Empirical Evidence based on Text Analysis Methods. *Economist* **2021**, *33*, 41–51.
38. Wang, S.; Xu, X.; Liu, Y. Will Digital Transformation of Enterprises Reduce the Risk of Debt Default. *Secur. Mark. Her.* **2022**, *32*, 45–56.
39. Xu, H.; Zhang, Y.; Cao, Y. Digital Economy, Technology Spillover and Dynamic Coopetition Policy. *Manag. World* **2020**, *36*, 63–84.
40. Shi, S.; Wang, Y. The Influence of Business Environment on Enterprise Digital Transformation: Facts and Mechanisms. *J. Beijing Jiaotong Univ.* **2022**, *21*, 14–28.

sustainability

Article

Corporate Social Responsibility of Chinese Multinational Enterprises: A Review and Future Research Agenda

Shu-Yun Du [1], Xiao-Chen Shao [2,3,*], Alfredo Jiménez [4] and Jeoung Yul Lee [5,6,*]

1 School of Management, Zhengzhou University, Zhengzhou 450001, China
2 Graduate School, Zhengzhou University, Zhengzhou 450001, China
3 Graduate School, Hongik University, Sejong 30016, Republic of Korea
4 Department of Management, Kedge Business School, 33405 Talence, France
5 School of Business Management, Hongik University, Sejong 30016, Republic of Korea
6 National Research Base of Intelligent Manufacturing Service, Chongqing Technology and Business University, Chongqing 400067, China
* Correspondence: shao1603@mail.hongik.ac.kr (X.-C.S.); jeoungyul@hongik.ac.kr (J.Y.L.)

Abstract: This study analyzes papers on the corporate social responsibility (CSR) of Chinese multinational enterprises (CMNEs) published in top-tier management and international business journals. We extracted six key constructs from these studies, examined their interconnections, and identified five themes. These themes are (1) the relationship between corporate governance and CSR practice, (2) the relationship between institutional environments and CSR practice, (3) the relationship between resources and capabilities and CSR practice, (4) the relationship between strategy/activity and CSR practice, and (5) the relationship between corporate performance and CSR practice. Our study aim is to reveal research gaps that have not been identified in other previous review articles. Thus, based on the research gaps identified through a review of previous studies, we identified that there is a strong relationship between CSR and national cultural contexts; however, most current research on CSR has focused on Western cultural contexts. Thus, to further explore how CSR of CMNEs may differ from other countries (e.g., Western countries) that is our review aim, we provide five directions for future CSR research on CMNEs. Finally, we theoretically and conceptually analyze recent studies on the impacts of corporate governance, resources, and capabilities on CMNEs' CSR practices in relation to corporate performance through a theoretical framework and identify future research directions on Chinese MNEs' CSR by reviewing various theories and perspectives over the last 13 years.

Keywords: Chinese multinational enterprises; corporate social responsibility; stakeholder theory; institutional theory; agency theory

Citation: Du, S.-Y.; Shao, X.-C.; Jiménez, A.; Lee, J.Y. Corporate Social Responsibility of Chinese Multinational Enterprises: A Review and Future Research Agenda. *Sustainability* **2022**, *14*, 16199. https://doi.org/10.3390/su142316199

Academic Editor: Ioannis Nikolaou

Received: 15 October 2022
Accepted: 29 November 2022
Published: 5 December 2022

1. Introduction

With the development of the global economy and the increasing diversity of discussions about balancing corporate and societal interests, the concept of corporate social responsibility (CSR) has evolved [1]. In most research, CSR has been defined as a society's expectations for enterprises in terms of economy, law, ethics, and discretion [2]. Some scholars believe that CSR supplements corporate, economic, and legal responsibilities, while corporate shareholders maximize profits and maintain and promote social interests [3]. However, some see CSR primarily as an approach to raising profits [3]. Our paper argues that CSR is reflected in a company's pursuit of economic profitability along with environmentally and socially responsible practices [4].

Multinational enterprises (MNEs) need to respond to the complex needs of multiple stakeholders and be socially responsible to different host communities [5,6], i.e., (1) CSR in a home country, (2) CSR in different host countries, and (3) global international CSR [7]. CSR activities conducted by MNEs not only contribute to the economic growth of the host country but also to the general welfare of society. Therefore, CSR as a non-market coping mechanism can help subsidiaries reduce stakeholder pressure from unfamiliar host countries and facilitate the acquisition of local legitimacy [8], especially for emerging market MNEs [6]. To respond better to isomorphic pressures from various host communities and gain internal and external legitimacy for MNEs operating in emerging Asian markets [9], a global CSR strategy aligned with the home country and a local CSR strategy aligned with local needs must be adopted [10].

Some current studies have illustrated the significance of CSR from different perspectives, such as the examination of the necessity of CSR from the perspective of institutional theory, agency theory, and upper echelons theory [8,11–13], and the relationship between CSR and corporate social, financial, and environmental performance based on stakeholder theory, resource-based view, and resource dependence theory [14,15]. Under the influence of global trade processes and the COVID-19 epidemic, the field of CSR research in the context of MNEs is trending towards the dynamic characteristics of social expectations, the non-fixed needs of stakeholders, the factors that impede CSR, and the integration of dynamic corporate capabilities with social needs [14,16].

Our study aim is to reveal research gaps that have not been identified in other previous review articles on the relevant topics. Thus, in this way, our study contributes to filling the Chinese MNEs' (CMNEs') CSR literature research gap that is the focus of our review article. Many studies have explored the concept of CSR. Research on CSR practices of MNEs is also increasing, but most studies focus on Western cultural contexts [16]. The CSR of MNEs involves the home country, host country, and the entire international community, which distinguishes it from the CSR of non-MNEs [17]. Given the relationship between CSR and national cultural background, Chinese firms' CSR dimensions may differ from those of other countries (e.g., Western countries) [18]. We highlight prior literature on CSR in CMNEs, which contributes to a better understanding of MNE CSR activities in emerging Asia. Additionally, by reviewing the literature, we identified the factors that influence CMNEs' CSR and the effect of CSR practices on corporate performance, which can provide some direction for corporations in the design and implementation of CSR strategies.

In the global trade market, China's outbound investment has increased with the support of the Chinese government's Belt and Road Initiative and other policies. From January to May 2022, China's domestic investors' cumulative non-financial investment in overseas enterprises reached USD 44.6 billion, up 3% year on year. The investment range includes 3302 abroad firms from 157 countries and regions [19]. While the average net worth of companies in mainland China (including Hong Kong) (USD 43.18 billion) exceeds the Fortune 500 average in 2022, the average return on sales (at 5.1%) and return on net assets (at 9.5%) still lag the Fortune 500 average [20].

In terms of the CSR practices of CMNE, most studies use the SNAI (Shanghai National Accounting Institute) Chinese firms' social responsibility index to assess Chinese CSR through SA8000 (Social Accountability International), GRI3 (Global Reporting Initiative), and the "Global Compact" project (The United Nations) [21]. In this system, a listed company's CSR index is divided into eight areas and 36 subcategories as follows: environment, energy savings, employees, employment and fair promotion, social problems, consumers, other stakeholders, law, and business ethics [21]. While Chinese enterprises' CSR practices are constantly standardized due to a lack of global responsibility awareness and ineffective governance mechanisms, some enterprises fail to fulfill their responsibilities in overseas investment [22]. Based on the background of China's multinational business development, CSR issues in CMNEs show a variety of trends.

This study has at least three contributions and implications. First, we learn about the application of CSR-related theories and concepts to the study of Chinese MNEs by reviewing research published in top journals over the last 13 years. Second, we categorize the existing research and present each topic in the form of a conceptual framework to analyze studies on the impacts of Chinese MNEs' governance structures, resources, and capabilities, including institutional environments and strategies, on CSR practices and corporate performance, providing a systematic overview of the most recent research on the subject. Third, based on previous research, we identify future research directions for CSR in CMNEs, such as the adaptation of CSR practices to emergency responses under the influence of the COVID-19 pandemic. Through a review and extension of the literature, we argue that the research area is rich, and we hope that this study will contribute to the development of CSR theory related to CMNEs.

This paper is organized as follows. First, we discuss the CSR theories used to study CME. Next, we review 16 top-tier journals' articles in the management and international business (IB) fields, summarize the research topic, and outline the research framework. We then identify CSR concepts from these articles. Finally, we provide suggestions for future research based on previous studies and describe our contributions in the conclusion.

2. Literature Review Methodology

We used a semi-systematic analysis to review theories, concepts, and findings from the literature and identified themes [12]. First, we selected journals or articles published by reputable publishers to exclude technical reports and online presentations [23]. To more efficiently map the direction of the research area, we focused on the University of Texas at Dallas (UTD) list of top 24 journals in the business administration field, from UTD the Top 100 Business School Research Rankings in 2020 for management and IB journals (i.e., *Academy of Management Journal, Administrative Science Quarterly, Journal of International Business Studies, Management Science, Organization Science,* and *Strategic Management Journal*) and nine highly reputed journals primarily in the field of IB and area studies listed on the 2021 UK Chartered Association of Business Schools Research Rankings (ABS) 3 or 4 (e.g., *Asia Pacific Journal of Management, Global Strategy Journal, International Business Review, Journal of International Management, Business Ethics Quarterly, Journal of World Business, Journal of Business Ethics,* and *Management and Organization Review*).

Then, by referring to the PRISMA guidelines and the keyword search algorithm created by Pisani [24] using standard Boolean operators, we identified the keywords: "corporate social responsibility", "CSR", "social responsibility", "corporate social irresponsibility", "CSIR", "environment sustainable", "environmental sustainability", "social sustainable", "social sustainability", "economic sustainable", "economic responsibility", "stakeholder", "multinational enterprise", "MNE", "multinational corporation", "MNC", "Chinese multinational enterprise", "Chinese MNE", Chinese multinational corporation", "Chinese MNC", "Chinese firm", "corporate ethics", "corporate philanthropy", "international", "multinational", "transnational", and "global". To ensure the timeliness of the research findings, we searched for papers between 2010 and 2022 by Google Scholar and Web of Science using the above keywords in the titles, abstracts, and keywords of the journals [25,26], and after removing those that appeared more than once in the different searches, we obtained a total of 82 articles. Next, we screened the literature. In the first stage, we read the title and abstract of each paper to check if the topic was related to MNEs' CSR, which reduced the initial number of articles to 72. In the second step, we removed CSR studies of MNEs that were not relevant to the Chinese context. Based on these two screenings, 55 papers were selected for review [27,28].

The authors completed the framework of CMNE's CSR literature review using the following steps. First, based on the title, abstract, keywords, theoretical lens, and logical structure of the paper, two authors created initial tables summarizing the journal sources, years, theoretical perspectives, and core viewpoints of previous related research, and drew the initial frame. The three authors then worked together to examine and modify the framework and tables. Then, all authors made several more adjustments to the framework in the subsequent writing process, resulting in the Figure and Tables [28]. Figure 1 depicts the distribution of research topics in CMNE CSR over the last ten years, with research gaps or rarely studied or understudied issues noted in grey. In order to clearly represent the relationships between the constructs, we indicated the causal relationships with numbers [27]. We can easily find abundant academic literature to propose new ideas for future agendas [12].

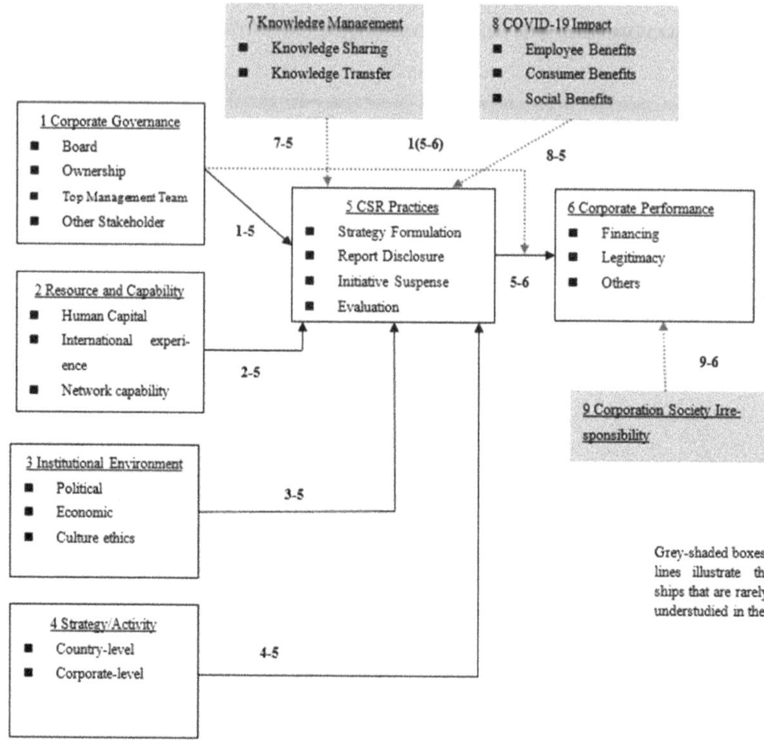

Figure 1. Conceptual framework.

Table 1 presents the number of journal publications over time. According to the statistics in the table, the number of papers on CSR in Chinese firms shows a relatively stable fluctuation each year. Since 2010, every five years has increased to a maximum number comparable to the previous fifth year; for example, in 2010, 2015, and 2020, the numbers were 8,7, and 7, respectively. Furthermore, business ethics and Asian journals have the most publications, except for the Strategic Management Journal (5). Next, we provide statistics on the number of times each theory is used every year, as shown in Table 2. As mentioned above, Institutional theory and Shareholder theory are the most frequently used theories in the research field of CMNE CSR, followed by agency theory, upper echelons theory, legitimacy theory, and resource dependence theory.

We classify six research topics and several key concepts based on the core ideas of each paper, which are examined in detail below. Table 3 shows the number of times each topic was studied each year. From this table, we can observe the influence of the institutional environment and corporate government on CSR practices and the relationship between CSR and corporate performance is the largest number. In Table 4, we select concepts related to CMNEs' CSR from each study. CSR disclosures, legitimacy, reporting, and strategies have appeared most often. Additionally, in Appendix A, we list all the papers discussed in the form of a table.

Table 1. Journal and year of the articles on Chinese MNEs' CSR 2010–2022.

Journal	2010	2011	2012	2013	2014	2015	2016	2017	2018	2019	2020	2021	2022	Total
Academy of Management Journal								2			1			3
Administrative Science Quarterly														0
Asia Pacific Journal of Management					1	1			1	1	2	2		8
Business Ethics Quarterly							2							2
Global Strategy Journal														0
International Business Review												1		1
Journal of International Business Studies											1			1
Journal of International Management														0
Journal of Business Ethics	6	4	2	1		3	2				2	1	1	22
Journal of World Business	1				1									2
Management and Organization Review						3	1	2			1			7
Management International Review	1			1										2
Management Science														0
Organization Science				2										2
Strategic Management Journal				1	1				1	1			1	5
Total	8	4	2	5	3	7	5	4	2	2	7	4	2	55

Table 2. Theory and year of the articles on Chinese MNEs' CSR.

Theory	2010	2011	2012	2013	2014	2015	2016	2017	2018	2019	2020	2021	2022	Total
Agency theory	1			1	1		1		1					5
Attention-based view										1				1
Boundary-spanning learning													1	1
Chief sustainability officer view										1	1			2
Collective action theory	1													1
Corporate social irresponsibility										1				1
Critical mass theory									1					1
Cross-cultural perspective													1	1
direct benefits/indirect costs											1			1
Elaboration Likelihood Model		1												1
Grounded-theory-building			2											2
Human capital management perspective													1	1
Information asymmetry theory			1								1			2
Information Theory		1							1					2
Institutional Theory	1			3	1	2	1	2	1		3	2	1	17
Integrative social contracts theory							1							1
International business theory		1												1
legitimacy theory							1				2		1	4
Neoclassical trade theory						1								1
Organizational Theory							1	2						3
Portfolio theory		1												1
Product classification theory		1												1
Reputation risk view											1			1
Resource-based View													1	1
Resource dependence theory					1									1
Risk mitigation theory		1												1
Signaling theory								1					1	2
Societal marketing perspective				1										1
Social stratification view												1		1
Stakeholder theory	1	1		1	4	5	2	1				1	1	17
Strategic view													1	1
Task interdependence													1	1
Type II agency problem	1													1
Upper echelons theory						2					2	1		5
Total	5	7	3	6	7	10	7	6	4	3	11	5	10	84

Table 3. Topic and year of the articles on Chinese MNEs' CSR.

Topic	2010	2011	2012	2013	2014	2015	2016	2017	2018	2019	2020	2021	2022	Total
Corporate Governance → CSR	2					2	2	1	1		2		1	11
CSR → Performance	2	3	1	2	1	3	1	1	1		2	1	1	19
Institutional environments → CSR	2		1	1	2	1	2	2	1		3	1	1	17
Resource and Capability → CSR					1						2		1	4
Strategy/Activity → CSR				2		1					1			4
Total	6	3	2	5	4	7	5	4	3	0	10	2	4	55

Table 4. Concepts related to Chinese MNEs' CSR.

Concepts	2010	2011	2012	2013	2014	2015	2016	2017	2018	2019	2020	2021	2022	Total
Corporate ethics					2				1					3
CSR assurance									1	1				2
CSR Commitment						1		1	1					3
CSR communication				1			1					1		3
CSR donation				1					1	1	1		1	5
CSR diffuse			1					1			2	1		5
CSR disclosures					1				1	1	2	2		7
CSR security					1			1						2
CSR initiatives legitimacy			1			1	2	1						5
CSR reporting					1		1	1	2	2	2	1	1	11
CSR strategies				1	1	1	2	1	1	2	1	1	1	12
CSR suspension						1			1					2
Corporate philanthropy	1	1	1	1	1			1	1					7
Corporate volunteer assignments											1			1
Environmental CSR						1			2			1		4
external-oriented CSR practices.								1			1			2
Globalization of CSR							1				1	1		3
intangible assets												1		1
Internal CSR structures								1			2			3
Rankins CSR Ratings		2					1				2			5
Reputation risk spillover													1	1
Self-Presentation of CSR				1			1							2
Total	1	3	3	5	7	5	9	9	12	7	15	9	4	88

On this basis, we also found that the existing research is divided into two main areas: one part is the research that discusses the factors that influence CSR practices in the Chinese context, such as corporate governance, resource and capability, institutional environment, and corporate strategy (Figure 1). Most of them have been concluded through quantitative studies by collecting data from Chinese companies or by comparing the differences with Western CSR practices using qualitative methods; the other part discusses the role of corporate CSR practices on corporate performance; the other part discusses the effect of corporate CSR practices on corporate performance, as in Figure 1, mainly regarding the impact on financial and legitimacy performance, through quantitative analysis.

3. Research on the CMNEs' CSR

CSR implementation by MNEs in the world has always been an interesting topic for scholars in the field of business ethics [25]. We focus on CMNEs in emerging Asian markets implementing global CSR activities. As a result, we classify six research topics and several key concepts based on the core ideas of each paper, which are examined in detail below. First, we found that, with the exception of non-MNEs, MNEs may consider stakeholders such as the home country, the host country, and even the entire world in a more complex political, economic, and cultural environment [6].

Second, many studies have proposed that CSR performance in China differs from that in Western countries because of the sociocultural context [18]. Besides similar dimensions, i.e., economic, legal, environmental, consumer, employee, and social charity dimensions, the Western CSR system regarding profits for shareholders also has dimensions in racial and gender equality, as well as equal opportunity for underprivileged groups and regional development, which are of less concern to Chinese corporations. For Chinese corporations, the first dimension that is of greater concern is good faith, which is reflected in the sense of cooperation and business ethics related to fair prices and genuine goods. The second is employment, which is typically required by firms to provide more jobs to alleviate China's labor shortage. The third distinct dimension is social stability and progress, which is like Gallo's [29] "correcting or stopping a behavior that is detrimental to social matters," but also has its own unique meaning related to China, i.e., ensuring social stability and harmony [18]. Next, we will analyze in detail the key findings of the six themes.

3.1. The Relationship between Corporation Governance and CSR Practices

Since the governance structure of MNEs demonstrates multiple trends [30], it is more conducive to directly comprehending the CSR implementation process of MNEs [11], which is useful for CSR analysis in the Chinese context. Most previous studies, from the perspective of the CMNE governance structure, such as board composition and firm ownership, as well as top management team (TMT) characteristics, examine its role in the implementation of CSR strategies, CSR evaluation, and CSR disclosure. In Table 5, we list the main findings of the current studies on CSR in CMNEs, including theories and concepts. As it can be seen from the table, the main theories used on this theme are institutional theory, agency theory, stakeholder theory, upper echelon theory, etc. The concepts related to it that are discussed more frequently are CSR strategies, CSR reporting, CSR disclosures, and the legitimacy of CSR initiatives. We can see from Figure 1 for 1–2 that there is a bidirectional relationship between corporate and CSR practice.

Based on the upper echelons theory, Wang et al. [31,32] proposed that government, customer, competitor, employee, and shareholder pressures all influence corporate CSR managerial decision making. In the implementation of CMNEs' CSR practices, the issue concerning the role of government and public ownership is still a concern for many scholars, since it influences the adoption of corporate internationalization strategies and the relationship with stakeholders [33,34]. Khalid et al. [35], according to legitimacy theory and stakeholder theory, proposed that the laws and regulations promulgated by a country's legislative body serve as the foundation for the execution of the country's CSR policies, concluding that when the government is both a stakeholder and the organization's owner, it applies different rules to state-owned enterprises than it does to non-state-owned enterprises; this may also lead to the different international performance of SOEs and non-SOEs in terms of environmental, social and governance. Based on institutional and agency theory, Lau and Lu [11] emphasized the unique characteristics of corporate governance structures and mechanisms in the Chinese context and proposed that the structure of state ownership has an impact on CSR discolors and that ownership concentration reduces the diversity of CSR activities. Therefore, state-controlled firms with dispersed equity perform better than private enterprises with concentrated equity. This finding implies that in a diverse governance environment, Chinese MNEs may broaden the scope of CSR in internationalization [35].

Regarding the implementation of CSR activities at the company's board and TMT levels, according to Lau and Lu [11], board members are external supervisors or representatives from the perspective of stakeholders. In comparison to the internal TMT level, the board may elicit the CMNE's social responsibility to serve the public's performance positively and effectively. For board CSR performance, some studies, based on resource dependence theory, mention that joint ventures need to connect to more external resources to provide support for CSR activities [36,37]. Liao et al. [36], from an agency perspective, also mention that a larger board size, more female directors, and increased international experience of CEOs can devote more energy and resources to social responsibility assurance. Indeed, the above incentives also stimulate CSR performance at the TMT level at the same time; moreover, philanthropy in CSR also has an impact on the legitimacy of external stakeholders and the persistence of internal stakeholders [38].

Furthermore, Fu et al. [39] proposed that establishing a chief sustainability officer (CSO) in a corporation can increase CSR activities while decreasing socially irresponsible activities (CSIR). However, if initiatives are not enhanced, it may even lead to governance failure. For example, some MNEs in the oil and gas industry may experience governance failures owing to insufficient CSR and policy initiatives [40]. As a result, the approach to addressing the issue will require additional research in the future.

Table 5. Research on the effect of corporation governance on CSR practices.

Authors	Year	Theory	Concepts	Findings
Lau et al. [11]	2016	Institutional theory, Agency theory, Upper echelons theory	CSR disclosures, CSR strategies	Compared to TMT, board may have a more active and effective elicit CMNE's CSR to serve the performance of public
Khalid et al. [35]	2021	Legitimacy theory Stakeholder Theory	Environmental CSR, Globalization of CSR	Chinese non-state-owned MNEs outperform their peers on environmental and governance performance.
Wang et al. [31]	2015	Upper echelons theory	CSR donation	Pressure from stakeholders influences the perception of corporate charitable giving management decisions
Zamirl and Saeed [41]	2020	Legitimacy theory and institutional theory	CSR disclosures, CSR reporting	MNEs close to financial centers exhibit more CSR disclosure.
Liao et al. [36]	2018	Resource dependence theory, agency theory, and critical mass theory	CSR assurance	MNEs with larger boards, more women directors can devote more energy and resources.
Fu et al. [39]	2020	Upper echelons theory	CSR Commitment	The presence of a chief sustainability officer (CSO) increases CSR activities and reduces corporate social irresponsibility activities (CSIR)

3.2. The Relationship between Institutional Environment and CSR Practices

Institutional logic aims to understand how the cognition and behavior of organizations and individuals are influenced by various belief systems as well as being reshaped [6]. Institutional infrastructure and cultural ethics will have a long-term impact on emerging economies' CSR approaches and when faced with global isomorphic challenges, Chinese MNEs will adapt to corresponding strategies [14,42]. Through a review of the literature, we also find that in addition to institutional theory, scholars have drawn on stakeholder theory, upper echelons theory, and Grounded-theory-building to analyze topics related to CSR practices, involving concepts such as CSR strategies, CSR diffuse, CSR reporting, external-oriented CSR practices, globalization of CSR, CSR disclosures and CSR initiatives legitimacy, as shown Table 6. This section discusses the role of the national institutional environment in CMNE CSR implementation from political, economic, and social perspectives, as shown in Figure 1 for 3–5.

Among the studies about the political-institutional environment on CSR, Miska et al. [43] believe that the characteristics of the home country are decisive factors for MNEs to implement CSR strategies in emerging Asian markets. The political environment in China also has an impact on the adoption of CSR strategies. Most studies concentrate on the degree of connection with the state. Ge and Zhao [44] examined that corporations with a closer bureaucratic linkage to the state are more likely to focus on external-oriented CSR practices, while those with closer relationships with states through political or semi-political associations with the state are more likely to adopt strategies to improve the internal structure of CSR [44].

Regarding the motivation of corporations to implement government CSR initiatives, Li and Lu [45] from the institutional view developed a dual-agency model, explored the interplay of corporate motivation to implement CSR initiatives and human agents (government officials, corporate CEOs), and conclude that corporations are more likely to increase CSR when public agents are more motivated to seek promotion to central government or when private agents are more concerned with legitimacy. Liu et al. [14], from upper echelons theory and stakeholder theory, examined that private Chinese enterprises with a high social status are more willing to expand their national connections through CSR activities to maintain their dominant position in the local market. Furthermore, Marquis et al. [33] established a state-mediated globalization mechanism based on institutional theory to guide corporations on how to adopt and adapt to global CSR practices to meet the adaptability abroad and legitimacy in home countries for CMNE's overseas subsidiaries.

Based on some studies, CMNEs' CSR practices are influenced by local economic circumstances during the globalization process [46]. For example, a company in a region with a weaker economic institutional environment can reduce the quality of CSR disclosure and increase the cost of corporate bonds [47]. Companies in Asian economic markets located closer to financial centers exhibit more CSR disclosures than their counterparts located further away [41]. Sun et al. [48], from the perspective of institutional theory, discovered that banks are more likely to actively publish CSR reports in communities where enterprises generally publish more CSR reports or where CSR report guidelines. Moreover, at the industry level, large firms affiliated with the extractive and manufacturing industries, typically China's SOEs state-owned enterprises (SOEs), which have more government-funded projects, perform more and higher-quality CSR activities [49].

Cultural traditions and ethical differences play leading roles in CSR implementation. Hah and Freeman [6,50], based on stakeholder theory and institutional theory, suggest that MNEs are driven to engage in socially responsible activities by host country stakeholders when the ethical standards of the host country differ from those of the home country. According to Barin Cruz and Boehe [51], China adapts headquarters CSR practices to respond to the needs of local host societies to be regarded as locally responsive to particular cultural circumstances. Furthermore, regarding the ideological elements of religion and law, Du et al. [52] found that the religious climate has a positive effect on CSR behavior and that the religious climate of the informal system and law enforcement of the formal system has a substitutable effect.

In general, institutional environment factors influence corporate CSR strategies, and some studies have found that CSR activities may assist Chinese MNEs in better adapting to the global homogeneous model while complying with the requirements of home institutions, thereby promoting the diversification of CSR evaluation criteria in the Chinese context [43].

3.3. The Relationship between CSR Practice and Corporate Performance

This theme examines how CSR practices affect corporate performance (finance and operational legitimacy), as shown in Figure 1 for 5–6. As shown in Table 7, we could identify from the review that scholars more commonly use stakeholder theory, agency theory, institutional theory, information theory, and signaling theory, and that CSR reporting, CSR disclosure, CSR donation, CSR strategies, corporate philanthropy, environmental CSR, and CSR initiatives legitimacy are the concepts that are more frequently mentioned in relation to corporate performance studies. We discovered that scholars mainly examine the relationship in two directions: financial and legitimacy, with financial performance, being the most studied.

In the review, we found that CSR improves enterprise performance by positively influencing a firm's reputation, particularly in the context of ethical leadership. Many studies have found that companies that actively engage in CSR activities can improve their performance [54–56]. However, as a potential component that may conflict with shareholder interests in management, some studies have found that high CSR performance may result in undesirable outcomes in corporate operations [57,58].

Table 6. Research on the effect of Institutional Environment on CSR Practices.

Authors	Year	Theory	Concepts	Findings
Marquis et al. [33]	2017	Stakeholder theory	CSR diffuses, CSR reporting	The political mechanisms of state-mediated globalization allow corporations to adopt and adapt global normative practices while meeting the political legitimacy needs of key stakeholders.
LI and LU [53]	2020	Institutional theory	CSR reporting, external-oriented	Corporations are more likely to increase CSR when public agents are more motivated to seek promotion to the central government, or when private agents are more concerned with legitimacy.
Du et al. [52]	2016	Legitimacy theory	Rankins CSR Ratings	Religious climate plays an important role in strengthening CSR and has a substitute role with law enforcement.
Yin and Zhang [42]	2012	Grounded theory-building	CSR diffuses, Corporate philanthropy	Institutional infrastructure and cultural ethics have a continuing impact on the approach to CSR in emerging economies
Liu et al. [14]	2021	Upper echelons theory and stakeholder theory,	CSR strategies	Entrepreneurs with higher social status in China are more inclined to CSR efforts.
Hah and Freeman [6]	2014	Stakeholder theory and institutional theory	Corporate ethics, CSR security	MNEs are pressured by host country constituencies to engage in CSR activities when the ethical standards of the host and home countries differ.

For corporate financial performance, we find that it mainly involves effects on market valuation, bank credit, and the cost of debt financing. Hah, and Freeman [6] use shareholder theory to further conclude that CSR sponsors with high-quality CSR reports have higher market valuations. From the perspectives of stakeholder theory and signaling theory, Huang et al. [47] explained that CSR can reflect external stakeholders' evaluations of the corporation and thus have an impact on the corporation's access to loans. Gong et al. [56] used information asymmetry theory and verified that conducting CSR activities can partially offset CMNE's negative impact on the cost of debt due to corporate law violations. On the other hand, other studies have suggested that CSR practices may have negative effects on financial investment and too high or too low CSR performance may result in adverse investor reactions [58,59].

As for the performance of business and political legitimacy of corporations, many studies explain it from the perspective of institutional theory. Its application is primarily discussed from two aspects: institutional isomorphism and institutional logic [8,60]. Institutional isomorphism emphasizes the various isomorphic pressures that host countries exert on foreign subsidiaries, often persuading them to change or reshape their operations according to local social values. From the perspective of contending, institutional logic emphasizes the social ethical norms of how foreign subsidiaries balance heterogeneity and homogeneity while maintaining their expectations [8,61]. Hah and Freeman [6] explored how subsidiaries adopt CSR strategies (global/local strategy) to build internal/external legitimacy in the smaller Asian emerging market context while facing isomorphic pressures. They provided four specific approaches (negotiation, camouflage, compliance, and defiance) to balance the gambling relationship between CSR security in the parent company and local ethical pressure in a host country.

In terms of other aspects of corporate performance, such as market performance, Zhang et al. [62] suggest from an agency theory perspective that corporate philanthropic activities can enhance advertising intensity and thus increase corporate competitiveness. From the perspective of partnership identification and institutional learning, Gatigno [63] explored how developing employees' awareness of CSR values can reduce the risk of interdependence with nonprofit organizations due to boundary-spanning CSR programs. Furthermore, some studies have suggested that CSR activities should adapt to different environments rather than remain constant; for example, when facing a business recession, firms may reduce or suspend CSR initiatives [53]. Duanmu et al. [59] proposed a negative relationship between firms' environmental performance and current market competition. The causes and manifestations of CSR's negative impact on corporate performance could be explored further.

Table 7. Research on the effect of CSR Practice on Corporate Performance.

Authors	Year	Theory	Concepts	Findings
Wang et al. [58]	2011	Portfolio theory Stakeholder theory	Rankins CSR Ratings	Too low or too high CSR performance may lead to adverse reactions from investors.
Huang et al. [47]	2022	Signaling theory Stakeholder theory	CSR disclosure	CSR performance is associated with access to bank credit facilities, and this positive relationship is more pronounced in long-term loans
Zhang et al. [62]	2010	Agency theory	Corporate philanthropy	Advertising intensity is positively correlated with the category of CSR
Gong et al. [56]	2021	Information asymmetry theory	CSR reporting	Conducting CSR activities can partially offset CMNE's negative impact on the cost of debt due to corporate law violations.
Zhao [49]	2012	Grounded theory	CSR initiatives legitimacy	MNEs may regard CSR as an extension of their efforts to seek legitimacy in the state.
Zhang et al. [64]	2020	Institutional theory	CSR legitimacy	Conformity in CSR legitimizes enterprises in the analyst group and positively affects analyst coverage.
Ye and Zhang [65]	2011	Risk mitigation theory	CSR reporting Corporate philanthropy	The u-shaped relationship between CSR and the cost of debt financing in China in the context of emerging markets.
Liu et al. [53]	2015	stakeholder theory.	CSR suspension	Suspension of CSR can harm stakeholder relationships and threaten the survival of the business.

3.4. The Relationship between Strategy/Activity and CSR Practice

This topic discusses the effect of strategies or activities carried out by a country or enterprise on CSR practices such as national macro-development policies, as shown in Figure 1 for 4–5. Through the literature review, as shown in Table 8, we found that the most used theories related to this theme are institutional theory, shareholder theory, and stakeholder theory, and the concepts discussed with them are self-presentation of CSR, CSR donation, corporate philanthropy, etc. Next, we review both strategies and activities.

The impact of strategy on corporate CSR is mainly based on national policies. China's sustainability strategy emphasizes that the focus of economic development should shift from resource-based expansion to CSR initiatives [16]. Hence, the government implements some agendas related to this issue, and Ma and Bu [16] apply institutional theory and confirmed this result. Yang et al. [5] also indicated that the Belt and Road Initiative (BRI) would have a significant and positive impact on Chinese MNEs' overall CSR, especially for Chinese state-owned MNEs [5].

In the study of CSR practices by corporate strategies or activities, Zhang and Luo [66,67], from the viewpoint of social movement and taking the MNE online charitable donation event during the Wenchuan earthquake in Sichuan, China in 2018 as an example, proposed that an online campaign can support MNEs in establishing a response mechanism to social issues. Corporate philanthropy activities would compensate for the absence of CSR standards and regulations, as well as market institutions [66]. Moreover, Zeng et al. [68] applied institutional theory and proposed that corporate societal marketing activities enable multinational corporations to establish a CSR image in their home country or the host country, which can not only directly improve the company's operational performance but also benefit foreign subsidiaries by gaining external and internal legitimacy [68].

Table 8. Research on the effect of Strategy/Activity on CSR Practice.

Authors	Year	Theory	Concepts	Findings
Yang et al. [5]	2020	Institutional theory	CSR strategies	The positive impact of Belt and Road on the CSR performance of MNEs is stronger in host countries with higher levels of institutional pressure
Zhang and Luo [66]	2013	Agency theory and institutional theory	Self-Presentation of CSR, CSR donation, and corporate philanthropy	CSR increase the importance of external social forces that motivate MNEs to act.
Zeng et al. [68]	2013	Institutional theory	CSR reporting, Environmental CSR	Conducting marketing activities contribute to building CSR legitimacy

3.5. The Relationship between Resource/Capacity and CSR Practice

This theme explores the impact of resources and capabilities on the implementation of CSR, as shown in Figure 1 for 2–5. Through a literature review, as shown in Table 9, we found that network capabilities, human capital, international education, and work experience were the most discussed in past studies. Regarding the application of theories on this theme, there are legitimacy theory, stakeholder theory, a resource-based view, the upper echelons theory, and CSR-related concepts such as CSR diffuse, CSR disclosures, and CSR Commitment. Compared with other topics, the number of studies on this topic is still relatively small, and subsequent studies can continue to expand corporate resource capabilities and deepen the changes in CSR practices.

According to the resource-based view theory, the company controls resources and capabilities that are valuable, rare, difficult to imitate, and not substitutable, which enables the board to develop more effective CSR strategies to maintain the company's sustained competitive advantage [15]. Li et al. [15] suggested that a director's network is an important cornerstone for acquiring knowledge, intelligence, and expert resources, and legitimacy theory and stakeholder theory examine independent directors' network capacity can achieve superior CSR disclosure quality [15].

Some studies have examined the effects of managers' academic resources, international work, and educational experience on corporate governance. Ma et al. [46] showed that top executives with an academic background not only bring more professional CSR information to stakeholders but also have higher ethical standards for self-regulation in work compared to their non-academic counterparts. This can enable companies to proactively increase voluntary CSR disclosures by having higher ethical standards for self-regulation in work execution [69]. Furthermore, if the company has more directors and TMT members with international education and work experience, it will be better able to adapt to the internationalization process by diversifying its CSR performance [15].

Table 9. Research on the effect of Resource/Capacity on CSR Practice.

Authors	Year	Theory	Concepts	Findings
Li et al. [15]	2022	Legitimacy theory Stakeholder theory Resource-based view	CSR disclosures	Director network centrality has a significant positive effect on the quality of CSR disclosure, especially when the board devotes less to advertising
Ma et al. [69]	2020	Upper echelons theory	CSR disclosure	Executives with academic backgrounds are more willing to provide stakeholders with more CSR disclosure information
Cui et al. [55]	2015	Stakeholder theory	CSR Commitment	The relationship between private MNE commitment to CSR and average sales growth in the weak institutional environment

4. Results

Based on the above literature review and our analysis, we summarize our results in the following three points. First, by reviewing past studies published in top-tier journals in the last 13 years, we learned about the most recent trend in CMNEs' CSR. In terms of the number of studies, we find that the number of papers on CSR in Chinese corporations fluctuates steadily each year, and most papers are published in business ethics journals and Asian journals; in terms of theoretical foundations, the literature mainly focuses on the use of institutional theory, stakeholder theory, agency theory, and upper echelons theory and Resource Dependence Theory. For the frequency of research on concepts related to CSR, the existing studies involving CSR disclosures, legitimacy, and reporting are the most numerous. Regarding the research methods, most of the studies mainly use qualitative or quantitative methods, but quantitative research is the main research method.

Second, we divide the existing research into two main directions: one discusses the factors that influence CSR practices in the Chinese context (corporate governance, resource, and capability, institutional environment, and corporate strategy); the other discusses the role of corporate CSR practices on corporate performance outcomes (finance, legitimacy, etc.). In the following, we propose these relationships as a conceptual framework and summarize five themes, in which the impact of institutional environments and corporate governments on CSR practices is the most frequent.

Thirdly, we believe that CMNEs' CSR is a timely and critical agenda in IB and CSR, both theoretically and conceptually. Further research in this area is still needed because it can provide a new perspective on the development of CSR theory, for example, from a Chinese perspective, while notifying the exploration of the relationship between globalization and local management. This will help to recognize the specific CSR practices within the context of the Chinese government's proposed sustainable development strategy policy, for example, by examining the social mandates accomplished by CMNEs to their stakeholders in the era of the COVID-19 pandemic.

There are still some limitations of the study in this paper: first, we do not have empirical data to conduct a quantitative analytical analysis, a limitation that is common in other previous review articles including several published in top-tier or high-quality journals (e.g., [70–72]). Second, in terms of choosing the range of journals, we mainly focused on articles from 3 and 4/4* of the ABS rankings. For future research, we can collect data and expand the scope by including 1, 2, books, cook chapters, unpublished dissertations, etc., by using quantitative analytical methods to review, thus enlarging our understanding of the relationship between CSR and CMNEs.

5. Suggestions for Future Research Directions

We examined existing CSR articles for CMNEs and concluded with five themes: (1) the relationship between corporate governance and CSR practices, (2) the relationship between the institutional environment and CSR practices, (3) the relationship between corporate governance and CSR practices, (4) the relationship between strategy activities and CSR practice, and (5) the relationship between resource/capacity and CSR practice. Then, based on a large amount of accumulated literature, we explained the relationships between constructs and then illustrated the conceptual framework, as shown in Figure 1.

According to previous research, we found that there is much discussion on how to create a global code for CSR conduct. This is also of profound significance for improving the CSR practices of CMNE, which began to develop late, although from a universalistic rather than a particularistic perspective [16]. Of course, we found research on CSR implementation by enterprises in the context of China in some IB and IBE journals. In addition to research on CMNE's domestic and foreign operations, research on foreign subsidiaries operating in China is also included. However, considering that national culture is an important factor in the development of CSR, as an emerging economy, Chinese enterprises are still in the preliminary stage of development; therefore, we need to continue to explore issues [16] such as what are the indigenous characteristics of CMNEs' CSR, and how to integrate the

Chinese background into the global ·CSR standard with the contextualization approach. Establishing and improving CMNEs' CSR implementation systems can improve CSR performance in global operations.

We provide potential references and suggestions for future research on CMNEs' CSR based on previous research. We have highlighted rarely studied or understudied issues in Figure 1 with grey boxes

5.1. Developing CSR Theory on Chinese MNEs

Existing theories are mainly developed from Western to Chinese contexts [16]. We call for more local research to explore CSR theory in the Chinese context. In the future, we can further compare and analyze the differences in CSR implementation between Chinese firms and other countries, focusing on the operation of foreign subsidiaries in host countries, and then extend CSR theory. For example, a study on the CSR strategies of CMNEs for foreign subsidiaries.

Previous research has proposed some ethical approaches that foreign subsidiaries may adopt when faced with homogenization pressure, such as studies on MNEs' use of CSR strategies to reduce local ethical pressure and reshape their core values in the host country [60]. Some studies have shown that CSR strategy, as a bridge between business and the state, has become a strategy for MNEs to establish legitimacy overseas [49]. We also need to know whether national and local institutional contextualization factors, such as political and economic factors, can be better integrated into decision making and whether they can be used as CSR performance evaluation components for CMNE. Previous studies have discussed the moderating role of institutional factors in the relationship between CSR strategy and firm performance, and in the future, we can explore in depth the impact of different dimensions of CSR strategy on firm performance under the influence of institutional factors. Overall, integrating each unique local context with a globalized economic environment may enable a better extension of the CSR theory.

5.2. The Relationship between Corporate Governance and CSR in CME

A second direction for future research is to gain more insight into the relationship between the CMNE government and CSR. Ownership of equity in Chinese corporations is divided into state-owned, domestic private, and foreign-invested enterprises. Because the ownership structure differs, as does the proportion of state ownership; the scope of CSR differs as well. Future research could compare and analyze the CSR implementation of different companies' ownership. Specifically, SOEs have a high proportion of state ownership, which carries the universal recognition of the world's obligations such as economic and legal but also undertakes the responsibility of job creation, social stability, and national progress [73].

Although we found some studies on the CSR performance of state-owned MNEs, the number is limited. We also need to investigate more pertinent issues such as whether CSR activities have changed in China's changing business environment. How do SOEs' widely implied social commitments (such as employment stability, childcare, and school provision) interact with the responsibilities of operating in the host country? Furthermore, the influence of SOEs' degree of political dependency on CSR performance differs from that of other types of ownership, which should be investigated further in the future.

Then, regarding the Board and TMT level research, although previous studies have mentioned that investing in the employee dimension of CSR can increase employee loyalty and organizational identity, which helps companies to gain more value from intangible assets such as knowledge and experience through MNE employees working together across inter-regional departments. However, we also need to understand how intangible assets affect CSR practices, for example, does knowledge transfer and sharing in companies contribute to changes in CSR evaluation criteria? Additionally, does the increase in corporate research and technical staffing increase CSR disclosure voluntariness? This should be investigated further in future research.

5.3. CMNEs' Corporation Society Irresponsibility

The fourth research direction is the discussion of CMNEs' corporate society irresponsibility (CSIR). Luo et al. [74] found that CSR investments can be used to provide a function similar to reputational insurance for businesses. For example, increasing CSR donations can reduce the risk of an oil company's market value falling because of poor performance. CSR investment can compensate for inappropriate outbound investments because of inefficient home-country institutions [75]. Therefore, when implementing CSR activities, businesses may be unmotivated to actively improve social welfare and may also tend to coexist with CSIR behaviors [76]. In today's global economic depression caused by COVID-19, how companies' reputations are not affected to maintain good business is an urgent concern. Future research should focus on CSIR behaviors, such as how to improve CSR evaluation standards from a balanced perspective and scientifically explain and measure CSIR behaviors. Answering these questions will help improve CMNEs' CSIR mechanism of CMNEs.

5.4. Impact of COVID-19 on CSR of Chinese MNEs

The fifth research direction is the practice of CSR in CMNEs during COVID-19. COVID-19 has severely affected the operations of multinational corporations, leading to a new trend in CSR. Cui and Peng [77] confirmed that CSR is more inclined to focus on employees, consumers, communities, and social interests associated with COVID-19. Huang [78] argued that building CSR is the process of redefining China's social policies, which is not just related to the division of labor between China and the country's social duties, it also includes a variety of associations and social organizations. Future studies can further explore which CSR practices should be adopted to respond to the new requirements of all stakeholders when companies face changing environments.

Cui and Peng [77] mentioned that the length of CSR reports, framework criteria, and other aspects will be adjusted to follow the changes in the epidemic. However, there is a need to further explore companies' emergency response capabilities, such as how to adapt CSR strategies quickly and efficiently in response to public health emergencies and how CSR reports should represent the current state of the environment.

Finally, regarding the construction of new CSR evaluation criteria, Tan Yusheng believed that CSR issues should be considered from the perspective of value distribution in the global industry through a more equitable global benefit-sharing mechanism jointly established by global consumers, multinational companies, and local enterprises. Future research could further discuss how to use new technologies, such as data mining, to construct new indices of Chinese MNEs' CSR in global business in the context of COVID-19.

5.5. Methodological Approaches

Finally, more research is required to investigate the uniqueness of CMNEs' CSR. For example, an experimental or longitudinal study has been conducted. Most studies on Chinese companies' CSR use cross-sectional data. Although some studies use different statistical techniques to avoid endogeneity factors, a longer period can improve the restriction of causality [14] and facilitate an understanding of the basic causes of challenges in CSR implementation. For example, some researchers collected specific data on a CMNE's CSR activities over a long period to gain a better understanding of how companies use CSR activities to improve corporate performance and the quality of their CSR reports. In terms of collecting CMNE CSR cases or sample data, future research should consider the diversification of types, such as collecting multinational companies established in different regions of China and further dividing them according to corporate ownership type (private, state-owned, and foreign-funded enterprises). Tsui [79] observed that Chinese subgroups differ in many ways, including the economic and political environment, values, communication style, personality, and cognitive style. This heterogeneity may have resulted in significant differences between regions. Future research can use the potential heterogeneity characteristics to further investigate CSR-related issues that still require continuous attention or resolution, such as enhancing the indices of Chinese MNEs' CSR in global business. Furthermore, it can test whether regional heterogeneity in China affects the relationship between enterprise governance and CSR outcomes.

Author Contributions: Methodology, X.-C.S.; Supervision, S.-Y.D. and J.Y.L.; Writing—original draft, X.-C.S. and J.Y.L.; Writing—review & editing, A.J. and J.Y.L. All authors have read and agreed to the published version of the manuscript.

Funding: This research received no external funding.

Informed Consent Statement: Not applicable.

Conflicts of Interest: The authors declare no conflict of interest.

Appendix A

Table A1. The research on CSR of Chinese multinational enterprises.

Authors	Year	Sample Period	Theory leans	Focus	Findings
Luo et al. [80]	2017	2008–2011	Organizational theory	3–5	CSR reporting is seen as an organizational response to the institutional complications resulting from conflicting requirements of central and local government
LI and LU [45]	2020	Not specified	Institutional theory	3–5	Corporations are more likely to increase CSR when public agents are more motivated to seek promotion to central government.
Zhu et al. [54]	2014	Not specified	Stakeholder theory	2–5	There is a positive relationship between ethical leadership and CSR.
Du et al. [52]	2016	2007–2009	Legitimacy theory	3–5	Religious climate plays an important role in strengthening CSR and has a substitute role with law enforcement.
Zamir and Saeed [41]	2020	2010 to 2015	Legitimacy theory Institutional theory	3–5	Corporations faced institutional pressures depending on location, with those close to financial centers more legally committed to CSR disclosure.
Shen et al. [81]	2020	2012	Institutional perspective	2–5	Investing in CSR can help corporations create value from intangible assets.
Yang et. al [5]	2020	Not specified	Institutional theory	4–5	The positive impact of Belt and Road on the CSR performance of MNEs is stronger in host countries with higher levels of institutional pressure
Ding et al. [82]	2022	2008–2015	Institutional theory Strategic view	1–5	Board interlocking causes an integration in the CSR structure of the interlocked companies, increasing the probability that CSR activities will be implemented, which facilitates CSR discussion.
Zhang et al. [64]	2020	2008–2014	Institutional theory	5–6	Conformity in CSR legitimizes enterprises in the analyst group and positively affects analyst coverage.
Miska et al. [43]	2016	2012	Institutional theory	3–5	States effect Chinese MNEs' global CSR integration and local CSR responsiveness strategies.
Zhou and Wang [83]	2020	2009–2016	Reputation risk view	3–5	The positive relationship between parent company reputation risk and CSR activities of foreign subsidiaries is impacted by differences in institutional context between host and home countries.

Table A1. *Cont.*

Authors	Year	Sample Period	Theory leans	Focus	Findings
Wang, et al. [31]	2015	Not specified	Stakeholder theory and upper echelons theory	1–5	Personal values and perceptions of the CEO's attitudes toward philanthropy can influence corporate charitable donation decisions.
Li et al. [15]	2022	2010–2018	Legitimacy theory Stakeholder theory Resource-based view	2–5	Director network centrality has a significant positive effect on the quality of CSR disclosure, especially when the board devotes less to advertising.
Moon J, Shen [84]	2010	1993–2007	Not specified	3–5	The focus of CSR in Chinese enterprises has evolved from ethical issues to social, environmental and stakeholder focus.
Li and Zhang, [21]	2010	2008	Type II agency problem	1–5	Dispersion of corporate ownership mitigates the risk of minority shareholders' self-interest. For non-SOEs, the dispersion of corporate ownership is positively related to CSR
Xu and Yang [18]	2010	2006	Not specified	3–5	CSR dimensions of Chinese enterprises are strongly linked to their socio-cultural background and are different from those of Western countries.
Wang et al. [58]	2011	2007–2008	Portfolio theory and stakeholder theory	5–6	Avoid investing too little or too much in CSR may mitigate adverse investor reactions resulting in low financial performance
Ye and Zhang [65]	2011	2007–2008	Risk mitigation theory	5–6	The u-shaped relationship between CSR and the cost of debt financing in China in the context of emerging markets
Liu et al. [53]	2015	2009–2011	Stakeholder theory.	5–6	Suspension of CSR can harm stakeholder relationships and threaten the survival of the business.
Yin and Zhang [42]	2012	2009	Grounded-theory-building	3–5	Institutional infrastructure and cultural ethical factors have a strong relationship with the CSR performance of Chinese corporations.
Hah and Freeman [6]	2014	Not specified	Stakeholder theory and institutional theory	3–5	MNE subsidiaries respond to pressures from host countries by adopting globally integrated or locally responsive (or a combination of both) CSR strategies.
Cumming et al. [85]	2016	1982–2014	Not specified	5	Trust and fraud issues related to CSR are a rising concern for Chinese enterprises.
Lau et al. [11]	2016	2010–2011	Stakeholder theory Agency theory	1–5	The concentration of shareholding can reduce the diversity of CSR activities. Compared to the TMT, the board may have a more active and effective elicit CMNE's CSR to serve the performance of the public.
Wang and Li [86]	2016	2007–2012.	Stakeholder theory.	5–6	The market valuations of CSR initiators dominated by central and local governments are lesser than those of non- initiators and those owned by private shareholders.
Liao et al. [36]	2018	2008–2012	Resource dependence theory Agency theory Critical mass theory	1–5	Corporations with larger boards, more female directors, and separate CEO and board positions can dedicate more effort and resources and are more prone to CSR assurance
Gong et al. [87]	2018	2010–2013	Information theory	5–6 3–5	The stronger the negative relationship between the quality of CSR disclosure and the cost of corporate bonds when corporations are located in areas with weak corporate governance and institutional environments

Table A1. *Cont.*

Authors	Year	Sample Period	Theory leans	Focus	Findings
Ma and Bu [16]	2021	Not specified	Not specified	5	In order to explore CSR performance in CMNES′, contextualized CSR theories need to be developed by combining Chinese social contexts.
Gong et al. [56]	2021	2011–2017	Information asymmetry theory	5–6	Conducting CSR activities can partially offset CMNE's negative impact on the cost of debt due to corporate law violations.
Liu et al. [14]	2021	2000–2012	Upper echelons theory Stakeholder theory Social stratification view	3–5	Enterprises make strategic CSR decisions to satisfy their stakeholders (employees, environmental agencies, and communities). Entrepreneurs with higher social status and stronger political ties are more inclined to commit to CSR.
Tsoi [88]	2010	2004–2005	Stakeholder theory	5–6	Local and regional stakeholders believe that CSR is important to primarily export-oriented businesses.
Zheng et al. [38]	2015	2006–2008	Stakeholder theory Institutional theory	5–6	Corporations can pursue stakeholder legitimacy through strategies of passive conformity and intentional adaptation to stakeholder CSR requirement.
Sun et al. [48]	2015	2006-2011	Institutional theory	3–5	If banks in communities where more companies report CSR or where there are principles encouraging CSR practices, they are more probable to be early adopters of CSR reporting.
Cui et al. [55]	2015	2008	Stakeholder theory	5–6	The relationship between privately-owned enterprises' commitment to CSR and average sales growth is related to the size of the enterprise.
Han and Zheng [89]	2016	2004–2005	Organizational theory	1–5	the imprinting effects of a company's founding ownership on labor and environmental protections, two critical CSR practices.
Ge, and Zhao [44]	2017	2006	Organizational theory Institutional theory	3–5	The choice of external or internal CSR practices is related to how strongly the enterprise is linked to the state system.
Marquis and Qian [73]	2014	2009–2013	Stakeholder theory	3–5	The political mechanisms of state-mediated globalization allow corporations to adopt and adapt global normative practices while meeting the political legitimacy needs of key stakeholders.
Ma et al. [69]	2020	2008–2014	Upper echelons theory	2–5	Executives with academic backgrounds are more willing to provide stakeholders with more CSR disclosure information.
Li et al. [90]	2010	Not specified	Institutional theory	1–5	Corporations with a high percentage of outside directors tend to have stronger corporate governance and more CSR.
Zeng et al. [68]	2013	2010–2011	Institutional theory	4–5,5–6	Social marketing activities that contribute to the legitimacy of CSR and positive corporate performance.
Marquis et al. [33]	2017	2009–2013	Stakeholder theory	1–5	The Chinese government, as a stakeholder, can guide enterprises in employing and adapting global CSR practices.
Cheng et al. [91]	2014	Not specified	Agency theory Stakeholder theory	5–6	Transparency in CSR performance is essential to reducing capital constraints.
Flammer [92]	2015	1972–2005	Neoclassical trade theory Stakeholder theory	4–5	Trade liberalization is an important factor in shaping CSR practices.

Table A1. *Cont.*

Authors	Year	Sample Period	Theory leans	Focus	Findings
Duanmu, et al. [59]	2018	2000–2005	Institutional theory	5	It should be considered prudent to invest in CSR strategies as a competitive approach, due to enterprises are unable to avoid competition by environmental differentiation.
Fu et al. [39]	2020	2005–2014	Upper echelons theory	1–5	The presence of a chief sustainability officer (CSO) increases CSR activities and reduces corporate social irresponsibility activities (CSIR)
Gatignon [63]	2022	Not specified	Human capital management perspective	5–6	boundary-spanning CSR program and nonprofit peer mission-dependent employee identity pressure can be reduced by developing a sense of CSR among employees.
Doh et al. [93]	2013	Not specified	Stakeholder theory Institutional theory	3–5 5–6	Under the influence of institutional hollowness and duality, DMNEs use CSR as a signaling mechanism to obtain legitimacy and a "license to operate" in developed countries.
Huang et al. [47]	2022	2009–2016,	Signaling theory	5–6	CSR performance is related to access to bank credit, and this positive relationship is more significant for long-term loans than for short-term loans.
Tian et al. [94]	2011	2009	Information Theory	5–6	Corporations that sell experiential products (as opposed to seek-and-trust products) are more likely to obtain positive consumer evaluate with products and purchase by CSR practices
Luger et al. [95]	2022	Not specified	Cross-cultural perspective	3–5	consumer attitudes toward CSR in advanced European markets and emerging Asian markets and confirms that consumers' attitudes toward CSR support influence their purchasing behavior.
Zhang et al. [62]	2010	2008	Agency theory	5–6	Advertising intensity is positively correlated with the category of CSR
Zhao [49]	2012	2009	Grounded-theory-	5–6	MNE may regard CSR as an extension of their efforts to seek legitimacy in the state
Wei et al. [96]	2017	Not specified	Signaling theory Institutional theory	5–6	Environmental Corporate social responsibility can impact business and political legitimacy, as well as corporate performance.
Wang et al. [31]	2015	Not specified	Upper echelons theory	1–5	Pressure from stakeholders influences the perception of corporate charitable giving management decisions
Zamirl and Saeed [41]	2020	2010–2015.	Legitimacy theory and institutional theory	1–5	MNE close to financial centers exhibit more CSR disclosure.
Zhang and Luo [66]	2013	2008	Agency theory and institutional theory	4–5	CSR increase the importance of external social forces that motivate MNE to act.

Note: This table lists the main points of all the papers reviewed in this paper.

References

1. Ma, Z. The status of contemporary business ethics research: Present and future. *J. Bus. Ethics* **2009**, *90*, 255–265. [CrossRef]
2. Carroll, A.B. A three-dimensional conceptual model of corporate performance. *Acad. Manag. Rev.* **1979**, *4*, 497–505. [CrossRef]
3. Friedman, M.A. Friedman doctrine: The social responsibility of business is to increase its profits. *N.Y. Times Mag.* **1970**, *13*, 32–33.
4. Aguilera, R.V.; Rupp, D.E.; Williams, C.A.; Ganapathi, J. Putting the S back in corporate social responsibility: A multilevel theory of social change in organizations. *Acad. Manag. Rev.* **2007**, *32*, 836–863. [CrossRef]
5. Yang, N.; Wang, J.; Liu, X.; Huang, L. Home-country institutions and corporate social responsibility of emerging economy multinational enterprises: The belt and road initiative as an example. *Asia Pac. J. Manag.* **2020**, *39*, 927–965. [CrossRef]

6. Hah, K.; Freeman, S. Multinational enterprise subsidiaries and their CSR: A conceptual framework of the management of CSR in smaller emerging economies. *J. Bus. Ethics* **2014**, *122*, 125–136. [CrossRef]
7. Cui, X.J. A study on using foreign investment to accelerate the construction of innovative countries under the current situation. *Int. Econ. Coop.* **2017**, *9*, 23–27.
8. Campbell, J.T.; Eden, L.; Miller, S.R. Multinationals and corporate social responsibility in host countries: Does distance matter. *J. Int. Bus. Stud.* **2012**, *43*, 84–106. [CrossRef]
9. Husted, B.W.; Allen, D.B. Corporate social responsibility in the multinational enterprise: Strategic and institutional approaches. *J. Int. Bus. Stud.* **2006**, *37*, 838–849. [CrossRef]
10. Muller, A. Global versus local CSR strategies. *Eur. Manag. J.* **2006**, *24*, 189–198. [CrossRef]
11. Lau, C.M.; Lu, Y.; Liang, Q. Corporate social responsibility in China: A corporate governance approach. *J. Bus. Ethics* **2016**, *136*, 73–87. [CrossRef]
12. Snyder, H. Literature review as a research methodology: An overview and guidelines. *J. Bus. Res.* **2019**, *104*, 333–339. [CrossRef]
13. Garriga, E.; Mele, D. Corporate social responsibility theories: Mapping the territory. *J. Bus. Ethics* **2004**, *53*, 51–71. [CrossRef]
14. Liu, Y.; Dai, W.; Liao, M.; Wei, J. Social status and corporate social responsibility: Evidence from Chinese privately owned firms. *J. Bus. Ethics* **2021**, *169*, 651–672. [CrossRef]
15. Li, W.; Zhang, J.Z.; Ding, R. Impact of Directors' Network on Corporate Social Responsibility Disclosure: Evidence from China. *J. Bus. Ethics* **2022**, 1–33. [CrossRef]
16. Ma, Z.; Bu, M. A new research horizon for mass entrepreneurship policy and Chinese firms' CSR: Introduction to the thematic symposium. *J. Bus. Ethics* **2021**, *169*, 603–607. [CrossRef]
17. Cui, X.J. The conceptual framework of social responsibility of multinational corporations. *World Econ. Stud.* **2007**, *4*, 64–68.
18. Ye, S.; Yang, R. Indigenous characteristics of Chinese corporate social responsibility conceptual paradigm. *J. Bus. Ethics* **2010**, *93*, 321–333.
19. Ministry of Commence of The People's Republic of China. 2022 January-May China's Foreign Direct Investment in the Whole Industry Concise Statistics. Available online: http://www.mofcom.gov.cn/article/tongjiziliao/dgzz/202206/20220603322653.shtml (accessed on 28 June 2022).
20. Fortune China. Fortune 500 List for 2022. Available online: http://www.fortunechina.com/fortune500/c/2022-08/03/content_415683.htm (accessed on 3 August 2022).
21. Li, W.; Zhang, R. Corporate social responsibility, ownership structure, and political interference: Evidence from China. *J. Bus. Ethics* **2010**, *96*, 631–645. [CrossRef]
22. Li, X.; Zhou, Y.M. Offshoring pollution while offshoring production? *Strateg. Manag. J.* **2017**, *38*, 2310–2329. [CrossRef]
23. Xiao, Y.; Watson, M. Guidance on conducting a systematic literature review. *J. Plan. Educ. Res.* **2019**, *39*, 93–112. [CrossRef]
24. Pisani, N.; Kourula, A.; Kolk, A.; Meijer, R. How global is international CSR research? Insights and recommendations from a systematic review. *J. World Bus.* **2017**, *52*, 591–614. [CrossRef]
25. Rodriguez, P.; Siegel, D.S.; Hillman, A.; Eden, L. Three lenses on the multinational enterprise: Politics, corruption, and corporate social responsibility. *J. Int. Bus. Stud.* **2006**, *37*, 733–746. [CrossRef]
26. Torraco, R.J. Writing integrative literature reviews: Guidelines and examples. *Hum. Resour. Dev. Rev.* **2005**, *4*, 356–367. [CrossRef]
27. Colli, A.; Colpan, A.M. Business groups and corporate governance: Review, synthesis, and extension. *Corp. Gov. Int. Rev.* **2016**, *24*, 274–302. [CrossRef]
28. Holmes, R.M., Jr.; Hoskisson, R.E.; Kim, H.; Wan, W.P.; Holcomb, T.R. International strategy and business groups: A review and future research agenda. *J. World Bus.* **2018**, *53*, 134–150. [CrossRef]
29. Gallo, M.A. The Family Business and Its Social Responsibilities. *Fam. Bus. Rev.* **2014**, *17*, 135–148. [CrossRef]
30. Meyer, K.E.; Li, C.; Schotter, A.P.J. Managing the MNE subsidiary: Advancing a multi-level and dynamic research agenda. *J. Int. Bus Stud.* **2020**, *51*, 538–576.
31. Wang, S.; Gao, Y.; Hodgkinson, G.P.; Rousseau, D.M.; Flood, P.C. Opening the black box of CSR decision making: A policy-capturing study of charitable donation decisions in China. *J. Bus. Ethics* **2015**, *128*, 665–683. [CrossRef]
32. Gulzar, M.A.; Cherian, J.; Hwang, J.; Jiang, Y.; Sial, M.S. The impact of board gender diversity and foreign institutional investors on the corporate social responsibility (CSR) engagement of Chinese listed companies. *Sustainability* **2019**, *11*, 307. [CrossRef]
33. Marquis, C.; Yin, J.; Yang, D. State-mediated globalization processes and the adoption of corporate social responsibility reporting in China. *Manag. Organ. Rev.* **2017**, *13*, 167–191. [CrossRef]
34. Zhang, Y.; Wang, P.; Kwon, J. CSR in China: Does being close to the central or local government matter? *Sustainability* **2021**, *13*, 8770. [CrossRef]
35. Khalid, F.; Sun, J.; Huang, G.; Su, C.Y. Environmental, social and governance performance of Chinese multinationals: A comparison of state-and non-state-owned enterprises. *Sustainability* **2021**, *13*, 4020. [CrossRef]
36. Liao, L.; Lin, T.P.; Zhang, Y. Corporate board and corporate social responsibility assurance: Evidence from China. *J. Bus. Ethics.* **2018**, *150*, 211–225. [CrossRef]
37. Hillman, A.; Cannella, A.; Paetzold, R. The resource dependence role of corporate directors: Strategic adaptation of board composition in response to environmental change. *J. Manag. Stud.* **2000**, *37*, 213–255. [CrossRef]
38. Zheng, Q.; Luo, Y.; Maksimov, V. Achieving legitimacy through corporate social responsibility: The case of emerging economy firms. *J. World Bus.* **2015**, *50*, 389–403. [CrossRef]

39. Fu, R.; Tang, Y.; Chen, G. Chief sustainability officers, and corporate social (Ir) responsibility. *Strateg. Manag. J.* **2020**, *41*, 656–680. [CrossRef]
40. Frynas, J.G. Corporate social responsibility and societal governance: Lessons from transparency in the oil and gas sector. *J. Bus. Ethics* **2010**, *93*, 163–179. [CrossRef]
41. Zamir, F.; Saeed, A. Location matters: Impact of geographical proximity to financial centers on corporate social responsibility (CSR) disclosure in emerging economies. *Asia Pac. J. Manag.* **2020**, *37*, 263–295. [CrossRef]
42. Yin, J.; Zhang, Y. Institutional dynamics and corporate social responsibility (CSR) in an emerging country context: Evidence from China. *J. Bus. Ethics* **2012**, *111*, 301–316. [CrossRef]
43. Miska, C.; Witt, M.A.; Stahl, G.K. Drivers of global CSR integration and local CSR responsiveness: Evidence from Chinese MNEs. *Bus. Ethics Q.* **2016**, *26*, 317–345. [CrossRef]
44. Ge, J.; Zhao, W. Institutional linkages with the state and organizational practices in corporate social responsibility: Evidence from China. *Manag. Organ. Rev.* **2017**, *13*, 539–573. [CrossRef]
45. Li, S.; Lu, J.W. A dual-agency model of firm CSR in response to institutional pressure: Evidence from Chinese publicly listed firms. *Acad. Manag. J.* **2020**, *63*, 2004–2032. [CrossRef]
46. Wei, Z.; Wu, S.; Li, C.; Chen, W. Family control, institutional environment and cash dividend policy: Evidence from China. *China J. Account. Res.* **2011**, *4*, 29–46. [CrossRef]
47. Huang, G.; Ye, F.; Li, Y.; Chen, L.; Zhang, M. Corporate social responsibility and bank credit loans: Exploring the moderating effect of the institutional environment in China. *Asia Pac. J. Manag.* **2022**, 1–36. [CrossRef]
48. Sun, J.; Wang, F.; Wang, F.; Yin, H. Community institutions and initial diffusion of corporate social responsibility practices in China's banking industry. *Manag. Organ. Rev.* **2015**, *11*, 441–468. [CrossRef]
49. Zhao, M. CSR-based political legitimacy strategy: Managing the state by doing good in China and Russia. *J. Bus. Ethics* **2012**, *111*, 439–460. [CrossRef]
50. Freeman, S.; Edwards, R.; Schroder, B. How smaller born-global firms use networks and alliances to overcome constraints to rapid internationalization. *J. Int. Mark.* **2006**, *14*, 33–63. [CrossRef]
51. Cruz, L.B.; Boehe, D.M. How do leading retail MNCs leverage CSR globally? Insights from Brazil. *J. Bus. Ethics* **2010**, *91*, 243–263. [CrossRef]
52. Du, X.; Du, Y.; Zeng, Q.; Pei, H.; Chang, Y. Religious atmosphere, law enforcement, and corporate social responsibility: Evidence from China. *Asia Pac. J. Manag.* **2016**, *33*, 229–265. [CrossRef]
53. Liu, Y.; Feng, T.; Li, S. Stakeholder influences and organization responses: A case study of corporate social responsibility suspension. *Manag. Organ. Rev.* **2015**, *11*, 469–491. [CrossRef]
54. Zhu, Y.; Sun, L.Y.; Leung, A.S.M. Corporate social responsibility, firm reputation, and firm performance: The role of ethical leadership. *Asia Pac. J. Manag.* **2014**, *31*, 925–947. [CrossRef]
55. Cui, Z.; Liang, X.; Lu, X. Prize or price? Corporate social responsibility commitment and sales performance in the Chinese private sector. *Manag. Organ. Rev.* **2015**, *11*, 25–44. [CrossRef]
56. Gong, G.; Huang, X.; Wu, S.; Tian, H.; Li, W. Punishment by securities regulators, corporate social responsibility and the cost of debt. *J. Bus. Ethics* **2021**, *171*, 337–356. [CrossRef]
57. Cheung, Y.L.; Tan, W.; Ahn, H.J.; Zhang, Z. Does corporate social responsibility matter in Asian emerging markets? *J. Bus. Ethics* **2010**, *92*, 401–413. [CrossRef]
58. Wang, M.; Qiu, C.; Kong, D. Corporate social responsibility, investor behaviors, and stock market returns: Evidence from a natural experiment in China. *J. Bus. Ethics* **2011**, *101*, 127–141. [CrossRef]
59. Duanmu, J.L.; Bu, M.; Pittman, R. Does market competition dampen environmental performance? Evidence from China. *Strateg. Manag. J.* **2018**, *39*, 3006–3030. [CrossRef]
60. DiMaggio, P.J.; Powell, W.W. The iron cage revisited: Institutional isomorphism and collective rationality in organizational fields. *Am. Sociol. Rev.* **1983**, *48*, 147–160. [CrossRef]
61. Alford, R.R.; Friedland, R. *Powers of Theory: Capitalism, the State, and Democracy*; Cambridge University Press: New York, NY, USA, 1985; pp. 11–75. ISBN 0-521-31635-9.
62. Zhang, R.; Zhu, J.; Yue, H.; Zhu, C. Corporate philanthropic giving, advertising intensity, and industry competition level. *J. Bus. Ethics* **2010**, *94*, 39–52. [CrossRef]
63. Gatignon, A. The double-edged sword of boundary-spanning Corporate Social Responsibility programs. *Strateg. Manag. J.* **2022**, *43*, 2156–2184. [CrossRef]
64. Zhang, Y.; Wang, H.; Zhou, X. Dare to be different? Conformity versus differentiation in corporate social activities of Chinese firms and market responses. *Acad. Manag. J.* **2020**, *63*, 717–742. [CrossRef]
65. Ye, K.; Zhang, R. Do lenders value corporate social responsibility? Evidence from China. *J. Bus. Ethics* **2011**, *104*, 197–206. [CrossRef]
66. Zhang, J.; Luo, X.R. Dared to care: Organizational vulnerability, institutional logics, and MNCs' social responsiveness in emerging markets. *Organ. Sci.* **2013**, *24*, 1742–1764. [CrossRef]
67. Zhang, Q.; de Vries, A. Seeking Moral Legitimacy through Corporate Social Responsibility: Evidence from Chinese Manufacturing Multinationals. *Sustainability* **2022**, *14*, 5245. [CrossRef]

68. Zeng, F.; Li, J.; Zhu, H.; Cai, Z.; Li, P. How international firms conduct societal marketing in emerging markets. *Manag. Int. Rev.* **2013**, *53*, 841–868. [CrossRef]
69. Ma, Z.; Zhang, H.; Zhong, W.; Zhou, K. Top management teams' academic experience and firms' corporate social responsibility voluntary disclosure. *Manag. Organ. Rev.* **2020**, *16*, 293–333. [CrossRef]
70. Juergensen, J.J.; Narula, R.; Surdu, I. A systematic review of the relationship between international diversification and innovation: A firm-level perspective. *Int. Bus. Rev.* **2021**, *31*, 101955. [CrossRef]
71. Michailova, S.; Fee, A.; DeNisi, A. Research on host-country nationals in multinational enterprises: The last five decades and ways forward. *J. World Bus.* **2022**, *58*, 101383. [CrossRef]
72. Ponomareva, Y.; Uman, T.; Bodolica, V.; Wennberg, K. Cultural diversity in top management teams: Review and agenda for future research. *J. World Bus.* **2022**, *57*, 101328. [CrossRef]
73. Marquis, C.; Qian, C. Corporate social responsibility reporting in China: Symbol or substance? *Organ. Sci.* **2014**, *25*, 127–148. [CrossRef]
74. Luo, J.; Kaul, A.; Seo, H. Winning us with trifes: Adverse selection in the use of philanthropy as insurance. *Strateg. Manag. J.* **2018**, *39*, 2591–2617. [CrossRef]
75. Kotchen, M.; Moon, J.J. Corporate social responsibility for irresponsibility. *BE J. Econ. Anal. Policy* **2012**, *12*. [CrossRef]
76. Strike, V.M.; Gao, J.; Bansal, P. Being good while being bad: Social responsibility and the international diversification of US firms. *J. Int. Bus. Stud.* **2006**, *37*, 850–862. [CrossRef]
77. Cui, X.J.; Peng, X.H. New trends in the corporate social responsibility of multinational companies under the impact of COVID-19. *Int. Trade* **2020**, *9*, 14–21.
78. Huang, Y.J. Technological progress under open conditions—From technology introduction to independent innovation. *World Econ. Stud.* **2008**, *6*, 14–18+37+86.
79. Tsui, A.S. Contributing to Global Management Knowledge: A Case for High Quality Indigenous Research'. *Asia Pac. J. Manag.* **2004**, *21*, 491–513. [CrossRef]
80. Luo, X.R.; Wang, D.; Zhang, J. Whose call to answer: Institutional complexity and firms' CSR reporting. *Acad. Manag. J.* **2017**, *60*, 321–344. [CrossRef]
81. Shen, N.; Au, K.; Li, W. Strategic alignment of intangible assets: The role of corporate social responsibility. *Asia Pac. J. Manag.* **2020**, *37*, 1119–1139. [CrossRef]
82. Ding, H.; Hu, Y.; Yang, X.; Zhou, X. Board interlock and the diffusion of corporate social responsibility among Chinese listed firms. *Asia Pac. J. Manag.* **2022**, *39*, 1287–1320. [CrossRef]
83. Zhou, N.; Wang, H. Foreign subsidiary CSR as a buffer against parent firm reputation risk. *J. Int. Bus. Stud.* **2020**, *51*, 1256–1282. [CrossRef]
84. Moon, J.; Shen, X. CSR in China research: Salience, focus and nature. *J. Bus. Ethics* **2010**, *94*, 613–629. [CrossRef]
85. Cumming, D.; Hou, W.; Lee, E. Business ethics and finance in greater China: Synthesis and future directions in sustainability, CSR, and fraud. *J. Bus. Ethics* **2016**, *138*, 601–626. [CrossRef]
86. Wang, K.T.; Li, D. Market reactions to the first-time disclosure of corporate social responsibility reports: Evidence from China. *J. Bus. Ethics* **2016**, *138*, 661–682. [CrossRef]
87. Gong, G.; Xu, S.; Gong, X. On the value of corporate social responsibility disclosure: An empirical investigation of corporate bond issues in China. *J. Bus. Ethics* **2018**, *150*, 227–258. [CrossRef]
88. Tsoi, J. Stakeholders' perceptions and future scenarios to improve corporate social responsibility in Hong Kong and Mainland China. *J. Bus. Ethics* **2010**, *91*, 391–404. [CrossRef]
89. Han, Y.; Zheng, E. Why firms perform differently in corporate social responsibility? Firm ownership and the persistence of organizational imprints. *Manag. Organ. Rev.* **2016**, *12*, 605–629. [CrossRef]
90. Li, S.; Fetscherin, M.; Alon, I.; Lattemann, C.; Yeh, K. Corporate social responsibility in emerging markets. *Manag. Int. Rev.* **2010**, *50*, 635–654. [CrossRef]
91. Cheng, B.; Ioannou, I.; Serafeim, G. Corporate social responsibility and access to finance. *Strateg. Manag. J.* **2014**, *35*, 1–23. [CrossRef]
92. Flammer, C. Does product market competition foster corporate social responsibility? Evidence from trade liberalization. *Strateg. Manag. J.* **2015**, *36*, 1469–1485. [CrossRef]
93. Doh, J.; Husted, B.; Yang, X. Ethics, Corporate Social Responsibility, and Developing Country Multinationals. *Bus. Ethics Q.* **2013**, *23*, 638–639. [CrossRef]
94. Tian, Z.; Wang, R.; Yang, W. Consumer responses to corporate social responsibility (CSR) in China. *J. Bus. Ethics* **2011**, *101*, 197–212. [CrossRef]
95. Luger, M.; Hofer, K.M.; Floh, A. Support for corporate social responsibility among generation Y consumers in advanced versus emerging markets. *Int. Bus. Rev.* **2022**, *31*, 101903. [CrossRef]
96. Wei, Z.; Shen, H.; Zhou, K.Z.; Li, J.J. How does environmental corporate social responsibility matter in a dysfunctional institutional environment? Evidence from China. *J. Bus. Ethics* **2017**, *140*, 209–223. [CrossRef]

sustainability

Article

Foreign Shareholders' Social Responsibility, R&D Innovation, and International Competitiveness of Chinese SOEs

Yuying Zhou [1,*], Chu Lei [1] and Alfredo Jiménez [2]

[1] School of Business English, Sichuan International Studies University, Chongqing 400013, China; leichu@stu.sisu.edu.cn
[2] Department of Management, KEDGE Business School, 31405 Talence, France; alfredo.jimenez@kedgebs.com
* Correspondence: zhouyuying@sisu.edu.cn

Abstract: Despite the increasing use of mixed ownership (domestic and foreign shareholders) in Chinese state-owned enterprises (SOEs), the role and performance of foreign ownership is still a controversial topic. In this paper we empirically examine the effects of foreign shareholders' social responsibility on the international competitiveness of SOEs and the moderating effect of R&D innovation. Drawing on a sample of Chinese listed SOEs with international market operations over the period 2011–2019, we find empirical evidence supporting that foreign shareholders' social responsibility is effective in enhancing the international competitiveness of Chinese SOEs. We also find that R&D innovation strengthens the effect between foreign shareholders' social responsibility and enterprises' international competitiveness. These findings are valid after controlling for robustness and endogeneity factors. Furthermore, we find that the promoting effect of foreign shareholders' social responsibility on Chinese SOEs' international competitiveness, as well as the moderating effect of R&D innovation, is more pronounced among Chinese local SOEs, business SOEs, and manufacturing SOEs. The research in this paper contributes to the current debate and deepens our understanding regarding the role and performance of foreign shareholders in the process of mixed-ownership reform.

Keywords: international competitiveness; foreign shareholders' social responsibility; R&D innovation; Chinese SOEs

Citation: Zhou, Y.; Lei, C.; Jiménez, A. Foreign Shareholders' Social Responsibility, R&D Innovation, and International Competitiveness of Chinese SOEs. *Sustainability* **2022**, *14*, 1746. https://doi.org/10.3390/su14031746

Academic Editor: Carlos Rodríguez Monroy

Received: 28 December 2021
Accepted: 19 January 2022
Published: 2 February 2022

1. Introduction

As an essential part of China's economic development after its reform and opening up, foreign investment in China has undergone a gradual evolution from quantity to quality in both development scale and quality after the pilot start-up stage, rapid development stage, high-level development stage, and new stage of all-round opening up. Quantitatively, the total actual utilization of foreign capital in China has increased more than 60 times from USD 2.260 billion in 1983 to USD 138.135 billion in 2019 (see Figure 1). Foreign capital has helped China move into a new stage of high-quality economic development through the economic growth effect, industrial structure upgrading effect, income effect, etc. [1,2]. In recent years, along with the advance of a mixed-ownership reform of Chinese SOEs, foreign shareholders have not only brought more capital, resources, and experience in the process of entering Chinese SOEs, but also upgraded enterprises' governance mechanisms by reducing the cost of Chinese state-owned agents. Finally, the business performance of Chinese SOEs has been well improved [3,4].

However, in the process of Chinese SOEs utilizing foreign capital, problems such as misconceptions about foreign shareholders, poor utilization of foreign capital, and the late priority of foreign shareholders during mixed-ownership reform have partly curbed the performance of foreign shareholders. In this regard, the report of the 19th National Congress of the Communist Party of China clearly states that it is necessary to "deepen the reform of state-owned enterprises, develop a mixed-ownership economy, and cultivate world-class enterprises with global competitiveness". The introduction of foreign shareholders would help Chinese SOEs solve the problem of combining Chinese state-owned capital with a market economy, boost the marketization of Chinese SOEs, and especially provide Chinese SOEs with better access to international markets. Besides, the organic integration between Chinese state-owned capital and foreign capital is expected to improve the liquidity of Chinese state-owned capital, build up complementary strengths of different kinds of capital, and make Chinese SOEs more internationally competitive [5]. However, these expectations have not been adequately analyzed empirically in the literature. To address this gap in the literature, in this paper we study the international competitiveness of Chinese SOEs from the perspective of foreign shareholders' social responsibility not only to provide a new perspective on the study of the mixed-ownership reform of Chinese SOEs at the theoretical level, but also to empirically analyze Chinese SOEs' sustainable development in the context of global economic integration at the practical level.

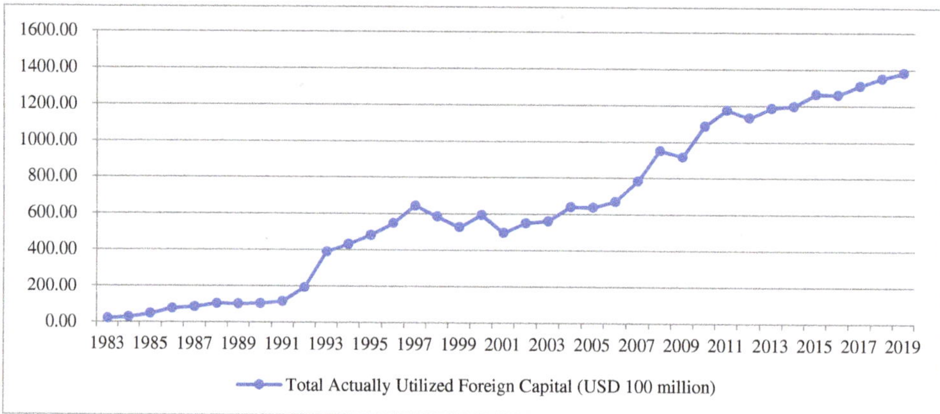

Figure 1. Total actual utilization of foreign investment in China from 1983 to 2019.

The arrival of foreign shareholders in Chinese SOEs offers sufficient capital elements, advanced technology, as well as desirable social responsibility concepts and practices. Since foreign shareholders tend to introduce their own advanced and mature social responsibility concepts to enterprises, they would serve as a demonstration to motivate enterprises to better fulfill their social responsibility through learning and imitation [6]. The existing literature also indicates that the inclusion of foreign shareholders has played a constructive role in elevating the social responsibility commitment of Chinese enterprises. Thus, previous studies underline that the inclusion of foreign shareholders efficiently reduces the incidence of labor workers' rights being violated in domestic enterprises [7], witnessing an improvement in employees' rights and interests in corporate social responsibility (CSR). It has been pointed out that Chinese enterprises tend to bring in foreign shareholders from developed regions such as Europe and the United States who generally place more emphasis on social responsibility, leading Chinese enterprises to better perform CSR correspondingly [8]. Also, it has been suggested that the presence of foreign shareholders actively affected Chinese enterprises' CSR performance through the channel of supply chain pressure [9], and that the entry of foreign shareholders is an incentive to foster social responsibility in host enterprises since a higher shareholding ratio is a prerequisite for making foreign shareholders work [10].

However, the existing literature only presents empirical evidence that the introduction of foreign shareholders enables host enterprises to deliver better CSR performance without considering the economic consequences brought along with it. For instance, China's export-oriented economy has made it possible for Chinese SOEs to introduce foreign shareholders.

The empirical evidence that the existing literature fails to deliver regards whether the introduction of foreign shareholders into Chinese SOEs is able to help Chinese SOEs better adapt to the international market and sharpen their international competitiveness, supposing that foreign shareholders will perform their social responsibilities well. We precisely aim to fill this gap in the literature and thus advance collective wisdom on the international competitiveness of Chinese SOEs. From a theoretical point of view, foreign shareholders can effectively attract more overseas investors for Chinese SOEs by fulfilling their social responsibility and satisfying the interests of different stakeholders, thereby making Chinese SOEs with better CSR engagement dominate and stand out in the international market. Furthermore, foreign shareholders' actions on social responsibility will upgrade Chinese SOEs' CSR performance and help create a sound image in overseas markets, making it easier for Chinese SOEs to explore international markets, build brands, and improve their international competitiveness.

Foreign shareholders value social responsibility fulfillment as well as R&D innovation. Foreign shareholders aim for better R&D innovation, technology spillovers, and improved productivity when supervising the management of Chinese SOEs [11]. The presence of foreign shareholders can effectively help Chinese SOEs develop technology while exploring capital and markets, sharpen R&D edges, reduce related costs, and gain a competitive advantage in the international market. At the same time, R&D innovation constitutes an important part of foreign shareholders' social responsibility. Foreign shareholders require enterprises to place great emphasis on CSR performance while developing new products, technologies, and business models, contributing to a virtuous cycle in social responsibility fulfillment, R&D investment, and market competition [12].

We empirically examine the impact of foreign shareholders' social responsibility on the competitiveness of Chinese SOEs, and the moderating effect of R&D innovation, based on the sample of Chinese SOEs with international market operations during 2011–2019. Our study makes several contributions: first, by focusing on foreign shareholders we contribute to extending the relatively scarce literature on the mixed-ownership reform of Chinese SOEs, and we do so by analyzing the benefits that foreign shareholders can bring to Chinese SOEs. Second, we delineate the social-responsibility-related mechanism through which foreign shareholders play an important role in and affect the international competitiveness of Chinese SOEs. Third, we provide empirical evidence on the improvement of international competitiveness in Chinese SOEs when foreign shareholders are included, which can be of great reference value to Chinese SOEs implementing mixed-ownership reforms and policy-makers of related policies.

2. Theoretical Analysis and Research Hypotheses

2.1. Foreign Shareholders' Social Responsibility and Enterprises' International Competitiveness

A number of enterprises in Asian emerging-capital-market countries, especially Chinese ones, tend to bring in foreign shareholders from developed European and American countries with Western management practices. These foreign shareholders normally not only require themselves to fulfill their own social responsibility, but also infuse this self-behavior into the enterprise as a way of improving overall social responsibility concepts and standards [13,14]. Foreign shareholders face the disadvantage of being outsiders in the process of entering the host-country enterprises. Therefore, social responsibility represents a good tool for foreign shareholders to protect their own interests, which includes, first, the protection of foreign shareholders' interests, and second, the need for foreign shareholders to reduce information asymmetry between themselves and management through disclosure of social responsibility information, so as to mitigate the loss of interests caused by information discrepancies [15]. Given this, in the process of fulfilling social responsibility, foreign shareholders typically try to strengthen the firm´s international competitiveness by emphasizing CSR performance as well as business performance, etc.

The fulfillment of social responsibility by foreign shareholders produces a competitive effect, prompting enterprises to explore special resources suitable for their own development, thus sharpening their competitive edge. Foreign shareholders come with more capital in the process of entering Chinese enterprises, and this capital exists both within the enterprise and within the industry, pushing both competitions forward. Foreign shareholders' acting on social responsibility reallocates corporate resources since enterprises' own operating costs and relationships with others in the industry are affected, which in turns shapes enterprises' competitive advantage [16]. In particular, as market consumers are sensible to CSR, they are more likely to purchase products from socially responsible companies, and the phenomenon exists in both domestic and international markets [17]. This allows shareholders to put more emphasis on social responsibility as well as its performance, and makes enterprises willing to obtain the economic foundation to be internationally competitive by fulfilling social responsibility. Besides, foreign shareholders' performing social responsibility will bring enterprises more special resources, particularly resources in overseas markets such as goodwill in international markets to create a favorable external environment and shape unique internal competitiveness in international market competition.

Moreover, foreign shareholders' social responsibility performance has a demonstration effect, motivating other shareholders to do the same and thus shaping competitiveness of enterprises commonly. Foreign shareholders bring advanced and mature social responsibility concepts of their home countries to the investee companies and integrate their own social responsibility preferences in the process of corporate governance, providing access to other shareholders to improve their own social responsibility performance through learning and imitation, guiding the investee companies to make more decisions favoring social responsibility undertakings [13]. The demonstration role enables enterprises faced with international market competition to provide upstream enterprises with higher-quality intermediate products and more comprehensive after-sales services, etc., so as to improve product and service quality. Advanced technology, information, organizational management mechanisms, etc., are expected to support downstream enterprises to assist the supplier in providing qualified raw materials [18,19]. As a result, foreign shareholders, by fulfilling their social responsibility, inject sustainability and long-term development prospects into the international market competition in shaping better international community relations and generating desirable long-term financial performance [20]. In this way, both the economic value and the international competitiveness of enterprises are raised [21].

Finally, the social responsibility behavior of foreign shareholders creates a signaling effect and delivers more information related to enterprises to the international market, contributing to a favorable atmosphere for enhancing its international competitiveness. Foreign shareholders aim to build their strengths in the international market by fulfilling their social responsibility, proactively sending positive signals to their stakeholders, spreading internal management results to international markets in different dimensions, generating positive feedback benefits, and further directing the inflow of international resources [22]. Besides, as one of the stakeholders, foreign shareholders' positive social responsibility signals can reduce the agency costs between them and the management as well as minimize moral hazard and adverse selection caused by information asymmetry. In this connection, the uncertainty of engaging in international markets is lowered, and enterprises are led toward better access to international market resources while maintaining and consolidating relationships with global customers and suppliers, thus laying a solid foundation to be internationally competitive [23].

We therefore propose the following research hypothesis:

Hypothesis 1 (H1). *There is a positive relationship between the social responsibility of foreign shareholders and the international competitiveness of enterprises.*

2.2. Foreign Shareholders' Social Responsibility, R&D Innovation, and Enterprises' International Competitiveness

As global science and technology advance, the innovation-driven model has emerged as a new model for sustainable economic growth across the world. Enterprises in various countries have been engaged in enhancing efficiency and deepening the effect of R&D innovation by pouring upfront investment into it in the hope of delivering better performance in international competition [24]. The inclusion of R&D innovation while formulating development strategy motivates enterprises to secure sustainable development and consolidate their existing competitive advantage in order to put themselves in a more favorable position in market competition [25]. Chinese listed SOEs involved in international competition mainly resorted to low-priced labor for gaining advantages in labor-intensive industries in the early years, but currently they stand out in technology-intensive industries with top-notch technological advances as well. In fact, the contribution of R&D innovation to China's economic growth has increased from 31.46% in 1991 to 58.36% in 2017 [26]. Given the current global digital economy, the continuous flow of data from R&D to production and from sales to service during use is what it takes to make enterprises continuously create economic value and elevate competitiveness [27]. It is noticeable that R&D innovation, which has received a lot of attention from an increasing number of Chinese companies, can also function as a new driving force to lead Chinese enterprises to compete in the international market.

Foreign shareholders have also realized the importance of R&D innovation. For enterprises in emerging markets, a motive for introducing foreign shareholders is to create technology spillover and technology transfer effects with technological advantages brought by foreign shareholders, thereby driving their own technological progress [28]. Similarly, in the process of fulfilling social responsibility, foreign shareholders also stress the need to enhance social responsibility performance by practical effects of promoting R&D innovation. Foreign shareholders, by fulfilling their social responsibility, can reduce various risk constraints that may exist in R&D innovation activities, thus increasing related future benefits. Although R&D innovation activities may restrict resources and capital due to their higher cost, social responsibility, as an intangible resource, works to help enterprises capture consumer brand loyalty as well as a good reputation and to foster investors' confidence. What is more, foreign shareholders own the foundation for implementing R&D innovation, thus ensuring that they can achieve the goal of fulfilling social responsibility through feasible R&D innovation activities [29]. Furthermore, R&D innovation and social responsibility are mutually promoted, allowing foreign shareholders to leverage the effect of R&D innovation activities to enhance social responsibility performance. CSR and R&D innovation are capital investment activities with similarities, bringing enterprises favorable social and moral capital as well as positive feedback from capital markets [30]. It is noteworthy that R&D innovation activities will be gradually optimized during CSR performance, and more R&D investment along with it will promote CSR performance and improve innovation capacity, contributing to a "win-win" solution [31].

We contend that R&D innovation might affect the relationship between the social responsibility of foreign shareholders and the international competitiveness of enterprises. Firstly, the complementarity between R&D innovation and social responsibility enables R&D innovation to mitigate the increased costs of social responsibility to a certain extent and better facilitate foreign shareholders to enhance their international competitiveness by social responsibility engagement. Since foreign shareholders with a better performance of social responsibility tend to think highly of R&D innovation activities, they are more courageous in bearing the risks of R&D innovation and work hard to make it targeted and feasible [32]. Foreign shareholders may use possible future benefits of R&D innovation to compensate for current costs of fulfilling social responsibility and minimize the uncertainty of future benefits for different stakeholders. Therefore, foreign shareholders will actively promote R&D the innovation behaviors of enterprises, especially internationally, during social responsibility performance as a way of establishing R&D innovation in international markets and enhancing the international competitiveness of enterprises. Secondly, R&D innovation is expected to be an effective channel for foreign shareholders' social responsibility to promote the international competitiveness of enterprises, encouraging foreign shareholders to complete social responsibility performance with R&D innovation. Accordingly, both performance effects and international competitiveness are improved. During this process, foreign shareholders can reduce heterogeneous resources required for their R&D innovation. For instance, capital and technology advantages of foreign shareholders, competitive advantage, demonstration advantage, and signal advantage generated by social responsibility of foreign shareholders achieve full utilization. Sound R&D innovation and social responsibility of foreign shareholders are better signaled to the capital and business markets [33].

We therefore propose the following research hypothesis:

Hypothesis 2 (H2). *R&D innovation strengthens the positive relationship between foreign shareholders' social responsibility and enterprises' international competitiveness.*

3. Study Design

3.1. Variable Design

3.1.1. Dependent Variable: International competitiveness

International competitiveness (*IC*): Building on [34], this paper constructs an international competitiveness indicator system based on four dimensions: management ability, financial status, investment performance, and development potential, as shown in Table 1. The indicators selected in Table 1 are homogenized and then standardized in accordance with the Z-value method, after which the international competitiveness index of Chinese SOEs is constructed in factor analysis.

Table 1. The international competitiveness evaluation system of Chinese listed SOEs.

First Level Indicators	Second Level Indicators	Third Level Indicators	Attribute
Management ability	Market scale	Market value per share, net profit per share, net assets per share	Positive indicators
	Ownership concentration	Shareholding ratio of the first largest shareholder, concentration of shares held by top ten shareholders	Positive indicators
	Insider incentive	Executive compensation level, executive shareholding ratio	Positive indicators
Financial Status	Viability	Liquidity ratio, quick ratio, total asset turnover	Positive indicators
		Asset-liability ratio	Negative indicators
	Profitability	Net profit margin, return on total assets, return on equity, return on invested capital	Positive indicators
		Ratio of sales to cost	Negative indicators
	Developing ability	Total assets growth rate, increase rate of main business revenue, net profit growth rate, equity multiplier	Positive indicators
Investment performance	Market performance	Alpha, Beta, Sharpe	Positive indicators
	Valuation ability	Price earnings ratio, price-to-book ratio	Moderation indicators
		Dividend yield ratio, earnings per share, free cash flow per share	Positive indicators
Development potential	Growth potential	Proportion of intangible assets to total assets, proportion of fixed assets to total assets	Positive indicators
	R&D ability	proportion of R&D expenses to total assets	Positive indicators
	Degree of internationalization	Proportion of overseas revenue to operating revenue	Positive indicators

3.1.2. Independent Variable: Social Responsibility of Foreign Shareholders

Social Responsibility of Foreign Shareholders (*SRFS*): Hexun.com (www.hexun.com, accessed on 15 February 2021) provides the total social responsibility score of Chinese listed companies based on a comprehensive consideration of corporate responsibility to shareholders, employees, suppliers, customers and consumers, the environment, and society. Higher scores imply better CSR performance. Since the score includes shareholder responsibility efforts and the study mainly focuses on the score for the social responsibility of foreign shareholders, the score is multiplied by the shareholding ratio of foreign shareholders to obtain the social responsibility performance that foreign shareholders achieved. Likewise, a higher calculated score means better social responsibility fulfillment of foreign shareholders.

3.1.3. Moderating Variable: R&D innovation

R&D Innovation (*R&D*): This variable is based on the natural logarithm of annual R&D investment of the focal Chinese SOE.

3.1.4. Controlled Variables

Building on previous research, the following controlled variables are included in the model.

Enterprise Attribute (*EA*): measured as the attribute of whether the sample enterprise is a Chinese central SOE or a local SOE; EA = 1 if the sample enterprise is Chinese central SOE, otherwise EA = 0.

Total Assets (*TA*): measured as the natural logarithm of the total assets of the sample enterprise at the end of the year.

Asset-liability Ratio (*ALR*): measured as the ratio of total liabilities to total assets of the sample enterprise at the end of the year.

Return on Assets (*ROA*): measured as the ratio of net income to average total assets of the sample enterprise at the end of the year.

Ownership Concentration (*OC*): measured by the sum of squared shareholdings of the top 10 shareholders of the sample enterprise at the end of the year.

Proportion of Independent Directors (*PID*): measured by the proportion of independent directors to the board of directors of the sample enterprise at the end of the year.

3.2. *Empirical Model Design*

3.2.1. Baseline Regression Test Model Design

To explore the relationship between the social responsibility of foreign shareholders and the international competitiveness of enterprises, we tested the following empirical regression model:

$$IC_{i,t} = \alpha_1 SRFS_{i,t} + \alpha_i Control\_Variable_{i,t} + Year + Industry + C + \varepsilon_{i,t} \quad (1)$$

In addition, in order to examine the moderating effect of R&D innovation in the relations between foreign shareholders and the international competitiveness of enterprises, we tested the following empirical model:

$$\begin{aligned} IC_{i,t} = \alpha_1 SRFS_{i,t} + \alpha_2 SRFS_{i,t} \times R\&D_{i,t} + \alpha_3 R\&D_{i,t} + \alpha_i Control_{Variablei,t} \\ + Year + Industry + C + \varepsilon_{i,t} \end{aligned} \quad (2)$$

In Equations (1) and (2), *Control_Variable* is control group and C is the constant term. Both the annual factor (Year) and the industry factor (Industry) of the sample enterprises are controlled.

3.2.2. Endogeneity Test Model Design

A possible endogeneity relationship between the social responsibility of foreign shareholders and the international competitiveness of enterprises should be taken into account, i.e., foreign shareholders may deliberately fulfill their social responsibility in light of some external factors, resulting in a spurious relationship between the social responsibility of foreign shareholders and international competitiveness. Therefore, we employed the Heckman two-stage regression model for endogeneity testing. In this case, the first stage works to estimate instrumental variables on explanatory variables $SRFS_{i,t}$, namely:

$$SRFS_{i,t} = \alpha_1 TPA_{i,t} + \alpha_i Control\_Variable_{i,t} + Year + Industry + C + \varepsilon_{i,t} \quad (3)$$

In Equation (3), the variable $TPA_{i,t}$ is an instrumental variable, measured as a dummy variable of whether the sample enterprise is engaged in targeted poverty alleviation, i.e., if yes, $TPA_{i,t} = 1$, otherwise $TPA_{i,t} = 0$. The reason for choosing this instrumental variable is that, firstly, targeted poverty alleviation has represented an important solution for fighting poverty in China in recent years. Chinese SOEs, as an essential mainstay of China's economic development, play a major role in this fight. Meanwhile, foreign shareholders rise as new forces, indicating that foreign shareholders who are willing to participate in targeted poverty alleviation will better perform their social responsibility. Therefore, the instrumental variable is proved to be relevant. Secondly, whether enterprises are engaged in targeted poverty alleviation or not makes no difference to their international competitiveness, and the exogeneity condition of instrumental variables is satisfied as well.

3.3. Data Selection and Description

Since many Chinese SOEs have undergone mixed-ownership reform by introducing foreign shareholders for the past few years, a rising number of them have opted to enhance their competitiveness through international markets along with the growth of China's export-oriented economy. We selected a sample of Chinese SOEs listed in Shanghai and Shenzhen A-shares with international market operations during 2011–2019 for empirical testing in this paper.

From the initial overall sample, we excluded the following cases: (1) firms in the finance, insurance, and securities industries; (2) firms with special treatment; (3) firms listed for the first time; (4) firms with data missing. Finally, 3030 observations of 641 Chinese listed SOEs during 2011–2019 are included in the final sample.

4. Results and Analysis of Empirical Tests

4.1. Descriptive Statistical Results and Analysis

Table 2 reports the descriptive statistical results of the full sample. The variable $IC_{i,t}$ has a mean value of 0.190, which shows that the current international competitiveness of Chinese SOEs is relatively weak, and there exist certain differences in international competitiveness across different Chinese SOEs. The mean value of variable $SRFS_{i,t}$ is 0.367; likewise, Chinese SOEs also differ in their foreign shareholders' social responsibility performance. The mean value of variable $R\&D_{i,t}$ is 15.858, which is relatively low. The average annual R&D investment of Chinese SOEs is about 7.71 million RMB; nevertheless, R&D investment varies greatly among different Chinese SOEs.

Table 3 reports the descriptive statistical results of groups. Regarding the grouping descriptive statistical results with a median value of variable $SRFS_{i,t}$, both mean and median values of variable $IC_{i,t}$ are higher in the high $SRFS_{i,t}$ group, and both met the significance test at the conventional confidence level. Chinese listed SOEs with foreign shareholders better fulfilling social responsibility present higher international competitiveness.

4.2. Correlation Test Results and Analysis

Table 4 reports the correlation test results. Firstly, the correlation coefficient values between variable $IC_{i,t}$ and variable $SRFS_{i,t}$ are significantly positive, indicating a positive relationship between foreign shareholders' social responsibility and international competitiveness of Chinese SOEs; the correlation coefficient values between variable $IC_{i,t}$ and variable $R\&D_{i,t}$ are also significantly positive, suggesting a positive relationship between R&D innovation and the international competitiveness of Chinese SOEs. Secondly, the correlation coefficient values between the variables are not high, showing that there is no multicollinearity between the variables.

Table 2. Descriptive Statistical Results of Full Sample.

Variable	Mean	Median	Standard Deviation	5%	25%	75%	95%
$IC_{i,t}$	0.190	0.176	0.065	0.125	0.152	0.216	0.297
$SRFS_{i,t}$	0.367	0.000	1.241	0.000	0.000	0.119	2.306
$R\&D_{i,t}$	15.858	17.982	6.250	0.000	16.416	19.237	20.757
$EA_{i,t}$	0.286	0.000	0.452	0.000	0.000	1.000	1.000
$TA_{i,t}$	22.728	22.570	1.292	20.821	21.786	23.735	24.965
$ALR_{i,t}$	0.522	0.532	0.198	0.184	0.371	0.689	0.826
$ROA_{i,t}$	0.043	0.041	0.058	-0.043	0.023	0.070	0.128
$OC_{i,t}$	0.180	0.155	0.123	0.034	0.090	0.264	0.407
$PID_{i,t}$	0.372	0.357	0.080	0.286	0.333	0.429	0.500

Table 3. Descriptive Statistical Results of Groups.

Variable	**High $SRFS_{i,t}$**			**Low $SRFS_{i,t}$**			***T* Test**	**Wilcoxon *Z***
	N	**Mean**	**Median**	***N***	**Mean**	**Median**		
$IC_{i,t}$	777	0.208	0.188	2253	0.183	0.172	9.358 ***	8.882 ***
Variable	High $R\&D_{i,t}$			Low $R\&D_{i,t}$			*T* test	Wilcoxon *Z*
	N	Mean	Median	*N*	Mean	Median		
$IC_{i,t}$	1515	0.198	0.181	1515	0.182	0.170	6.765 ***	7.262 ***

Note: *** indicates that they have passed the significance test at the 1 confidence levels.

Table 4. Correlation Test Results.

	$IC_{i,t}$	$SRFS_{i,t}$	$R\&D_{i,t}$	$EA_{i,t}$	$TA_{i,t}$	$ALR_{i,t}$	$ROA_{i,t}$	$OC_{i,t}$	$PID_{i,t}$
$IC_{i,t}$	1								
$SRFS_{i,t}$	0.169 ***	1							
$R\&D_{i,t}$	0.078 ***	0.036 **	1						
$EA_{i,t}$	0.067 ***	−0.018	0.062 ***	1					
$TA_{i,t}$	0.079 ***	0.115 ***	0.154 ***	−0.003	1				
$ALR_{i,t}$	−0.164 ***	−0.081 ***	-0.024	−0.032 *	0.426 ***	1			
$ROA_{i,t}$	0.418 ***	0.219 ***	0.046 **	−0.047 **	0.089 ***	−0.287 ***	1		
$OC_{i,t}$	0.102 ***	0.058 ***	0.021	0.029 *	0.284 ***	0.024	0.119 ***	1	
$PID_{i,t}$	−0.023	−0.031*	0.018	−0.011	0.139 ***	0.037 **	−0.006	0.083 ***	1

Note: ***, **, and * indicate that they have passed the significance test at the 1%, 5%, and 10% confidence levels, respectively.

4.3. Baseline Regression Test Results and Analysis

Table 5 reports the results of the baseline regression test. Before including control variables, the coefficient value of variable $SRFS_{i,t}$ in regression result (1) is positive and significant, showing that better social responsibility performance of foreign shareholders produces stronger international competitiveness of Chinese SOEs. Foreign shareholders' social responsibility engagement would create more international market resources, bringing Chinese SOEs international market recognition to further expand international market resources and occupy more market shares, and consequently increase international competitiveness, in line with H1. In regression result (2), the coefficient of the variable $R\&D_{i,t}$ is also positive and significant, revealing that higher investment in R&D innovation will make Chinese SOEs more internationally competitive. It is noted that well-developed R&D innovation also works to stimulate Chinese SOEs to improve their international competitiveness. Increasing investment in R&D innovation is expected to help Chinese SOEs secure more growth potential and space, expand market share, stand out in the international market with new technologies, products, and packaging as a way of enhancing international competitiveness. Further, in regression result (3), which includes the moderating effect of the variable $R\&D_{i,t}$, the coefficient value of the variable $SRFS_{i,t}$ is still positive and significant, and so is the coefficient value of the interaction term $SRFS_{i,t} \times R\&D_{i,t}$, reflecting a greater impact of foreign shareholders' social responsibility on the international competitiveness of Chinese SOEs when R&D innovation is included. Foreign shareholders themselves would attach great importance to R&D innovation and consider it as an essential part of fulfilling their social responsibility aiming to elevate enterprises' performance, satisfying the interests of different stakeholders, and exploring more opportunities in international market competition. Therefore, H2 is verified.

Table 5. Baseline Regression Test Results.

	(1)	(2)	(3)	(4)	(5)	(6)
$SRFS_{i,t}$	0.089 ***		0.078 ***	0.382 ***		0.330 ***
	(0.010)		(0.014)	(0.089)		(0.022)
$SRFS_{i,t}$ ×			0.006 ***			0.042 ***
$R\&D_{i,t}$			(0.001)			(0.012)
$R\&D_{i,t}$		0.081 ***	0.073 ***		0.454 ***	0.438 **
		(0.019)	(0.019)		(0.174)	(0.180)
$EA_{i,t}$				0.012 ***	0.011 ***	0.012 ***
$TA_{i,t}$				0.003 ***	0.003 ***	0.003 ***
$ALR_{i,t}$				−0.025 ***	−0.025 ***	−0.023 ***
$ROA_{i,t}$				0.422 ***	0.436 ***	0.422 ***
$OC_{i,t}$				0.020 **	0.021 **	0.021 **
$PID_{i,t}$				−0.021 *	−0.024*	−0.021 *
Year	Yes	Yes	Yes	Yes	Yes	Yes
Industry	Yes	Yes	Yes	Yes	Yes	Yes
Constant	0.187 ***	0.177 ***	0.175 ***	0.112 ***	0.105 ***	0.114 ***
Adj R^2	0.028	0.006	0.033	0.194	0.191	0.196
F-statistics	89.083 ***	18.424 ***	35.277 ***	105.370 ***	103.302 ***	82.831 ***

Note: ***, **, and * indicate they have passed the significance test at the 1%, 5%, and 10% confidence levels, respectively.

When the control variables are added, similar test results appear in regression results (3)–(5), i.e., the coefficient value of variable $SRFS_{i,t}$ is positive and significant, and so is the coefficient value of the interaction term $SRFS_{i,t} \times R\&D_{i,t}$. This proves that the social responsibility behavior of foreign shareholders is able to promote the international competitiveness of Chinese SOEs, and R&D innovation could exert a moderating effect between them. Consequently, this further confirms H1 and H2. The traditional corporate competitiveness measured by indicators such as ROA and revenue is relatively manifest, easily quantifiable, and widely accepted in the modern accounting system [35]. However, these indicators may cause inconclusive results in the literature due to sampling problems, reliability, and validity of measures [36,37]. Competitiveness captures not only the manifest indicators but also the latent factors such as potential and process [38]; a wide range of indicators has been included in this study to form a composite index to indicate corporate competitiveness, which can, to some extent, relieve the issue about previous measures. We document a positive association between *SRFS* and competitiveness. This study argues that CSR engagement will attract valuable resources such as reputation and talents for companies, which help them gain competitiveness in a market.

We conducted several sensitivity tests in order to examine the robustness of our empirical results. Firstly, in view of large differences in economic and market development among different provinces and cities in China, administrative differences may cause resource inequality for SOEs in their regions reflected in foreign capital introduction and international competition. Therefore, we conducted a robustness test after excluding SOEs with operations in Beijing, Shanghai, Tianjin, and Chongqing. Secondly, given the possible influence of extreme values, we Winsorized extreme values (0–1% and 99–100% of the sample) and obtained results consistent with those reported previously. Thirdly, the CSR indicators given by Hexun.com include both the total score of social responsibility and the sub-scores of shareholder responsibility, employee responsibility, supplier–customer and consumer-rights responsibility, environmental responsibility, and social responsibility. We considered the five sub-indicators as the dependent variable. The results do not differ substantially from the results previously reported.

4.4. Endogeneity Regression Test Results and Analysis

Table 6 reports the results of the endogeneity test. In the regression results of the 1st Stage, the coefficient value of the variable $TPA_{i,t}$ is positive and significant, indicating that foreign shareholders deliver better social responsibility performance among Chinese SOEs involved in targeted poverty alleviation compared with those do not, which validates the relevance of the instrumental variables. In the 2nd Stage regression results, the coefficient of the variable $SRFS_{i,t}$ is still positive and significant, and so is the coefficient of the interaction term when included. Even after taking endogeneity into account, our results show that a better social responsibility performance by foreign shareholders is associated with stronger international competitiveness of Chinese SOEs. Moreover, R&D innovation also moderates the relationship between social responsibility of foreign shareholders and international competitiveness of Chinese SOEs, strengthening the effect. Besides, in the regression results (2)–(5) in Table 6, the Sargan test values exhibited by the J statistic validate the instrumental variables chosen for the endogeneity test.

Table 6. Endogeneity Regression Test Results.

	1st Stage	**2nd-Stage Dependent Variable**			
	$SRFS_{i,t}$	$IC_{i,t}$	$IC_{i,t}$	$IC_{i,t}$	$IC_{i,t}$
	(1)	**(2)**	**(3)**	**(4)**	**(5)**
$TPA_{i,t}$	0.206 *** (0.088)				
$SRFS_{i,t}$		0.057 *** (0.011)	0.010 *** (0.001)	0.083 *** (0.022)	0.044 ***(0.003)
$SRFS_{i,t} \times R\&D_{i,t}$				0.099 *** (0.019)	0.079 *** (0.017)
$R\&D_{i,t}$				0.035 *** (0.004)	0.020 *** (0.003)
Control_Variable	Yes	No	Yes	No	Yes
Year	Yes	Yes	Yes	Yes	Yes
Industry	Yes	Yes	Yes	Yes	Yes
Constant	0.392 ***	0.186 ***	0.130 ***	0.180 ***	0.130 ***
Adj R^2	0.014	0.056	0.189	0.056	0.188
F-statistics	19.989 ***	80.006 ***	45.386 ***	27.237 ***	35.358 ***
J-statistics	—	0.444	0.708	0.582	0.726

Note: (1) *** indicates that they have passed the significance test at the 1% confidence levels. (2) The sample interval for the endogeneity test in Table 6 is 2016–2019 with a sample size of 1335, as Chinese enterprises started to publicly disclose information on targeted poverty alleviation in 2016.

4.5. Heterogeneity Grouping Regression Test Results and Analysis

4.5.1. Grouping Test between Central SOEs and Local SOEs

Chinese SOEs are divided into central SOEs and local SOEs, which differ in business objectives, business practices, corporate governance, and property rights objectives [39]. In the sample of the study, central SOEs accounted for 28.61% of the total, while local SOEs accounted for 71.39%. We therefore tested whether differences exist in the impact of social responsibility of foreign shareholders on the international competitiveness of central SOEs and local SOEs.

Table 7 presents the grouping test results for central SOE and local SOE samples. The coefficient value of the variable *SRFSi,t* remains positive and significant in both central and local SOE samples, and the coefficient value of the interaction term *SRFSi,t* × *R&Di,t* is also positive and significant, implying that social responsibility of foreign shareholders can boost the international competitiveness of both central and local SOEs. The moderating effect of R&D innovation is also observed. Both Chinese central and local SOEs share a unified development mindset and philosophy, and therefore foreign shareholders' social responsibility performance would fully leverage international competitiveness. Furthermore, a comparison of the results of different sample tests reveals that the coefficient values are greater for the Chinese local SOE sample. This implies that social responsibility of foreign shareholders exercises a greater impact on international competitiveness among Chinese local SOEs.

Table 7. Grouping Test Results for Central SOEs and Local SOEs.

	Sample of Central SOEs				Sample of Local SOEs			
	(1)	(2)	(3)	(4)	(5)	(6)	(7)	(8)
$SRFS_{i,t}$	0.023 *** (0.002)	0.005 *** (0.002)	0.015 *** (0.003)	0.008 ** (0.003)	0.041 *** (0.001)	0.010 *** (0.001)	0.022 *** (0.003)	0.010 *** (0.002)
$SRFS_{i,t} \times R\&D_{i,t}$			0.020 *** (0.002)	0.022 *** (0.002)			0.013 *** (0.001)	0.011 *** (0.002)
$R\&D_{i,t}$			0.013 *** (0.003)	0.028 *** (0.008)			0.049 ** (0.023)	0.043 ** (0.020)
Control_Variable	No	Yes	No	Yes	No	Yes	No	Yes
Year	Yes	Yes	Yes	Yes	Yes	Yes	Yes	Yes
Industry	Yes	Yes	Yes	Yes	Yes	Yes	Yes	Yes
Constant	0.195 ***	0.145 ***	0.174 ***	0.139 ***	0.183 ***	0.102 ***	0.175 ***	0.106 ***
N	867	867	867	867	2163	2163	2163	2163
Adj R^2	0.011	0.126	0.026	0.132	0.035	0.211	0.037	0.212
F-statistics	10.627 ***	21.787 ***	8.700 ***	17.430 ***	79.137 ***	97.381 ***	28.504 ***	73.534 ***

Note: *** and ** indicate they have passed the significance test at 1% and 5% confidence levels.

4.5.2. Grouping Test of Commercial SOEs and Public Welfare SOEs

On December 27, 2015, China's State-owned Assets Supervision and Administration Commission (SASAC), Ministry of Finance, and National Development and Reform Commission issued the Guidance on the Functional Definition and Classification of State-owned Enterprises. SOEs are divided into commercial SOEs and public welfare SOEs, and different categories of SOEs require corresponding market mechanisms and market environments [40], coupled with various performance evaluation indicators. Therefore, different types of SOEs face separate requirements while expanding overseas markets and enhancing competitiveness in international markets. In this sample, commercial SOEs account for 66.63% of the total, while public welfare SOEs account for 33.37%. We conducted a group test to examine whether there is a difference in the impact of the social responsibility of foreign shareholders on international competitiveness among commercial SOEs and public welfare SOEs.

Table 8 presents the grouping tests results for the samples of commercial SOEs and public welfare SOEs. The coefficient value of the variable $SRFS_{i,t}$ remains positive and significant in both commercial and public welfare SOE, and the coefficient value of the interaction term $SRFS_{i,t} \times R\&D_{i,t}$ is also positive and significant, indicating that foreign shareholders' social responsibility boosts the international competitiveness of commercial and local Chinese SOEs, and that R&D innovation strengthens this effect. Both commercial and public welfare SOEs are well positioned to fully play the role of foreign shareholders' social responsibility engagement during international competition so as to better seize competitive opportunities supported by R&D innovation. We also find that the coefficient values of Chinese commercial SOEs are greater after further comparing the results of different sample tests. This implies that the social responsibility of foreign shareholders could have a stronger impetus on the international competitiveness of Chinese commercial SOEs, which is also related to the fact that commercial SOEs face fiercer market competition and more intense market resource grabbing, making it more imperative for foreign shareholders to strengthen their international competitiveness by fulfilling social responsibility.

Table 8. Grouping Test Results for Commercial SOEs and Public Welfare SOEs.

	Sample of Commercial SOEs				Sample of Public Welfare SOES			
	(1)	(2)	(3)	(4)	(5)	(6)	(7)	(8)
$SRFS_{i,t}$	0.040 *** (0.001)	0.011 *** (0.001)	0.080 *** (0.003)	0.015 *** (0.004)	0.032 *** (0.001)	0.006 *** (0.001)	0.031 *** (0.002)	0.006 *** (0.001)
$SRFS_{i,t} \times R\&D_{i,t}$			0.026 *** (0.002)	0.025 *** (0.002)			0.043 *** (0.002)	0.041 *** (0.001)
$R\&D_{i,t}$			0.093 *** (0.002)	0.056 *** (0.002)			0.036 *** (0.003)	0.029 *** (0.003)
Control_Variable	No	Yes	No	Yes	No	Yes	No	Yes
Year	Yes	Yes	Yes	Yes	Yes	Yes	Yes	Yes
Industry	Yes	Yes	Yes	Yes	Yes	Yes	Yes	Yes
Constant	0.191 ***	0.022 ***	0.176 ***	0.025 ***	0.178 ***	0.245 ***	0.172 ***	0.252 ***
N	2019	2019	2019	2019	1011	1011	1011	1011
Adj R^2	0.031	0.224	0.037	0.225	0.028	0.186	0.037	0.193
F-statistics	65.790 ***	83.992 ***	26.808 ***	66.237 ***	30.334 ***	34.017 ***	14.014 ***	27.922 ***

Note: *** indicates they have passed the significance test at the 1% confidence level.

4.5.3. Grouping Test of Manufacturing SOEs and Non-Manufacturing SOEs

Industries differ in their social responsibility performance, with enterprises from the manufacturing industry receiving extra attention. The reason behind this is that manufacturing enterprises are often faced with problems such as environmental pollution in production and operation. Nevertheless, in recent years, Chinese manufacturing companies, especially major ones, have been devoted to conceiving and practicing social responsibility [41]. In our sample, manufacturing SOEs account for 70.30% of the total, while non-manufacturing SOEs account for 29.70%. Next, we test whether the influence of the social responsibility of foreign shareholders on international competitiveness differs between manufacturing SOEs and non-manufacturing SOEs.

Table 9 reports the grouping test results for manufacturing SOE and non-manufacturing SOE samples. The coefficient value of the variable $SRFS_{i,t}$ remains positive and significant for both manufacturing SOE and non-manufacturing SOE samples, while the coefficient value of the interaction term $SRFS_{i,t} \times R\&D_{i,}$ is also positive and significant, showing that social responsibility of foreign shareholders increases the international competitiveness of Chinese SOEs and that R&D innovation strengthens this effect. Both manufacturing SOEs and non-manufacturing SOEs fully deliver the role of foreign shareholders' social responsibility performance, while pressures and motivation thus generated make Chinese SOEs more internationally competitive. Further, a comparison of different sample test results reveals that the coefficient values of the test results are greater in the Chinese manufacturing SOE sample, which indicates that social responsibility of foreign shareholders could better propel the international competitiveness of Chinese manufacturing SOEs. This may be due to stronger social responsibility expectations and actions of manufacturing enterprises. For instance, some manufacturing enterprises are expected to achieve full coverage of green management, R&D innovation, production, and marketing processes from the organizational level through green consciousness and technology innovation involved in social responsibility, and finally shape a green brand image and win consumers' trust as a way of capturing a greater international market [42]. For another thing, in recent years, an increasing number of Chinese manufacturing SOEs have made full use of foreign shareholders imported through mixed-ownership reform. More Chinese manufacturing

SOEs have entered into international competition and made themselves known in the international market.

Table 9. Grouping Test Results for Manufacturing SOEs and Non-manufacturing SOEs.

	Sample of Manufacturing SOEs				Sample of Non-Manufacturing SOEs			
	(1)	(2)	(3)	(4)	(5)	(6)	(7)	(8)
$SRFS_{i,t}$	0.049 *** (0.012)	0.012 *** (0.001)	0.064 *** (0.005)	0.017 *** (0.006)	0.042 *** (0.012)	0.008 *** (0.001)	0.046 *** (0.002)	0.004 * (0.002)
$SRFS_{i,t} \times R\&D_{i,t}$			0.083 *** (0.028)	0.030 *** (0.003)			0.019 *** (0.005)	0.016 *** (0.001)
$R\&D_{i,t}$			0.050 *** (0.003)	0.015 *** (0.003)			0.032 *** (0.002)	0.025 *** (0.002)
Control_Variable	No	Yes	No	Yes	No	Yes	No	Yes
Year	Yes	Yes	Yes	Yes	Yes	Yes	Yes	Yes
Industry	Yes	Yes	Yes	Yes	Yes	Yes	Yes	Yes
Constant	0.187 ***	0.091 ***	0.161 ***	0.092 ***	0.185 ***	0.131 ***	0.181 ***	0.135 ***
N	2130	2130	2130	2130	900	900	900	900
Adj R^2	0.038	0.213	0.046	0.213	0.012	0.151	0.013	0.151
F-statistics	85.850 ***	83.399 ***	34.912 ***	65.143 ***	11.942 ***	23.847 ***	4.982 ***	18.787 ***

Note: ***, * indicate they have passed the significance test at the 1% and 10% confidence levels, respectively.

5. Conclusions

Over the past few years, a rising number of Chinese SOEs have introduced foreign shareholders through mixed-ownership reform as a way of standing out in international market competition with capital, technology, information, and management brought along with it. Foreign shareholders' emphasis on social responsibility aims to make Chinese SOEs internationally competitive. Therefore, in this paper we empirically examine the impact of foreign shareholders' social responsibility on the international competitiveness of Chinese SOEs and the moderating effect of R&D innovation. Specifically, we draw on a sample of Chinese listed SOEs with international market operations during 2011–2019. We find that foreign shareholders' social responsibility can effectively enhance the international competitiveness of Chinese SOEs, i.e., the better foreign shareholders perform social responsibility, the stronger the international competitiveness of Chinese SOEs will be. Moreover, we find that R&D innovation has a strengthening and a moderating effect between foreign shareholders' social responsibility and enterprises' international competitiveness, that is, greater R&D innovation of Chinese SOEs makes the contribution of foreign shareholders' social responsibility to international competitiveness stronger. These findings are also valid after controlling for several robustness tests and endogeneity issues. Additional tests show that the contribution of foreign shareholders' social responsibility to the international competitiveness of Chinese SOEs is more pronounced among Chinese local SOEs, commercial SOEs, and manufacturing SOEs, and the same is true for the moderating effect.

Our study, therefore, makes several contributions to the literature. By focusing on foreign shareholders and by analyzing the benefits that foreign shareholders can bring to Chinese SOEs, we contribute toward extending the relatively scarce literature on the mixed-ownership reform of Chinese SOEs. Specifically, we believe our findings are useful as they offer empirical evidence on how foreign shareholders and their social responsibility performance promote Chinese SOEs. In that sense, they deepen our understanding of the reasons why Chinese SOEs introduce foreign shareholders and their roles in the mixed-ownership reform. Our study underlines social responsibility as one important mechanism through which foreign shareholders play a significant role in and affect the international competitiveness of Chinese SOEs.

Our study also makes important contributions for practitioners and policy-makers. Building on our results, our study suggests several measures that can be taken in order to enhance the international competitiveness of Chinese SOEs: first, the role of foreign shareholders is underlined. In the mixed-ownership reform of Chinese SOEs, private shareholders are still preferred, with foreign shareholders ranked after. Nevertheless, foreign shareholders are less associated with state-owned shareholders, leading to governance advantages in particular. In that way, Chinese SOEs could achieve better results if they embrace mixed-ownership reform. Secondly, the advantages provided by foreign shareholders should be fully exploited. Some Chinese SOEs have introduced foreign shareholders but failed to utilize them effectively. Given this, it could be convenient to grant foreign shareholders more autonomy in the enterprise, such as participating in management and increasing voting rights, so that foreign shareholders can provide not only capital, but also technology and management, all of which is conducive to the sound growth of SOEs. Overall, the empirical evidence provided in this paper about the improvement of the international competitiveness of Chinese SOEs when foreign shareholders are included can be of great reference value to Chinese SOEs implementing mixed-ownership reforms and to policy-makers of related policies.

Limitations and Avenues for Future Research

Our study is naturally subject to limitations. First, specific firm-level characteristics could play an important role in and affect the relationships analyzed in this paper. For example, the age of the firm can be an important factor affecting the development of its operations, which deserves further attention in future studies. Second, although we included industry dummies in our models, we must acknowledge that specific industry characteristics may affect the international competitiveness of Chinese SOEs. We therefore encourage scholars to conduct further analyses of specific industries as well as in-depth comparative analyses of different industries to enlarge our knowledge of the specificities of each sector.

Author Contributions: Conceptualization, Y.Z., C.L. and A.J.; methodology, Y.Z., C.L. and A.J.; formal analysis, Y.Z., C.L. and A.J.; investigation, Y.Z., C.L. and A.J.; writing—original draft preparation, Y.Z. and C.L.; writing—review and editing, A.J.; funding acquisition, Y.Z. and C.L. All authors have read and agreed to the published version of the manuscript.

Funding: This research was funded by the Chongqing Social Science Planning Youth Project, grant number 2018QNGL37, and Youth Fund of Humanities and Social Sciences, Ministry of Education of China, grant number 18YJC630087.

Institutional Review Board Statement: Not applicable.

Informed Consent Statement: Not applicable.

Data Availability Statement: The data presented in this study are available on request from the corresponding author. The data are not publicly available due to privacy.

Conflicts of Interest: The authors declare no conflict of interest.

References

1. Jiang, X.J. On the Transformation of Models of Use of Foreign Capital versus the Transformation of Economic Growth Models. *Manag. World* **1999**, *15*, 7–15.
2. Li, Z.C.; Ma, X.M.; Chen, Y. Practice, Effect, Experience and Countermeasures of China's Utilization of Foreign Capital Since the Reform and Open Up. *Intertrade* **2019**, *38*, 58–67.
3. Wu, C.Q.; Lv, Z.Y. Privatization, Foreign Shareholder and Embeddedness: Evidence from China. *Bus. Manag. J.* **2011**, *33*, 51–58.
4. Deng, Z.L.; Chen, Y. The Influence of Foreign Direct Investment on the Survival of State-owned Enterprises: A Study based on the Heterogeneity of Enterprises. *J. World Econ.* **2013**, *36*, 53–69.
5. Ma, L.F.; Wang, L.L.; Zhang, Q. Pecking Order of Mixed Ownership: The Logic of Market. *China Ind. Econ.* **2015**, *33*, 5–20.
6. Letchumanan, R.; Kodama, F. Reconciling the Conflict Between the 'Pollution-Haven' Hypothesis and an Emerging Trajectory of International Technology Transfer. *Res. Policy* **2000**, *29*, 59–79. [CrossRef]
7. Shao, M.; Bao, Q. The Influence of FDI on China's Domestic Labor Rights and Interests. *Manag. World* **2013**, *29*, 32–43.
8. Wang, H.M.; Lv, X.J.; Lin, W.F. The Effect of Foreign Equity Participation,Executive Ownership,Institutional Ownership on Corporate Social Responsibility. *Account. Res.* **2014**, *35*, 81–87.

9. Huang, W.; Chen, Z. Foreign Capital Entry, Supply Chain Pressure and Chinese Corporate Social Responsibility. *Manag. World* **2015**, *31*, 91–100.
10. Bu, D.L.; He, C.; Wen, C.H. How does Foreign Shareholder Affect Corporate Social Responsibility. *Account. Res.* **2021**, *42*, 86–101.
11. Aggarwal, R.; Ere, I.; Ferreira, M.; Matos, P. Does Governance Travel around the World: Evidence from Institutional Investors. *J. Financ. Econ.* **2011**, *100*, 154–181. [CrossRef]
12. Gangi, F.; Mustilli, M.; Varrone, N. The Impact of Corporate Social Responsibility (CSR) Knowledge on Corporate Financial Performance: Evidence from the European Banking Industry. *J. Knowl. Manag.* **2019**, *23*, 110–134. [CrossRef]
13. Child, J. A Foreign Perspective on the Management of People in China. *Int. J. Hum. Resour. Manag.* **1991**, *2*, 93–107. [CrossRef]
14. Chapple, W.; Moon, J. Corporate Social Responsibility (CSR) in Asia: A Seven-Country Study of CSR Web Site Reporting. *Bus. Soc.* **2005**, *44*, 415–441. [CrossRef]
15. Barako, D.G.; Hancock, P.; Izan, H.Y. Factors Influencing Voluntary Corporate Disclosure by Kenyan Companies. *Corp. Gov. Int. Rev.* **2006**, *14*, 107–125. [CrossRef]
16. In, F.; Kim, M.; Park, R.J. Competition of Socially Responsible and Conventional Mutual Funds and Its Impact on Fund Performance. *J. Bank. Financ.* **2014**, *44*, 160–176. [CrossRef]
17. Ma, L.L. Research on the Influence Mechanism of Corporate Social Responsibility on Consumers' Purchase Intention. *Manag. World* **2011**, *27*, 120–126.
18. Lall, S. Vertical Inter-Firm Linkages in LDCs: An Empirical Study. *Oxf. Bull. Econ. Stat.* **1980**, *42*, 203–226. [CrossRef]
19. Zheng, S.F.; Huang, L.Y. Impact of Foreign Direct Investment Entry on Corporate Social Responsibility: Based on Intra-industry and Inter-industry Spillover Effects. *J. Int. Trade* **2018**, *44*, 116–129.
20. Ruf, B.M.; Muralidhar, K.; Brown, R.M.; Janney, J.J.; Paul, K. An Empirical Investigate of the Relationship between Change in Corporate Social Performance and Financial Performance: A Stakeholder Theory Perspective. *J. Bus. Ethics* **2001**, *32*, 143–156. [CrossRef]
21. Petersen, H.L.; Vredenburg, H. Morals or Economics: Institutional Investor Preferences for Corporate Social Responsibility. *J. Bus. Ethics* **2009**, *90*, 1–14. [CrossRef]
22. Lin, B.; Rao, J. Why do Listed Companies Disclose the Auditor's Internal Control Reports Voluntarily: An Empirical Study Based on Signaling Theory in China. *Account. Res.* **2009**, *30*, 45–52.
23. Friedman, M. The Social Responsibility of Business is to Increase its Profit. *N. Y. Times Mag.* **1970**, *13*, 122–126.
24. Du, W.J.; Li, M.J. A Research on Enterprise Innovation-Driven Mechanism in the Open Economy. *Sci. Res. Manag.* **2018**, *39*, 91–98.
25. Küçükoglu, M.T.; Pınar, R.İ. Positive Influences of Green Innovation on Company Performance. *Procedia-Soc. Behav. Sci.* **2015**, *195*, 1232–1237. [CrossRef]
26. Zheng, S.L.; Zhang, M.C. Estimating the Contribution of China's Scientific and Technological Progress to Economic Growth: 1990–2017. *J. World Econ.* **2019**, *42*, 73–97.
27. Li, X.H.; Wang, Y.F. Data Value Chain and the Mechanism of Value Creation. *Econ. Rev. J.* **2020**, *36*, 54–62.
28. Cheng, K.Y.; Lin, P. Spillover Effects of FDI on Innovation in China: Evidence from Provincial Data. *China Econ. Rev.* **2004**, *15*, 25–44. [CrossRef]
29. Ortas, E.; Gallego-Alvarez, I.; Etxeberria, I.A. Financial Factors Influencing the Quality of Corporate Social Responsibility and Environmental Management Disclosure: A Quantile Regression Approach. *Corp. Soc. Responsib. Environ. Manag.* **2015**, *22*, 362–380. [CrossRef]
30. Brammer, S.; Millington, A. Corporate Reputation and Philanthropy: An Empirical Analysis. *J. Bus. Ethics* **2005**, *61*, 29–44. [CrossRef]
31. Carrasco, I.; Buendia, M. Corporate Social Responsibility: A Crossroad between Changing Values, Innovation and Internationalization. *Eur. J. Int. Manag.* **2013**, *7*, 295–314.
32. Luong, H.; Moshirian, F.; Nguyen, L.; Tian, X.; Zhang, B. How do Foreign Institutional Investors Enhance Firm Innovation. *J. Financ. Quant. Anal.* **2017**, *52*, 1449–1490. [CrossRef]
33. Iyer, D.N.; Miller, K.D. Performance Feedback, Slack, and the Timing of Acquisitions. *Acad. Manag. J.* **2008**, *51*, 808–822.
34. Chen, H.; Xu, R. Research on the International Competitiveness of Chinese and American Listed Companies: An Empirical Analysis Based on High-end Manufacturing and Information Technology Industry. *Stud. Int. Financ.* **2016**, *33*, 49–61.
35. Long, W.; Li, S.; Wu, H.; Song, X. Corporate social responsibility and financial performance: The roles of government intervention and market competition. *Corp. Soc. Responsib. Environ. Manag.* **2020**, *27*, 525–541. [CrossRef]
36. Margolis, J.D.; Walsh, J.P. Misery loves companies: Rethinking social initiatives by business. *Adm. Sci. Q.* **2003**, *48*, 268–305. [CrossRef]
37. Orlitzky, M.; Schmidt, F.L.; Rynes, S.L. Corporate social and financial performance: A meta-analysis. *Organ. Stud.* **2003**, *24*, 403–441. [CrossRef]
38. Buckley, P.J.; Pass, C.L.; Prescott, K. Measures of international competitiveness: A critical survey. *J. Mark. Manag.* **1988**, *4*, 175–200. [CrossRef]
39. Chen, S.H.; Lu, C.C. Can the Governance Participation of Party Organizations in State-owned Enterprises Effectively Curb the 'Loss of State-owned Assets' in Mergers and Acquisitions. *Manag. World* **2014**, *30*, 106–120.
40. Xie, L.Y. The Boundary between Government and Market in the Classification Reform of State-owned Enterprises. *Dyn. Soc. Sci.* **2017**, *40*, 35–39.

41. Feng, D.L. Trends and Problems of China's Manufacturing Large Enterprises Outward Internationalization and Its Countermeasures. *Intertrade* **2020**, *39*, 31–37.
42. Sueyoshi, T.; Wang, D. Radial and Non-Radial Approaches for Environmental Assessment by Data Envelopment Analysis: Corporate Sustainability and Effective Investment for Technology Innovation. *Energy Econ.* **2014**, *45*, 537–551. [CrossRef]

sustainability

MDPI

Article

Digital Competency, Innovative Medical Research, and Institutional Environment: A Global Context

Whan Shin [1] and Byungchul Choi [2,*]

1 Department of Obstetrics and Gynecology, CHA Bundang Medical Center, CHA University, 59 Yatap-ro, Bundang-gu, Seongnam 13496, Gyeonggi-do, Republic of Korea
2 College of Business, Hankuk University of Foreign Studies, Seoul 02450, Republic of Korea
* Correspondence: bchoi@hufs.ac.kr

Abstract: The use of digital technology accelerates the progress of medical research through improving the quality of clinical trials and medical education. However, empirical evidence on how digital competency contributes to the innovativeness of medical research and influence of institutional environment has received scant attention. Based on the data of 63 nations, this study explores the question of how national-level digital competency impacts the innovativeness of medical research reflected in research publications and examines the moderating effect of government and the economic environment. We find that national digital competency positively impacts the innovativeness of medical research in the focal nation. However, this relationship is positively or negatively modulated by diverse institutional environments. Our study contributes to innovation and institutional perspective literature in the context of digital technologies for medical research.

Keywords: national digital competency; innovative medical research; institutional environment

Citation: Shin, W.; Choi, B. Digital Competency, Innovative Medical Research, and Institutional Environment: A Global Context. *Sustainability* **2022**, *14*, 16887. https://doi.org/10.3390/su142416887

Academic Editor: Hao-Chiang Koong Lin

Received: 31 October 2022
Accepted: 12 December 2022
Published: 16 December 2022

1. Introduction

The use of digital technology has great potential for medical research. Particularly, the COVID-19 pandemic has played a central role in accelerating the process of development and sophistication of digital technology in medical research [1,2]. Appropriately employing digital technology can significantly increase both efficiency and efficacy in clinical trials and medical education, which are key to the advancement of medical research [3–6]. More specifically, digital technology can contribute to the development of medical research by improving the efficiency of participant recruitment and retention, health data collection, and data analysis in clinical trials. It also increases the accuracy of the analysis by facilitating communication with the participants of an experiment and reducing the time for data collection. Thus, the development of digital technology is closely related to advances in medical research.

In a global perspective, the COVID-19 pandemic provides many countries with an opportunity to recognize the importance of employing digital technologies to respond to global challenge. Research collaboration for the development and distribution of vaccines, the prediction and tracking of confirmed cases, and the sharing of information have become globally critical issues. The role of digital technologies in medicine has received steady attention from scholars from diverse domains. In the field of medicine, researchers have mainly studied how digital technology contributes to the treatment or surgery of patients in specific fields. [7–9]. Scholars from engineering fields have focused on data sharing, protection, and management including the interface, integration, and coordination of data [10,11]. Business researchers have predominantly investigated digital health ecosystem and interactions among various stakeholders from an ecosystem perspective [12–14]. Although these existing studies have offered valuable and diverse insights, these studies have been conducted mainly in the context of specific types of organizations (e.g., hospital, biotech company, etc.) or industries (e.g., biotech industry, pharmaceutical industry, etc.), and national or global-level perspectives have been somehow neglected in this stream of research.

However, how digital competency contributes to the innovativeness of medical research has received scant attention and is barely supported by empirical evidence. Based on the awareness of this issue, this study examines how national digital competency impacts the innovativeness of medical research in a global context. As medical research is highly diversified, this study will pay special attention to the effects of national digital competency on the research performance of vital areas in medicine—a medical terminology—that comprehensively refers to four areas: (1) surgery; (2) internal medicine; (3) pediatrics, perinatology, and child health; and (4) obstetrics and gynecology. These areas are major disciplines in the field of medicine, encompassing various subfields. For example, geriatrics is included in internal medicine. (Pediatrics, etc., are included in this category not to distinguish a specific age group, but because babies and children require a fundamentally different medical approach than adults). The reason for focusing on those vital areas is because the research performance of those areas is straightly associated with fatalities through the whole lifespan of human. Knowledge in vital areas particularly becomes significant during pandemics, experiencing a new disease for which epidemiologic data have not been accumulated rapidly, and the death rate is determined within a short time. This is because knowledge about the effects of infectious diseases on body parts is directly related to human lives and forms the gist of coping with unprecedented pandemics. For example, at the beginning of the COVID-19 outbreak, many pediatric patients suffered due to a lack of adaptation period to changes in surgical environments and methods [15]. In addition, many people have experienced unexpected pains due to a lack of knowledge about complications or organ damage caused by COVID-19.

In addition, as it takes time for the institution to embrace various effects of rapidly developed knowledge, drastic progress in digital technology in terms of both development and utilization could cause particular social interest in the process of taking advantage of such benefits. This is a social phenomenon that is often accompanied by radically innovative knowledge, and it is not uncommon. Therefore, researchers have recognized the importance of understanding how institutional environments influence the progress of medical research [16–19], but enough empirical evidence still has not been found. Hence, we examined how various institutional factors moderate this relationship. We support our arguments using digital competencies, publications, and diverse institutional data of 63 countries. Our conceptual framework is depicted in Figure 1.

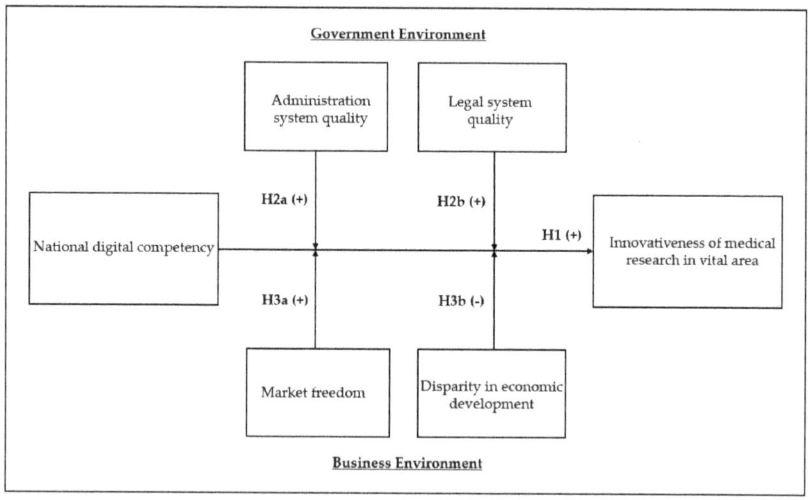

Figure 1. Conceptual Framework.

The remainder of this paper is organized as follows. First, we discuss how national digital competencies impact the degree of innovation research in medicine, and consequently, how this association is moderated by the government and business environments. Second, drawing on data from multiple databases, we provide the results of an empirical test. Third, we address the implications and contributions of this study.

2. Hypotheses Development

2.1. Digital Competency and Innovative Medical Research

Recent medical research requires an integrated system consisting of diverse digital technologies. These technologies typically include the Internet of Things [20], big data analysis [21], AI [22], and blockchains [23]. These digital technologies comprise digital health systems in hospitals or clinics [1]. Clinical trials play a crucial role in medical research by providing researchers with the basic knowledge and data to estimate causality when verifying the efficacy and safety of new therapies and devices as well as prevention and diagnosis [4]. However, conducting clinical trials efficiently is often challenging as inherent inefficiencies are embedded in each stage of procedure, including the identification and recruitment of participants, data collection, and analysis of participants, which result in poor clinical trial participation rates. For instance, cancer-related clinical trials secure only 8% of cancer patients [24]. Furthermore, financial burden caused by the physical distance between the patient and hospital as well as complicated scheduling problems lower the participation rates in clinical trials [25]. However, the experiment environments for clinical research have improved quite slowly over the years, thereby keeping them demanding and expensive. However, employing digital technology provides a stepping stone for improving clinical trials both qualitatively and quantitatively. It allows various clinical trials to be virtually implemented [5] and improves the quality of clinical trials in two aspects.

First, the adoption of digital technology contributes to the accuracy of clinical trials by making the key steps in clinical trials more reliable. According to Inan et al. (2020), digital clinical trials comprise three key steps: digital recruitment and retention, which is responsible for the participation and management of participants; digital data collection, comprising data mining and processing; and digital analytics, including data analysis and modeling. By utilizing digital technology, it is possible to increase the participation and communication levels of subjects through social media engagement and online consent. By using wearable and mobile sensing technologies, real-time data collection is possible, and various analyses and modeling are possible using AI. In other words, the digital clinical trial removes various obstacles that act as constraints in the existing clinical trials, thereby enabling the qualitative improvement of the clinical trial itself while saving resources.

The second aspect is medical education, which is an essential element for nurturing highly qualified medical researchers, armed with rigorous knowledge. The level of medical knowledge has a decisive influence on the ideas and conduction of clinical trials. However, there is a gap between the education provided by medical institutions and the knowledge required to conduct actual clinical trials [26]. In fact, it is difficult to practice all the theoretically learned medical tests in real life. However, this limitation can be overcome by using digital twin technology, as it can reproduce reality in a virtual space. Students can learn medical knowledge and experience diverse medical situations based on repeatable training such as a 3D surgery simulator using haptic technology. These increasing learning opportunities can have a direct impact on the innovativeness of clinical trials. The study of Chen et al. (2022) presented various application methods, such as medical education training, health and behavior tracking, operation playback and reproduction, and medical knowledge popularization, which can be useful when digital twin technology is used in medical education.

In summation, digital technology dramatically improves the quality of clinical trials and medical education that is critical to innovative medical research. Therefore, we propose the following hypothesis:

H1. *National digital competency will have a positive impact on the innovativeness of medical research.*

2.2. Moderating Effect of the Institutional Environment

The institutional environment significantly influences the strategic choices of the various actors in both the private and public sectors [27–29]. North (1990) provides a theoretical landscape of such changes, in which formal rules, structured incentives and constraints form the institutional matrix. Although our baseline proposition suggests that national digital competency will, in general, have a positive effect on innovative medical research, we anticipate that these positive effects can be contingent upon the institutional environment. In this context Salman et al. (2014) states that the quality of the public system and management system are the two key elements that should be considered when conducting medical research. Therefore, as investing in and conducting innovative research is inherently uncertain and risky, an appropriate level of stability in regulatory and economic systems is an inevitable environmental factor. In this study, we investigated how government and economic environments moderate the association between national digital competency and the innovativeness of medical research.

2.2.1. Government Environment: Quality of Administration and Legal System

In order for new knowledge to be used in a critical sector, such as medical research, the institutions and social systems that enable a country to manage the utilization of such knowledge, a stable market system, infrastructure, and high digital literacy must also be in place [30–33]. According to the OCED—a consortium of advanced countries—for digital technologies to be effectively utilized, the following must be available: infrastructure, public services, and data; effective use of digital data; data-driven and digital innovation; and social institutions such as labor markets and trust in society (https://goingdigital.oecd.org/dimensions, accessed on 11 October 2022). In other words, it is important to have a variety of institutional supports that enable the effective and efficient use of digital knowledge throughout society. Regarding legal and regulation aspects, numerous studies have addressed the quality of the legal system as medical research is closely and sensitively related to personal data, thus the need for ethical protocols, and there remains a responsibility issue for experiments that can critically influence the stability of society [16–19]. Therefore, we predict that countries with a high level of administrative and legal systems will have a more effective utilization of digital technology for medical research. Hence, we propose the following hypotheses:

H2a: *The quality of the administrative system will positively moderate the association between national digital competency and the innovativeness of medical research.*

H2b: *The quality of the legal system positively moderates the association between national digital competency and the innovativeness of medical research.*

2.2.2. Business Environment: Market Freedom and Disparity in Economic Development

Market freedom has been considered one of the major institutional environments [34,35]. Market freedom enhances the accessibility to resources [36] and reduces information asymmetry between investors and research teams through improved monitoring systems [37]. It also enables research teams to utilize their resources more [38] and make more explorative projects feasible options.

However, if a nation has an unevenly developed economy, a certain area may suffer from low accessibility to medical facilities and information due to the lack of basic digital infrastructure, such as the internet or network, or medical facilities [33,39]. As these areas have limited access to basic medical information, along with low participation rates in clinical trials, they lack the chance to experience improved medical knowledge ([40,41]. Digital technologies such as IoT, AI, and blockchain are applied technologies that can only be operated if basic infrastructure and devices such as computer hardware and wireless networks are available.

Further, vulnerable socioeconomic environments lead to low information utilization problems [6,42,43]. Even if the focal region has an adequate level of technological infrastructure that enables people to have high accessibility to information or participate in various clinical trials, limitations in time owing to low income, physical disability, and limited public service due to racial discrimination may reduce the chances of enjoying the benefits of using digital technologies. For example, during the COVID-19 pandemic, low-income residents even in New York City suffered significantly owing to serious health inequalities because of an uneven chance to utilize digital technology [43]

Furthermore, given that digital technology is closely related to cutting-edge knowledge, consistent investment is required in its development, diffusion, and market development. In fact, economic level has been cited as a source of various digital disparities, as well as healthcare, and this is clearly observed in the digital health market [42]. A region's economic level is an important factor influencing the stable development of digital technology as well as market formation. If the growth of the digital health market is difficult, the need for medical research to support it will also decrease. Combining all the discussions presented above, we postulate the following two propositions:

H3a: *The degree of market freedom will positively moderate the association between national digital competency and the innovativeness of medical research.*

H3b: *The degree of disparity in economic development will negatively moderate the association between national digital competency and the innovativeness of medical research.*

3. Methods

Using 62 national-level panel data, we investigate the effect of national digital competency on the innovativeness of medical research and how government and business environmental factors moderate that relationship.

3.1. Data and Sample

For empirical analysis, we utilize multiple databases. Regarding national digital competency (NDC), we draw the data from the World Digital Competency data provided by the International Institute for Management Development (IMD), which is a top-tier global research institute in Switzerland. Since the late 1980s, the IMD's annual report on national competency based on relevant proxies has been widely acknowledged by researchers in various disciplines [44–46].

To estimate the innovativeness of medical research, we use the data from the Journal and the Country Rank database offered by SCImago, which is an established data-mining and visualization group in Spain that provides a wide range of bibliometric data including journals and citations. The data of SCImago has demonstrated reliability in bibliometric research including top-tier medicine journals, such as *Nature* and *Lancet* [47,48]. We obtained the raw numerical values of published medical documents and citation data for each nation and constructed the dependent variable. For control variables, drawing on multiple databases, we collected nation-level data on innovation index health infrastructure, political rights index, globalization index, services sector value-adding, gross domestic product (GDP), government protectionism, science research legislation, and innovation index. We offer the details of these variables in the next section.

The final sample of our study comprises 63 countries with 341 nation-year observations between 2015 and 2020. The list of sample countries is shown in Table 1. In total, there are 33 countries from Europe, 8 countries from South America, 2 countries from North America, 14 countries from Asia and the Pacific, 5 countries from Middle East, and 1 country from Africa. Our sample include a wide range of countries, including both advanced economies and catching-up economies. We used 2015 as the starting year because interest in digital health has drastically increased based on the emergence of digital transformation, as illustrated in Figure 1. We use 2020 as the cutoff year as forward citation information generally suffer from the truncation issue [49].

Table 1. The 63 countries by regional classification.

Europe (33)		America (10)	Asia and Pacific (14)
Austria	Lithuania	Argentina	China
Belgium	Luxembourg	Australia	Hong Kong
Bulgaria	Netherlands	Brazil	India
Croatia	Norway	Canada	Indonesia
Cyprus	Poland	Chile	Japan
Czechia.	Portugal	Colombia	Kazakhstan
Denmark	Romania	Mexico	Malaysia
Estonia	Russia	Peru	Mongolia
Finland	Slovakia	USA	New Zealand
France	Slovenia	Venezuela	Philippines
Germany	Spain	**Middle East (5)**	Singapore
Greece	Sweden	Israel	South Korea
Hungary	Switzerland	Jordan	Taiwan
Iceland	Turkey	Qatar	Thailand
Ireland	Ukraine	Saudi Arabia	**Africa (1)**
Italy	United Kingdom	UAE	South Africa
Latvia			

3.2. Variable Descriptions

Dependent variable. To estimate our dependent variable, the innovativeness of medical research, we use the number of forward citations per document published in the fields of Surgery, Pediatrics, Perinatology and Child Health, Obstetrics and Gynecology, and Internal Medicine based on the Journal and Country Rank from the Scimago database. Many researchers address that highly cited research is highly likely to be conducted based on combinations of a broad range of knowledge domains that provide an explorative perspective to researchers and enable them to avoids intellectual lock [50]. Similarly, combinative knowledge from exploratory search can produce more innovative scientific research that ultimately becomes highly cited [51,52]. Therefore, the number of forward citations has been widely acknowledged and employed as a proxy for the innovativeness of research in prior studies [53–55].

We first calculate the total number of published and citable documents in each of the vital areas in medicine and the total number of forward citations that those documents received. Both numbers are aggregated at the nation level. Then, consistent with previous literature, we estimate medical research performance as:

$$\textbf{Innovativeness of Medical Research}_{\,i,t,c} = \frac{\textbf{Total forward citations}_{\,i,t,c}}{\textbf{Citatable document}_{i,t,c}}$$

where citable document i,t,c represents the number of citable documents published by country i in medical field c at the time of year t. Total forward citations i,t,c represents the number of forward citations (the document receives after published) of the focal citable document.

Independent variable. National digital competency (NDC) is measured based on the digital competency ranking data from the IMD *World Competency Yearbook*, which offers a comprehensive estimation of the digital and technological level of each nation country by combining statistical and survey data.

Moderating Variables. We draw institutional data from the Global Economy database. The quality of the administration system is measured as Government effectiveness index from the Global Economy Database. This measure captures the quality of public services, the quality of the civil service and the degree of its independence from political pressures, the quality of policy formulation and implementation, and the credibility of the government's commitment to such policies. Regarding the quality of the legal system, we employ the rule of law index from the same database. This indicator captures perceptions of the extent to which agents have confidence in and abide by the rules of society, the quality of contract enforcement, property rights, the police, and the courts, as well as the likelihood of crime and violence. To capture the quality of market freedom, we use the business freedom index from the Global Economy database constructing this measure based on the World Bank's Doing Business study. Lastly, the disparity of economic development is measured as the uneven economic development index from the Global Economy database.

Control Variables. The research can be affected by the overall innovation environment. Therefore, we used the innovation index of a nation from the Global Economy database. The Global Economy database measured the innovation index (country level) using data from Cornell University, INSEAD, and the World Intellectual Property Organization, which provide an innovation index that comprehensively captures each country's quality of institutions, human capital and research, infrastructure, and market and business sophistication. We use the World Bank's gross domestic product (GDP) data as our control variable. Economic level has been cited as an indicator of digital technologies in healthcare [42]. We also controlled for policy instruments that might have influenced the quality and application of the research. Based on the IMD National Competitiveness Data, we controlled for the nations' government protectionism and scientific research legislation (laws relating to scientific research encourage innovation). The IMD also offers the measure of health infrastructure, the degree to which it meets the social needs of the focal society, of each nation. We also control the degree of globalization that may facilitate the innovative research in medicine and political rights index that can potentially influence the credibility of governmental policy. We also control for the portion of the services sector that can affect the business activities in the healthcare industry. Appendix A provides detailed information for variable descriptions regarding measurement and source.

3.3. *Models*

Using unbalanced panel data, we employed a fixed-effect regression model to investigate the effect of national digital competency on the innovativeness of medical research in vital areas and moderating effects delivered by various environmental factors. To control unobserved heterogeneity, we employed a fixed-effects regression model instead of a random-effects model based on the Hausman test [56]. We considered the time lag (two years) between the dependent and independent variables with consideration because the bibliometric information (documents and citations) includes the past two years.

(1) IMR_1 (S, P, O, I) $_{i,t+2} = \alpha_{0i} + \alpha_1$Natioanl digital competency (NDC) $_{i,t}$ +. α_2Controls $_{i,t} + e_{i,t}$

(2) IMR $_1$ (S, P, O, I) $_{i,t+3} = \beta_{0i} + \beta_1$Natioanl digital competency (NDC) $_{i,t}$ +. β_2*Natioanl* digital competency (NDC) x Institutional environment factors B_3Controls $_{i,t} + e_{i,t}$

where α0i represents country fixed effects and $e_{i,t}$ is the random error. IMR (S), IMR (P), IMR (O), and IMR (I) refer to the innovativeness of medical research in Surgery, Pediatrics, Perinatology and Child Health, Obstetrics and Gynecology, and Internal Medicine, respectively.

4. Results

Tables 2 and 3 present the descriptive statistics and correlation matrices, respectively. Considering space limitations, we used an abbreviated name of each variable for the correlation matrix. The summary statistics indicated that national digital competency (NDC) was positively correlated with forward citations per document in all vital fields, including Surgery ($\rho = 0.30$, $p < 0.05$), Pediatrics, Perinatology, Child Health ($\rho = 0.21$, $p < 0.05$), Obstetrics and Gynecology ($\rho = 0.20$, $p < 0.5$), and Internal Medicine ($\rho = 0.30$, $p < 0.05$). The relatively high correlation among dependent variables could be attributed to their academic relatedness. However, no dependent variable is used in the same regression equation, and hence, multicollinearity was not a major concern in analyses.

Table 2. Descriptive statistics.

Variables Description	Abbreviation	Mean	S.D.	Min	Max
Innovativeness of Research in Surgery	IRS	6.81	5.88	0.10	57.17
Innovativeness of Research in Pediatrics, Perinatology and Child Health	IRP	6.74	6.02	0.25	43.33
Innovativeness of Research in Obstetrics and Gynecology	IRO	7.96	7.19	0.00	39.25
Innovativeness of Research in Internal Medicine	IRI	11.62	9.81	0.32	63.60
National digital competency	NDC	7.30	0.97	4.67	9.47
Quality of administration system	QAS	0.91	0.74	−1.17	2.23
Quality of legal system	QLS	0.81	0.89	−1.91	2.12
Market freedom	MF	76.08	12.50	37.00	100.0
Disparity of economic development	DED	4.18	1.80	0.70	8.10
Innovation index	II	46.69	9.86	25.70	68.40
Political rights index	PRI	2.12	1.72	1.00	7.00
Globalization index	GI	78.68	8.29	53.21	91.31
Services sector value-adding	SBA	60.72	8.49	30.32	88.70
Gross domestic product [a]	GDP	5.90	1.50	2.48	9.93
Science research legislation	SRP	5.37	1.58	1.81	8.43
Health infrastructure	HI	5.83	2.02	0.86	9.25

N = 341; [a] logarithm

Table 3. Correlation.

	IRS	IRP	IRO	IRI	DC	QAS	QLS	MF
IRS	1.00							
IRP	0.68	1.00						
IRO	0.72	0.61	1.00					
IRI	0.73	0.72	0.68	1.00				
DC	0.30	0.21	0.20	0.30	1.00			
QAS	0.21	0.16	0.09	0.26	0.58	1.00		
QLS	0.21	0.18	0.11	0.28	0.54	0.96	1.00	
MF	0.25	0.22	0.19	0.31	0.39	0.75	0.75	1.00
DED	−0.10	−0.02	−0.04	−0.10	−0.39	−0.74	−0.77	−0.60
II	0.22	0.16	0.12	0.25	0.51	0.89	0.88	0.69
PRI	−0.16	−0.14	−0.10	−0.16	−0.17	−0.41	−0.51	−0.30
GI	0.16	0.12	0.13	0.20	0.37	0.74	0.79	0.59
SBA	0.09	0.06	0.03	0.12	0.32	0.59	0.59	0.50
GDP	−0.15	−0.14	−0.20	−0.11	0.12	0.19	0.12	0.06
SRP	0.11	0.08	0.00	0.17	0.57	0.80	0.76	0.59
HI	0.10	0.07	0.02	0.16	0.50	0.80	0.74	0.56
	DED	**II**	**PRI**	**GI**	**SBA**	**GDP**	**SRP**	**HI**
UED	1.00							
II	−0.70	1.00						
PRI	0.46	−0.46	1.00					
GI	−0.74	0.76	−0.57	1.00				
SBA	−0.47	0.62	−0.42	0.54	1.00			
GDP	0.02	0.28	0.04	0.05	0.16	1.00		
SRP	−0.49	0.76	−0.09	0.50	0.46	0.32	1.00	
HI	−0.62	0.70	−0.17	0.59	0.47	0.29	0.73	1.00

All correlations with magnitude > |0.1| are significant at the 0.05 level.

Table 4 demonstrate the results of the main effect. Hypothesis 1 predicts that NDC will have a positive impact on the innovativeness of medical research in the field of the vital area. In Table 4, there are positive coefficients of Model 1 ($\beta = 3.664$, $p < 0.001$), Model 3 ($\beta = 3.826$, $p < 0.01$), Model 5 ($\beta = 3.403$, $p < 0.05$), and Model 7 ($\beta = 5.148$, $p < 0.01$), providing support for Hypothesis 1 with the baseline regression model. These results indicate that a national digital capability positively influences research performance in vital areas. These results are held after employing full model regression in Model 2 ($\beta = 2.449$,

$p < 0.05$), Model 4 ($\beta = 2.606$, $p < 0.05$), Model 6 ($\beta = 1.841$, $p < 0.05$), and Model 8 ($\beta = 3.251$, $p < 0.01$).

Table 4. Fixed-Effect Regression of National Digital Competency (NDC) on Innovativeness of Medical Research Vital Performance.

Variables	**Surgery**		**Pediatrics, Perinatology and Child Health**		**Obstetrics and Gynecology**		**Internal Medicine**	
	Model 1	**Model 2**	**Model 3**	**Model 4**	**Model 5**	**Model 6**	**Model 7**	**Model 8**
NDC	3.664 ***	2.449 ***	3.826 ***	2.606 ***	3.403 ***	1.841 *	5.148 ***	3.251 **
	(0.674)	(0.646)	(0.695)	(0.684)	(0.808)	(0.794)	(1.118)	(1.104)
II		0.500*		0.671 **		0.410		0.886 *
		(0.213)		(0.225)		(0.261)		(0.363)
PRI		0.282		1.228		−1.085		−0.230
		(1.207)		(1.278)		(1.484)		(2.061)
GI		−2.043 ***		−1.466 ***		−2.007 ***		−1.874 ***
		(0.329)		(0.348)		(0.404)		(0.561)
SBA		−0.410 *		−0.634 **		−0.667 ***		−0.971 ***
		(0.161)		(0.170)		(0.198)		(0.275)
GDP		−13.63 ***		−10.44 ***		−14.96 ***		−23.63 ***
		(3.163)		(3.350)		(3.889)		(5.403)
SRP		−3.006 ***		−2.853 ***		−3.464 ***		−4.958 ***
		(0.786)		(0.833)		(0.967)		(1.343)
HI		0.868		2.512 ***		2.033 **		2.662 *
		(0.627)		(0.664)		(0.771)		(1.071)
R^2	0.091	0.003	0.046	0.008	0.041	0.01	0.087	0.005
F	29.57	15.09	30.28	12.67	17.76	10.83	21.22	11.00
N	341	341	341	341	341	341	341	341

* $p < 0.05$, ** $p < 0.01$, *** $p < 0.001$.

Next, we shift our attention to investigate how the main effect is moderated by various institutional variables. Hypothesis 2a posits that the quality of administration will enhance the positive impact of NDC on innovativeness of medical research. In Table 5, the positive coefficients of Model 2 ($\beta = 3.052$, $p < 0.001$), Model 4 ($\beta = 2.531$, $p < 0.01$), Model 6 ($\beta = 3.359$, $p < 0.01$), and Model 8 ($\beta = 5.482$, $p < 0.001$) provide support for Hypothesis 2a. Figure 2 provides a plot to understand these results. The plot indicates that the impact of national digital competency (NDC) on the innovativeness of medical research is contingent on the quality of the administration system.

Table 5. Fixed-Effect Regression for Moderating Effect: Quality of Administration System (QAS).

Variables	**Surgery**		**Pediatrics, Perinatology and Child Health**		**Obstetrics and Gynecology**		**Internal Medicine**	
	Model 1	**Model 2**	**Model 3**	**Model 4**	**Model 5**	**Model 6**	**Model 7**	**Model 8**
NDC	2.447 ***	−0.188	2.532 ***	0.346	1.813 *	−1.086	3.158 **	−1.575
	(0.649)	(0.984)	(0.684)	(1.047)	(0.797)	(1.216)	(1.105)	(1.673)
QAS	0.144	−22.8 ***	4.465	−14.61 +	1.698	−23.60 **	5.591	−35.71 **
	(2.732)	(7.085)	(2.882)	(7.537)	(3.359)	(8.748)	(4.655)	(12.04)
NDC × QAS		3.052 ***		2.531 **		3.358 **		5.482 ***
		(0.871)		(0.926)		(1.075)		(1.480)
Controls	YES	YES	YES	YES	YES	YES	YES	YES
R^2	0.31	0.337	0.277	0.297	0.242	0.268	0.248	0.284
F	9.95	13.76	11.59	11.42	9.63	9.92	9.95	10.75
N	341	341	341	341	341	341	341	341

+ $p < 0.1$, * $p < 0.05$, ** $p < 0.01$, *** $p < 0.001$.

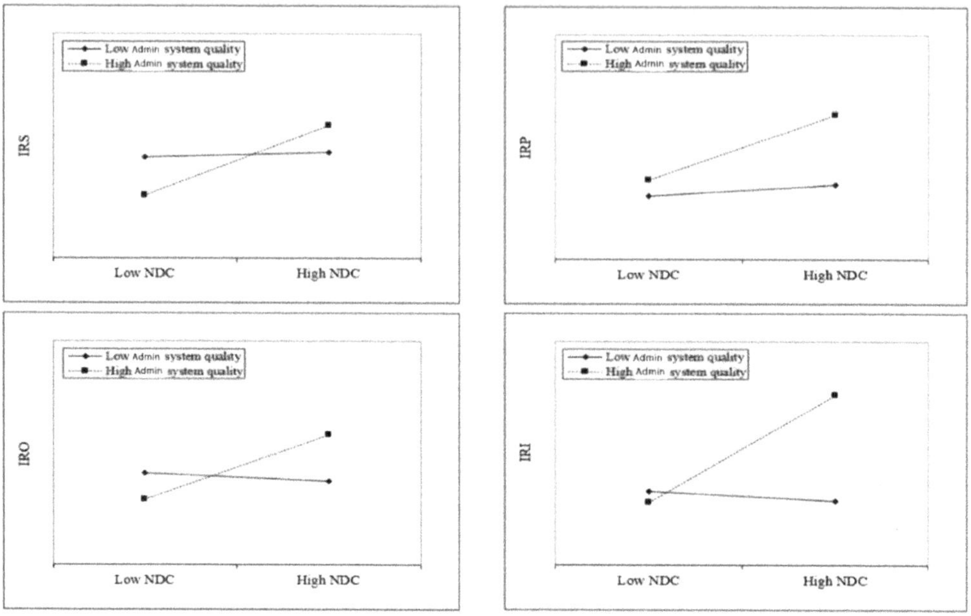

Figure 2. Moderating Effect of Administration System Quality.

Hypothesis 2b predicts that quality of the legal system will strengthen the positive effect of NDC on the innovativeness of medical research. In Table 6, the positive coefficients of Model 2 (β = 2.661, $p < 0.001$), Model 4 (β = 1.668, $p < 0.05$), Model 6 (β = 2.641, $p < 0.00$), and Model 8 (β = 4.720, $p < 0.001$) offer support for Hypothesis 2b. To aid in understanding these results, we plotted the interaction effects in Figure 3. The slope of the high administration system quality line changes steeply over the high vs. low NDC in the areas of Surgery (IRS) and Obstetrics and Gynecology (IRO), which are more strongly moderated than the others.

Table 6. Fixed-Effect Regression for Moderating Effect: Quality of Legal System (QLS).

Variables	**Surgery**		**Pediatrics, Perinatology and Child Health**		**Obstetrics and Gynecology**		**Internal Medicine**	
	Model 1	**Model 2**	**Model 3**	**Model 4**	**Model 5**	**Model 6**	**Model 7**	**Model 8**
NDC	2.277 ***	−0.007	2.335 ***	0.902	1.491 +	−0.776	2.704 **	−1.356
	(0.646)	(0.900)	(0.676)	(0.957)	(0.781)	(1.098)	(1.078)	(1.498)
QLS	7.013 *	−12.23 *	11.06 ***	−0.999	14.29 ***	−4.803	22.30 ***	−11.89
	(3.131)	(6.208)	(3.279)	(6.599)	(3.788)	(7.568)	(5.226)	(10.32)
NDC × QLS		2.661 ***		1.668 *		2.641 **		4.729 ***
		(0.746)		(0.794)		(0.910)		(1.242)
Controls	YES	YES	YES	YES	YES	YES	YES	YES
	(0.622)	(0.610)	(0.652)	(0.649)	(0.753)	(0.744)	(1.039)	(1.016)
R^2	0.319	0.349	0.300	0.311	0.278	0.300	0.291	0.327
F	14.17	14.57	12.95	12.25	11.68	11.64	12.42	13.18
N	341	341	341	341	341	341	341	341

+ $p < 0.1$, * $p < 0.05$, ** $p < 0.01$, *** $p < 0.001$.

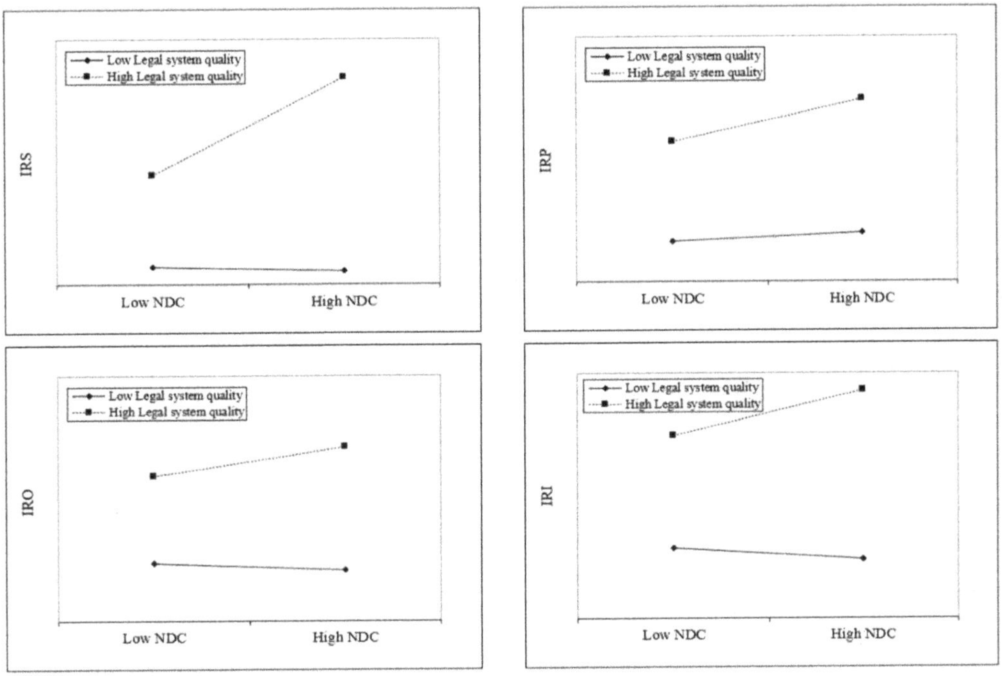

Figure 3. Moderating Effect of Legal System Quality.

Hypothesis 3a postulates that market freedom will augment the positive impact of NDC on the innovativeness of medical research. In Table 7, the positive coefficients of Model 2 (β = 0.089, $p < 0.05$), Model 4 (β = 0.095, $p < 0.05$), Model 6 (β = 0.101, $p < 0.05$), and Model 8 (β = 0.218, $p < 0.01$) provide support for Hypothesis 3a. Figure 4 offers a plot to understand these results, and the slope of the high market freedom line increases steeply over the high vs. low NDC in the area of Internal Medicine (IRI) compared with the others.

Table 7. Fixed-Effect Regression for Moderating Effect: Market Freedom (MF).

Variables	**Surgery**		**Pediatrics, Perinatology and Child Health**		**Obstetrics and Gynecology**		**Internal Medicine**	
	Model 1	**Model 2**	**Model 3**	**Model 4**	**Model 5**	**Model 6**	**Model 7**	**Model 8**
NDC	2.170 ***	−4.357	2.309 ***	−4.704	1.491 +	−5.960	2.647 *	−13.32 *
	(0.631)	(3.151)	(0.668)	(3.336)	0.774 ***	(3.874)	1.056	(5.228)
MF	0.365 ***	−0.312	0.38 ***	−0.339	0.458	−0.315	0.789 ***	−0.868
	(0.087)	(0.332)	(0.093)	(0.352)	0.107	(0.408)	0.146	(0.551)
NDC × MF		0.089 *		0.095 *		0.101 *		0.218 **
		(0.042)		(0.045)		(0.052)		(0.070)
Controls	YES	YES	YES	YES	YES	YES	YES	YES
R^2	0.005	0.007	0.013	0.016	0.018	0.02	0.011	0.015
F	16.16	15.18	13.90	13.14	12.26	11.53	14.01	13.98
N	341	341	341	341	341	341	341	341

+ $p < 0.1$, * $p < 0.05$, ** $p < 0.01$, *** $p < 0.001$.

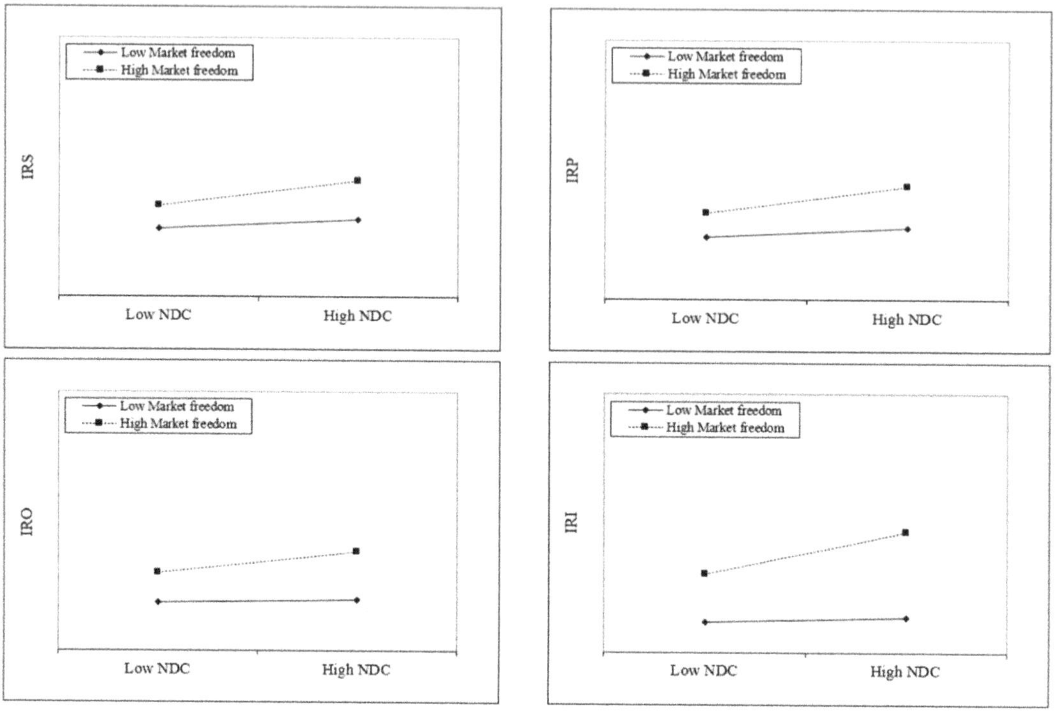

Figure 4. Moderating Effect of Market Freedom.

Hypothesis 3b anticipates that disparity in the economic development system will diminish the positive effect of NDC on the innovativeness of medical research. In Table 8, the negative coefficients of Model 2 (β = −0.702, $p < 0.05$) and Model 8 (β = −1.274, $p < 0.01$) offer partial support for Hypothesis 3b. To help in understanding these results, we plotted the interaction effects in Figure 5.

Table 8. Fixed-Effect Regression for Moderating Effect: Disparity of Economic Development (DED).

Variables	Surgery		Pediatrics, Perinatology and Child Health		Obstetrics and Gynecology		Internal Medicine	
	Model 1	**Model 2**	**Model 3**	**Model 4**	**Model 5**	**Model 6**	**Model 7**	**Model 8**
NDC	1.259 **	4.112 **	1.312 *	2.631 +	0.243	2.446	1.537	6.713 **
	(0.564)	(1.330)	(0.593)	(1.411)	(0.672)	(1.595)	(1.017)	(2.400)
DED QAS	7.721 ***	12.55 ***	8.345 ***	10.57 ***	10.24 ***	13.97 ***	11.05 ***	19.81 ***
	(0.758)	(2.176)	(0.798)	(2.309)	(0.904)	(2.611)	(1.368)	(3.928)
NDC × DED		−0.702 *		−0.324		−0.542		−1.274 **
		(0.297)		(0.315)		(0.356)		(0.536)
Controls	YES	YES	YES	YES	YES	YES	YES	YES
R^2	0.004	0.0026	0.0003	0.0001	0.0002	0.0001	0.0001	0.0002
F	30.04	28.05	27.88	25.20	28.33	25.86	19.30	18.23
N	339	339	339	339	339	339	339	339

+ $p < 0.1$, * $p < 0.05$, ** $p < 0.01$, *** $p < 0.001$.

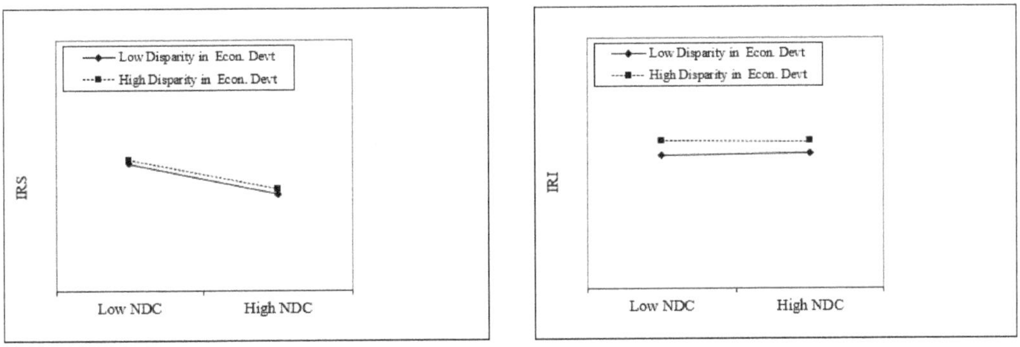

Figure 5. Moderating Effect of Disparity in Economic Development.

5. Discussion and Conclusions

5.1. Summary and Implications

As seen in the COVID-19 crisis, the development and utilization of digital technologies in medicine is becoming a global issue, not just a matter of individual hospitals or companies. However, while the usage of digital technologies for medical purposes has been studied in various fields including medicine, engineering, and business, the predominant interests of existing studies have been the quality of medical services, data management, and interests of individual institutions in the ecosystem, with micro-level perspectives. The main purpose of our study is to expand interest in digital competency and medical research to the national-level perspective.

Accelerated by the COVID-19 pandemic, the development of digital technology has provided significant benefits. Our study used data from 63 nations to demonstrate that digital competency positively impacts the innovativeness of medical research in vital areas: Surgery, Pediatrics, Perinatology, Child Health, Obstetrics and Gynecology, and Internal Medicine, and we discuss how this association varies in different institutional environments. This is an important finding for medical research because producing innovative results is critical to the sustainable progress of the field. In addition, our analysis provides several insights into the use of digital technologies for medical research, which is meaningful to researchers, practitioners, and policymakers.

First, while we find a positive association between digital competency and innovativeness in medical research, the benefit of digital competency is notably contingent upon different types of institutional environments. The institutional environment likely modulates the positive impact of digital competency on the innovativeness of medical research. While the quality of administration, legal system, and market liberalization strengthen the main effect, the disparity in economic development alleviates the positive impact of digital competency. When a new technology brings about a macro-level socioeconomic change, how much and in what direction it is affected by institutional influence is a significant concern for innovation and institutional perspectives. As innovative medical research is an important criterion for determining digital health systems, it has received many institutional benefits or constraints. Our study provides a more detailed picture of the important institutional factors in medical research by suggesting two dimensions of the institutional environment—the government's executive capacity and the economic system—and their impact.

Second, despite explicit benefits, the rapid adoption of new technologies may result in unintended or unexpected side effects. For example, economic inequality within the same country significantly reduces the positive impact of digital capabilities. This is because it implies the development and a distribution gap. In other words, although digital technology can facilitate the development of medical research, the benefits are not evenly distributed across people or regions. Consequently, many researchers focus on health inequality arising from the increased use of digital technology in medicine [3,39]. In other words, although the medical benefits significantly increase with digital technology for individuals (or groups) with the accessibility and ability to utilize such technology, for the remaining individuals (or groups), this change may leave them far behind where they are less likely to leverage these benefits. Hence, future studies can recognize this health inequality and develop digital health technologies to solve social problems.

The third important implication is for policymakers and institutions. Our findings support the most vital areas of medicine, but different results were obtained for some regions. For example, Pediatrics, Perinatology, Child Health, Obstetrics and Gynecology are unaffected by economic disparities. This could mean the system weakly affects children's health or important health issues such as cancer. Therefore, these blind spots should be carefully considered when designing a system.

As seen during the COVID-19 pandemic, if a global infectious disease such as a pandemic re-emerges, ultimately, the collective intelligence through research collaboration can make an effective global response the key to cope with the crisis. Countries that adhere to closed systems may be able to keep their distance from some issues that can be potentially problematic, but they will be excluded from many of the great benefits that those collaborations will bring. To make those collaborations effective and efficient, in-depth understanding of the digital competency and institutional environment of individual countries must be a precedent. Our study empirically demonstrates that digital competency is conducive to the innovativeness of medical research at the country level. However, sophisticated design for the institutional environment must be concurrently considered to maximize its positive impact.

5.2. Limitations and Suggestions for Future Research

Our study has several limitations. Although it measured the innovativeness of medical research using established measures, due to the intrinsic characteristics of medicine, experimentations, services, and practices are critical to realizing the innovativeness of new knowledge. There can be limitations in accurately reflecting the degree of innovativeness using a document-based measure. Future research could conduct an in-depth analysis to investigate how innovative publications are utilized in digital health systems.

The scope of the medical research used in this study can be extended. Although this is important because of its direct linkage to mortality, recent medical services and practices require extensive cooperation within medicine, such as anesthesiology or radiology, and across other fields, such as material and biomedical engineering. Hence, further studies should be conducted using more comprehensive data. In addition, while we use the simple slope analysis to depict our moderating effects due to the methodological limitation, future study can employ more sophisticate analysis techniques to investigate the detailed mechanisms of moderating effects.

Author Contributions: W.S.: conceptualization, methodology, writing—original draft, writing—review & editing, formal analysis, visualization, B.C.: conceptualization, methodology, writing—original draft, writing—review and editing, formal analysis, visualization. All authors have read and agreed to the published version of the manuscript.

Funding: This research was funded by CHA Bundang Medical Center, CHA University. This work was supported by Hankuk University of Foreign Studies research fund.

Data Availability Statement: The data that support the findings of this study are available upon reasonable request from the authors.

Conflicts of Interest: The authors declare no conflict of interest.

Appendix A. Variable Description and Summary

Variable Name	Measurement	Database
	Dependent variables	
Innovativeness of Research in Surgery Innovativeness of Research in Pediatrics, Perinatology and Child Health Innovativeness of Research in Obstetrics and Gynecology Innovativeness of Research in Internal Medicine	• The ratio of the total number of published and citable documents in the focal country for each of vital areas in medicine to total number of forward citations that those documents received. • Reference: https://www.scimagojr.com/, (accessed on 11 October 2022).	Journal and Country Rank from Scimago
	Independent variable	
National digital capacity	• Comprehensive estimation of the digital and technological level of each country based on a combination of statistical and survey data (IMD website description) • Measure: point (0–10) • Reference: https://www.imd.org/centers/world-competitiveness-center/rankings/world-digital-competitiveness/, (accessed on 11 October 2022)	International Institute for Management Development (IMD) Digital Competitiveness
	Moderating variables	
Quality of administration system	• The index of government effectiveness captures perceptions of the quality of public services, the quality of the civil service and the degree of its independence from political pressures, the quality of policy formulation and implementation, and the credibility of the government's commitment to such policies (GED website description) • Measure: point (−2.5 to +2.5) • Raw data source: The World Bank • Reference: https://www.theglobaleconomy.com/, (accessed on 11 October 2022)	Global Economy Database (GED)
Quality of legal system	• The index for Rule of Law of GED. It captures perceptions of the extent to which agents have confidence in and abide by the rules of society, and in particular the quality of contract enforcement, property rights, the police, and the courts (GED website description) • Measure: point (−2.5 to +2.5) • Raw data source: The World Bank • Reference: https://www.theglobaleconomy.com/, (accessed on 11 October 2022)	
Market freedom	• The business freedom index of GED. It is based on 10 indicators, using data from the World Bank's Doing Business study: Starting a business—procedures (number), time (days), cost (% of income per capita), and minimum capital (% of income per capita); Obtaining a license—procedures (number), time (days), and cost (% of income per capita); Closing a business—time (years), cost (% of estate), and recovery rate (cents on the dollar). (GED website description) • Measure: point (0–100) • Raw data source: The Heritage Foundation • Reference: https://www.theglobaleconomy.com/, (accessed on 11 October 2022)	

Variable Name	Measurement	Database
Disparity of economic development	• The uneven economic development index of the GED. It considers inequality within the economy, irrespective of the actual performance of an economy. The higher the value of the index, the higher the inequality in the country's economy (GED website description) • Measure: point (0–10) • Raw data source: Fund for Peace • Reference: https://www.theglobaleconomy.com/, (accessed on 11 October 2022)	
	Control variables	
Innovation index	• The Global Innovation Index includes two sub-indices: the Innovation Input Sub-Index and the Innovation Output Sub-Index. The first sub-index is based on five pillars: Institutions, Human capital and research, Infrastructure, Market sophistication, and Business sophistication. The second sub-index is based on two pillars: Knowledge and technology outputs and Creative outputs. Each pillar is divided into sub-pillars and each sub-pillar is composed of individual indicators (GED website description) • Measure: point (0–100) • Raw data source: Cornell University, INSEAD, and the World Intellectual Property Organization (WIPO) • Reference: https://www.theglobaleconomy.com/, (accessed on 11 October 2022)	Global Economy Database (GED)
Political rights index	• Reference: https://www.theglobaleconomy.com/, (accessed on 11 October 2022) • Score ratings from the Freedom House evaluate three categories: electoral process, political pluralism and participation, and the functioning of government indicators (GED website description). • Measure: point (1–7) • Raw data source: The Freedom House • Reference: https://www.theglobaleconomy.com/, (accessed on 11 October 2022)	
Globalization index	• Globalization index of GED. It covers the economic, social, and political dimensions of globalization. Higher values denote greater globalization. • Measure: point (0–100) • Raw data source: The Swiss Institute of Technology • Reference: https://www.theglobaleconomy.com/, (accessed on 11 October 2022)	
Services sector value-adding	• Services correspond to International Standard Industrial Classification (ISIC) divisions 50–99. Value added is the net output of a sector after adding up all outputs and subtracting intermediate inputs. It is calculated without making deductions for the depreciation of fabricated assets or depletion and degradation of natural resources (GED website description) • Measure: percent • Raw data source: The World Bank • Reference: https://www.theglobaleconomy.com/, (accessed on 11 October 2022)	

Variable Name	Measurement	Database
Gross domestic product	• Standard measure of the value added created through the production of goods and services in a country during a certain period • Reference: https://data.worldbank.org/, (accessed on 11 October 2022)	
Science research legislation	• Science research legislation indicator (to facilitate innovation) of IMD national competitiveness It is based on a comprehensive estimation of various factors of each country based on a combination of statistical and survey data • Reference: https://www.imd.org/centers/world-competitiveness-center/rankings/world-competitiveness/, (accessed on 11 October 2022)	IMD national competitiveness
Health infrastructure	• Health infrastructure indicator of IMD national competitiveness. It is based on a comprehensive estimation of various factors of each country based on a combination of statistical and survey data • Reference: https://www.imd.org/centers/world-competitiveness-center/rankings/world-competitiveness/, (accessed on 11 October 2022)	

References

1. Ting, D.S.W.; Carin, L.; Dzau, V.; Wong, T.Y. Digital technology and COVID-19. *Nat. Med.* **2020**, *26*, 459–461. [CrossRef] [PubMed]
2. Tan, R.K.J.; Wu, D.; Day, S.; Zhao, Y.; Larson, H.J.; Sylvia, S.; Tang, W.; Tucker, J.D. Digital approaches to enhancing community engagement in clinical trials. *NPJ Digit. Med.* **2022**, *5*, 37. [CrossRef] [PubMed]
3. Inan, O.T.; Tenaerts, P.; Prindiville, S.A.; Reynolds, H.R.; Dizon, D.S.; Cooper-Arnold, K.; Turakhia, M.; Pletcher, M.J.; Preston, K.L.; Krumholz, H.M.; et al. Digitizing clinical trials. *NPJ Digit. Med.* **2020**, *3*, 101. [CrossRef] [PubMed]
4. Steinhubl, S.R.; Wolff-Hughes, D.L.; Nilsen, W.; Iturriaga, E.; Califf, R.M. Digital clinical trials: Creating a vision for the future. *NPJ Digit. Med.* **2019**, *2*, 126. [CrossRef] [PubMed]
5. Rosa, C.; Marsch, L.A.; Winstanley, E.L.; Brunner, M.; Campbell, A.N. Using digital technologies in clinical trials: Current and future applications. *Contemp. Clin. Trials* **2021**, *100*, 106219. [CrossRef] [PubMed]
6. Jenssen, B.P.; Mitra, N.; Shah, A.; Wan, F.; Grande, D. Using Digital Technology to Engage and Communicate with Patients: A Survey of Patient Attitudes. *J. Gen. Intern. Med.* **2016**, *31*, 85–92. [CrossRef]
7. Devine, K.A.; Viola, A.S.; Coups, E.J.; Wu, Y.P. Digital health interventions for adolescent and young adult cancer survivors. *JCO Clin. Cancer Inform.* **2018**, *2*, 1–15. [CrossRef]
8. Roberts, A.L.; Fisher, A.; Smith, L.; Heinrich, M.; Potts, H.W.W. Digital health behaviour change interventions targeting physical activity and diet in cancer survivors: A systematic review and meta-analysis. *J. Cancer Surviv.* **2017**, *11*, 704–719. [CrossRef]
9. Fallahzadeh, R.; Rokni, S.A.; Ghasemzadeh, H.; Soto-Perez-De-Celis, E.; Shahrokni, A. Digital health for geriatric oncology. *JCO Clin. Cancer Inform.* **2018**, *2*, 1–12. [CrossRef]
10. Demirkan, H. A Smart Healthcare Systems Framework. *IT Prof.* **2013**, *15*, 38–45. [CrossRef]
11. Dong, H.; Hussain, F.K.; Chang, E. A framework for discovering and classifying ubiquitous services in digital health ecosystems. *J. Comput. Syst. Sci.* **2011**, *77*, 687–704. [CrossRef]
12. Schiavone, F.; Mancini, D.; Leone, D.; Lavorato, D. Digital business models and ridesharing for value co-creation in healthcare: A multi-stakeholder ecosystem analysis. *Technol. Forecast. Soc. Chang.* **2021**, *166*, 120647. [CrossRef]
13. Hermes, S.; Riasanow, T.; Clemons, E.K.; Böhm, M.; Krcmar, H. The digital transformation of the healthcare industry: Exploring the rise of emerging platform ecosystems and their influence on the role of patients. *Bus. Res.* **2020**, *13*, 1033–1069. [CrossRef]
14. Frow, P.; McColl-Kennedy, J.R.; Payne, A. Co-creation practices: Their role in shaping a health care ecosystem. *Ind. Mark. Manag.* **2016**, *56*, 24–39. [CrossRef]
15. Dedeilia, A.; Esagian, S.M.; Ziogas, I.A.; Giannis, D.; Katsaros, I.; Tsoulfas, G. Pediatric surgery during the COVID-19 pandemic. *World J. Clin. Pediatr.* **2020**, *9*, 7–16. [CrossRef] [PubMed]
16. Donnelly, M.; McDonagh, M. Health research, consent and the GDPR exemption. *Eur. J. Health Law* **2019**, *26*, 97–119. [CrossRef] [PubMed]
17. Rumbold, J.M.M.; Pierscionek, B. The effect of the general data protection regulation on medical research. *J. Med. Internet Res.* **2017**, *19*, e7108. [CrossRef] [PubMed]
18. Chassang, G. The impact of the EU general data protection regulation on scientific research. *Ecancermedicalscience* **2017**, *11*, 709. [CrossRef]

19. Salman, R.; Beller, E.; Kagan, J.; Hemminki, E.; Phillips, R.S.; Savulescu, J.; Macleod, M.; Wisely, J.; Chalmers, I. Increasing value and reducing waste in biomedical research regulation and management. *Lancet* **2014**, *383*, 176–185. [CrossRef]
20. Ting, D.; Lin, H.; Ruamviboonsuk, P.; Wong, T.; Sim, D. Artificial intelligence, the internet of things, and virtual clinics: Ophthal mology at the digital translation forefront. *Lancet Digit. Health* **2019**, *2*, E8–E9. [CrossRef]
21. Shilo, S.; Rossman, H.; Segal, E. Axes of a revolution: Challenges and promises of big data in healthcare. *Nat. Med.* **2020**, *26*, 29–38. [CrossRef] [PubMed]
22. LeCun, Y.; Bengio, Y.; Hinton, G. Deep learning. *Nature* **2015**, *521*, 436–444. [CrossRef] [PubMed]
23. Heaven, D. Bitcoin for the biological literature. *Nature* **2019**, *566*, 141–142. [CrossRef] [PubMed]
24. Murthy, V.H.; Krumholz, H.M.; Gross, C.P. Participation in cancer clinical trials. *JAMA* **2004**, *291*, 2720–2726. [CrossRef] [PubMed]
25. Anderson, D. Digital R&D: Four Ways to Maximize Patient Engagement in Clinical Trials, Deloitte Consulting LLP. 2018. Available online: https://www2.deloitte.com/us/en/blog/health-care-blog/2018/digital-rd-four-ways-to-maximize-patient-engagement-in-clinical-trials.html (accessed on 7 October 2022).
26. Chen, M.; Wang, R.; Zhou, Y.; He, Z.; Liu, X.; He, M.; Wang, J.; Huang, C.; Zhou, H.; Hong, P.; et al. Digital medical education empowered by intelligent fabric space. *Natl. Sci. Open* **2022**, *1*, 10. [CrossRef]
27. North, D.C. *Institutions, Institutional Change and Economic Performance*; Cambridge University Press: Cambridge, UK, 1990.
28. Powell, W.W.; DiMaggio, P. (Eds.) *The New Institutionalism in Organizational Analysis*; University of Chicago Press: Chicago, IL, USA, 1991; pp. 183–203.
29. Scott, W.R. Institutional Theory: Contributing to a Theoretical Research Program. In *Great Minds in Management: The Process of Theory Development*; Smith, K.G., Hitt, M.A., Eds.; Oxford University Press: New York, NY, USA, 2005; pp. 460–484.
30. Kruse, C.; Betancourt, J.; Ortiz, S.; Luna, S.M.V.; Bamrah, I.K.; Segovia, N. Barriers to the use of mobile health in improving health outcomes in developing countries: Systematic review. *J. Med. Internet Res.* **2019**, *21*, e13263. [CrossRef]
31. Mahmood, S.; Hasan, K.; Carras, M.C.; Labrique, A. Global preparedness against COVID-19: We must leverage the power of digital health. *JMIR Public Health Surveill.* **2020**, *6*, e18980. [CrossRef]
32. Dadaczynski, K.; Okan, O.; Messer, M.; Leung, A.Y.M.; Rosário, R.; Darlington, E.; Rathmann, K. Digital Health Literacy and Web-Based Information-Seeking Behaviors of University Students in Germany during the COVID-19 Pandemic: Cross-sectional Survey Study. *J. Med. Internet Res.* **2021**, *23*, e24097. [CrossRef]
33. Fagherazzi, G.; Goetzinger, C.; Rashid, M.A.; Aguayo, G.A.; Huiart, L. Digital Health Strategies to Fight COVID-19 Worldwide: Challenges, Recommendations, and a Call for Papers. *J. Med. Internet Res.* **2020**, *22*, e19284. [CrossRef]
34. Zahra, S.A.; Ireland, R.D.; Gutierrez, I.; Hitt, M.A. Privatization and Entrepreneurial Transformation: Emerging Issues and a Future Research Agenda. *Acad. Manag. Rev.* **2000**, *25*, 524. [CrossRef]
35. Park, S.H.; Li, S.; Tse, D.K. Market Liberalization and Firm Performance during China's Economic Transition. *J. Int. Bus. Stud.* **2006**, *37*, 127–147. [CrossRef]
36. La Porta, R.; Lopez-De-Silanes, F.; Shleifer, A.; Vishny, R. Legal Determinants of External Finance. *J. Financ.* **1997**, *52*, 1150. [CrossRef]
37. Gang, K.W.; Woo, H.G.; Lee, C. The Transformation of Ownership Structure and Changes in Principal-Principal Conflicts: Evidence from Corporate Governance Reforms in South Korea. *Int. J. Corp. Gov.* **2018**, *8*, 281–301.
38. Kim, H.; Kim, H.; Hoskisson, R.E. Does Market-Oriented Institutional Change in an Emerging Economy Make Business-Group-Affiliated Multinationals Perform Better? An Institution-Based View. *J. Int. Bus. Stud.* **2010**, *41*, 1141–1160. [CrossRef]
39. Noonan, D.; Simmons, L.A. Navigating nonessential research trials during COVID-19: The push we needed for using digital technology to increase access for rural participants? *J. Rural. Health* **2021**, *37*, 185. [CrossRef] [PubMed]
40. Young, L.; Barnason, S.; Do, V. Review Strategies to Recruit and Retain Rural Patient Participating Self-management Behavioral Trials. *Online J. Rural Res. Policy* **2015**, *10*, 1–12. [CrossRef]
41. Unger, J.M.; Moseley, A.; Symington, B.; Chavez-MacGregor, M.; Ramsey, S.D.; Hershman, D.L. Geographic Distribution and Survival Outcomes for Rural Patients With Cancer Treated in Clinical Trials. *JAMA Netw. Open* **2018**, *1*, e181235. [CrossRef]
42. Yamin, C.K.; Emani, S.; Williams, D.H.; Lipsitz, S.R.; Karson, A.S.; Wald, J.S.; Bates, D.W. The Digital Divide in Adoption and Use of a Personal Health Record. *Arch. Intern. Med.* **2011**, *171*, 568–574. [CrossRef]
43. Eruchalu, C.N.; Pichardo, M.S.; Bharadwaj, M.; Rodriguez, C.B.; Rodriguez, J.A.; Bergmark, R.W.; Bates, D.W.; Ortega, G. The Expanding Digital Divide: Digital Health Access Inequities during the COVID-19 Pandemic in New York City. *J. Urban Health* **2021**, *98*, 183–186. [CrossRef]
44. Cheung, H.Y.; Chan, A.W. Increasing the competitive positions of countries through employee training: The competency motive across 33 countries. *Int. J. Manpow.* **2012**, *33*, 144–158. [CrossRef]
45. Ciocanel, A.B.; Pavelescu, F.M. Innovation and competitiveness in European context. *Procedia Econ. Financ.* **2015**, *32*, 728–737. [CrossRef]
46. Fonseca, L.M.; Lima, V.M. Countries three wise men: Sustainability, innovation, and competitiveness. *J. Ind. Eng. Manag.* **2015**, *8*, 1288–1302. [CrossRef]
47. Butler, D. Free journal-ranking tool enters citation market. *Nature* **2008**, *451*, 6. [CrossRef] [PubMed]
48. El-Azami-El-Idrissi, M.; Lakhdar-Idrissi, M.; Ouldim, K.; Bono, W.; Amarti-Riffi, A.; Hida, M.; Nejjari, C. Improving medical research in the Arab world. *Lancet* **2013**, *382*, 2066–2067. [CrossRef] [PubMed]

49. Choi, B.; Kumar, M.V.S.; Zambuto, F. Capital structure and innovation trajectory: The role of debt in balancing Exploration and exploitation. *Organ. Sci.* **2016**, *27*, 1183–1201. [CrossRef]
50. Gavetti, G.; Levinthal, D. Looking forward and looking backward: Cognitive and experiential search. *Adm. Sci. Q.* **2000**, *45*, 113–137. [CrossRef]
51. Phene, A.; Fladmoe-Lindquist, K.; Marsh, L. Breakthrough innovations in the US biotechnology industry: The effects of technological space and geographic origin. *Strateg. Manag. J.* **2006**, *27*, 369–388. [CrossRef]
52. Rosenkopf, L.; Nerkar, A. Beyond local search: Boundary-spanning, exploration, and impact in the optical disk industry. *Strateg. Manag. J.* **2001**, *22*, 287–306. [CrossRef]
53. Alvesson, M.; Sandberg, J. Has management studies lost its way? Ideas for more imaginative and innovative research. *J. Manag. Stud.* **2013**, *50*, 128–152. [CrossRef]
54. Kaplan, S.; Vakili, K. The double-edged sword of recombination in breakthrough innovation. *Strat. Manag. J.* **2015**, *36*, 1435–1457. [CrossRef]
55. Fleming, L.; Sorenson, O. Science as a map in technological search. *Strat. Manag. J.* **2004**, *25*, 909–928. [CrossRef]
56. Wooldridge, J.M. *Econometric Analysis of Cross Section and Panel Data*; MIT Press: Cambridge, MA, USA, 2010.

sustainability

MDPI

Article

The Influence of Reverse Technology Spillover of Outward Foreign Direct Investment on Green Total Factor Productivity in China's Manufacturing Industry

Yan Li, Xiaohan Zhang, Chenxin Jin and Qingbo Huang *

School of Maritime Economics and Management, Dalian Maritime University, Dalian 116026, China
* Correspondence: huangqingbo@dlmu.edu.cn

Abstract: Outward foreign direct investment (OFDI) is an important channel for China to obtain advanced technology spillover to promote green production upgrading. As a pillar of the national economy and also a large-scale pollution emission industry, can the manufacturing industry benefit from the reverse technology spillover of OFDI and improve its green total factor productivity (GTFP)? Based on the provincial data of China from 2005 to 2019, this paper analyzes the effect and moderating mechanism of reverse technology spillover of OFDI on domestic manufacturing GTFP theoretically and empirically. The results show that the reverse technology spillover of OFDI cannot significantly promote the growth of manufacturing GTFP in the sample period. The heterogeneity analysis further proves that the inhibition effect similar to that of the whole sample appears in the eastern region, but in the central and western regions, the reverse technology spillover of OFDI can significantly improve the manufacturing GTFP, and this positive effect in the central region is greater. Additionally, absorptive capacity characterized by human capital, economic development and financial development can actively adjust the impact of reverse technology spillover of OFDI on manufacturing GTFP, of which the positive moderating effect of financial development is the most significant.

Keywords: outward foreign direct investment; reverse technology spillover; green total factor productivity; absorptive capacity; moderating effect

Citation: Li, Y.; Zhang, X.; Jin, C.; Huang, Q. The Influence of Reverse Technology Spillover of Outward Foreign Direct Investment on Green Total Factor Productivity in China's Manufacturing Industry. *Sustainability* **2022**, *14*, 16496. https://doi.org/10.3390/su142416496

Academic Editors: Jeoung Yul Lee, Dilek Zamantili Nayir and Charles Chen

Received: 24 October 2022
Accepted: 2 December 2022
Published: 9 December 2022

Publisher's Note: MDPI stays neutral with regard to jurisdictional claims in published maps and institutional affiliations.

1. Introduction

As an important pillar of China's national economy, the manufacturing industry has played a decisive role in promoting the rapid economic development. However, its extensive development mode with high input, high energy consumption and high emission has led to serious resource waste and environmental pollution, which has become an important factor restricting high-quality economic development for a long time [1]. According to the 2020 Global Environmental Performance Index (EPI) Assessment Report [2], China ranks only 120th out of 180 countries, which illustrates the urgency of paying attention to environmental pollution. The report of the 19th National Congress of the Communist Party of China pointed out that "green development is an important means to transform the mode of economic development, and improving green total factor productivity (GTFP) is the key to achieving green development" [3]. GTFP can fully consider both energy input and environmental pollution in the process of economic development, which is more in line with the requirements of high-quality and sustainable economic development [4]. As the main source of energy consumption and environmental pollution emissions, upgrading the GTFP of the manufacturing industry and realizing its green transformation is the inevitable choice for China to achieve high-quality economic development.

The upgrading of the manufacturing GTFP cannot be separated from scientific and technological innovation. In the context of economic globalization, it is often difficult for a country, especially a developing country, to gain absolute technological advantage only by relying on its own strength. In this case, access to foreign technology spillovers through multiple channels can give play to the "late-mover advantage" of developing countries and achieve technology catch-up and upgrading [5]. There are three main forms of international technology spillovers, including trade, foreign direct investment (FDI) and outward foreign direct investment (OFDI) [6,7]. However, due to the protection of developed countries, it is often difficult for developing countries to obtain core technologies at the international frontier. Compared with the first two ways, the reverse technology spillover obtained through OFDI can be more targeted and proactive [8]. Nowadays, OFDI has become an important way for the international community, especially developing countries, to integrate into the global economy and acquire international advanced technology and other strategic assets [9–11]. In recent years, China has further expanded its opening up to the outside world, actively attracting foreign capital and encouraging local enterprises to "go global" [12,13]. Some other emerging countries have also boosted local economies through OFDI and upgraded their position in global value chains by promoting technological progress and improving the status of trade networks [14,15]. In 2020, China's OFDI flow reached USD 153.71 billion, and the stock had risen to USD 2580.66 billion. Can OFDI of such a large scale help improve the GTFP of domestic manufacturing industry by obtaining advanced technology spillover from abroad? An accurate answer to this question is of crucial relevance and theoretical value for the green development of the manufacturing industry and for the choice of China's future OFDI development direction.

Scholars have discussed this research topic from different perspectives and made various findings. The study of Kogut and Chang [9] first confirms that OFDI can indeed bring reverse technology spillovers to home countries through investment and learning from developed countries. Hong et al. [10] and Fahad et al. [11] further provide the similar conclusion that OFDI is actually an effective way to acquire advanced technologies. Based on this, some scholars directly affirmed the positive linear influence of OFDI on green production activities of the home country [16,17]. At the regional level, Pan et al. [18] proved that reverse technology spillover of China's OFDI can significantly promote the growth of total factor carbon productivity (TFCP) according to provincial panel data and found that the reverse technology spillover of OFDI can increase the TFCP of neighboring provinces through the spatial spillover mechanism. At the firm level, Bai et al. [12] examined that OFDI to developed countries can transfer reverse green technology and promote the environmental innovation of manufacturing enterprises in emerging economies. Song et al. [13] found a similar significant positive impact of OFDI on GTFP using Chinese firm-level data and discussed the heterogeneity of the impact for different firm nature, different OFDI types and different regions. However, there are also some studies drawing the opposite conclusion that the promotion effect of reverse technology spillover of OFDI in the home country is not significant [19] or even negative [20,21]. Lee [22] empirically tested the relationship between reverse technology spillover of OFDI and home country productivity by taking OECD countries as research objects and concluded that the former does not play a significant positive role. Bitzer and Kerekes [23] believe that OFDI has a negative effect on the improvement of total factor productivity through analyzing the industrial level data of OECD countries, but this effect is significantly different among different countries. The research of Li et al. [24] found that reverse technology spillover of OFDI has a significant inhibitory effect on TFP growth in the home country which is more obvious when the market mechanism of the host country is not sound.

Different from the above studies, some scholars believe that the impact of reverse technology spillover of OFDI on green production in home countries is nonlinear. The research results of Zhu and Ye [25] show that only OFDI flowing to developed countries can bring significant technology spillover effect and promote China's green technology progress, while this effect is insignificant for OFDI flows to transition countries or developing countries. He et al. [26] found that the impact of reverse technology spillover of OFDI on total factor energy efficiency is nonlinear, and that there is a single threshold effect at the regional level and a double threshold effect at the industry level. Some other scholars propose that the impact of OFDI reverse technology spillovers on green production in the home country is limited by other factors such as environmental regulation [27,28], institutional quality [29], national culture [30] and absorptive capacity [7]. Among these, absorptive capacity is one of the key capabilities of the home country in the process from acquiring foreign technologies to domestic effective application, which is manifested in financial, human and other aspects [31,32]. Tian [33] argues that OFDI can significantly improve GTFP and digital inclusive finance can strengthen the promoting effect. Zhou et al. [34] verify that whether China's OFDI has green spillover effect on domestic economy depends on the heterogeneity of absorptive capacity and environmental supervision strength of provinces.

The above literature has highlighted the impact of OFDI on the green production of the home country from different perspectives, but the research strand on the impact of reverse technology spillover of OFDI on GTFP is relatively small. Therefore, this paper attempts to supplement some research gaps and makes several marginal contributions. First, many studies fail to fully consider the bidirectional impact of OFDI on GTFP in theory, so the estimation results may be biased. This paper considers the multiple effects in the whole process of a country obtaining foreign technology spillovers through OFDI and affecting the GTFP of the industry, providing a solid theoretical framework for the research. Second, many existing studies assess the impact of OFDI on green production in the home country from the perspective of OFDI flow or stock scale, which may cause deviation due to the selection of indicators. This paper directly calculates the reverse technology spillovers of OFDI and selects manufacturing industry as the research object, hoping to improve the accuracy and pertinence of the research conclusions. Third, many studies only select one variable as a reference when studying the moderating effect of absorptive capacity, which may not be comprehensive. In this paper, human capital, economic development and financial development are all included in the test of the moderating effect, which can not only make the regression results more convincing, but also draw more effective policy enlightenment through comparison.

Generally, the main objective of this paper is to analyze whether and how reverse technology spillover of OFDI can affect the domestic manufacturing GTFP theoretically and empirically. To achieve this, this paper (1) adopts the baseline regression to test the influence of reverse technology spillover of OFDI on domestic manufacturing GTFP; (2) constructs heterogeneity analysis to discuss the different performance of this influence in different regions; and (3) studies the moderating effect of absorptive capacity including human capital, economic development and financial development.

The rest of this work is organized as follows. Section 2 illustrates the mechanism function of reverse technology spillover of OFDI on GTFP. The design of the research scheme, including model introduction, indicator selection and data source, is shown in Section 3. The empirical results and analysis are presented in Section 4. Finally, Section 5 gives the conclusions and puts forward the policy implications.

2. Theoretical Analysis

2.1. Process of Reverse Technology Spillover of OFDI

The process of a country obtaining foreign technology spillovers through OFDI can be divided into three stages: acquisition stage, transfer stage and diffusion stage [35,36].

In the technology acquisition stage, multinational corporations can acquire advanced technologies in the host countries three ways. First is cross-border mergers and acquisitions (M&A). OFDI can be achieved through greenfield investment and M&A, which can bypass the protection barriers of developed countries to advanced technologies. In this way, the patent and production process, scientific and technological R&D and other tacit knowledge of the acquired company can be transferred to the subsidiary in the host country quickly and conveniently. Second is overseas R&D cooperation. By setting up R&D institutions in the host country and cooperating with local universities and research institutes, multinational corporations can make full use of local advanced technologies and resources, which is conducive to a more in-depth and intuitive understanding of the cutting-edge areas of technology development. Third is industrial agglomeration. After entering the technology-intensive industrial cluster area of the host country through OFDI, multinational companies can not only get in touch with the frontier development field of their own industries, but also acquire advanced technologies through communication and learning with other enterprises in the cluster.

In the technology transfer stage, the subsidiary in the host country needs to transfer the information resources, acquired technical knowledge and R&D achievements to the parent company, and the parent company subsequently digests and absorbs these technologies and finally puts them into production and operation. In order to realize this process, the government of the home country can attract the parent company, actively promoting the overseas subsidiary to transfer new technologies and skills back to home through policy incentives at the macro level. For example, governments can provide preferential policies for domestic multinational corporations investing in advanced technology industries in developed countries to save investment costs and increase profits. The micro transmission for enterprise level is mainly based on two-way personnel flow. On the one hand, the parent company can send domestic technicians overseas for training and learning, so that technicians can master overseas skills and then return to apply what they have learned to domestic production practice and product R&D. On the other hand, the parent company can also directly introduce talents from the overseas subsidiary to exchange and work domestically, which can not only shorten the cycle of reverse technology spillover, but also help the home country to absorb sophisticated technologies.

In the technology diffusion stage, the parent company should first identify and screen out the overseas technologies that are valuable to the home country and fit its situation. Subsequently, the parent company needs to make a localized interpretation of the technologies that meet the screening conditions, and combine the core and key technologies with each production link, to lay the foundation for technology transformation and application. Finally, these modified and innovative technologies will be applied to the production practice of the multinational corporations and even the whole industry. This way, reverse technology spillover completes the value embodiment in the internal optimization process of the home country.

2.2. *Effect of Reverse Technology Spillover of OFDI on GTFP*

In the process of reverse technology spillover of OFDI, the green production activities of the home country will be affected in many aspects [19,26,37], resulting in the change in GTFP. The influence effects mainly include:

(1) R&D feedback effect. On the one hand, OFDI activities can help enterprises in the home country gain direct access to advanced green production technologies in the host country, so as to help the parent company learn and imitate, and eventually apply these technologies to the whole industry. On the other hand, the transfer of foreign technologies to the home country will also stimulate local enterprises' sense of competition, to maintain or increase their market share. Overall, the R&D feedback from reverse technology spillovers of OFDI will drive enterprises to learn and compete, thereby increasing the GTFP across the industry.

(2) Cost allocation effect. For manufacturing enterprises, it is essential to maintain technological advantages through increasing R&D expenses. However, excessive R&D costs have become invisible capital pressure on enterprises with relatively backward and unsophisticated production systems. OFDI activities can expand overseas markets for these enterprises, increase their income and reduce the pressure of R&D expenses. At the same time, when investing in a host country that actively welcomes overseas capital, it can also obtain tax and fiscal policy support from the host government which is conducive to share R&D costs. An example from India confirms this—to realize the "Made in India" plan, the Indian government has created some key factors to attract FDI investment, including establishing high-level government support and maintaining a large number of sustainable financial resources. According to the World Investment Report 2022, these measures have enabled India's FDI inflows to reach USD 81.973 billion between 2020 and 2021, which

created a record level and an increase of 10% over the previous fiscal year. With the fiscal support of the host government, the R&D cost pressure of the parent company could be reduced, which better helps improve the green production efficiency of the home country.

(3) Resource optimization effect. Through OFDI activities, the bi-directional flow of production factors at home and abroad will be promoted, especially the internalization of international resources. Since enterprises may tend to protect their core technologies, OFDI is somewhat easier than other routes, such as trade, to weaken technological barriers and help the home country gains access to advanced overseas production factors. At the same time, OFDI also facilitates the cross-border flow of human capital, and enterprises in the home country can hire high-level technical personnel from the host country to optimize local production resources and strengthen green production capacity.

(4) Capital crowding-out effect. OFDI activities are also essentially part of enterprises' limited capital allocation. When large OFDI accelerates the outflow of domestic capital, resource allocation on other production links may change greatly. Crucially, funds which are originally available for independent R&D and innovation of enterprises may be partly occupied. Especially for enterprises with strong independent R&D capabilities, the negative impact of the crowding-out effect will be more obvious. In addition, due to the risks in the OFDI process, enterprises may suffer losses in overseas investment. This may also lead to insufficient supply of domestic R&D funds, which is not conducive to the development of enterprises' independent innovation.

(5) External dependence effect. Although the reverse technology spillover of OFDI can help enterprises imitate innovation to a certain extent, it can also cause some excessive dependence on external technologies. For example, in order to save time and promote production, some enterprises tend to directly assign overseas technicians to take charge of the core production link, without digesting and absorbing the advanced technologies needed in this link. In the long run, the enthusiasm of enterprises for independent innovation will be reduced, and the independent innovation ability cannot be really improved. In other words, this mentality of dependence on external technologies will lead to local enterprises being locked in behind the advanced foreign technologies, thereby depressing the GTFP of the whole industry in the home country.

2.3. Moderating Effect of Absorptive Capacity on Reverse Technology Spillover of OFDI

Whether reverse technology spillovers of OFDI can improve the technology level of the parent company depends, to some extent, on whether the parent company can identify, absorb and transform the advanced technologies transferred back from its subsidiaries. In other words, absorptive capacity plays an important role in the process of reverse technology spillover of OFDI affecting GTFP in the home country. For different enterprises, even if the technical knowledge transferred back by their overseas subsidiaries is similar, the intensity of reverse technology spillover will be different due to different absorption capacities. Factors affecting the absorption capacity of spillover technology in the home country mainly include:

(1) Human capital. The level of human capital determines the ability of knowledge accumulation, and the knowledge system originally possessed by domestic human capital can effectively complement advanced foreign knowledge. High-quality human capital will help promote the progress that reverse spillover technology elements can be digested, absorbed and recreated after entering the home country [32]. Therefore, the improvement of human capital can make each absorption step of the home country gain more benefits, and further strengthen the effect of reverse technology spillover of OFDI.

(2) Economic development. First, the better the local economy develops, the more complete the construction of transportation, communication and other facilities, and the more conducive for enterprises to absorb foreign technologies. Second, economic development will improve the economic vitality of the region, thus enhancing the effectiveness of market competition. Under the pressure of competition, enterprises in the market will focus on R&D and innovation, which can actively improve the absorption and digestion

of technological knowledge in the whole region. Third, economic development can drive regional market demand. This will encourage local enterprises to actively absorb foreign technologies in order to make them better localized and cater to local needs [34].

(3) Financial development. The improvement of the financial development level is conducive to relaxing the financing constraints of regions on enterprises. On the one hand, this will enable enterprises to increase their R&D investment, and gradually enhance their ability to absorb and digest foreign technologies while repeatedly learning and creating technologies [31]. On the other hand, the frequency of enterprises' outward investment will be increased, which can help enterprises skillfully handle foreign technologies, so as to improve the overall technology absorption capacity of the region [33].

3. Research Design

3.1. Research Scheme

Many previous studies on this topic have laid the foundation for this paper, whose methods, variables, data and conclusions are shown in Appendix A. However, as mentioned in the introduction, although these literature works have studied relevant issues from multiple perspectives, there are still some research gaps that can be supplemented. Based on the above theoretical analysis, this paper proposes that the reverse technology spillover of OFDI promotes GTFP of the home country through R&D feedback effect, cost allocation effect and resource optimization effect, and inhibits through capital crowding-out effect and external dependence effect. It is worth noting that the performance of these effects may be different in different regions. At the same time, the impact of reverse technology spillover of OFDI on GTFP is affected by the heterogeneity of absorptive capacity. Basis on these, the complete mechanism function and empirical tests taken in this paper to verify the following three hypotheses are shown in Figure 1.

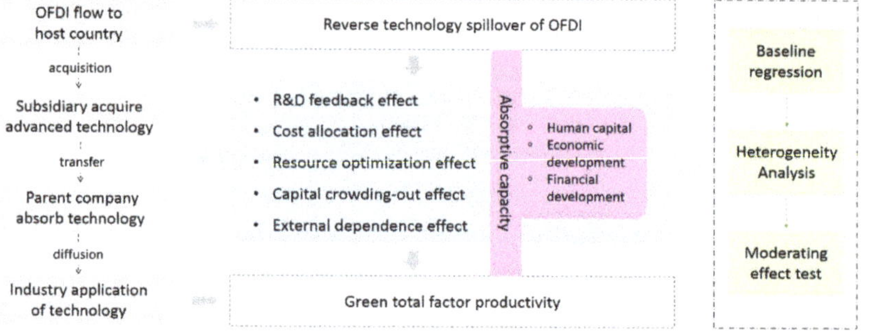

Figure 1. Diagram of the mechanism function and empirical tests.

Hypothesis 1. *Reverse technology spillover of OFDI can significantly affect the manufacturing GTFP of the home country.*

Hypothesis 2. *There is regional heterogeneity in the impact of reverse technology spillover of OFDI on the manufacturing GTFP.*

Hypothesis 3. *Absorption capacity plays a moderating role in the impact of reverse technology spillover of OFDI on GTFP.*

3.2. Model Specification

Coe and Helpmen [38] proposed the international R&D spillover model, believing that a country's technological progress can be affected by not only by domestic but also foreign R&D level. On this basis, Lichtenberg and Potterie [39] introduced OFDI as an important channel of foreign R&D spillover and further constructed the L-P model, which provided research thinking for testing the impact of OFDI on technological progress. In this paper, the L-P model is referenced to investigate the impact of reverse technology spillover of OFDI on GTFP, which is described as:

$$\ln GTFP_{i,t} = \alpha_0 + \alpha_1 \ln SOFDI_{i,t} + \alpha_2 Controls_{i,t} + \varepsilon_{i,t} \quad (1)$$

Among them, the subscripts i and t stand for provincial region and year, respectively. $\ln GTFP$ is the explained variable of this paper and denotes the logarithm value of GTFP. $\ln SOFDI$ is the core explanatory variable of this paper and denotes the logarithm value of reverse technology spillover of OFDI. *Controls* represents a series of control variables. $\varepsilon_{i,t}$ represents the random error term and α_0 represents constant.

In addition, considering the continuity of the growth for GTFP, this paper adds $\ln GTFP_{i,t-1}$, the lag term of GTFP, to the empirical model, as shown in Equation (2). At the same time, there may be a bidirectional causality between the reverse technology spillover of OFDI and the GTFP, that is, the improvement of the GTFP in turn affects enterprises to "going out" and obtain foreign technologies. Therefore, endogeneity inevitably exists, and it is scientifically feasible to use the generalized method of moments (GMM) to overcome the problem when the lag term of the explained variable has been introduced in the model. Since the SYS-GMM is more suitable for solving the problem of weak instrumental variables than the DIF-GMM, this paper selects the former as the empirical estimation method to verify Hypothesis 1.

$$\ln GTFP_{i,t} = \beta_0 + \beta_1 \ln SOFDI_{i,t} + \beta_2 \ln GTFP_{i,t-1} + \beta_3 Controls_{i,t} + \varepsilon_{i,t} \quad (2)$$

Subsequently, to verify Hypothesis 3, this paper sets the following mechanism model to examine the "moderating effect" of absorptive capacity in the impact of reverse technology spillover of OFDI on GTFP, which is described as:

$$\ln GTFP_{i,t} = \gamma_0 + \gamma_1 \ln SOFDI_{i,t} + \gamma_2 \ln GTFP_{i,t-1} + \gamma_3 INTER_{i,t} + \gamma_4 Controls_{i,t} + \varepsilon_{i,t} \quad (3)$$

Among them, $INTER_{i,t}$ denotes the interactive item between absorptive capacity and reverse technology spillover of OFDI. The variables representing absorption capacity are included in the control variables, which are described in the following sections.

3.3. Data Sources

Taking the data availability into consideration, this paper selects the manufacturing industry of 30 Chinese provincial regions from 2005 to 2019 as samples (except Tibet, Hong Kong, Macao and Taiwan). The original data come from the Statistical Bulletin of China's Outward Foreign Direct Investment, the Organization for Economic Co-operation and Development Database (OECD), the World Bank Database, China Industry Statistical Yearbook, China Statistical Yearbook of Science and Technology, China Labor Statistical Yearbook, China Energy Statistical Yearbook, China Statistical Yearbook on Environment and statistical yearbooks of every provincial region.

3.4. Definition of Variables

3.4.1. Explained Variable

GTFP ($GTFP_{i,t}$) is employed as the explained variable in this paper. Referring to the methods of Tone [40] and Oh [41], the SBM-GML model considering unexpected output is adopted for its widely use in dealing with the relationship between multiple inputs and outputs to evaluate efficiency. The selection and detailed description of input and output indicators are shown below [19,26,33].

Input indicators: (1) labor input, which is expressed as the year-end number of employed people in the manufacturing industry of every provincial region; (2) capital input, which is expressed as additional fixed capital and calculated using the perpetual inventory method; (3) energy input, which is expressed as the industrial energy consumption converted to standard coal of every provincial region.

Output indicators: (1) expected output, which is expressed as the industrial sale value after deflating by the producer price index (PPI) of industrial products in each year; (2) unexpected output, which is expressed as comprehensive environmental pollution index synthesized by entropy method using industrial wastewater discharge, industrial smoke and dust discharge, industrial sulfur dioxide discharge and solid waste discharge.

Based on the above, this paper sets the GTFP of 2005 as 1, and the calculated change rate is multiplied to obtain the GTFP level from 2006 to 2019 of the whole China as well as eastern, central and western regions. To reduce the heteroscedasticity, logarithmic form is taken when the model is regressed.

3.4.2. Explanatory Variable

Reverse technology spillover of OFDI ($SOFDI_{i,t}$) is taken as the core explanatory variable in this paper. Referring to the common practices in the existing literature [11,26], it can be measured by calculating the international R&D capital stock obtained from OFDI, as shown below:

$$SOFDI_{p,t} = \sum_q OFDI_{p,q,t} \times \frac{S_{q,t}}{GDP_{q,t}} \tag{4}$$

Among them, the subscripts p and q stand for home and host region, respectively. $OFDI_{p,q,t}$ stands for the investment stock from region p to q in period t; $GDP_{q,t}$ and $S_{q,t}$ stand for the gross domestic product (GDP) and R&D capital stock of the host region q, respectively. $S_{q,t}$ can be further expressed as:

$$S_{q,t} = S_{q,t-1} \times (1 - \delta) + RD_{q,t} \tag{5}$$

Among them, δ denotes the depreciation rate, set as 5%; $RD_{q,t}$ stands for the R&D expenditure of region q in period t. Considering that the sample period of this paper starts from 2005, $S_{q,2005}$ can be calculated as:

$$S_{q,2005} = \frac{RD_{q,2005}}{g + \delta} \tag{6}$$

Among them, g denotes the average growth rate of R&D expenditure from 2005 to 2019. The R&D expenditure is obtained by multiplying the R&D intensity of country q by its GDP denominated in USD. In order to eliminate the influence of price factors, the consumer price index of each country from 2005 to 2019 is used to convert the R&D expenditure with 2005 as the constant price. Based on data availability, and considering that technology seeking OFDI going to developed economies can better realize learning of foreign advanced technologies, this paper selects 11 countries and regions as the main sources for China to absorb international technology spillover: Hong Kong, Japan, South Korea, Singapore, Russia, Germany, The Netherlands, the United Kingdom, the United States, Canada and Australia. By the end of 2020, China's OFDI stock in the aforementioned 11 countries and regions had totaled USD 1706.92 billion, accounting for 66.14% of China's global OFDI stock. Using the R&D stock in 2005 of 11 countries and regions, $S_{q,t}$ from 2006 to 2019 can be obtained, which is further summed up to calculate international R&D capital stock from OFDI of the whole China.

Based on the above, reverse technology spillover of OFDI for every provincial region can be calculated using Equation (7), where $OFDI_{i,t}$ and $OFDI_{p,t}$ stand for non-financial OFDI stocks of provincial region i and the whole China, respectively.

$$SOFDI_{i,t} = SOFDI_{p,t} \times \frac{OFDI_{i,t}}{OFDI_{p,t}} \tag{7}$$

3.4.3. Control Variables

Referring to existing literature [12–14,18,19], this paper includes the following control variables:

(1) Lag term of GTFP ($GTFP_{i,t-1}$). The growth of GTFP may be continuous, and the previous period of GTFP may lead the growth of the later. Logarithmic form is taken when the model is regressed to reduce the heteroscedasticity.

(2) Technology spillover of import ($SIMP_{i,t}$). Generally, the greater the actual import volume of a country, the stronger the reverse technology spillover. The calculation method of $SIMP_{i,t}$ is similar to that of reverse technology spillover of OFDI. Logarithmic form is taken when the model is regressed to reduce the heteroscedasticity.

(3) R&D stock of domestic manufacturing ($SRD_{i,t}$). Due to the relative lack of R&D data for provincial manufacturing, this paper uses the internal expenditure of R&D funds of industrial enterprises above the scale in every provincial region to replace the R&D funds of the manufacturing industry, and adopts the perpetual inventory method to convert it into stock data. Logarithmic form is taken when the model is regressed to reduce the heteroscedasticity.

(4) Human capital ($HUM_{i,t}$). The higher the level of human capital, the more conducive to the development of technological innovation. According to Barro and Lee [42], this paper employs the average years of education of the labor force to approximate the level of human capital. Logarithmic form is taken when the model is regressed to reduce the heteroscedasticity.

(5) Economic development ($GDP_{i,t}$). A higher level of economic development means a higher level of scientific and technological research and innovation in the region, and a stronger ability to absorb advanced technologies. The level of economic development is generally expressed by regional GDP. In order to eliminate the influence of population factors on GDP, this paper uses per capita GDP as the representation of economic development level.

(6) Financial development ($FIN_{i,t}$). The higher the level of financial development, the smaller the financing constraints of regional enterprises, and the more favorable it is for enterprises to carry out foreign investment activities. In this paper, the ratio of year-end credit to GDP of financial institutions is selected as the proxy index of financial development level.

Among the above control variables, human capital, financial development and economic development can reflect the local absorptive capacity for advanced technology spillover. Therefore, this paper selects these three variables as the moderating variables in the mechanism model, forming an interactive item with the core explanatory variable. That is, $INTER_{i,t}$ in Equation (3) can be expressed as $HUM_{i,t} \times SOFDI_{i,t}$, $GDP_{i,t} \times SOFDI_{i,t}$ and $FIN_{i,t} \times SOFDI_{i,t}$. Descriptive statistics of each variable are shown in Table 1.

Table 1. Descriptive statistics of variables.

Variables	Obs	Mean	Std	Min	Max
$\ln GTFP$	450	0.028	0.397	−1.337	1.278
$\ln SOFDI$	450	−0.634	2.1	−7.247	4.039
$\ln SIMP$	450	2.241	0.133	1.861	2.632
$\ln SRD$	450	3.12	1.63	−1.39	6.573
$\ln HUM$	450	3.858	1.643	−3.429	7.26
GDP	450	0.641	0.417	0.065	2.381
FIN	450	3.005	1.146	1.288	8.131

4. Empirical Results and Description

In order to avoid spurious regression of panel data in empirical analysis, this paper tests the stationarity of data before regression analysis. CADF test and CIPS test are used to improve the accuracy, and the null hypothesis of both tests is that there is a unit root. The results show that all variables have no unit root, that is, the variables are stationary.

4.1. Baseline Regression

The regression results of the baseline model are presented in Table 2. Through stepwise regression, variables that may cause multicollinearity are eliminated. The P value of the Hansen test in column (7) is 0.465, which is smaller than 0.1, indicating that there is no over identification problem for the tool variables selected in the model, and the selection of tool variables is effective; the p value of the AR (2) test is 0.384, indicating that the random disturbance term of the residual does not have second-order sequence correlation, and the endogenous problem of the model has been well solved.

Table 2. Empirical results of baseline model using SYS-GMM model.

Variables	(1)	(2)	(3)	(4)	(5)	(6)	(7)
$\ln SOFDI$	−0.186 * (−1.83)	−0.020 *** (−3.07)	−0.040 *** (−3.43)	−0.040 ** (−2.41)	−0.070 *** (−3.03)	−0.928 ** (−2.58)	−0.810 *** (−3.25)
$\ln GTFP_{t-1}$		0.991 *** (16.22)	0.959 *** (25.65)	0.974 *** (28.39)	0.943 *** (25.36)	0.785 *** (26.24)	0.860 *** (26.37)
$\ln SIMP$			0.057 *** (3.76)	0.057 *** (3.76)	0.052 *** (3.04)	0.533 *** (3.40)	0.574 *** (3.78)
$\ln SRD$				0.026 (1.25)	0.014 (0.91)	0.345 (1.55)	0.288 ** (1.83)
$\ln HUM$					0.483 *** (3.05)	5.782 ** (2.43)	3.287 ** (2.38)
GDP						−1.197 ** (−2.22)	−1.560 *** (−2.88)
FIN							0.318 ** (2.14)
Constant	−0.090 (−0.83)	−0.019 (−1.82)	−0.280 *** (−3.84)	−1.930 *** (−2.79)	−1.420 *** (−3.12)	−8.667 * (−2.49)	−11.100 *** (−3.07)
AR(2)	1.59 (0.112)	0.43 (0.669)	0.89 (0.376)	0.79 (0.429)	1.01 (0.313)	0.79 (0.432)	0.87 (0.384)
Hansen	20.36 (0.119)	28.38 (0.291)	28.21 (0.453)	27.87 (0.472)	27.96 (0.467)	15.0 (0.307)	12.78 (0.465)
N	450	450	450	450	450	450	450

Note: (1) The numbers in brackets are the t statistics corresponding to the regression coefficient; ***, ** and * indicate that they have passed the significance test at the 1%, 5% and 10% confidence levels, respectively, with the same interpretations below. (2) The numbers in brackets of Hansen test are the P statistics to check the rationality of tool variables, the same as in the following table.

The regression results of columns (1)–(7) robustly show that the coefficient of reverse technology spillover of OFDI ($SOFDI$) is always significant. That is to say, Hypothesis 1 raised in the theoretical analysis is acceptable. From the sign of coefficient, it can be observed that the impact of reverse technology spillover of OFDI on GTFP is negative. This is consistent with the research conclusions of Bitzer and Kerekes [23] and Li et al. [24]. Column (5) is the result of using the complete Equation (2), indicating that GTFP decreases by 0.81% for every 1% increase in reverse technology spillover of OFDI. This may be because the negative impact of China's OFDI to developed countries, such as capital crowding-out effect and external dependence effect, is more obvious than the positive impact of R&D feedback effect, cost allocation effect and resource optimization effect.

The coefficient of lag term of GTFP ($GTFP_{t-1}$) is 0.860, which is significant at the level of 1%, indicating that the growth of GTFP of the manufacturing industry is not only affected by explanatory variables, but also by the GTFP of the previous year, and the GTFP of the last year plays a positive demonstration role for this year. For other control variables, the coefficient of technology spillover obtained through import ($SIMP$) is 0.574 and significant at the level of 1%, indicating that every 1% increase in technology spillover obtained through import will drive the GTFP of the manufacturing industry up by 0.574%. Import trade provides opportunities for domestic enterprises to learn, imitate and absorb foreign advanced technologies, thus improving the level of domestic manufacturing GTFP. R&D stock of domestic manufacturing (SRD) is significant at the level of 5%, with a coefficient of 0.288, indicating that the more domestic R&D investment accumulation to the purchase of advanced equipment and the introduction of technical personnel, the more it promotes the improvement of manufacturing GTFP. The coefficient of human capital level (HUM) is 3.287 and significantly positive, indicating that the higher the level of human capital, the better domestic enterprises can learn, identify and absorb foreign advanced technical knowledge. At the same time, the improvement of human capital will also promote the independent technological innovation of enterprises to a certain extent, thereby further driving the improvement of GTFP. The coefficient of economic development (GDP) equals −1.56 and significant at the level of 1%, indicating that the economic development level has a certain inhibiting effect on the manufacturing GTFP. The possible reason is that the improvement of China's economic development level during the sample period is still based on large-scale energy consumption, and the economic development is not fully compatible with green development. The coefficient of financial development (FIN) is significantly positive, indicating that China's financial development has actively promoted the absorption of reverse technology spillovers. Reverse technology spillover of OFDI is mainly concentrated in high-tech fields with high investment and risk. A sound financial system can facilitate enterprise financing, reduce financing costs and improve financing efficiency, thus promoting technology diffusion, transfer and absorption.

4.2. Robustness Test

Two methods are adopted for robustness testing in this section. First, this paper uses practice of Zhang and Li [43] for reference, removes 1% of the minimum and maximum values of GTFP and re-estimates Equation (2) to overcome the influence of the abnormal values and non-randomness of explained variable on the regression. Secondly, this paper adjusts the calculation method of core explanatory variables referring to the methods of Rong et al. [44], that is, replace $GDP_{q,t}$ with $K_{q,t}$ in the calculation formula of reverse technology spillover of OFDI. Based on this, Equation (4) is reformulated as below:

$$SOFDI_{p,t} = \sum_q OFDI_{p,q,t} \times \frac{S_{q,t}}{K_{q,t}} \tag{8}$$

The robustness test results are shown in Table 3. It can be seen that the two methods both pass the Hansen test, and the values of AR (2) are greater than 0.1. The coefficients of the core explanatory variables are significantly negative at the levels of 5% and 1%, respectively, and all the other control variables pass the significance test except R&D stock of domestic manufacturing (SRD) in column (1), which is basically the same as the results in the baseline regression. The above results demonstrate that the conclusion of this paper is robust.

Table 3. Empirical results of robustness test using SYS-GMM model.

Variables	(1)	(2)
$\ln SOFDI$	−0.785 ** (−2.64)	−0.793 *** (−3.28)
$\ln GTFP_{t-1}$	0.830 *** (6.45)	0.844 *** (6.48)
$\ln SIMP$	0.558 *** (2.92)	0.570 *** (3.87)
$\ln SRD$	0.268 (1.65)	0.287 * (1.77)
$\ln HUM$	2.957 * (2.01)	3.107 *** (2.35)
GDP	−1.466 ** (−2.20)	−1.540 *** (−2.84)
FIN	0.305 * (1.79)	0.326 *** (2.23)

Table 3. *Cont.*

Variables	(1)	(2)
Constant	−10.369 ** (−2.55)	−10.807 *** (−3.10)
AR(2)	−0.51 (0.608)	0.92 (0.358)
Hansen	13.54 (0.331)	12.41 (0.495)
N	441	450

Note: ***, ** and * indicate significance at the 1%, 5%, and 10% levels, respectively.

4.3. Heterogeneity Analysis

Different regions are quite different in resource endowment, economic development basis, policy support and technological innovation capacity, so the overall sample may be difficult to make a reasonable assessment of how reverse technology spillover of OFDI affect GTFP in different regions of China. It is of great practical significance to further analyze the regional heterogeneity. Thus, this paper divides 30 regions into the eastern region, the central region and the western region, and performs sub-sample regression to verify Hypothesis 2. On the basis of the baseline regression model, the heterogeneity analysis takes the eastern region as the reference system, introduces two dummy variables representing the central and western regions, and also employs the SYS-GMM method to estimate the dynamic panel. See Table 4 for the estimation results.

Table 4. Empirical results of regional heterogeneity test using SYS-GMM model.

Variables	Eastern	Central	Western
$\ln SOFDI$	−1.260 * (−2.08)	0.741 * (1.88)	0.678 * (1.86)
$\ln GTFP_{t-1}$		1.182 *** (5.25)	
$\ln SIMP$		0.474 * (2.06)	
$\ln SRD$		0.436 * (1.99)	
$\ln HUM$		2.063 (1.66)	
GDP		−1.463 * (−1.72)	
FIN		0.450 * (1.79)	
Constant		−8.698 ** (−2.20)	
AR(2)		0.34 (0.735)	
Hansen		14.36 (0.349)	
N		450	

Note: ***, ** and * indicate significance at the 1%, 5%, and 10% levels, respectively.

The regression results show that the impact of reverse technology spillover of OFDI on manufacturing GTFP varies significantly among regions. In the central and western regions, reverse technology spillover of OFDI play a positive role in promoting GTFP significantly with coefficients of 0.741 and 0.678, respectively, of which the effect in the central region is slightly greater than that in the western region. However, the coefficient of core explanatory variable in the eastern region is −1.260, indicating that for every 1% increase in reverse technology spillover of OFDI, the manufacturing GTFP in the eastern region will decline by 1.260%. This partly explains the results of full sample regression, as more than 80% of

China's technology seeking OFDI flowing to developed countries come from the eastern region. Although OFDI in the central and western regions has grown rapidly in recent years, their overall scales are still small.

Why does reverse technology spillover of OFDI in the eastern region inhibit domestic manufacturing GTFP? The core reason may be that enterprises in the eastern region have stronger independent R&D ability, a smaller technology gap with overseas and a larger scale of OFDI compared with the central and western regions. According to the conditional convergence theory, when the technology gap between the two countries is small, the technology learning space of OFDI activities will be limited, because the subsidiary in the host country can hardly acquire more advanced knowledge and cannot provide much help for the green production of the parent company in the home country. In this case, from the perspective of technology acquisition, a larger scale of OFDI from the eastern region will squeeze more investment in independent R&D of enterprises in the home country. Especially when there is "incomplete information" in OFDI activities, the R&D spillover investment of the host country will also have "repeated consumption" with the domestic R&D funds, resulting in resource waste. As a result, the crowding-out effect caused by reverse technology spillover of OFDI will be amplified in the eastern region, while the positive effects such as R&D feedback and resource optimization are relatively insignificant, which eventually lead to the suppression of manufacturing GTFP.

4.4. Moderating Analysis

The results of baseline regression show that reverse technology spillover of OFDI fails to promote the GTFP of the manufacturing industry in the sample period. So, does an increase in domestic absorptive capacity help ameliorate this negative effect? To answer this question, Hypothesis 3 is proposed in the theoretical analysis, and interactive items composed of human capital, economic development, financial development and reverse technology spillover of OFDI are added as auxiliary explanatory variables in the baseline model. The regression results using SYS-GMM are shown in Table 5.

It can be found that the coefficients of the three interactive items in the regression results are all significantly positive, and the coefficients of the core explanatory variables are still significantly negative, but their absolute values are reduced compared with those of baseline regression. On this basis, Hypothesis 3 is validated: the improvement of absorptive capacity can weaken the negative impact of reverse technology spillover of OFDI on manufacturing GTFP, and promote the improvement effect of the former on the latter. By contrast, the coefficient of the interactive item composed of financial development and core explanatory variable is equal to 0.030, which is significant at the 5% level and relatively higher than that of the other two groups representing absorptive capacity. This means that financial development can play a more active role in the process of reverse technology spillover of OFDI affecting the manufacturing GTFP. Through relaxing regional financial constraints, enterprises can gradually enhance the ability to absorb and digest foreign technologies acquired through OFDI, and amplify positive effects such as R&D feedback. At the same time, enterprises can also invest sufficient funds to improve their independent R&D capabilities, thereby weakening the crowding-out effect of reverse technology spillover of OFDI, and comprehensively promote the manufacturing GTFP. The coefficients of the other two interactive items are both equal to 0.020, significant at the 5% level. This indicates that the accumulation of human capital and the promotion of regional economic development can both effectively improve the absorptive capacity of local enterprises to advanced technologies, and then help enterprises to better use the reverse technology spillover of OFDI to improve the GTFP of the whole manufacturing industry.

Table 5. Empirical results of moderating effect test using SYS-GMM model.

Variables	(1)	(2)	(3)
$\ln SOFDI$	−0.611 *** (−3.56)	−0.668 *** (−3.51)	−0.636 *** (−3.50)
$HUM \times SOFDI$	0.020 ** (2.13)		
$GDP \times SOFDI$		0.020 ** (2.12)	
$FIN \times SOFDI$			0.030 ** (1.85)
$\ln GTFP_{t-1}$	0.864 *** (8.17)	0.842 *** (7.30)	0.850 *** (7.59)
$\ln SIMP$	0.407 *** (3.82)	0.455 *** (3.84)	0.430 *** (3.65)
$\ln SRD$	0.204 * (1.91)	0.228 ** (1.89)	0.219 * (1.90)
$\ln HUM$	2.500 ** (2.46)	2.766 ** (2.48)	2.599 ** (2.43)
GDP	−1.080 *** (−2.92)	−1.260 *** (−2.96)	−1.143 ** (−2.72)
FIN	0.200 * (1.87)	0.229 * (1.90)	0.207 * (1.74)
$Constant$	−8.320 *** (−3.20)	−9.210 *** (−3.22)	−8.687 (−3.15)
AR(2)	0.13 (1.49)	0.15 (1.44)	0.14 (1.46)
Hansen	0.223 (16.51)	0.251 (15.97)	0.244 (16.09)
N	450	450	450

Note: ***, ** and * indicate significance at the 1%, 5%, and 10% levels, respectively.

5. Conclusions and Policy Implications

This paper clarifies the impact of reverse technology spillover of OFDI on the GTFP of China's manufacturing industry by first conducting mechanism analysis theoretically. Then, the panel data of the manufacturing industry in 30 provinces of China and SYS-GMM regression model are adopted to quantitatively analyze the impact of reverse technology spillover of OFDI on GTFP and the moderating role of absorptive capacity in it. The results indicate that reverse technology spillover of OFDI has a negative effect on manufacturing GTFP on the whole. This conclusion is still valid after changing the sample size and the calculation method of the core explanatory variable. At a regional level, heterogeneity is reflected in that the reverse technology spillover of OFDI significantly inhibits manufacturing GTFP in the eastern region, while it has a positive impact both in the central and western regions, and the impact in the central region is greater than that in the western region. Moreover, the impact of reverse technology spillover of OFDI on manufacturing GTFP can be moderated by absorptive capacity. With the improvement of human capital, economic development and financial development, the inhibiting effect of reverse technology spillover of OFDI on manufacturing GTFP will be weakened, and the promoting effect will be enhanced. Among them, the moderating role of financial development as absorptive capacity is more positive than the other two indicators.

Based on the results of the empirical analysis, the following policy implications are put forward. First, it is necessary to implement regionally differentiated investment and improve investment quality. Due to the large differences in the scale of OFDI in different regions, reverse technology spillover of OFDI has different effects on manufacturing GTFP. Therefore, differentiated investment strategies should be implemented according to the actual region situation to maximize the positive effects of reverse technology spillover. For example, reverse technology spillover of OFDI in the central and western regions can significantly promote manufacturing GTFP, so regional governments should continue to provide various investment related policies and actively encourage enterprises to "go global". For the eastern region, large-scale overseas investment cannot promote the upgrading of regional manufacturing GTFP. The underlying reason may be that despite the large scale of OFDI in the eastern region, the proportion of technology acquisition is relatively low, and domestic R&D investment may be squeezed at the same time. Therefore, enterprises in the eastern region should improve the quality of OFDI through targeted investment in projects whose technology spillovers are needed by local development. At the same time, the government should pay more attention to maintaining the ability of independent innovation and promote the green development of the manufacturing industry in a two-pronged approach. Second, the government should improve the regional absorptive capacity and actively transform foreign advanced technologies. Absorptive capacity, which can be reflected in the accumulation of human capital, economic development and financial development, can help to reduce the negative effect of reverse technology spillover of OFDI on GTFP and magnify the positive effect. Therefore, the local government should pay attention to the introduction and training of high-tech personnel through strengthening the cooperation between domestic and foreign universities and research institutes, promote local economic development to tap market demand matching advanced technology and promote technological competition, and build a more active financial support system and improve the level of regional financial development to reduce the financing constraints of enterprises in the process of "going global".

To sum up, this paper takes China's manufacturing industry as the research object to verify the effect and moderating mechanism of reverse technology spillover of OFDI on domestic manufacturing GTFP theoretically and empirically. The results show that the reverse technology spillover of OFDI cannot significantly promote the growth of manufacturing GTFP based on the provincial data of China from 2005 to 2019, which is contrary to the research conclusions of Pan et al. [18], Bai et al. [12] and Song et al. [13], but supports the findings of Zhang and Ren [21] and Li et al. [24] to some extent. On this basis, this paper also verifies the heterogeneity of the above relationship in the eastern, central and western regions, which can provide targeted OFDI development reference according to the actual region situation. This is one of the important application contributions of this study. Moreover, this paper further explores the moderating mechanism of absorptive capacity, finding that human capital, economic development and financial development can all play important roles in the impact of reverse technology spillover of OFDI on GTFP, of which the positive moderating effect of financial development is the most significant. This can help China's manufacturing industry to select targeted forms and paths to amplify the positive promotion effect of OFDI on GTFP and encourage enterprises to carry out reverse technology spillover in the process of "going global".

This study provides a theoretical basis and policy reference for China to promote reverse technology spillover of OFDI and improve GTFP in the manufacturing industry. Nonetheless, this study has the following limitations. First, because of the data limitations, the time span chosen in this study to examine the impact of reverse technology spillover of OFDI on manufacturing GTFP is from 2005 to 2019, and the latest relationship after the pandemic cannot be analyzed. Second, the enterprise is the main element of OFDI, but due to the restriction of database, we only conducted research through industry panel data, without exploring typical cases or conducting research. In future research, we will seek breakthroughs in these aspects.

Author Contributions: Conceptualization, Y.L. and X.Z.; methodology, Y.L.; software, Y.L. and X.Z.; validation, X.Z., C.J. and Q.H.; formal analysis, X.Z.; data curation, C.J.; writing—original draft preparation, Y.L. and C.J.; writing—review and editing, X.Z. and Q.H.; funding acquisition, Q.H. All authors have read and agreed to the published version of the manuscript.

Funding: This research was funded by the Shenzhen Key Research Base Project of Humanities and Social Sciences: Research Center of Global Ocean Center City (grant number 2020 SZJD 07) and the Liaoning New Think Tank Project of Colleges and Universities: Research Center of Marine Economic Management (grant number 2020-10151-002).

Institutional Review Board Statement: Not applicable.

Informed Consent Statement: Not applicable.

Data Availability Statement: Not applicable.

Conflicts of Interest: The authors declare no conflict of interest.

Appendix A

Table A1. Literature comparison.

Reference	Methods	Variables	Data	Conclusions
Pan et al. 2020 [18]	Spatial measurement model	OFDI; Total factor carbon productivity	Period of 2004–2016; 30 provinces in China	Positive
Song et al. 2021 [13]	SYS-GMM	OFDI; Green total factor productivity	Period of 2000–2013; 412,654 firms in China	Positive
Dai et al. 2021 [19]	SYS-GMM	OFDI; Green innovation	Period of 2006–2017; 30 provinces in China	Negative but not significant
Luo and Liang 2017 [20]	Spatial measurement model	OFDI; Green technology innovation efficiency	Period of 2004–2015; 30 provinces in China	Negative
Zheng and Ran 2018 [21]	SYS-GMM	OFDI; Green total factor productivity	Period of 2003–2015; 30 provinces in China	Negative
He et al. 2022 [26]	Threshold model	OFDI; Total factor energy efficiency	Period of 2004–2017; 30 provinces in China	Nonlinear
Ren et al. 2022 [29]	Threshold model	OFDI; Green total factor energy efficiency	Period of 2006–2017; 30 provinces in China	Nonlinear

References

1. Cheng, M.L.; Shao, Z.; Yang, C.H.; Tang, X.A. Analysis of Coordinated Development of Energy and Environment in China's Manufacturing Industry under Environmental Regulation: A Comparative Study of Sub-Industries. *Sustainability* **2019**, *11*, 6510. [CrossRef]
2. 2020 Global Environmental Performance Index Assessment Report. Available online: https://envirocenter.yale.edu/2020-environmental-performance-index (accessed on 14 October 2022).
3. Report of the 19th National Congress of the Communist Party of China. Available online: http://english.mofcom.gov.cn/article/zt_19da/ (accessed on 14 October 2022).
4. Sun, Y.L.; Tang, Y.W.; Li, G. Economic growth targets and green total factor productivity: Evidence from China. *J. Environ. Plan. Manag.* **2022**, *4*, 2061335. [CrossRef]
5. Sarker, B.; Serieux, J. Foreign-invested and domestic firm attributes and spillover effects: Evidence from Brazil. *J. Multinatl. Financ. Manag.* **2022**, *63*, 100719. [CrossRef]
6. Salim, A.; Razavi, M.R.; Afshari-Mofrad, M. Foreign direct investment and technology spillover in Iran: The role of technological capabilities of subsidiaries. *Technol. Forecast. Soc. Chang.* **2017**, *122*, 207–214. [CrossRef]
7. Brandao, L.G.L.; Ehrl, P. International R&D spillovers to the electric power industries. *Energy* **2019**, *182*, 424–432.
8. Wang, Z.B.; Zhang, L.; Han, L.Y. Knowledge-seeking and firm international performance: Evidence from Chinese multinational enterprises. *Int. Rev. Financ. Anal.* **2021**, *77*, 101823. [CrossRef]
9. Kogut, B.; Chang, S.J. Technological capabilities and Japanese foreign direct investment in the United States. *Rev. Econ. Stat.* **1991**, *73*, 401–413. [CrossRef]
10. Hong, J.; Zhou, C.Y.; Wu, Y.R.; Wang, R.C.; Marinova, D. Technology Gap, Reverse Technology Spillover and Domestic Innovation Performance in Outward Foreign Direct Investment: Evidence from China. *China World Econ.* **2019**, *27*, 1–23. [CrossRef]
11. Fahad, S.; Bai, D.B.; Liu, L.C.; Dagar, V. Comprehending the environmental regulation, biased policies and OFDI reverse technology spillover effects: A contingent and dynamic perspective. *Environ. Sci. Pollut. Res.* **2022**, *29*, 33167–33179. [CrossRef]
12. Bai, Y.; Qian, Q.Q.; Jiao, J.L.; Li, L.L.; Li, F.Y.; Yang, R.R. Can environmental innovation benefit from outward foreign direct investment to developed countries? Evidence from Chinese manufacturing enterprises. *Environ. Sci. Pollut. Res.* **2020**, *27*, 13790–13808. [CrossRef]

13. Song, Y.G.; Hao, F.; Hao, X.Z.; Gozgor, G. Economic Policy Uncertainty, Outward Foreign Direct Investments, and Green Total Factor Productivity: Evidence from Firm-Level Data in China. *Sustainability* **2021**, *13*, 2339. [CrossRef]
14. Li, X.; Zhou, W.; Hou, J. Research on the impact of OFDI on the home country's global value chain upgrading. *Int. Rev. Financ. Anal.* **2021**, *77*, 101862. [CrossRef]
15. Hasanat Shah, S.; Ameer, W. The impact of outbound foreign direct investment on export and private investment: Comparative analysis of emerging and developed countries. *Aust. Econ. Pap.* **2021**, *60*, 674–692. [CrossRef]
16. Hao, Y.; Guo, Y.X.; Guo, Y.T.; Wu, H.T.; Ren, S.Y. Does outward foreign direct investment (OFDI) affect the home country's environmental quality? The case of China. *Struct. Chang. Econ. Dyn.* **2020**, *52*, 109–119. [CrossRef]
17. Liu, H.Q.; Peng, C.A.L.; Chen, L.X. The impact of OFDI on the energy efficiency in Chinese provinces: Based on PVAR model. *Energy Rep.* **2022**, *8*, 84–96. [CrossRef]
18. Pan, X.F.; Li, M.N.; Wang, M.Y.; Chu, J.H.; Bo, H.G. The effects of outward foreign direct investment and reverse technology spillover on China's carbon productivity. *Energy Policy* **2020**, *145*, 111730. [CrossRef]
19. Dai, L.H.; Mu, X.R.; Lee, C.C.; Liu, W. The impact of outward foreign direct investment on green innovation: The threshold effect of environmental regulation. *Environ. Sci. Pollut. Res.* **2021**, *28*, 34868–34884. [CrossRef] [PubMed]
20. Luo, L.W.; Liang, S.R. The spatial effect of international R&D capital technology spillovers on the efficiency of China's green technology innovation. *Bus. Manag. J.* **2017**, *39*, 21–33.
21. Zheng, Q.; Ran, G.H. Effects of two-way FDI on green productivity spillover in China: An empirical test based on dynamic panel model. *J. Stat. Inform.* **2018**, *33*, 54–61.
22. Lee, G. The effectiveness of international knowledge spillover channels. *Eur. Econ. Rev.* **2006**, *50*, 2075–2088. [CrossRef]
23. Bitzer, J.; Kerekes, M. Does foreign direct investment transfer technology across borders? New evidence. *Econ. Lett.* **2008**, *100*, 355–358. [CrossRef]
24. Li, C.C.; Luo, Y.; De Vita, G. Institutional difference and outward FDI: Evidence from China. *Empir. Econ.* **2020**, *58*, 1837–1862. [CrossRef]
25. Zhu, S.P.; Ye, A.Z. Does the Impact of China's Outward Foreign Direct Investment on Reverse Green Technology Process Differ across Countries? *Sustainability* **2018**, *10*, 3841. [CrossRef]
26. He, Y.; Zuo, H.Y.; Liao, N. Assessing the impact of reverse technology spillover of outward foreign direct investment on energy efficiency. *Environ. Dev. Sustain.* **2022**, *2*, 02204. [CrossRef]
27. Liu, L.Y.; Zhao, Z.Z.; Zhang, M.M.; Zhou, C.X.; Zhou, D.Q. The effects of environmental regulation on outward foreign direct investment's reverse green technology spillover: Crowding out or facilitation? *J. Clean Prod.* **2021**, *284*, 124689. [CrossRef]
28. Luo, Y.S.; Salman, M.; Lu, Z.N. Heterogeneous impacts of environmental regulations and foreign direct investment on green innovation across different regions in China. *Sci. Total Environ.* **2021**, *759*, 143744. [CrossRef]
29. Ren, S.Y.; Hao, Y.; Wu, H.T. The role of outward foreign direct investment (OFDI) on green total factor energy efficiency: Does institutional quality matters? Evidence from China. *Resour. Policy* **2022**, *76*, 102587. [CrossRef]
30. Long, W.B.; Luo, L.; Sun, H.F.; Zhong, Q.Q. Does going abroad lead to going green? Firm outward foreign direct investment and domestic environmental performance. *Bus. Strateg. Environ.* **2022**, *5*, 3156. [CrossRef]
31. Jiang, M.R.; Luo, S.M.; Zhou, G.Y. Financial development, OFDI spillovers and upgrading of industrial structure. *Technol. Forecast. Soc. Chang.* **2020**, *155*, 119974. [CrossRef]
32. Martinez-Sanchez, A.; Vicente-Oliva, S.; Perez-Perez, M. The strategy of human resource flexibility versus absorptive capacity of knowledge An integrative framework in industrial firms. *Eur. J. Innov. Manag.* **2021**, *24*, 315–337. [CrossRef]
33. Tian, G. How Does Outward Foreign Direct Investment Affect Green Total Factor Productivity? Evidence from Increment and Quality Improvement. *Sustainability* **2022**, *14*, 11833. [CrossRef]
34. Zhou, Y.; Jiang, J.J.; Ye, B.; Hou, B.J. Green spillovers of outward foreign direct investment on home countries: Evidence from China's province-level data. *J. Clean Prod.* **2019**, *215*, 829–844. [CrossRef]
35. Liang, W.H.; Liu, H. The Mechanism and Empirical Study of FDI Driving China's Technological Progress: A Comparative Perspective. *Inq. Econ. Issues* **2017**, *2*, 111–117.
36. Su, R.J.; Li, L. Reverse Technology Spillover Effect of FDI in Manufacturing Industry: An Analysis Based on the Impact of Technology Gap. *Macroecon.* **2021**, *7*, 66–78+126.
37. Wu, F.; Fu, X.P.; Zhang, T.; Wu, D.; Sindakis, S. Examining Whether Government Environmental Regulation Promotes Green Innovation Efficiency-Evidence from China's Yangtze River Economic Belt. *Sustainability* **2022**, *14*, 1827. [CrossRef]
38. Coe, D.T.; Helpman, E.; Hoffmaister, A.W. International R&D spillovers and institutions. *Eur. Econ. Rev.* **2009**, *53*, 723–741.
39. van Pottelsberghe, B.; Lichtenberg, F. Does foreign direct investment transfer technology across borders? *Rev. Econ. Stat.* **2001**, *83*, 490–497.
40. Tone, K. A slacks-based measure of efficiency in data envelopment analysis. *Eur. J. Oper. Res.* **2001**, *130*, 498–509. [CrossRef]
41. Oh, D.H. A global Malmquist-Luenberger productivity index. *J. Prod. Anal.* **2010**, *34*, 183–197. [CrossRef]
42. Barro, R.J.; Lee, J.W. International comparisons of educational attainment. *J. Monetary Econ.* **1993**, *32*, 363–394. [CrossRef]
43. Zhang, J.; Li, Z.F. Does OFDI Promote Green TFP Growth in China: An Empirical Study Based on Dynamic System GMM Estimation and Threshold Model. *J. Int. Trade* **2020**, *9*, 159–174.
44. Rong, S.; Yang, M.H.; Zeng, J.; Gui, X.L. Does the Goverment Support Policy Promote the Reverse Technology Spillover of OFDI in China? Based on the Threshold Effect Analysis. *Macroeconomics* **2020**, *11*, 86–101.

sustainability

MDPI

Review

Managerial Dilemmas and Entrepreneurial Challenges in the Ambidexterity of SMEs: A Systematic Review for Execution System

Gayoung Kim [1], Woo Jin Lee [2] and Hoshik Shim [1,*]

1 College of Business Administration, Kookmin University, Seoul 02707, Republic of Korea
2 Graduate School of Global Entrepreneurship, Kookmin University, Seoul 02707, Republic of Korea
* Correspondence: Correspondence: hsshim@kookmin.ac.kr; Tel.: +82-2-910-5658

Abstract: According to the organizational learning theory, there are two types of corporate activities, exploitation and exploration, for enhancing and improving corporate performance. However, organizations are continually faced with choosing between these two conflicting activities that require different organizational structures, strategies, and environments, respectively. This study's objective is to use a systematic review methodology to investigate how implementing organizational ambidexterity affects managerial performance in small- and medium-sized enterprises (SMEs). Although there is a general consensus about the relationship between ambidexterity and firm performance, few studies have probed into the mechanism of how it is applied to management process and what antecedents affect the implementation of OA in SMEs. The qualitative method was conducted to investigate the influence of the ambidexterity strategy of SMEs on firm performance. According to the findings, organizational ambidexterity in SMEs has a positive impact on the firm's managerial performance. SMEs must make decisions that consider environmental factors. Making practical decisions based on accurate formation, considering organizational human resources for implementing ambidexterity, and sharing specific performance goals are all important considerations. This study is also important for SMEs' top management teams to make proper decisions for the firm's sustainable growth via OA, and shed new light on the literature of organization theory that operates in a more turbulent environment.

Keywords: SMEs; organizational ambidexterity; organizational learning theory; systematic review

Citation: Kim, G.; Lee, W.J.; Shim, H. Managerial Dilemmas and Entrepreneurial Challenges in the Ambidexterity of SMEs: A Systematic Review for Execution System. *Sustainability* **2022**, *14*, 16550. https://doi.org/10.3390/su142416550

Academic Editors: Jeoung Yul Lee, Dilek Zamantili Nayir and Charles Chen

Received: 28 October 2022
Accepted: 6 December 2022
Published: 9 December 2022

1. Introduction

The company maximizes corporate operation efficiency by maximizing the exploitation of accumulated resources through management. However, in today's market environment of high market uncertainty, businesses must explore new opportunities. Exploration activities at a company can capitalize on opportunities for new products, services, and innovative technologies. So, in today's companies, exploitation should be performed simultaneously with exploration. Companies must establish a process that balances exploitation and exploration [1]. Large enterprises have relatively abundant resources. However, because resources are always scarce, it is difficult for small- and medium-sized enterprises (SMEs) and ventures (hereinafter referred to as SMEs) to balance exploitation and exploration [2]. Various studies suggest approaches for carrying out these two activities. Organizational ambidexterity refers to an organization's ability to pursue and balance these two activities at the same time. Recently, SMEs and ventures have also adopted an ambidexterity strategy that simultaneously operates exploitation and exploration for performance and survival [3,4].

This research looked at the ambidexterity strategies of SMEs that are growing with limited resources. Various methods of implementing ambidexterity have been studied according to the environment and situation of the enterprise. Due to a lack of resources and management skills, SMEs always face greater challenges when seeking ambivalence [5]. This is especially likely for SMEs in transitional and high-growth industries, where top management teams are confronted with and must choose from a plethora of future business opportunities. Many previous studies have discussed OA in SMEs, but there is no integrated research and, therefore, no clear implications that SMEs could apply to their business.

The goal of this study is to expand on previous research on organizational ambidexterity in SMEs by looking into the factors that influence the relationship between OA and SME performance. Although many scholars have studied the relationship between ambidexterity and firm performance, few studies have looked into how it is applied to management processes and what factors influence OA implementation in SMEs. The research questions of this study are as follows:

(1) What factors influence the implementation of organizational ambidexterity in SMEs, and how do different types of organizational ambidexterity affect SMEs' performance?
(2) How should SMEs that have been through the effectuation process develop an ambidexterity strategy?

Some of the additional research questions that could flow from this main question are: Do SMEs that were developed on the basis of the effectuation process after startup choose organizational ambidexterity for their firm's future growth? Can SMEs expect the same effect as large firms through the implementation of organizational ambidexterity? Although scholars have studied this emerging topic for more than 15 years, there has been limited research conducted in the field of SMEs. This study is also important for SMEs' top management teams to make proper decisions for the firm's sustainable growth via OA. Undertaking a careful analysis of the mechanism of organizational ambidexterity in SMEs, this study may shed new light on the literature of organization theory that operates in a more turbulent environment.

2. Literature Review

2.1. The Concept of Exploitation and Exploration

March (1991) [2] published a key paper on exploitation and exploration in organizational learning, which clearly stated the notion of the activities required by the firm. Exploitation implies an organization's activities, such as efficiency, selection, execution, production, as well as firms learning to enhance their existing capabilities and competencies, using existing knowledge, focusing on current activities, mitigating risks, and predicting outcomes through exploitation in their existing business [3,6,7]. Organizational activities associated with exploration include variation, new knowledge, experimentation, flexibility, long-term needs, risk-taking, entrepreneurship, and innovation [8–10]. Exploration, in other words, refers to the development of new organizational routines, as well as the discovery of new technologies, products, business opportunities, and processes [9,11,12].

Based on the conceptual understanding of exploitation and exploration, previous studies have identified what each activity produces as an outcome within the organization. Juni et al. (2013) [3] found that exploratory activity was primarily related to the firm's long-term growth in their meta-analysis. While the firm's exploration activities may not impact immediate profit, they eventually positively impact growth [13]. In contrast, firms pursuing productivity efficiency rather than innovation were the focus of exploitation activity [3,14]. That is, the firm's exploitative activities mainly relate to the firm's current profits but do not closely relate to growth [3]. Organizations may abandon a promising and seemingly attractive business opportunity because stakeholders perceive the opportunity as overly disruptive. [15].

Because it is hard to choose just one of the two strategies, previous research on ambidexterity has argued that firms must balance exploitation and exploration [16]. The ability to aim and apply exploration and exploitation has been suggested as essential for the long-term performance and survival of organizations [3,4]. Furthermore, according to Schumpeterian theory, innovative organizations outperform noninnovative ones, and ambidextrous organizations outperform businesses that focus solely on one strategy, such as exploitation or exploration [17].

However, organizational ambidexterity is recognized as a paradoxical characteristic in the sense of pursuing two different activities at the same time as evidenced by the use of various terminologies in various studies. Scholars, for example, assert that causation and effectuation are not mutually exclusive but rather interactive relationships [18,19] and that these two strategies can be viewed as distinct types of exploitation and exploration [2,20,21], cost leadership and differentiation [22], competition and collaboration [23], and efficiency and flexibility [24,25].

2.2. Characteristics of SMEs

SMEs face greater difficulties than large corporations when pursuing an ambidexterity strategy. The majority of previous studies on ambidexterity have concentrated on large corporations. However, in recent years, there has been a growing body of literature studying the practice of ambidexterity at the scope of SMEs, such as ventures, high-tech startups, and entrepreneurial firms [26]. Many SMEs face managerial quandaries regarding their growth, such as whether to pursue differentiation or low cost as a strategy, adopt a mechanistic or flexible structure, or prioritize control or autonomy [27]. SMEs may require a new logic to effectively manage their resources and introduce entrepreneurial bricolage, which is defined as "making do by applying combinations of the resources at hand to new problems and opportunities" [28]. SMEs' core competencies and management skills are to overcome scarce resources and operate ambidextrous organizations.

This study helps to broaden the recognition and integration of organizational ambidexterity in SMEs, as well as the practical difficulties and factors that affect their ability to engage in two different activities related to SMEs' performance.

2.3. Features of Organizational Ambidexterity

Firms can use organizational ambidexterity to solve conflict and the dilemma of paradoxes by employing a few typologies. In previous studies, two ambidextrous methods, contextual and structural ambidexterity, were most representatively presented. Structural ambidexterity is defined as the separation of individuals or groups based on the action plan of an organization [29–31]. To address the conflict and dilemma created by the paradoxes of balancing exploration and exploitation, firms establish separate units that respond to environmental changes and communicate with external stakeholders.

On the other hand, contextual ambidexterity is defined as performing both two strategies at an individual level in the organizational unit [30]. Individuals focus on the organization's regular activities while also undertaking new activities [30]. According to this HRM viewpoint, an ambidextrous structure enables an organization to better take advantage of business opportunities while holding onto its current market share. However, when implementing contextual ambidexterity, an important question about who can manage an individual arises [5,32].

Previous literature suggests another pathway to achieve organizational ambidexterity for firms; sequential ambidexterity [31,33]. Sequential ambidexterity refers to an organization's focus on one of the competing objectives in turn.

Firms achieve different structural alternatives, such as structural or contextual separation, to resolve the organizational paradox. While earlier studies argued that firms should build separate organizational units to gain the benefits of adaptability and alignment at the same time [16,34,35]. However, the separated units may not be effective for SMEs due to their small size and limited resources. In reality, these structures hinder the sharing of knowledge and capabilities with the mainstream units. Thus, Duncan (1976) [36] suggests that organizations should implement a dual structure that allows them to structurally respond to their environment while pursuing both exploration and exploitation.

As a result, the focus of this research has been on the factors that enable organizations to create dual structures, as well as the systems and processes that facilitate ambidexterity for SME performance.

2.4. Performance in the SME Organizations

Empirical studies have already indicated that ambidextrous organizations have a positive effect on the firm's performance [4,5,33,37–41]. Many studies have proposed that organizational ambidexterity is related to a longer period of survival [42], better financial performance [43–45], and improved learning and innovation [46,47], whether directly related to the firm's performance or not.

However, scholars still have arguments that pursuing such organizational ambidexterity can be either beneficial or detrimental to firms [48–50]. The lack of empirical tests of the ambidexterity-performance relationship has been criticized by Raisch and Birkinshaw (2008) [31] and Andriopoulos and Lewis (2009) [51]. Few studies have provided empirical support for the hypothesis of ambidexterity and performance. For example, Bierly and Daly (2001) [52] investigated the impact of ambidexterity on firm performance in a sample of 98 manufacturing firms but found no significant results. Katila and Ahuja (2002) [53] discovered a positive relationship between the proclivity to cite different patents and the proclivity to cite specific patents repeatedly on new product development, but did not test the impact on firm performance [54].

These ambiguous findings encourage further investigation into whether ambidexterity has a significant impact on the performance and survival of SMEs. However, it is a challenge to capture when and how ambidexterity is implemented and results are created due to the nature of SMEs that operate firms with scarce resources.

Therefore, this study focuses on SMEs that are thriving with scarce resources, and analyzes the evidence of the relationship between organizational ambidexterity and performance. SME organizational performance indicators, such as SME innovation, financial gains, product innovation, sales, and investment scales, must be defined, as well as any qualitative outcomes presented in the literature. Simultaneously, the factors affecting SMEs' performance need to be studied. Scholars have discovered that organizational culture is one of the factors influencing firm performance [55–58]. Additionally, manager performance is regarded as the degree to which the manager meets the requirements of his/her general work context toward the firm's performance [59,60]. Thus, by investigating the factors influencing the firm's performance, this study will determine the relationship between SMEs' ambidexterity and performance and under what conditions.

3. Theoretical Framework

3.1. Organizational Learning Theory

Organizational adaptation capabilities are a core concept of organizational behavior theory, suggesting that exploitation and exploration activities are needed as a rational system for organizational sustainability. Organizational learning refers to the distribution, acquisition, storage, and interpretation of new knowledge, which are vital success factors of firms [61–63]. This study employs organizational learning theory from the perspective of adaptation to employ the ambidexterity strategy to overcome the company's uncertain environment.

March (1991) [2] stated that activities to improve corporate performance in terms of organizational learning can be divided into exploitation and exploration. Organizations are forced to concentrate on exploitation and exploration activities even though those activities are in conflict [30]. Therefore, companies must find a compromise to balance these two activities.

It is also necessary to consider a resource-based perspective (RBV), as companies will eventually be forced to respond to an uncertain environment based on the resources they own. RBV is a strategic position that governs how a company interacts with its tangible and intangible resources [64]. Many studies suggest that the concept of RBV is more suitable for exploitation than exploration. However, understanding how to apply the concept of RBV in an organization's activities is required to maintain an appropriate balance between exploration and exploitation. In most cases, businesses will focus and act on either exploration or exploitation. When a company focuses solely on one activity, path-dependent tendencies can be significant, increasing organizational inertia. This poses a risk to the organization in the long run. Based on organizational learning theory, this study explains how companies adapt to new activities that they have never engaged in before.

3.2. Conceptual Framework

Figure 1 shows the activities focused on exploitation and exploration based on large companies and SMEs (startups and ventures) [65]. Quadrant 4 (Q4) represents the activity of existing market participants. Q1 now represents startups entering the market and exploring new businesses. SMEs can exist in both of these areas. However, the premise that SMEs are close to startups and ventures was presented earlier in this study. Q1 and Q4 both choose a path toward Q2, completing an ambidexterity strategy by reinforcing an activity they were not focused on. Ferrary (2011) [66] described changes in an organization's internal processes toward Q2 after a large company acquisitioned and merged a startup. Startups that need to investigate stable businesses in the market focus mainly on exploration activities. However, most startups that are acquired by a larger company and primarily carry out the exploitation process are primarily engaged in exploitation activities. Ferrary (2011) [66] explains that it is not easy to implement an ambidexterity strategy unless companies are willing to do both. Based on the theory of the resource-based view, the merged firm has comparatively fewer resources, causing it to rely on the larger firm's resources following the M&A.

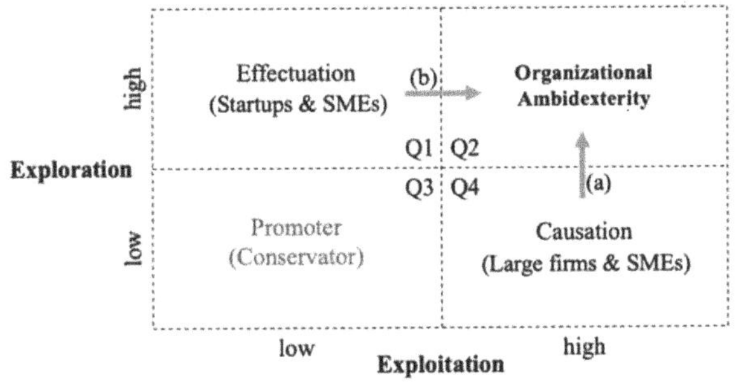

Figure 1. Theoretical framework (Modified from the work of Gedajlovic et al., 2012 [65]). Note. Path (a) suggests increasing exploration-related activities and path (b) implies increasing exploitation-related activities in firms.

According to organizational learning theory, SMEs have internal resources that can be used to quantify benchmarking and respond flexibly to environmental changes in a flexible manner. SMEs belonging to Q4 might be in the growing or mature stage of the firm where the SMEs already have exploitative capability and intention to adopt explorative activities. In contrast, SMEs in Q1 may be in the early stages of development, where the SMEs remain at the startup level and intend to increase the firm's efficiency level. According to Köllmann, Kuckertz, and Stöckmann (2009) [67], entrepreneurial growth companies that have just survived the birth stage still have exploratory behavior—and have entered the phase of rapid growth in which the venture is transferred into a managed firm [68–71]. Furthermore, traditional technological life cycle theory suggests that exploration may have the highest payoff in the early stage due to radical product innovation and competing product designs, whereas exploitation may have a higher payoff in the later stage due to cost savings in incremental process innovation [67]. Thus, exploration is a prerequisite for exploitation, but the advantage of exploration is also dependent on the knowledge gained through exploitation [72].

Previous research on organizational ambidexterity has been conducted mainly on large firms. The purpose of this research is to look at SMEs that are implementing organizational ambidexterity and analyze the factors that influence their ambidexterity and performance. Thus, as illustrated in Figure 2, a conceptual framework was constructed for this research.

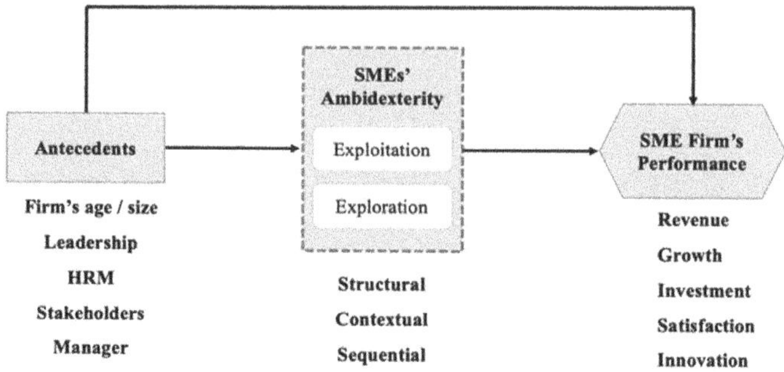

Figure 2. Conceptual framework. Source: author's elaboration.

4. Methods

This research employs systematic review (SR) methodology, which employs a structured process to identify trends and meaningful themes in a large body of literature on specific subjects and research questions. This SR methodology is part of the evidence-based management (EBMgt) movement. Evidence-based research synthesis is a valuable method for assessing, summarizing, and disseminating the findings of a large amount of data and scholarship, which is available in print and online databases [73]. Popay et al. (2006) [73] assert that the evidenced-based research synthesis is an invaluable method of assessing, recapping, and sharing the findings of a large amount of data and scholarship, which is available in print and online databases. Another strength of this method, as posited by Gough, Thomas and Oliver (2012) [74] is that the evidenced-based research synthesis is to demonstrate a transparent, thorough, and reliable process for evidence review. Evidence-based synthesis can be a useful tool to help transform contemporary management practice into evidence-based management (EBM). In addition, EBM can bridge the gap between the business and academic worlds by utilizing systematic reviews as the methodology for the decision-making process. The evidenced-based research synthesis has the potential to deliver the synthesis of many different situations by highlighting how certain mechanisms work in particular contexts [74].

SR is appropriate for this study because it allows us to examine a wide range of empirical studies on organizational ambidextrous approaches in SMEs and their performance. As a result, the SR approach enables us to examine the state of the research question in a short time. Finally, we can use sophisticated and well-structured search and synthesis techniques to draw meaningful conclusions about ambidexterity approaches in a variety of ways.

- According to Steven (2001) [75], an SR process should include formulating a clear question, locating all relevant research, and carefully evaluating the quality of each study to meet the rigor required for clinical decisions or, in the case of this review, management decisions (p. 532). The following research questions will be addressed through a synthesis of existing management theory and primary research studies. As previously stated, the methodology will be thematic synthesis. Relevant research will be found by employing carefully chosen inclusion/exclusion criteria, key terms, search strings, and the most applicable date ranges. The following is the methodological approach taken in this study. Identifying the question: this dissertation study's research question was to determine the antecedents to organizational ambidexterity in SMEs as an intervention within the entrepreneurial and managerial processes of organizational systems to achieve innovation and efficiency.

- Clarifying the purpose of the review: determining whether ambidexterity in SMEs will improve firm performance, allowing SMEs to seize new opportunities and increase efficiency.
- Articulating theories: because the implementation of ambidexterity involves numerous challenges and knowledge exchanges, the theory chosen is the basic principle that drives this mechanism.
- Search for the evidence: the nature and approach of the bibliographic search chosen to answer, obtain and identify bibliographic search engines containing appropriate scientific literature, subject matter experts, databases, and gray materials.
- Appraise the evidence: an appraised piece of evidence for trustworthiness, validity, and alignment to the research question.
- Extract the results: review cumulative findings from the literature and combine all the knowledge, from the evidence-based literature appraised and instructional strategies.
- Synthesize findings: evaluate the decision's effectiveness and efficiency, as well as its relevance in answering the research question and solving the business problem while making any necessary adjustments.
- Conclude and make recommendations: highlight gaps in the synthesis of the findings that need to be addressed in the future to develop a set of recommendations and document the implications for managers in SMEs.

To illustrate the entire process of selecting evidence and establishing the final sample set for this SR, a preferred reporting items for SRs and meta-analysis (Prisma) diagram is used. As shown in Figure 3, prisma is a preferred reporting chart for studies that were included and excluded from the SR. As stated by Gough et al. (2012) [74], Prisma is an essential component of the SR methodology because it allows the reader to follow the rigorous process of reviewing the evidence and establishing the final sample size.

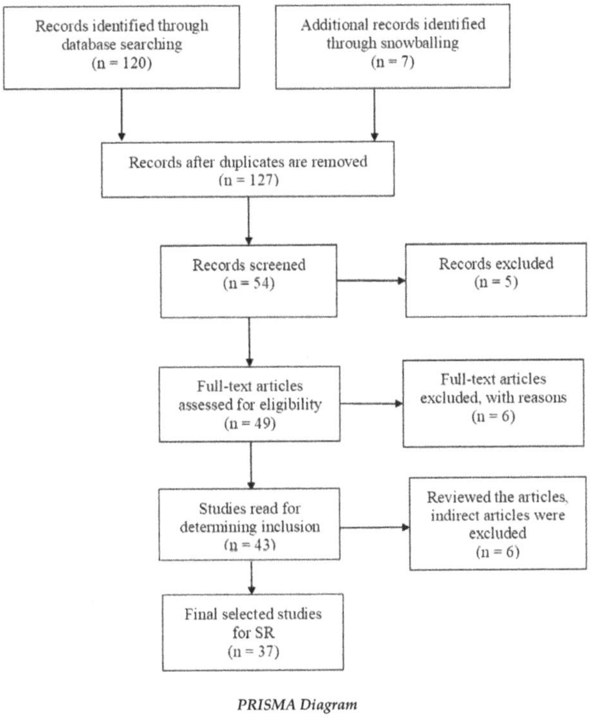

Figure 3. Prisma diagram of preferred reporting for systematic reviews.

5. Analysis and Findings

5.1. Description of the Data Set

For this study, evidence from the scholarly literature was selected from a wide range of contexts, including studies of firms of different SME sizes, industries, geographic locations (different countries), growth stages, and lifespan.

The companies examined in the included scholarly studies were from three continents. Given that the studies included in this study drew from firms in North and South America (35%, 13 studies), Europe (24%, 9 studies), and Asia (27%, 10 studies), the common themes extracted for this study may have cross-cultural applications, such as for firms from different geographical locations.

Only studies published after the year 2000 were considered, which was one of the key inclusion criteria. Given the relatively new and rapidly evolving theory development of organizational ambidexterity in SMEs, this criterion was used to review the most recent literature on ambidexterity-related topics.

The organizational level of analysis of this study was SMEs. Figure 4 also shows that there was insufficient research on OA-SMEs related to the research question in the early 2000s, with an increase in articles occurring in recent years. This rise could be attributed to changes in the market environment and a recognition of the importance of SMEs as a driver of economic growth.

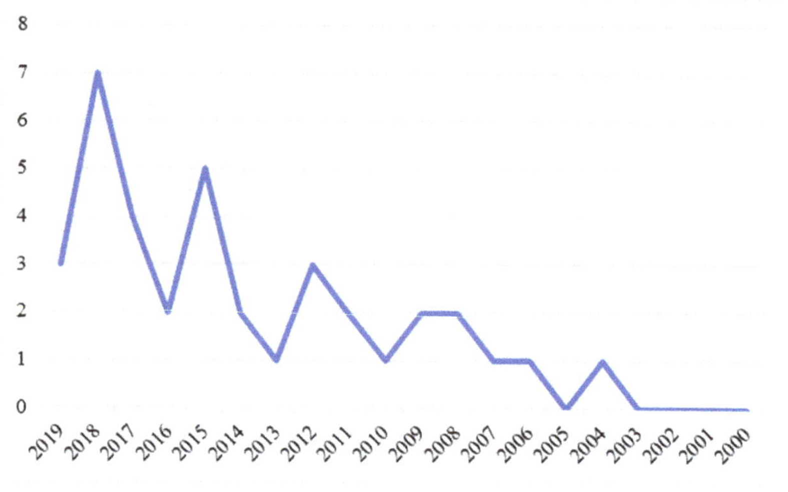

Figure 4. Number of studies by publication year (n = 37).

The distribution of the sample sizes was 37 studies. There were multiple studies for each of the sample groupings (interview, review, 0-10 samples, etc.). This distribution chart implies that the conclusions drawn from the evidence assessed in this SR of the literature might have broad application given the varying number of SMEs reviewed in the aggregate data. In addition, the type of research methodology for the 37 studies included in this SR of the literature is shown next to the sample size chart. Tables A2 and A3 in Appendix B contain more specific information, such as journal names, study context, the sample size for each article, and the main theory employed in the study.

The citations of a study represent the ripple effect of a certain research domain. The total number of citations for all studies examined in this study was 9290 with an average of 251 citations across 37 articles. However, we excluded four studies that had quite high citation numbers at the end of the process of article selection. Those studies with a high citation count were cited numerous times in recent studies chosen through library research, so there was a strong possibility that they would be redundant to the others. Articles for analysis were gathered with the most recent and influential articles in mind to draw meaningful conclusions. Tables A2 and A3 in Appendix B provides citation numbers for each study.

5.2. Antecedents of Ambidexterity in SMEs

Eighteen studies (49% of total articles) examined the causes of organizational ambidexterity or how specific factors influenced ambidexterity implementation in SMEs. Among these 18 studies, 14 provided evidence in the results section of the article based on various experiments conducted by each study, while four only provided antecedents in the literature review section of the study. The four studies that did not speak to the results were excluded, and only the factors from the study results of the 14 articles were aggregated. Table 1 shows how the antecedents were divided into eight categories.

Table 1. Key antecedents of SMEs ambidexterity as found in the systematic review.

Concept Category	Antecedents	Authors
Culture	organizational culture (bottom-up approach)	Ikhsan et al. (2017) [27]
Operation	leadership ambidexterity, centralization, connectedness	Chen and Kannan-Narasimhan (2015) [76]
HRM	HRM system, HRM practices, manager's fit, enhanced human resource capacity	Patel et al. (2013); Du and Chen (2018); Selcer and Decker (2012) [77–79]
Structure (legal)	top-management shareholdings, advisory boards, private companies	Gedajlovic et al. (2012) [65]; Kusumastuti (2018); Chebbi et al. (2015) [80,81]
Competency	creativity, long term consideration and entrepreneur's experience, entrepreneurial bricolage	Parmentier and Picq (2016) [82]; Chebbi et al. (2015) [81]; Günsel et al. (2018) [83]
Preparation	readiness for change, firm life cycle stage	Lillegraven et al. (2016) [84]; Günsel et al. (2018) [83]
Cooperation	Intra-firm knowledge exchange, inter-organizational coordination, cross-functional organization, unit inter-dependence	De Clercq et al. (2014) [85]; Ferrary (2011) [66]; Heavey et al. (2015) [86]
Support	leaders' commitment and support, senior team (rewards, social relationships)	Soares et al. (2018) [17]; Heavey et al. (2015) [86]

According to the literature uncovered for this SR, the most supportive mode to implement organizational ambidexterity in SMEs is a cooperative organizational tendency. Four of the studies support cooperation as an antecedent, including intra-firm knowledge exchange, inter-organizational coordination, cross-functional organization, and unit interdependence [27,66,77,82,85,86]. However, the authors who presented the cooperation antecedent also discovered preparation and support antecedents in their study.

These findings are in line with previous scholars who focused their research on the antecedents of organizational ambidexterity [5,30–32]. While earlier studies (e.g., [87,88]) provided empirical evidence of the importance of an organizational atmosphere based on employee and manager cooperation, the relationship between organizational support and new product development performance was not statistically significant [58,83]. The resources, care, and autonomy provided to employees were referred to as organizational support [89].

Although all eight antecedents identified in the body of evidence contribute to the implementation of AMB for SMEs, cooperation may be the most fundamental antecedent, in that it must be initiated before the other antecedents, such as leadership commitment, readiness for changes, connectedness, etc. can be realized. Cooperation is especially important in the pursuit of AMB in SMEs because knowledge utilization and sharing in organizations must be actively performed to overcome a lack of slack resources, which is common in SMEs.

5.3. Organizational Structure and Features of Ambidexterity in SMEs

For the second theme, almost all the studies chosen for the SR mentioned either structural or contextual ambidexterity in SMEs, however, only nine of the 37 studies provided evidence for the type of ambidexterity in the study's results and conclusions. After analysis, eight of the nine studies concluded that contextual ambidexterity should be implemented in SMEs. Although Ferrary (2011) [66] discussed the negative aspects of contextual ambidexterity in the organization, there was only one study that concluded that structural ambidexterity should be implemented in SMEs [89]. These findings demonstrate that for many scholars contextual design for ambidexterity is assumed to contribute to more valid results for SMEs than structural ambidexterity. In creative industries, SMEs lacked the human and financial resources required to conduct two types of activity to achieve an ambidextrous structure. As a result, Parmentier and Picq (2016) [82] argued that contextual ambidexterity models are better suited to SMEs than other models, particularly in the creative industries. Table 2 provides more information on the different types of structures and their components.

Table 2. Types and common theme of SMEs ambidexterity resulted in the literature reviewed.

AMB Type	Common Theme	Components	Selected Study
Structural	Structure	Need to separate the structures	Felício et al. (2019) [89]
Contextual	HR	The proper set of HR practices	Patel et al. (2013) [77]
		Negative interaction with internal rivalry	De Clercq et al. (2014) [85]
		Contextual is more critical for employees	Chang et al. (2009) [90]
		Make integrated behavior of employees	Du and Chen (2018) [78]
	Culture	The learning process (bottom-up culture)	Ikhsan et al. (2017) [27]
	Structure	No internal separation for AMB	Heavey et al. (2015) [86]
	Industry	Suite in the creative industries	Parmentier and Picq (2016) [82]
	Environment	The disadvantage in changing environment	Ferrary (2011) [66]

Chang et al. (2009) [90], Patel et al. (2013) [77], De Clercq et al. (2014) [85], and Du and Chen (2018) [78] discussed the importance of human resources in contextual ambidexterity, and Du and Chen (2018) [78] emphasized integrated-employee behavior as an advantage of contextual ambidexterity. According to this viewpoint, contextual ambidexterity is more likely to emerge from a distinct human resources base than from a set of practices. More specifically, ambidexterity is realized through the flexibility with which SMEs' human resources allocate their time and attention to exploration and exploitation.

Previous research has increasingly argued for evidence for the positive impact of contextual ambidexterity [38]. According to the findings of this study's SR of the literature, contextual ambidexterity in an organization required practices that work to improve resource flexibility in their human base so that employees have the discretion and motivation to devote their energy to activities associated with both exploitation and exploration. Exploitation, for example, is seen as a result of having clear performance standards and goals, rapid and open feedback systems, and consistency in how employees are managed. Exploration, on the other hand, refers to an organizational context in which employees actively and voluntarily push their standards and goals to higher levels. Therefore, the HR system in SMEs is highly important to produce these contextual elements. Finally, developing contextual ambidexterity within the HR system improves employees' practical activity in demonstrating exploitation and exploration across an entire business unit. HRM practices can help SMEs create a behavioral environment that encourages employees to explore and exploit.

In pursuing contextual ambidexterity, SMEs need to provide an appropriate environment for employees by offering social support and setting aggressive performance targets. That is, SMEs must provide employees with the appropriate set of HR practices for the development of both efficiency-related competencies and innovation-related competencies [77]. SMEs must ensure that their HR practices encourage cooperative behavior and mitigate internal rivalry because increasing internal rivalry among employees creates inefficiency in organizations because they compete for knowledge, information, and other types of resources [85].

5.4. Performance of SMEs

There were four operational factors influencing the performance of SMEs found in the synthesis of the literature: preparation, human resources, resources, and structure. Preparation was defined as readiness for change, goal setting, behavioral integration of the top management team, and a combination of exploitation and exploration that enabled SMEs to improve their firm's performance [5,21,79,84,91]. In addition to preparation, human resources are also emphasized as being a fundamental factor for performance in SMEs [54,77,92]. Human resources appear to be a major attribute of organizational ambidexterity because it has been identified as one of the most important subthemes for ambidexterity antecedents and it contributes to SME performance.

The results of analyzing the operational factors affecting performance in more detail are as follows. Patel et al. (2013) [77] concluded that HPWS affect SME performance and, more specifically, growth by producing an ambidextrous workforce in SMEs. In this study, the results provided robust evidence for the relationship between HPWS in SMEs and firm performance. Firms can expect the dynamic processes of knowledge exploration and exploitation as a key source of a firm's sustainable competitive edge by increasing the abilities of employees through the system [93].

De Clercq et al. (2014) [85] demonstrated a negative relationship between internal rivalry and firm performance and discovered that internal battles over a firm's resources can impede internal knowledge transfer. Employees must collaborate and interact with others to effectively meet the demands the firm faces rather than compete inside the firm [92].

Other studies [13,21,85,92] demonstrated the performance of SMEs in terms of the environment and government policy. Businesses should consider and capitalize on the direction of government policy. Combining exploitation and exploration can serve as a portfolio diversification function and, depending on the environment, SMEs should balance the contradictory activities. In a less uncertain environment, for example, SMEs should prioritize exploitation, while in a more uncertain environment, they should combine exploitation and exploration [21].

The performance literature was fairly homogeneous in terms of its assessment and value for ambidexterity in SMEs. SMEs that implement a combination of exploitation and exploration perform better overall, but younger or early-stage SME firms should prioritize one activity first to achieve higher performance [91]. Finally, Lubatkin et al. (2006) [5] proposed that behavioral integration of the top management team is critical for achieving an ambidextrous orientation that affects performance in SMEs.

In addition to investigating operational factors for performance in SMEs, it is also necessary to carefully explore the practical meanings of performance that operational factors affect. As we previously discussed, many other researchers have focused on the outcomes and impact of ambidexterity on performance. Among these studies, contextual ambidexterity appropriate for SMEs contributes to both financial and nonfinancial performance [94,95]. In the same vein, almost all the studies selected for the SR defined the word performance in each study. Revenue, revenue growth, sales growth, profit or profitability, and return on investment were all used to define performance (ROI). It was also defined in nonfinancial terms, such as perceived performance in comparison to competitors, user increases, innovation, firm growth, fulfillment of requirements in the firm, customer relationship, and commercialization of a firm's intellectual properties. Surprisingly, nonfinancial performance measures were more common in this SR than financial performance measures. This is most likely due to nonfinancial performance measures being more easily accessible through survey sampling than profitability estimates. Table 3 summarizes the financial and nonfinancial performance measures identified in this SR.

Table 3. Financial and nonfinancial measures of performance in the SR.

Attribute	Performance Measure	Selected Study
Financial performance	• Revenue • Revenue growth • Sales growth • Profit or profitability • Return on investment (ROI)	Battaglia et al. (2018); [91] Lillegraven et al. (2016); [84] Lubatkin et al. (2006); [5] Han and Celly (2008); [54] De Clercq et al. (2014); [85]
Nonfinancial performance	• Perceived performance compared to competitors • User increases • Innovation • Growth of the firm • Fulfillment of the requirement in the firm • Relationship with customers • Commercialization of the firm's intellectual properties	Yu et al. (2014); [21] Patel et al. (2013); [77] Lillegraven et al. (2016); [84] Chang et al. (2009); [90] Mom et al. (2015); [92] Selcer and Decker (2012); [79] Han and Celly (2008); [54] Cegarra-Navarro and Dewhurst (2007) [93]

5.5. *Organizational Resources and Dilemmas in SMEs*

Recall that studies indicated that there are often internal fights for a firm's resources in ambidextrous organizations [85]. March (1991) [2] previously assumed that simultaneously implementing exploitation and exploration in an organization resulted in a zero-sum game in which both approaches competed for scarce organizational resources. Exploitation and exploration generate tensions with a fundamentally different logic and compete for scarce resources, so the firm must weigh the two [38]. As a result, this situation leads to dilemmas or difficulties for SMEs, even with the implementation of ambidexterity.

As previously discussed in this study, dilemmas of the availability of resources, such as financial support, human resources, knowledge, and skills exist in the firm. Gedajlovic et al. (2012) [65] insisted that firms with better performance typically possess more slack resources to support exploitative and exploratory activities. Larger firms may have more slack resources than SMEs. Larger firms may engage more in strategic planning (due to their size) and are more likely to be ambidextrous due to resource constraints. However, the size of the firm is not an omniscient factor that always results in having the ability to better implement ambidexterity. According to Lillegraven et al. (2016) [84], firm size does not affect strategic planning and/or being ambidextrous. Larger established firms are also frequently slower to respond to opportunity than SMEs because their entrepreneurship ability deteriorates over time as their internal structures become increasingly laden with rules, procedures, and systems [5].

However, in most organizations, key resources appear to be predetermined and housed in core units. Most entrepreneurial or new venture units lack the core resources or the infrastructure required to transform an early-stage venture project into an established viable business [76]. These resources are typically housed within core business units.

6. Conclusions and Implication

This study's main goal was to determine whether ambidexterity, which has been described as a strategy for large corporations, can be applied to SMEs, and if so, what precedents there are for doing so and what effect these strategies would have on the performance of SMEs. The research question, "what are the determinants of ambidexterity, and what is the effect of organizational ambidexterity on corporate performance in SMEs?" can be answered in part by this study's findings.

An SR methodology was used in this study. An SR is an effective way to check the direction of previous studies on a research question. The SR of 37 studies has demonstrated that the original conceptual model should be revised. Figure 5 depicts the relationships discovered during the SR.

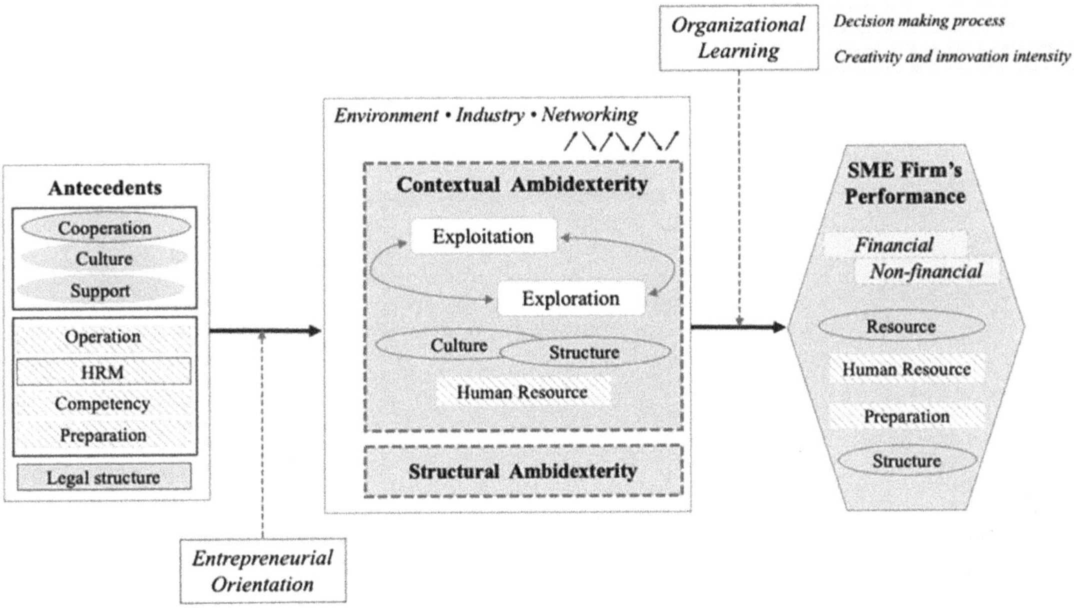

Figure 5. Postsynthesis conceptual model of the organizational ambidexterity in SMEs and its influence on firm performance.

According to the review, the organizational ambidexterity of SMEs is a key organizational component that affects the performance of businesses. Additionally, entrepreneurial orientation, where exploration is stronger than exploitation, creates a cooperative culture in the firm, which tends to form contextual ambidexterity in SMEs. Structural ambidexterity influences cooperative organizational culture and knowledge transfer. Additionally, firm performance was not supported by this study however. That is, depending on the firm's given situation, contextual or structural ambidexterity should be chosen, but most of the studies analyzed in this dissertation study supported contextual ambidexterity.

The initial conceptual model put forth the idea that organizational learning helps SMEs develop their ambidexterity. The key finding of the synthesis was that organizational learning not only improves contextual ambidexterity but also offers an experience that informs the decision-making process improvement, as well as creativity and innovation know-how to seize future opportunities and maintain current profit. The mechanism of the conceptual model is very crucial for SME organizations as this provides an opportunity to modify and adapt to a quickly changing environment. For SMEs, organizational ambidexterity can be invaluable in orchestrating changes to the organization's structure and how it handles potential future opportunities in the VUCA environment. This conceptual model as shown in Figure 5 can serve as a mechanism for the top management teams to implement ambidexterity in SMEs.

A total of 37 carefully chosen scholarly studies supported the aforementioned research question. In particular, corporate performance is more important than anything else, and ambidexterity has been shown to have a significant correlation with the performance improvement of SMEs. The company's resources, organizational structure, organizational goals, and vision are significant factors in implementing ambidexterity. The relevance to performance and the factors of execution provide an important foundation for the company's working manpower to establish a strategy. In the still underdeveloped field of SMEs, achieving successful results through an efficient blending of related elements can be good practice for ambidexterity. An important organizational decision is how a company will implement an ambidextrous strategy. Decisions made by business executives must take into account the organization's resource level and various environments.

The SR methodology used in this study gave management practitioners who implement organizational ambidexterity in their SMEs invaluable insight. We offer managers a framework for modifying organizational ambidexterity to shape overall innovation management and efficiency.

First, we discovered a strong correlation between organizational structure design and performance. The organizational structure should take into account the company's resources, core competencies, and environments because these choices have an impact on the company's sustainability. Since the ambidexterity structure requires a balance between exploitation and exploration as an organizational behavior, organizations must support their members to perform both types of activity because the ambidexterity structure necessitates a balance between exploitation and exploration as an organizational behavior. In this vein, temporal separation is considered for a manager to control organizational changes sequentially between phases of exploration and exploitation [96]. In this type of contextual ambidexterity model, organizations alternate between decentralized periods to foster innovations and centralized periods to increase efficiency. Thus, as a result of this dissertation study, this sequential approach is recommended for practitioners in SMEs.

Second, this study implies that contextual ambidextrous SMEs should pay attention to internal competition. Internal conflicts over a firm's resources may obstruct the transfer of internal knowledge according to De Clercq et al.'s (2014) [85] research, which established a negative correlation between internal rivalry and firm performance. Practitioners should lessen internal competition because employees need to work together and interact with others to effectively meet the demands the firm faces [92]. A reward system for sharing knowledge and skills could be suggested.

Third, this study shows the need for SMEs to increase knowledge exchange. From the organizational learning perspective, organizations learn to improve their capabilities, apply knowledge, and enhance competencies in their business [3,6,7]. To allow employees to share and learn about the other aspects of their work, firms hold regular project meetings or seminars.

Fourth, the systematic review suggests that the three activities should be used to further HRM. First of all, foster talents internally in the long term rather than recruit from outside. Establish precise criteria for hiring outside talent as well. Lastly, provide hands-on training programs and career development opportunities for employees.

7. Limitations and Future Research

This study has several limitations. First, it is possible that the systematic review methodology used in this dissertation study to extract constructs only adequately captured a subset of the distinction between exploitation and exploration. Future research needs to examine the usefulness of additional measures. Second, as market and technological dynamism change, the successful balance between exploration and exploitation may change significantly. Due to the selected articles' limitations, this study was only able to analyze specific industries and certain growing stages of firms. To provide more precise controls for industry and growing stage environmental factors, and to investigate how the ideal balance between exploration and exploitation may be dependent on such environmental factors, future research should bring together diverse SME samples. Third, due to sample limitations, this dissertation study could not investigate the impact of explorative and exploitative innovation on long-term performance; 10 years or more. This amount of time is required if we are to examine entrepreneurial orientation businesses in a VUCA setting. To address this issue, future research needs to assemble articles studying longitudinal data over a sufficiently long period.

Author Contributions: As main contributors, H.S. outlined and performed literature review, and conducted analysis; G.K. and W.J.L. reorganized the manuscript; conducted and additional literature review; conceptualized the work, research design, and discussion; and completed a reference check. W.J.L. and H.S.; Methodology, W.J.L. and H.S.; Investigation, G.K.; Data curation, G.K.; Writing—original draft, G.K., W.J.L. and H.S.; Visualization, W.J.L. All authors have read and agreed to the published version of the manuscript.

Funding: This research received no external funding.

Institutional Review Board Statement: Not applicable.

Informed Consent Statement: Not applicable.

Data Availability Statement: Not applicable.

Conflicts of Interest: The authors declare no conflict of interest.

Appendix A

Table A1. Quality Assessment Using Weight of Evidence.

#	Authors	WoE-A	WoE-B	WoE-C	WoE-D	Decision
1	Felício et al. (2019) [89]	2	3	3	8	H
2	Yu et al. (2018) [97]	2	3	3	8	H
3	Sussan et al. (2017) [13]	2	3	3	8	H
4	Gedajlovic et al. (2012) [65]	3	2	3	8	H
5	Patel et al. (2013) [77]	3	3	3	9	H
6	Clercq et al. (2014) [86]	3	2	3	8	H
7	Lillegraven et al. (2016) [84]	2	2	2	6	M
8	Ikhsan et al. (2017) [27]	2	2	2	6	M
9	Parmentier and Picq (2016) [82]	3	2	2	7	M
10	Ferrary (2011) [66]	3	2	2	7	M
11	Martínez-Climent et al. (2019) [98]	2	2	1	5	M
12	Ren and Jackson (2020) [99]	1	1	1	3	L
13	Chang et al. (2009) [90]	3	2	3	8	H
14	Soares et al. (2018) [17]	2	3	2	7	M
15	Mom et al. (2015) [92]	3	3	3	9	H
16	Du and Chen (2018) [78]	2	3	3	8	H
17	Chen and Kannan-Narasimhan (2014) [76]	3	3	3	9	H
18	Kusumastuti et al. (2018) [80]	2	2	1	5	M
19	Selcer and Decker (2012) [79]	2	2	2	6	M
20	Han and Celly (2008) [54]	3	3	3	9	H
21	Joharianzadeh et al. (2015) [100]	2	2	1	5	M
22	Kollmann et al. (2009) [67]	2	3	2	7	M
23	Chebbi et al. (2015) [81]	3	3	2	8	H
24	Heavey et al. (2015) [86]	3	3	3	9	H
25	He and Wong (2004) [38]	3	3	3	9	H
26	Cegarra-Navarro and Dewhurst (2007) [93]	2	2	3	7	M
27	Burpitt and Valle (2010) [72]	2	3	3	8	H
28	Park and Kim (2015) [101]	2	3	2	7	M
29	Liu, Wang, and Li (2019) [102]	2	3	3	8	H
30	Battaglia et al. (2018) [91]	2	3	3	8	H
31	Günsel et al. (2018) [83]	2	3	3	8	H

Table A1. *Cont.*

#	Authors	WoE-A	WoE-B	WoE-C	WoE-D	Decision
32	Soto-Acosta et al. (2018) [103]	3	2	2	7	M
33	Venugopal et al. (2018) [104]	2	2	2	6	M
34	Voss and Voss (2013) [105]	3	2	3	8	H
35	Chang et al. (2011) [106]	3	2	2	7	M
36	Chang and Hughes (2012) [107]	3	2	2	7	M
37	Lubatkin et al. (2006) [5]	3	2	3	8	H
38	Jansen et al. (2005) [96]	3	1	2	6	M
39	Cao et al. (2009) [20]	3	1	1	5	M
40	Tiwana (2008) [108]	3	1	1	5	M
41	O'Reilly and Tushman (2008) [109]	3	2	2	7	M

Note. Appraisal criteria: 3 = high quality (strong); 2 = medium (moderate); 1 = low quality (weak).

Appendix B

Table A2. Basic Description of Included Articles.

#	Database	Published Year	Cited	Authors	Journals
1	OneSearch	2019	0	Felício et al.	Journal of Business Research
2		2018	9	Yu et al.	Technological Forecasting and Social Change
3		2017	2	Sussan et al.	JOURNAL OF THE ASIA PACIFIC ECONOMY
4		2012	87	Gedajlovic et al.	Journal of Business Venturing
5		2013	310	PATEL et al.	Academy of Management Journal
6		2014	48	Clercq et al.	Small Bus Econ
7		2016	1	Lillegraven et al.	Nordicom Review
8		2017	3	Ikhsan et al.	International Journal of Business and Society
9		2016	12	Parmentier and Picq	Human Resources Management
10		2011	147	Ferrary	European Management Journal
11		2019	3	Martínez-Climent et al.	Sustainability
12		2009	165	Chang et al.	Research Policy
13		2018	0	Soares et al.	Journal of Technology Management and Innovation
14		2015	93	MOM et al.	Human Resource Management
15		2018	5	Du and Chen	International Journal of Innovation Studies
16		2014	23	Chen and Kannan-Narasimhan	R&D Management
17		2018	1	Kusumastuti et al.	Policy and Governance Review
18		2012	12	Selcer and Decker	The International Journal of Organization Innovation
19		2008	118	Han and Celly	Canadian Journal of Administrative Sciences
20		2015	1	Joharianzadeh et al.	International Journal of Management, Accounting, and Economics
21		2009	30	KOLLMANN et al.	Journal of Enterprising Culture
22		2015	33	CHEBBI et al.	Human Resource Management
23		2015	42	HEAVEY et al.	Human Resource Management
24		2004	3579	He and Wong	Organization Science
25		2007	106	Cegarra-Navarro and Dewhurst	The International Journal of Human Resource Management
26	ABI/INFORM	2010	12	Burpitt and Valle	Journal of Small Business Strategy
27		2015	19	Park and Kim	Asia Pacific Journal of Management

Table A2. *Cont.*

#	Database	Published Year	Cited	Authors	Journals
28	SCOPUS	2019	1	Liu, Wang, and Li	Frontiers of Business Research in China
29		2018	5	Battaglia et al.	Management Decision
30		2018	7	Günsel et al.	Kybernetes
31		2018	32	Acosta et al.	Journal of Knowledge Management
32		2017	5	Venugopal et al.	Management Decision
33		2013	228	Voss and Voss	Organization Science
34		2011	153	Chang et al.	Management Decision
35		2012	219	Chang and Hughes	European Management Journal
36	Snowballing	2006	1743	Lubatkin et al.	Journal of Management (from article #4)
37		2008	2036	O'Reilly and Tushman	Research in Organizational Behavior (from article #4)

Note. Cited: from an article published year until 3 November 2019.

Table A3. Sample, Methodology, and Theory Descriptions of Included Articles.

#	Authors	Study Context	Methodology (Sample Size)	Main Theory
1	Felício et al. (2019) [89]	Portugal SMEs	Quantitative (202 respondents)	Organizational learning theory, Behavioral theory
2	Yu et al. (2018) [97]	China software firms	Quantitative (312 firms)	Causation and Effectuation
3	Sussan et al. (2017) [13]	Korea high-tech firms	Quantitative (2800 firms)	Traditional strategy
4	Gedajlovic et al. (2012) [65]	China high-tech firms	Quantitative (122 firms)	Agency theory
5	Patel et al. (2013) [77]	US high-tech manufacturing SMEs	Quantitative (215 firms)	Behavioral theory
6	Clercq et al. (2014) [85]	Canadian SMEs	Quantitative (146 firms)	Contingency perspective
7	Lillegraven et al. (2016) [84]	US newspaper SMEs	Quantitative (143 firms)	Strategic management theory
8	Ikhsan et al. (2017) [27]	Indonesia SMEs	Quantitative (133 firms)	Organizational learning theory
9	Parmentier and Picq (2016) [82]	France's creative industry SMEs	Qualitative (11 firms)	Ambidexterity
10	Ferrary (2011) [66]	US corporations	Qualitative (2 Corp.–case study)	Open innovation
11	Martínez-Climent et al. (2019) [98]	(N/A)	Qualitative (review)	Resource-based view, theory of dynamic capabilities
12	Chang et al. (2009) [90]	Taiwan universities	Quantitative (229 respondents)	Institutional theory
13	Soares et al. (2018) [17]	Brazil's higher education institutions	Quantitative (79 respondents)	Institutional theory
14	Mom et al. (2015) [92]	Global 500 (service and manufacturing) firms	Quantitative (337 respondents)	Maturity degree of organizational ambidexterity
15	Du and Chen (2018) [78]	China high-tech SMEs	Qualitative (2 firms–case study)	Human resource management
16	Chen and Kannan-Narasimhan (2015) [76]	US Silicon Valley firms	Qualitative (51 interviewees)	(N/A)
17	Kusumastuti et al. (2018) [80]	Indonesia business group	Quantitative (450 respondents)	Formal integration mechanisms (OT)
18	Selcer and Decker (2012) [79]	US large oil and gas company	Qualitative (31 interviewees)	Resource-based view
19	Han and Celly (2008) [54]	Canada's international new venture firms	Quantitative (70 firms)	Structuration theory (loose-tight coupling)
20	Joharianzadeh et al. (2015) [100]	(N/A)	Qualitative (Propositions)	Theory of dynamic capability
21	Kollmann et al. (2009) [67]	(N/A)	Qualitative (Propositions)	(N/A)
22	Chebbi et al. (2015) [81]	France telecommunication market	Qualitative (interview)	(N/A)

Table A3. *Cont.*

#	Authors	Study Context	Methodology (Sample Size)	Main Theory
23	Heavey et al. (2015) [86]	US high-tech SMEs	Quantitative (99 firms)	Structural configurations theory
24	He and Wong (2004) [38]	US manufacturing firms	Quantitative (206 firms)	Social capital theory
25	Cegarra-Navarro and Dewhurst (2007) [93]	Spain optometry and telecommunication SMEs	Quantitative (269 firms)	Organization theory
26	Burpitt and Valle (2010) [72]	US furniture industry SMEs	Quantitative (94 firms)	Organizational learning theory
27	Park and Kim (2015) [101]	Korean government-sponsored companies	Quantitative (467 firms)	Behavioral theory, Resource-based view
28	Liu, Wang, and Li (2019) [102]	China SMEs	Qualitative (63 firms)	(N/A)
29	Battaglia et al. (2018) [91]	Italy's high and medium-tech industries	Quantitative (221 firms)	(N/A)
30	Günsel et al. (2018) [83]	Turkey SMEs	Quantitative (105 firms)	The emerging view of domain ambidexterity
31	Soto-Acosta et al. (2018) [103]	Spain manufacturing SMEs	Quantitative (429 firms)	Strategic management
32	Venugopal et al. (2018) [104]	India IT, electronics, biotech SMEs	Quantitative (78 firms)	Knowledge-based view
33	Voss and Voss (2013) [105]	US nonprofit theater industry SMEs	Quantitative (107 firms)	Behavioral integration
34	Chang et al. (2011) [106]	Scotland manufacturing and service SMEs	Quantitative (265 firms)	Strategic combinations
35	Chang and Hughes (2012) [107]	Scotland manufacturing and service SMEs	Quantitative (243 firms)	(N/A)
36	Lubatkin et al. (2006) [5]	US SMEs	Quantitative (139 firms)	(N/A)
37	O'Reilly and Tushman (2008) [109]	(N/A)	Qualitative (Propositions)	Echelon theory

Appendix C

Table A4. Contribution of Each Article in the Systematic Review.

#	Authors	A	S	P	M
1	Felício et al. (2019) [89]		O		
2	Yu et al. (2018) [97]			O	O
3	Sussan et al. (2017) [13]			O	
4	Gedajlovic et al. (2012) [65]	O			O
5	Patel et al. (2013) [77]	O	O	O	
6	Clercq et al. (2014) [86]	O	O	O	O
7	Lillegraven et al. (2016) [84]	O		O	
8	Ikhsan et al. (2017) [27]	O	O		O
9	Parmentier and Picq (2016) [82]	O	O		O
10	Ferrary (2011) [66]	O	O		
11	Martínez-Climent et al. (2019) [98]				O
12	Chang et al. (2009) [90]		O	O	
13	Soares et al. (2018) [17]	O			
14	Mom et al. (2015) [92]			O	
15	Du and Chen (2018) [78]	O	O		
16	Chen and Kannan-Narasimhan (2014) [76]	O			
17	Kusumastuti et al. (2018) [80]	O			

Table A4. *Cont.*

#	Authors	A	S	P	M
18	Selcer and Decker (2012) [79]	O		O	
19	Han and Celly (2008) [54]			O	
20	Johariаnzadeh et al. (2015) [100]	O		O	O
21	Kollmann et al. (2009) [67]		O		
22	Chebbi et al. (2015) [81]	O			
23	Heavey et al. (2015) [86]	O	O		
24	He and Wong (2004) [38]				O
25	Cegarra-Navarro and Dewhurst (2007) [93]			O	
26	Burpitt and Valle (2010) [72]		O		
27	Park and Kim (2015) [101]	O			
28	Liu, Wang and Li (2019) [102]	O			
29	Battaglia et al. (2018) [91]			O	
30	Günsel et al. (2017) [83]	O			O
31	Soto-Acosta et al. (2018) [103]	O			
32	Venugopal et al. (2017) [104]			O	
33	Voss and Voss (2013) [105]			O	O
34	Chang et al. (2011) [106]		O	O	
35	Chang and Hughes (2012) [107]		O	O	
36	Lubatkin et al. (2006) [5]	O		O	
37	O'Reilly and Tushman (2008) [109]		O	O	

Note. Cited: A: Antecedents, S: Structure of Ambidexterity, P: Performance in SMEs, M: Moderating/Mediating.

References

1. Kuran, T. The tenacious past: Theories of personal and collective conservatism. *J. Econ. Behav. Organ.* **1988**, *10*, 143–171.
2. March, J.G. Exploration and exploitation in organizational learning. *Organ. Sci.* **1991**, *2*, 71–87. [CrossRef]
3. Junni, P.; Sarala, R.M.; Taras, V.; Tarba, S.Y. Organizational ambidexterity and performance: A meta-analysis. *Acad. Manag. Perspect.* **2013**, *27*, 299–312.
4. Jansen, J.J.P.; Simsek, Z.; Cao, Q. Ambidexterity and performance in multiunit contexts: Cross-level moderating effects of structural and resource attributes. *Strateg. Manag. J.* **2012**, *33*, 1286–1303. [CrossRef]
5. Lubatkin, M.H.; Simsek, Z.; Ling, Y.; Veiga, J.F. Ambidexterity and performance in small-to medium-sized firms: The pivotal role of top management team behavioral integration. *J. Manag.* **2006**, *32*, 646–672.
6. Holmqvist, M. A dynamic model of intra-and interorganizational learning. *Organ. Stud.* **2003**, *24*, 95–123. [CrossRef]
7. Levinthal, D.A.; March, J.G. The myopia of learning. *Strateg. Manag. J.* **1993**, *14*, 95–112. [CrossRef]
8. Cameron, K.S.; Quinn, R.E. *Diagnosing and Changing Organizational Culture: Based on the Competing Values Framework*; John Wiley & Sons: New York, NY, USA, 2011.
9. Schulz, M. The uncertain relevance of newness: Organizational learning and knowledge flows. *Acad. Manag. J.* **2001**, *44*, 661–681.
10. Vermeulen, F.; Barkema, H. Learning through acquisitions. *Acad. Manag. J.* **2001**, *44*, 457–476. [CrossRef]
11. McGrath, R.G. Exploratory learning, innovative capacity, and managerial oversight. *Acad. Manag. J.* **2001**, *44*, 118–131. [CrossRef]
12. Eisenhardt, K.M.; Schoonhoven, C.B. Organizational growth: Linking founding team, strategy, environment, and growth among US semiconductor ventures, 1978–1988. *Adm. Sci. Q.* **1990**, *35*, 504–529. [CrossRef]
13. Sussan, F.; Acs, Z.J. The digital entrepreneurial ecosystem. *Small Bus. Econ.* **2017**, *49*, 55–73.
14. Sato, H. Routine-based view of organizational learning and mechanisms of myopia. *Ann. Bus. Adm. Sci.* **2012**, *11*, 45–54. [CrossRef]
15. Christensen, C.M.; Bower, J.L. Customer power, strategic investment, and the failure of leading firms. *Strateg. Manag. J.* **1996**, *17*, 197–218. [CrossRef]
16. Tushman, M.L.; O'Reilly, C.A., III. Ambidextrous organizations: Managing evolutionary and revolutionary change. *Calif. Manag. Rev.* **1996**, *38*, 8–29. [CrossRef]
17. Soares, J.L.; dos Reis, D.R.; da Cunha, J.C.; Neto, P.J.S. Organizational ambidexterity: A study in Brazilian higher education institutions. *J. Technol. Manag. Innov.* **2018**, *13*, 36–46.
18. Brettel, M.; Mauer, R.; Engelen, A.; Küpper, D. Corporate effectuation: Entrepreneurial action and its impact on R&D project performance. *J. Bus. Ventur.* **2012**, *27*, 167–184.

19. Reymen, I.M.M.J.; Andries, P.; Berends, H.; Mauer, R.; Stephan, U.; Van Burg, E. Understanding dynamics of strategic decision making in venture creation: A process study of effectuation and causation. *Strateg. Entrep. J.* **2015**, *9*, 351–379. [CrossRef]
20. Cao, Q.; Gedajlovic, E.; Zhang, H. Unpacking organizational ambidexterity: Dimensions, contingencies, and synergistic effects. *Organ. Sci.* **2009**, *20*, 781–796. [CrossRef]
21. Yu, C.; Zhang, M.; Ren, F. Collective learning for the emergence of social norms in networked multiagent systems. *IEEE Trans. Cybern.* **2014**, *44*, 2342–2355.
22. Porter, M. *Competitive Strategy*; Free Press: New York, NY, USA, 1980.
23. Li, M.; Nguyen, B.; Yu, X. Competition vs. collaboration in the generation and adoption of a sequence of new technologies: A game theory approach. *Technol. Anal. Strateg. Manag.* **2016**, *28*, 348–379. [CrossRef]
24. Adler, P.S.; Goldoftas, B.; Levine, D.I. Flexibility versus efficiency? A case study of model changeovers in the Toyota production system. *Organ. Sci.* **1999**, *10*, 43–68.
25. Ebben, J.J.; Johnson, A.C. Efficiency, flexibility, or both? Evidence linking strategy to performance in small firms. *Strateg. Manag. J.* **2005**, *26*, 1249–1259. [CrossRef]
26. Simon, H. *Hidden Champions of the Twenty-First Century: The Success Strategies of Unknown World Market Leaders*; Springer Science & Business Media: Berlin, Germany, 2009.
27. Ikhsan, K.; Almahendra, R.; Budiarto, T. Contextual ambidexterity in SMEs in Indonesia: A study on how it mediates organizational culture and firm performance and how market dynamism influences its role on firm performance. *Int. J. Bus. Soc.* **2017**, *18*, 369–390.
28. Baker, T.; Nelson, R.E. Creating something from nothing: Resource construction through entrepreneurial bricolage. *Adm. Sci. Q.* **2005**, *50*, 329–366. [CrossRef]
29. Benner, M.J.; Tushman, M.L. Exploitation, exploration, and process management: The productivity dilemma revisited. *Acad. Manag. Rev.* **2003**, *28*, 238–256. [CrossRef]
30. Gibson, C.B.; Birkinshaw, J. The antecedents, consequences, and mediating role of organizational ambidexterity. *Acad. Manag. J.* **2004**, *47*, 209–226.
31. Raisch, S.; Birkinshaw, J. Organizational ambidexterity: Antecedents, outcomes, and moderators. *J. Manag.* **2008**, *34*, 375–409.
32. Mom, T.J.M.; Van Den Bosch, F.A.J.; Volberda, H.W. Investigating managers' exploration and exploitation activities: The influence of top-down, bottom-up, and horizontal knowledge inflows. *J. Manag. Stud.* **2007**, *44*, 910–931. [CrossRef]
33. Simsek, Z.; Heavey, C.; Veiga, J.F.; Souder, D. A typology for aligning organizational ambidexterity's conceptualizations, antecedents, and outcomes. *J. Manag. Stud.* **2009**, *46*, 864–894. [CrossRef]
34. Puranam, P.; Singh, H.; Zollo, M. Organizing for innovation: Managing the coordination-autonomy dilemma in technology acquisitions. *Acad. Manag. J.* **2006**, *49*, 263–280. [CrossRef]
35. Rosenbloom, R.S.; Christensen, C.M. Technological discontinuties, organizational capabilities, and strategic commitments. *Ind. Corp. Change* **1994**, *3*, 655–685. [CrossRef]
36. Duncan, R.B. The ambidextrous organization: Designing dual structures for innovation. *Manag. Organ.* **1976**, *1*, 167–188.
37. Boumgarden, P.; Nickerson, J.; Zenger, T.R. Sailing into the wind: Exploring the relationships among ambidexterity, vacillation, and organizational performance. *Strateg. Manag. J.* **2012**, *33*, 587–610. [CrossRef]
38. He, Z.L.; Wong, P.K. Exploration vs. exploitation: An empirical test of the ambidexterity hypothesis. *Organ. Sci.* **2004**, *15*, 481–494. [CrossRef]
39. Li, Y.H.; Huang, J.W. Ambidexterity's mediating impact on product development proficiency and new product performance. *Ind. Mark. Manag.* **2012**, *41*, 1125–1132.
40. Im, G.; Rai, A. Knowledge sharing ambidexterity in long-term interorganizational relationships. *Manag. Sci.* **2008**, *54*, 1281–1296. [CrossRef]
41. Kostopoulos, K.C.; Bozionelos, N. Team exploratory and exploitative learning: Psychological safety, task conflict, and team performance. *Group Organ. Manag.* **2011**, *36*, 385–415.
42. Cottrell, T.; Nault, B.R. Product variety and firm survival in the microcomputer software industry. *Strateg. Manag. J.* **2004**, *25*, 1005–1025. [CrossRef]
43. Derbyshire, J. The impact of ambidexterity on enterprise performance: Evidence from 15 countries and 14 sectors. *Technovation* **2014**, *34*, 574–581. [CrossRef]
44. Govindarajan, V.; Trimble, C. Building breakthrough businesses within established organizations. *Harv. Bus. Rev.* **2005**, *83*, 58–68. [PubMed]
45. Kitapçi, H.; Çelik, V. Ambidexterity and firm productivity performance: The mediating effect of organizational learning capacity. *Procedia Soc. Behav. Sci.* **2013**, *99*, 1105–1113.
46. Eriksson, P.E. Exploration and exploitation in project-based organizations: Development and diffusion of knowledge at different organizational levels in construction companies. *Int. J. Proj. Manag.* **2013**, *31*, 333–341. [CrossRef]
47. Holmqvist, M. Experiential learning processes of exploitation and exploration within and between organizations: An empirical study of product development. *Organ. Sci.* **2004**, *15*, 70–81.
48. Agogué, M.; Levillain, K.; Hooge, S. Gamification of creativity: Exploring the usefulness of serious games for ideation. *Creat. Innov. Manag.* **2015**, *24*, 415–429. [CrossRef]

49. Fisher, G. Effectuation, causation, and bricolage: A behavioral comparison of emerging theories in entrepreneurship research. *Entrep. Theory Pract.* **2012**, *36*, 1019–1051.
50. Smolka, K.M.; Verheul, I.; Burmeister-Lamp, K.; Heugens, P.P.M.A.R. Get it Together! Synergistic Effects of Causal and Effectual Decision–Making Logics on Venture Performance *Get It Together*. *Entrep. Theory Pract.* **2018**, *42*, 571–604. [CrossRef]
51. Andriopoulos, C.; Lewis, M.W. Exploitation-exploration tensions and organizational ambidexterity: Managing paradoxes of innovation. *Organ. Sci.* **2009**, *20*, 696–717. [CrossRef]
52. Bierly, P.; Daly, P.S. Exploration and exploitation in small manufacturing firms. In Proceedings of the 61st Annual Meeting of the Academy of Management, Washington, DC, USA, 3–8 August 2001.
53. Katila, R.; Ahuja, G. Something old, something new: A longitudinal study of search behavior and new product introduction. *Acad. Manag. J.* **2002**, *45*, 1183–1194. [CrossRef]
54. Han, M.; Celly, N. Strategic ambidexterity and performance in international new ventures. *Can. J. Adm. Sci./Revue Canadienne des Sciences de l'Administration* **2008**, *25*, 335–349. [CrossRef]
55. Deshpandé, R.; Farley, J.U.; Webster, F.E., Jr. Corporate culture, customer orientation, and innovativeness in Japanese firms: A quadrad analysis. *J. Mark.* **1993**, *57*, 23–37. [CrossRef]
56. Ogbonna, E.; Harris, L.C. Leadership style, organizational culture and performance: Empirical evidence from UK companies. *Int. J. Hum. Resour. Manag.* **2000**, *11*, 766–788.
57. Fey, C.F.; Denison, D.R. Organizational culture and effectiveness: Can American theory be applied in Russia? *Organ. Sci.* **2003**, *14*, 686–706.
58. Wei, Y.; Morgan, N.A. Supportiveness of organizational climate, market orientation, and new product performance in Chinese firms. *J. Prod. Innov. Manag.* **2004**, *21*, 375–388. [CrossRef]
59. Griffin, M.A.; Neal, A.; Parker, S.K. A new model of work role performance: Positive behavior in uncertain and interdependent contexts. *Acad. Manag. J.* **2007**, *50*, 327–347. [CrossRef]
60. Ilgen, D.R.; Pulakos, E.D. (Eds.) Employee performance in today's organizations. In *The Changing Nature of Performance: Implications for Staffing, Motivation and Development*; Jossey-Bass: San Francisco, CA, USA, 1999; pp. 1–18.
61. Bong, S.H.; Lee, J.; Gil, Y. Effective team processes for technology internalisation with special emphasis on knowledge management: Successful late starter, Samsung case. *Int. J. Technol. Manag.* **2004**, *27*, 16–39. [CrossRef]
62. Hall, R.; Andriani, P. Managing knowledge associated with innovation. *J. Bus. Res.* **2003**, *56*, 145–152.
63. Huber, G.P. Organizational learning: The contributing processes and the literatures. *Organ. Sci.* **1991**, *2*, 88–115. [CrossRef]
64. Newbert, S.L. Empirical research on the resource-based view of the firm: An assessment and suggestions for future research. *Strateg. Manag. J.* **2007**, *28*, 121–146.
65. Gedajlovic, E.; Cao, Q.; Zhang, H. Corporate shareholdings and organizational ambidexterity in high-tech SMEs: Evidence from a transitional economy. *J. Bus. Ventur.* **2012**, *27*, 652–665. [CrossRef]
66. Ferrary, M. Specialized organizations and ambidextrous clusters in the open innovation paradigm. *Eur. Manag. J.* **2011**, *29*, 181–192.
67. Kollmann, T.; Kuckertz, A.; Stöckmann, C. Continuous innovation in entrepreneurial growth companies: Exploring the ambidextrous strategy. *J. Enterprising Cult.* **2009**, *17*, 297–322.
68. Kimberley, J.R.; Miles, R.H. *The Organizational Life Cycle: Issues in the Creation, Transformation and Decline of Organizations*; Jossey-Bass Publisher: San Francisco, CA, USA, 1980.
69. Churchill, N.C.; Lewis, V.L. The five stages of small business growth. *Harv. Bus. Rev.* **1983**, *61*, 30–50.
70. Smith, N.R.; Miner, J.B. Type of entrepreneur, type of firm, and managerial motivation: Implications for organizational life cycle theory. *Strateg. Manag. J.* **1983**, *4*, 325–340. [CrossRef]
71. Kazanjian, R.K. Relation of dominant problems to stages of growth in technology-based new ventures. *Acad. Manag. J.* **1988**, *31*, 257–279. [CrossRef]
72. Burpitt, W.J., Jr.; Valle, M. Balancing exploration and exploitation in a declining industry: Antecedents to firm adaptation strategy and performance. *J. Small Bus. Strategy* **2010**, *21*, 1–17.
73. Popay, J.; Roberts, H.; Sowden, A.; Petticrew, M.; Arai, L.; Rodgers, M.; Britten, N.; Roen, K.; Duffy, S. *Guidance on the Conduct of Narrative Synthesis in Systematic Reviews. A Product from the ESRC Methods Programme*; Version 1; Lancaster University: Bailrigg, UK, 2006; p. b92.
74. Gough, D.; Thomas, J.; Oliver, S. Clarifying differences between review designs and methods. *Syst. Rev.* **2012**, *1*, 28.
75. Stevens, K.R. Systematic reviews: The heart of evidence-based practice. *AACN Clin. Issues* **2001**, *12*, 529–538.
76. Chen, R.R.; Kannan-Narasimhan, R.P. Formal integration archetypes in ambidextrous organizations. *RD Manag.* **2015**, *45*, 267–286.
77. Patel, P.C.; Messersmith, J.G.; Lepak, D.P. Walking the tightrope: An assessment of the relationship between high-performance work systems and organizational ambidexterity. *Acad. Manag. J.* **2013**, *56*, 1420–1442.
78. Du, J.; Chen, Z. Applying Organizational Ambidexterity in strategic management under a "VUCA" environment: Evidence from high tech companies in China. *Int. J. Innov. Stud.* **2018**, *2*, 42–52.
79. Selcer, A.; Decker, P. The structuration of ambidexterity: An urge for caution in organizational design. *Int. J. Organ. Innov.* **2012**, *5*, 65–96.
80. Kusumastuti, R. Understanding Social Capital that Leads to Strategic Ambidexterity Practice in Family Firm Business. *J. Eng. Appl. Sci.* **2018**, *13*, 5317–5321.

81. Chebbi, H.; Yahiaoui, D.; Vrontis, D.; Thrassou, A. Building multiunit ambidextrous organizations—A transformative framework. *Hum. Resour. Manag.* **2015**, *54*, s155–s177.
82. Parmentier, G.; Picq, T. Managing creative teams in small ambidextrous organizations: The case of videogames. *Int. J. Arts Manag.* **2016**, *19*, 16–30.
83. Günsel, A.; Altındağ, E.; Kılıç Keçeli, S.; Kitapçı, H.; Hızıroğlu, M. Antecedents and consequences of organizational ambidexterity: The moderating role of networking. *Kybernetes* **2018**, *47*, 186–207.
84. Lillegraven, T.B.; Wilberg, E. Editors, Executive and Entrepreneur. *Nord. Rev.* **2016**, *37*, 115–130.
85. De Clercq, D.; Thongpapanl, N.; Dimov, D. Contextual ambidexterity in SMEs: The roles of internal and external rivalry. *Small Bus. Econ.* **2014**, *42*, 191–205.
86. Heavey, C.; Simsek, Z.; Fox, B.C. Managerial social networks and ambidexterity of SMEs: The moderating role of a proactive commitment to innovation. *Hum. Resour. Manag.* **2015**, *54*, s201–s221.
87. Amabile, T.M.; Conti, R.; Coon, H.; Lazenby, J.; Herron, M. Assessing the work environment for creativity. *Acad. Manag. J.* **1996**, *39*, 1154–1184.
88. Scott, S.G.; Bruce, R.A. Creating innovative behavior among R&D professionals: The moderating effect of leadership on the relationship between problem-solving style and innovation. In Proceedings of the 1994 IEEE International Engineering Management Conference-IEMC '94, Dayton North, OH, USA, 17–19 October 1994; pp. 48–55.
89. Felício, J.A.; Caldeirinha, V.; Dutra, A. Ambidextrous capacity in small and medium-sized enterprises. *J. Bus. Res.* **2019**, *101*, 607–614.
90. Chang, Y.C.; Yang, P.Y.; Chen, M.H. The determinants of academic research commercial performance: Towards an organizational ambidexterity perspective. *Res. Policy* **2009**, *38*, 936–946.
91. Battaglia, D.; Neirotti, P.; Paolucci, E. The role of R&D investments and export on SMEs' growth: A domain ambidexterity perspective. *Manag. Decis.* **2018**, *56*, 1883–1903.
92. Mom, T.J.M.; Fourné, S.P.L.; Jansen, J.J.P. Managers' work experience, ambidexterity, and performance: The contingency role of the work context. *Hum. Resour. Manag.* **2015**, *54*, s133–s153. [CrossRef]
93. Cegarra-Navarro, J.G.; Dewhurst, F. Linking organizational learning and customer capital through an ambidexterity context: An empirical investigation in SMEs. *Int. J. Hum. Resour. Manag.* **2007**, *18*, 1720–1735. [CrossRef]
94. Wang, C.L.; Rafiq, M. Ambidextrous organizational culture, Contextual ambidexterity and new product innovation: A comparative study of UK and Chinese high-tech Firms. *Br. J. Manag.* **2014**, *25*, 58–76.
95. Atuahene-Gima, K. Resolving the capability–rigidity paradox in new product innovation. *J. Mark.* **2005**, *69*, 61–83. [CrossRef]
96. Jansen, J.J.; Van Den Bosch, F.A.; Volberda, H.W. Exploratory innovation, exploitative innovation, and performance: Effects of organizational antecedents and environmental moderators. *Manag. Sci.* **2005**, *52*, 1661–1674. [CrossRef]
97. Yu, X.; Tao, Y.; Tao, X.; Xia, F.; Li, Y. Managing uncertainty in emerging economies: The interaction effects between causation and effectuation on firm performance. *Technol. Forecast. Soc. Change* **2018**, *135*, 121–131. [CrossRef]
98. Martínez-Climent, C.; Rodríguez-García, M.; Zeng, J. Ambidextrous leadership, social entrepreneurial orientation, and operational performance. *Sustainability* **2019**, *11*, 890.
99. Ren, S.; Jackson, S.E. HRM institutional entrepreneurship for sustainable business organizations. *Hum. Resour. Manag. Rev.* **2020**, *30*, 100691.
100. Joharianzadeh, F.; Sakhdari, K.; Ziyae, B.; Aghviyeh, M.A. Can franchisors balance adaptation and standardization? Toward theorizing ambidexterity in franchisors. *Int. J. Manag. Account. Econ.* **2015**, *2*, 1278–1289.
101. Park, J.; Kim, S. The differentiating effects of workforce aging on exploitative and exploratory innovation: The moderating role of workforce diversity. *Asia Pac. J. Manag.* **2015**, *32*, 481–503.
102. Liu, L.; Wang, F.; Li, X. Comparing the configured causal antecedents of exploration and exploitation: A fuzzy set qualitative comparative analysis. *Front. Bus. Res. China* **2019**, *13*, 1–25.
103. Soto-Acosta, P.; Popa, S.; Martinez-Conesa, I. Information technology, knowledge management and environmental dynamism as drivers of innovation ambidexterity: A study in SMEs. *J. Knowl. Manag.* **2018**, *22*, 824–849. [CrossRef]
104. Venugopal, A.; Krishnan, T.N.; Kumar, M. Identifying the Focal Role of Top Management Paradoxical Cognition in Ambidextrous Firms. 2018. Available online: https://www.emerald.com/insight/content/doi/10.1108/MD-04-2017-0402/full/html (accessed on 27 October 2022).
105. Voss, G.B.; Voss, Z.G. Strategic ambidexterity in small and medium-sized enterprises: Implementing exploration and exploitation in product and market domains. *Organ. Sci.* **2013**, *24*, 1459–1477. [CrossRef]
106. Chang, Y.Y.; Hughes, M.; Hotho, S. Internal and external antecedents of SMEs' innovation ambidexterity outcomes. *Manag. Decis.* **2011**, *49*, 1658–1676.
107. Chang, Y.Y.; Hughes, M. Drivers of innovation ambidexterity in small-to medium-sized firms. *Eur. Manag. J.* **2012**, *30*, 1–17.
108. Tiwana, A. Do bridging ties complement strong ties? An empirical examination of alliance ambidexterity. *Strateg. Manag. J.* **2008**, *29*, 251–272. [CrossRef]
109. O'Reilly, C.A., III; Tushman, M.L. Ambidexterity as a dynamic capability: Resolving the innovator's dilemma. *Res. Organ. Behav.* **2008**, *28*, 185–206. [CrossRef]

sustainability

Article

The Emergence of Resources Seeking Chinese Firms' Specific Advantages in Emerging Market

Ojo Olukayode Iwaloye [1,*], Hong Kei Im [1], Adeniyi Damilola Olarewaju [2], Ayantunji Gbadamosi [3], Jose Alves [4] and Michael Trimarchi [5]

1 School of Business, Macau University of Science and Technology, Macau SAR, China; hkim@must.edu.mo
2 Facultad: International Business, Tecnologico de Monterrey, Toluca 50110, Mexico; olarewajadeniyi@yahoo.com
3 Royal Docks School of Business and Law, University of East London, London E15 1NF, UK; a.gbadamosi@uel.ac.uk
4 Faculty of Business Administration, City University, Macau SAR, China; josealves@cityu.mo
5 Faculty of Business and Law, University of Saint Joseph, Macau SAR, China; michael.trimarchi@usj.edu.mo
* Correspondence: oiwaloye@must.edu.mo

Abstract: It is argued that the role of the Chinese government to support the cross-border operations of Chinese firms is to assist these firms in overcoming their limited established brands, and their disadvantages in technology and managerial resources, which were also the reasons why such firms decided to enter emerging markets instead of developed markets. This strategic choice is preferred to avoid direct confrontation with established firms from developed countries endowed with superior ownership advantages. Therefore, Chinese resources seeking firms innovate by increasing investment in developing and emerging markets to develop unique ownership advantages for sustainable market development and competitive advantage. This research investigates the ownership advantages of resources seeking Chinese firms in these markets using the OLI theory. The paper contributes to explaining the specific advantages of Chinese MNEs when entering emerging markets. The study applied a two-stage qualitative methodology to examine Chinese firms operating in Nigeria. The first stage included an exploratory study based on interviews with key informants and experts while the second stage included a case study methodology. The study focused on resources seeking Chinese MNEs operating in Nigeria.

Keywords: resources seeking MNEs; emerging markets; ownership advantages; OLI theory and Chinese firms

Citation: Iwaloye, O.O.; Im, H.K.; Olarewaju, A.D.; Gbadamosi, A.; Alves, J.; Trimarchi, M. The Emergence of Resources Seeking Chinese Firms' Specific Advantages in Emerging Market. *Sustainability* **2022**, *14*, 8345. https://doi.org/10.3390/su14148345

Academic Editors: Jeoung Yul Lee, Dilek Zamantili Nayir and Charles Chen

Received: 20 May 2022
Accepted: 29 June 2022
Published: 7 July 2022

1. Introduction

Ownership advantages are firm-specific competitive advantages that the firm possesses [1,2]. It is the why of MNEs activity [3] which are created through firm international experience, size, product differentiation, and product adaptability [4]. These intangible advantages create an added value to the firms and also aid the decision-making processes of these firms because it assists a firm in determining when these variables are transferable at a reasonable cost and in answering the question of why it should operate in another country. When firms have these advantages, they help to overcome the costs of cross-border production and increase the firm's revenue. It is seen as providing a competitive or monopolistic advantage to the firm when they derive economic rent [5]. These advantages are otherwise known as 'competitive' or 'monopolistic' advantages that compensate for the additional costs associated with setting up and operating abroad.

Dunning [3] identified several firm-specific advantages that give resource seeking MNEs an advantage over existing competitors in the host country [3]. They are capital, technology, access to market, complementary assets, size and negotiating strength, informational, management and marketing and organizational skills. These superior resources or capabilities [6] include surplus R&D capacity, economies of scale and scope, ability to generate brand, firm size and experience, know-how capability and production differentiation.

It has been noted that several firms from emerging markets, most especially Chinese resource seeking firms wishing to operate in developing markets, behaved differently due to the lack of these superior specific advantages over existing competitors [7,8]. Recent arguments of notable IB scholars, the likes of Buckley [9], Hernandez and Guillén [10], and He, Khan, Lew, and Fallon [11] supported the above statement that existing theories did not take into account the behavior of these firms. Nambisan and others [12], supported the informed contributions of these major theories as they served as theoretical foundations for most of the extant research in international business but most of them came up short in their applications to emerging market situations. Therefore, the emergence of resources seeking Chinese MNEs with large-scale business activities in emerging markets demands attention since they are not properly accommodated in most of the existing theories.

The emergence and large-scale operations of resource seeking Chinese MNCs in developing markets present considerable implications for international business theories. This study is advancing the applicability of existing OLI theory in relation to Matthew [7,13] and Luo and Zang's [14] advancement of other existing theories to provide relevant theories adequate for emerging MNEs' internalization. Dunning [15] and Narula [16] argued that the ownership, location, and internalization advantages (OLI) paradigm provides a theoretical basis for EMNCs' emergence and their internationalization behavior. These provided them the opportunity to move from the realm of imitators to fully globalized and innovative firms [13]. This study is to explore the advantages that orchestrated tremendous involvement of resources seeking Chinese operations in Nigeria.

2. Ownership Advantages of Chinese Resources Seeking Chinese

As mentioned, Dunning's OLI paradigm is among the leading theoretical approaches to explain the internationalization of activities of Western multinational corporations. This theory holds in the context of western multinationals but not necessarily for firms from emerging and developing countries. Research shows that the majority of ownership advantages are missing in Chinese multinationals [7,17] therefore the success of a Chinese firm's internalization activity cannot be based entirely on the ownership advantages that are present in western multinational enterprises [18,19], because conventional OLI theory doesn't fully account for Chinese MNES behavior and these firms' motivations differ from established Western MNEs [7,11,14,16]. However, OLI still provides a framework from which to build a new analytical framework to explain Chinese multinational firms in developing countries [15,16].

Resources seeking Chinese firms do not possess the same ownership advantages as Western companies due to different institutional factors, liabilities of foreignness, and liabilities of newness [20]. However, Chinese firms enjoy strong support from the Chinese government [21], allegedly overcoming their limited international experience and established brands [18,21]. Other advantages offered are sales channel power (monopolistic positioning), size and monetary resources, human capital, and technology [3,18,21–23]. The contrast between ownership advantages of resources seeking multinationals from developed countries and China are presented in Table 1, and each advantage is discussed in the following sections.

Table 1. Ownership advantages of resources seeking firms.

Resources Seeking MNEs	Chinese Resources Seeking MNEs
-Capital	-Government Support
-Technology	-Supporting network (Guanxi)
-Access to Markets	-Sales Channel Power
-Complementary Assets	-Size and monetary resources
-Size and Negotiating Strengths	-Technology

Source: Dunning, J. 2000 [3,4,15]; Alden, and Davies, 2006 [21]; Athreye et al. 2009 [18]; Morck and Zhao, 2008 [24].

2.1. Government Relationship

The relationship between the Chinese firms and the government is the core of China's economic reform [23]. The widespread involvement of the state in the international activities of Chinese firms helps them to maintain a symbiotic relationship of mutual interest with the government that is beyond commercial activities [23]. It is entangled with many facets of interest, including the Chinese government's ability to control its domestic economy, enhance state stability, and attain economic power in the global arena [25]. In some instances, companies such as China National Offshore Oil Corporation enjoy monopolistic privileges to operate in strategic industries [25].

Besides this, the Chinese government played a positive role by using a series of policies and state-owned financial institutions to support Chinese firms [26], including resources seeking Chinese firms [24]. Preferential arrangements include financial aids, management autonomy, profit retention, low-interest financing, favorable use of home currency for exchange, and reduced taxation [27].

2.2. Supporting Network

There has been growing interest among researchers in the influence of networking on operations of resources seeking Chinese firms in emerging markets. [28,29] pointed out that a supporting network is a key strategic instrument of Chinese firms' activities that links Chinese investors from home to host countries to promote professional *esprit de corps*, which leads to knowledge and experience sharing [30]. This practice is consistent with the concept of Guanxi, or social networking, which has been identified as one of the ownership advantages specific to the Chinese [19,23].

Chinese firms' interest in cross-border activity is highly encouraged by their extensive networking in other parts of the world [31]. Chinese firms are widely known to engage in extensive networking in search of opportunities to achieve corporate goals [7,32]. These forms of personal connection and special relationships are used as substitutes for formal institutional arrangements and are also employed to compensate for ownership and location disadvantages [23]. Chinese firms may be lacking in experience and established brands but supporting networks and the guanxi factor play a major role in the internalization drive of these companies. In Nigeria, a good number of Chinese investments were established through companies in Hong Kong and Taiwan [33,34].

2.3. Sales Channel Power

This is the ability of a channel member to control the marketing variables of any other member in a channel at a different level of distribution [35]. Channel members in China depend on the ownership structure and there are considerable unequal distributions of power among the different actors [36]. According to Polsa [36], Chinese state-owned actors tend to have management freedom, experience, and financial and social resources to operate more extensively than the other two actors. State-owned actors tend to dominate the distribution of material sources abroad. They are in a sort of monopolistic position against the other actors most especially in the private sector. Resource seeking Chinese firms' relationships with channel actors is positively linked to the concept of guanxi [22]. Network actors do most of the distribution within their network, and the source of their power is based on the value of their respective relationships in China.

2.4. Size and Enormous Resources

One of the important features of Chinese firms is their size and the monetary resources at their disposal [24,37]. The reform of large state-owned enterprises [37] provided resources seeking Chinese firms an advantage to access a large pool of capital [24]. Examples of preferential financial arrangements provided to these firms include financial aids, profit retention, low-interest financing, and reduced taxation [27]. Chinese firms possess access to special financing channels such as state allocation, state-owned national banks, and national government financial sources for the international market.

Dunning [38] noted that large firms endowed with resources such as skilled labor, monetary resources, and suitable investment opportunities have a greater tendency to move abroad. In this case, Chinese firms are no exception. Their size is related to resources which in turn is a strong determinant of growth through foreign direct investments [37].

2.5. Technology

Multinational enterprises should possess superior technology [17] to engage in cross-border activities. Some technology developed by Chinese firms in China was found to be unreliable and of low quality compared to foreign technology made in China [39]. The low level of Chinese technology [40] may not be adequate to compete favorably with their Western counterparts but it gives them unique leverage in developing countries [41]. Chinese technology has not only a cost advantage in developing countries, but its accessories are also unsophisticated [42,43], less expensive [44–46], and readily available [47].

Furthermore, emerging markets provide a suitable ground for Chinese firms to launch their brand of technology [41]. For example, recently, the Nigerian market was flooded with Chinese products with 100% Chinese technology, such as Chinese heavy-duty mining dump trucks, China-made Hono trucks, and Keno tractors. Another example in Nigeria is the electronic consumer market (televisions, air conditioners, refrigerators, and mobile phones). These products are cheaper than those from countries with advanced technology and they come with inexpensive spare parts. A good number of government and private contracts were also won and successively carried out by Chinese firms. One of these is the Dangote Cement plant in Ibese, Ogun State, built by Sinoma, a Chinese firm [48].

In summary, with the development of emerging market institutions and changes in environmental factors due largely to reforms and engagement with other emerging markets, there is pressure to examine the behavior of MNCs firms from these markets as they engage with each other. In this case, we deal with two countries, China and Nigeria, and the literature revealed that Chinese firms' internalization cannot be determined solely by ownership attributes experienced by Western firms. Unique factors such as Government relationship with Chinese MNCs, Home and abroad supporting networks, Chinese type of technology, Chinese MNCs' enormous resources, and an impregnable sales Channel network of Chinese MNCs are important factors that distinguish them from other MNCs in the Western world. Although terms such as technology; capital and size, and monetary resources are similar, government relationships, support networks, and sales power channels revealed the differences between developed markets and emerging market ownership advantages. Table 2 below showed the similarities and differences which are to be tested further in the exploratory stage of this research.

Table 2. Emerging and Developed Markets Ownership Advantages.

Similarities	Differences
1. Capital/Size and Monetary Resources 2. Technology	1. Government Relationship 2. Sales Channel Power 3. Supporting Network

3. Methods

The explorative nature of this investigation to draw a distinction between Western firms and emerging firms determined our consideration for the choice of qualitative research method with a focus on the case study. This method is adequate for this research because previous knowledge may not be adequate to shed light on the activities of emerging markets MNCs operating in emerging markets. Therefore, the choice is an important tool to identify and understand the new phenomenon that is rising rapidly concerning Chinese MNCs' activities in Nigeria. It is suited to opening the black box of the organization process [49].

Given the number of Chinese MNCs operating in Nigeria, it will also be a difficult task to adopt a quantitative research method even though it is considered the best approach for MNC study in IB. Its richness in developing new theory [50] and contributions to an in-depth understanding of the context in the real-world justify its adoption for this study. The study on resources seeking Chinese firms' ownership advantages applied a two-stage qualitative methodology [51] to revisit the specific ownership advantages of resources seeking Chinese firms operating in Nigeria.

As an exploratory empirical study, the aim of this paper is to capture and justify the appropriateness of the constructs assembled from the literature that were tested in stage two using the case study method. The new concepts from the literature cannot be used directly, they need to go through robust scrutiny, confirming identification and addition through several expert's involvement using open question interviews made this preliminary section inevitable. The second stage aimed to further address the issues identified in the first stage. It offers in-depth empirical inquiry to investigate contemporary issues within a real-life context to provide rich information through multiple sources to describe the phenomenon.

3.1. Preliminary Study

The first stage includes a preliminary study encompassing exploratory interviews for the first part of the investigation [49,50,52]. The exploratory research interview method is acknowledged for its effectiveness to justify the appropriateness of the resources seeking Chinese firms' ownership advantages constructs assembled in the research. Besides justifying and validating the relevance of the constructs, it also led to the identification of new concepts in the final development of the list of ownership advantages specific to Chinese resources seeking firms in emerging markets.

This exploratory research was in two phases. The first phase included a detailed review of the literature and face-to-face interviews with seven academic experts in the field of International Business, two academic experts in the field of China-African studies from Mainland China, and three from Hong Kong and two from Macau. Considering the goal of this paper, the second phase in the exploratory study involved six CEOs and fourteen Managers doing business in Nigeria and China as indicated in Table 3. The six CEOs participated in both exploratory and case study interviews. The remaining fourteen participants were seasoned managers involved in exportation and importation businesses across the two countries.

Table 3. Preliminary exploratory study interview participants.

Interviewees' Codes	**P1**	**P2**	**P3**	**P4**	**P5**	**P6**	**P7**	**P8**	**P9**	**P10**	**P11**	**P12**	**P13**	**P14**	**P15**	**P16**	**P17**	**P18**	**P19**	**P20**	**P21**	**P22**	**P23**	**P24**	**P25**	**P26**	**P27**
Language	1 2 3	1 2 3	1 2 3	1 2 3	1 2 4	1 5	1 5	1 4	1 2 3	1 3 4	1 2 5	1 3 5	1 3 4	1 2 3 5	1 2 3	1 2 3	1 2 3	1 6	1 6	1 4 6	1 5	1 5	1 4 5 6	1 5	1 5	1 4	1 3 4
Position	1	1	1	1	2	2	2	3	3	3	3	2	2	2	2	2	2	2	2	2	2	2	3	3	1	1	1
Nationality	1	1	1	1	2	2	2	2	1	2	2	2	2	2	1	1	1	1	1	2	2	2	2	2	2	2	2
Key	Language: English 1, Cantonese 2, Mandarin 3, Yoruba 4, Igbo 5, Hausa 6; Position: Academic Professor 1, Manager 2 and CEO 3; Nationality: Chinese 1, Nigerian 2; Location: Macau 1, China Mainland 2, Hong Kong 3																										

We start with a purposeful sampling strategy using a snowballing or chain sampling approach to gather Chinese and Nigerians doing business in China and Nigeria. The approach helps us locate information-rich informants [53] because the first respondents directed us to the next respondent who has vast knowledge and experience in the area of this study. [53]. These respondents were chosen because they all have a good number of years of dealing in business activities in Nigeria and Mainland China. All the respondents also speak English, and the majority of them can speak either Cantonese or Mandarin. This makes it very easy to conduct the interview with the assistance of two secretaries without missing important valued points. These 27 respondents were contacted, and the face-to-face interviews took place in Macau, Hong Kong, and Mainland China.

The data analysis process began with the transcription of responses from the interview because a majority of the interviewees did not agree to the use of audio and video materials. Therefore, qualified assistants were engaged to take notes along with me, to make sure every word was recorded, and not to lose the meanings of issues discussed by respondents during the interview. Next, themes drawn out from the discussions were categorized and differentiated by attaching labels such as phrases and sentences to 'chunk' the data from the 27 interviews. Finally, new codes and categories were added as they were discovered during the reading and revision of the data, which simplified the process of highlighting cogent quotes and themes necessary for the analysis of the data.

This first approach used in this paper allowed us to dig deeper into the phenomenon as it is appropriate for under-researched areas and also contributes to an in-depth understanding of the context in the real world [54] and solving practical research [55]. The Chinese firms' specific advantages such as government relationships, supporting networks, sales channel power, size, and monetary resources and technology, found in the literature were validated and considered appropriate for the exploratory study. The first stage findings revealed further that the two-stage research adopted is appropriate. There were modifications, and supporting networks and sales channel power were combined as supporting networks. On the other hand, 'Chinese technology' was adopted to differentiate from other technologies from advanced countries. Size and monetary resources also changed to size and enormous resources, and supporting infrastructures initially seen as a location advantage was considered as ownership advantages of Chinese MNEs.

3.2. Case Studies

Considering the difficulties associated with using quantitative survey instruments with Chinese firms operating in emerging markets as well as using exploratory research interviews alone is not sufficient for research of this nature. Therefore, the findings in the stage one exploratory research set the stage for the second stage study using multiple interview-based case studies to establish the final ownership advantages of Chinese MNEs in emerging markets. The approach appeals in its ability to collect data necessary to address all the issues identified in the exploratory stage of the research. The ownership advantages were developed into five concepts (identified in the literature and tested and explored in stage one of the research) to study the ownership advantages of resources seeking Chinese firms operating in emerging markets. The method offers the researcher the ability to substantiate the final part of the inductive processes because it offers a detailed investigation in terms of data analysis, vis-à-vis the application of preliminary interviews.

The second phase began with six in-depth cases, which included twelve main case interviews on the basis of purposeful sampling, identifying theoretical and literal replication as indicated in Table 4. They were top management personnel from the level of Senior Manager to Group Chairman. They were selected based on their understanding and involvement in bilateral trade agreements between Nigeria and China. Their roles and experience in managing Chinese resources seeking firms in Nigeria were considered important factors. Each of the participants was contacted by phone and a consent letter was immediately sent by mail. A detailed but brief explanation of the nature of the research was made by phone. The consent letter expressly detailed the purpose and benefits of collecting the information. Participation was made voluntary and the right to withdraw from the exercise was available. An assurance to protect privacy, respect identities, and the identification of the researcher and their affiliations were provided. A minimum of one and a half to two hours was assigned and devoted to each interview but the longest lasted about two hours and fifteen minutes.

Table 4. Cases and interviewees' profiles.

Case Codes	CA		CB		CC		CD		CE		CF	
Interviewees' Codes	CA1	CA2	CB1	CB2	CC1	CC2	CD1	CD2	CE1	CE2	CF1	CF2
Nationality	1	2	1	1	2	2	1	1	1	1	1	2
Key	Chinese 1, Nigerian 2 and Location: Macau 1, China Mainland 2, Hong Kong 3											

In the research, codes were developed to represent the identities of the respondents and their employers in the data. The quotes and perceptions of the interviewees were directly included in the analysis and research findings without disclosing their true identities [53,56]. These steps enhanced the quality of the data collected from each interviewee who felt at ease to give his/her maximum support to reveal enrich information as to whether the resources seeking Chinese firms' constructs should be considered as firms' specific advantage. The strategies help the researcher to entrench the rights of all the stakeholders and adhere to ethical considerations. The data collected were guided by the concepts analyzed.

All the interviewees occupied a top position at the time of interview.

4. Findings

Based on the convergence of seven experts in the field of International Business, six CEOs and fourteen Managers' views expressed in the interviews, the respondents involved ownership advantages popular with developed markets resources seeking MNEs such as capital, technology, access to markets, complementary assets and size and negotiating strengths into what they regarded as ownership advantages of Chinese resource seeking MNEs -*Chinese government relations, Chinese type of technology, supporting networks, enormous resources, and impregnable sales Channel networks of Chinese MNEs were identified as important factors that distinguish them from other MNEs.* They also agreed, through their preliminary interviews, that these five factors in the literature are useful constructs relevant for the case study of Chinese firms' ownership advantages specific to resources seeking Chinese MNCs. Therefore, the presentation of the findings is to synthesize the respondents' views from the exploratory stage and case studies in the form of the emergent themes related and linked to Chinese resources seeking ownership advantages in Nigeria. Each of the five specific concepts is discussed below.

4.1. Government Relationship

In stage one, Chinese managers mentioned frequently the role of the Chinese government in supporting the internationalization process. For example, P3 mentioned that "The objective of sourcing for raw materials to fuel Chinese growth and development make the home government to provide for the financial need of the Chinese firms in Nigeria". Another participant (CA1) in stage two emphasized that "Chinese government provided different opportunities and avenues to help (Chinese firms)... they have unhindered access to cheap loans through their export and import bank–(the) Export-Import Bank of China. Participant (P19) also mentioned that "over 3 billion US dollars has been invested by the Chinese government on Chinese firms operating in Nigeria", and participant CB2 confirmed vividly that "My government financially encouraged the move to Nigeria".

Nigerian managers also recognized the distinctive role of top Chinese and Nigerian leaders in helping Chinese firms to handle major projects in Nigeria. This indirectly opens financial sources for Chinese MNEs in Nigeria. Participants CB1reinforced the belief that "An agreement with Nigeria's Communications Ministry for a Telecom Network project was witnessed by the Presidents of China and Nigeria-Mr. Hu Jintao and Chief Olusegun Obasanjo in Beijing ... and CF1 summed it up rhetorically "with these types of people working for Chinese company success is sure in Nigeria, why do you think they would not like to do business in our country".

The experts and business executives unanimously identified that resource seeking Chinese firms are fulfilling their home country objectives as indicated by participants 3 and CC2 that "Nigeria is blessed with majority of natural resources such as oil and gas, iron ore, Kaolin, gold and cassava and the objective of sourcing for raw materials to fuel Chinese growth and development make the home government to provide for financial need of Chinese MNEs in Nigeria". It is evident from this plethora of views that the relationship between Chinese firms and their home government is a form of competitive advantage. Financial support, preferential treatment, and management autonomy were identified as important factors that establish the Chinese government's relationship with Chinese firms in Nigeria.

4.2. Supporting Network

Different networks were identified by the majority of the respondents such as the Nigerian-China network, old generation Chinese firm network, and new generation Chinese firm network. The majority of respondents in stage one of this research saw this as a link to their participation in trade and business-related activities in Nigeria and as an important factor attracting new Chinese firms to engage in business in Nigeria. For example, P16 confirmed that "No matter which of the networks on which they came into Nigeria, there is no distinction among these networks. Whether it is the Nigeria-Chinese government network with Nigeria government, old generation of Chinese firm's network and individual company network" This axiom was supported by Chinese manager (CB2) that "the network that brought us to Nigeria and other developing world is the network between our government and most of these countries".

It was confirmed in the two stages that this general attitude of Chinese firms working together was exploited to resolve common problems in Nigeria. For example, P6/CE2 stated that training and helping new members to negotiate contracts and agreements with local firms and fighting common problems such as double taxation and frequent public holidays make them even better than most Nigerian firms. In the same manner, its Chinese counterpart (CF1) established that "we provide information they required to start their business in Nigeria and whenever they run into troubles, we are willing hands to help them out of it". He further claimed that any new Chinese company that needs their assistance must be a member of the association. A few Chinese elites such as Philip Tung and Jacob Wood were mentioned. They are used to the Nigerian business environment and were mentioned with more than six decades of experience.

Interestingly, respondents tend to see congruence in supporting network and sales channel power as Chinese firms benefit from the symbiotic relationship among themselves. The influence of their interconnection, interaction, and cooperation is seen as a specific advantage in terms of a formidable network to support each other. Issues such as institutional distance and liabilities of foreignness were addressed through this type of experience-sharing framework. Many of the respondents believed that they are at home in Nigeria. For instance, CE1 set the record straight with "It is only Chinese people who know African people very well. Nigerian and Chinese have the same Culture". Finally, a Nigerian manager concluded that "these Chinese supporting network do influence most of Chinese firms to Nigeria".

4.3. Chinese Technology

The theme was captured within these four dimensions: affordability, availability, maintainability, and unavoidability considering the views of the majority of respondents from both stages one and two. For example, in stages one and two, Chinese managers P4/CD2 claimed that Chinese types of technology are affordable and available "Not only that they are fast moving products ... the price is affordable and they are everywhere in Nigeria ... investment cost is very low compare to when you have to import heavy machines from Europe". Likewise, senior Chinese managers recognized why the products are available at the lowest price and against the market price. CD1 insinuated that both

Nigerian and Chinese hugely contributed to the affordability of Chinese technology. "Low labor cost at home and host countries coupled with great talents to develop the best products at affordable price advantage".

One common thing about Chinese technology in Nigeria is that the cost of maintaining Chinese technology is really low and therefore accepted by users. CD2 established this fact when stating"It is not easy to find other accessories from other countries in Nigeria .... the reason is that Chinese tech parts are very cheap in Nigeria and they are able to buy them". A Chinese manager purposely claimed that they are able to achieve that because they are in the best position to meet Nigerian business needs, "you know that we are also from a developing country; we do understand what business environment in developing countries looks like". We fully understand what Nigeria needs from us (CB1). Therefore, CC1 concluded that "Nigerian consumers are faced with many Chinese brands that are very cheap at a reasonable good quality".

Chinese types of technology are not just available and affordable; they are meeting the needs of Nigerian users such as telecommunication companies even though there were slightly different opinions from some quarters. "The quality may be below what we use to get from Europe years back but is the right thing to have started during the time of President Obasanjo' (CE2)". A Chinese manager claimed that "We do not believe in substandard products because Hi-tech technology cannot be compromised at the level we operate". Apart from testimonies from Hi-tech companies, a Nigerian manager (CF1) working with hard resources seeking Chinese firm testified and provided examples of such products as the China Hono Truck, BZK D45 Dump Truck, Keno tractors, and other heavy-duty agricultural products by Beijing Zhonghua and Changzhou Dongfeng companies.

The participants claim that the Chinese level of technology was ideal for resource extractive activities in Nigeria since they do not only meet the need in this market but are also available and affordable and invariably become unavoidable. These are justifications for the theme of inclusion as an ownership advantage. It was repeatedly claimed as 'Chinese technology' to differentiate it from other technologies in advanced markets.

4.4. Size and Enormous Resources

Another important firm's specific advantage that emerged repeatedly from this study is the size and sufficient resources at the disposal of Chinese resource seeking firms operating in Nigeria. Evidence from stages one and two show that resources such as skilled labor, monetary resources, and technology were deployed for investment opportunities in Nigeria. A Nigerian businessman (P13) made the assertion that "They are not the type of organizations that wait for foreign government assistance before they realize their objectives". In stage two, a senior Chinese manager (CD2) provided the opinion that "The money they possess without considering what they get from my government to transact business for them is enough to take over business in Africa".

Resources seeking Chinese firms are known to be large because of their antecedent and capabilities in all business areas in Africa. For example, a Chinese manager in Nigeria confirmed that "Chinese firms in Nigeria such as ZTE, Huawei, SINOPEC, and CNOCC are big companies and are as big as other firms from other countries" (CD2). They become bigger in Nigeria due to their formation and structure. According to participant CF1, he claimed that "The first company my Grandfather established when he came to Nigeria was known a (large Chinese Company) ... he brought (three other large Chinese. companies to Nigeria) ... from Enamel wares, we moved into metals, plastic, glass, wastepipes, fibre weaving, iron, mining and steel" (CF1). Another Chinese Manager (CA1) confirmed the above statement "My company has not metamorphosed into any group like Lee Group, Wempco Group and other Chinese conglomerations ... but still in the process of becoming a big Chinese firms in Nigeria".

The size of their resources positions the Chinese firms to be recognized in Nigeria and other developing nations. Their ownership structure influences the nature and composition of each group of companies. The formation provides the opportunity to demonstrate their intention to work in different mining companies. It also reveals a unique capability that differentiates them with an added advantage from both local and foreign competitors.

4.5. Supporting Infrastructures

There were general indications from stages one and two that supporting infrastructures are inadequate for resources seeking Chinese firms to achieve their goals. It was reputedly mentioned by Chinese and Nigerian managers (CE1/CD1) that "Nigeria cannot be compared to China in term of infrastructures facilities but its government is trying to provide the basic ones" and "Nigeria is not having the best infrastructures now but they are still enough for Chinese companies to invest in Nigeria". In stage one, P1 and P6 supported CE1's assertion of what needs to be resolved in the provision of unavailable facilities in Nigeria before achieving their goals because of the poor state of infrastructures in Nigeria. "Chinese firms have started investing in infrastructures by bring in technology aim for infrastructures development ... Huge amount of resources was deplored into Nigeria to provide supporting infrastructures and engagement in providing facilities that will aid development to Nigeria".

Inadequate infrastructures pose complications in operating business in Nigeria. A Chinese manager rhetorically complained about the poor condition of Nigerian roads. "Nigerians roads have caused us so much when our Lorries involved in series of accidents...we have to cover so many distances on road since there are limited numbers of airport base in Nigeria" (CD2). In the same manner, another manager from China operating in Nigeria said to CC1 "Nigerian business men cry every day because of epileptic nature of power in the country; we do not complain. Instead we decided to generate power more than what we need. We give out to the nearby communities" a statement supported by a Nigerian manager CF1. Some of the firms from China knew that they needed to provide basic infrastructures before they can get what they want such as natural resources (CC1/CF1).

To resolve the inadequacies, Chinese resource seeking firms entered into an agreement with the Nigerian Government according to CC1. "Nigerian Government allowed these firms to create their own infrastructures ... to build, operate and transfer (BOT) at later date". In summary, the lack of quality supporting infrastructures in Nigeria should have discouraged Chinese firms from investing in the solid mineral sector as inadequacies had caused the majority of Chinese firms to lose properties, time, and lives. However, the decision or agreement to join forces with the Nigerian government in order to improve the standard of supporting facilities that will provide access to natural resources in Nigeria creates a sort of advantage for Chinese resources seeking Chinese firms.

4.6. Findings: Similarities and Differences

From Table 5 below, the findings confirm that there were similarities and differences in Dunning's lists of Ownership advantages and resources seeking Chinese MNCs. The literature review and exploratory study showed that capital/size and enormous resources are similar in nature compared to government relationships, support networks, and supporting infrastructures are features specific to Chinese MNCs. In the final stage, access to markets, complementary assets, and size and negotiating strengths are not specific features of Chinese MNCs.

Table 5. Similarities and Differences Identification in Research Stages.

Types	Literature Review	Exploratory Study	Case Study
Similarities	Capital/Size and Monetary Resources; Technology	Size and Enormous Resources; Chinese Technology	

Table 5. Cont.

Types		Literature Review	Exploratory Study	Case Study
Differences	Chinese MNCs	Government Relationship; Sales Channel Power; Supporting Network	Government Relationship; Supporting Network; Supporting Infrastructures	Government Relationship; Supporting Network; Size and Enormous Resources; Chinese Technology; Supporting Infrastructures
	Developed Market MNCs	Complementary Assets; Size and Negotiating Strengths; Access to Markets	Complementary Assets; Size and Negotiating Strengths; Access to Markets	Complementary Assets; Size and Negotiating Strengths; Access to Markets

5. Discussion

This finding provides empirical confirmation that Chinese government-firm relations manifested under the soft provisions from the parent body. For instance, financial support [21,57,58] preferential treatments [24], and management autonomy [59–61] provided resources seeking Chinese firms' additional advantages over their competitors in an emerging market. It was noted that the relationship between Chinese firms and their government is the core of China's economic reform [23]. This was due to long years of ownership structure between them, a strategic tool to achieve political and economic gains. On this ground, a series of policy tools and state-owned financial institutions were used to financially support Chinese firms [24]. Financial support, management autonomy, and preferential treatment are vividly reflected in resources seeking Chinese firms' performance in Nigeria.

The research further expanded the values associated with foreign supporting networks by Chinese firms operating outside their domain to demonstrate the development of core competence in relational/supporting networks termed *Guanxi* is an important form of Chinese firms' specific advantages [19,23,29]. The research confirmed that the institution distance and liabilities of the foreignness phenomenon were addressed by the role of business networking because Chinese firms earn support through the linking of individuals and institutions in a knowledge and experience sharing type of framework [30]. The support of the Chinese network is a cultural phenomenon in China. It is seen as a system of social networks and influential relationships in Chinese society and it plays some important roles such as business relationship development and supporting the growth of firms' operations both home and abroad. The research confirmed that Chinese firms are widely known to engage in extensive networking in search of opportunities and performance [7,32].

The research also found that availability [47], affordability [45,46,62], and the maintainability of Chinese technology in the emerging market make their substandard technology relevant. Chinese substandard technologies in this regard are a case of relative or comparative advantage for Chinese multinationals operating in emerging markets [41]. The firm's level of technology may not be adequate to compete favorably with their Western counterparts, but it gives them unique leverage in developing countries. Chinese technology is what developing countries need because of its cost advantage. The spare parts are readily available [41], unsophisticated [42,43] and less expensive [44–46].

Enormous resources such as skilled labor, monetary resources, technology, and suitable investment opportunities [63] are important features of Chinese firms [11]. The research found that the Chinese government used its control power over state-owned financial institutions to provide resources seeking Chinese firms' adequate sources of financial resources. Examples of preferential financial arrangements are financial aids, profit retention, low-interest financing, favorable exchange rate, and reduced taxation [27]. Other special financing channels are state allocation, state-owned national banks, and national government financial sources for the international market. From these indications, without the Chinese government's implicit and explicit control over these firms, the financial structures would not have been erected. Therefore, the ownership structure gives Chinese firms the advantage of access to a large pool of capital [37]. It was rightly indicated that financial support in the form of state allocation and low-interest loans from State-owned banks makes these Chinese firms super-rich to the extent that they do not wait for foreign government assistance before they realize their objectives of accessing natural resources in Nigeria.

Availability or improved supporting infrastructures such as power, water, transportation, telecommunications, and technology are critical for foreign direct investment into developing markets [4,64–68]. The research found that resources seeking Chinese firms made the inadequate resources adequate because inadequate infrastructures pose some form of complications in operating business in Nigeria. They also demonstrated their support to the Nigerian government to improve the existing facilities.

Resources seeking Chinese firms recognize the importance of quality supporting infrastructures; they entered into agreements to upgrade basic infrastructural facilities to facilitate their investments and also reduce the cost of operations. In reality, the lack of quality supporting infrastructures in Nigeria should have discouraged Chinese firms from operating in the solid mineral sector as most of the literature suggested, but the decision or agreement by resources seeking Chinese firms to join forces with the Nigerian government in order to improve the standard of supporting facilities was not confirmed from any literature. This effort to make the supporting infrastructures available at a better state categorized this element as resources seeking Chinese firm ownership advantage

Basically, the paper reaffirmed the importance of the international business theory of eclectic paradigm by looking into the activities of Chinese resources seeking firms in emerging markets. A total of five ownership advantages emerged that have been considered before, with a few factors that are somehow similar contextually but different when operationalized. These were the use of Government-firm relationships, Supporting networks, and Chinese Technology. Size and monetary resources and Supporting infrastructures factors are contributions to OLI theory by John Dunning within the emerging market context.

6. Implication for Theory, Policy and Practice

The literature review implies that prior research can provide a framework for new research and the perceptions of experts and international business executives are essential to explore and refine new concepts and constructs to understand the activities of resources seeking firms in Nigeria. An exploratory research study also would not have been enough for a theory-building study of this nature, but a two-stage research method provided the window to understand the reality that old theories are inadequate to make new MNCs sustainable in today's global markets.

A new approach of this nature also has implications for policymakers in emerging markets, and international business and marketing practitioners. The Chinese government can align with the Nigerian or other governments in emerging markets to further strengthen their bilateral relationship with elements that make resources seeking firms use these ownership advantages. The Nigerian government and other policymakers in emerging markets, provide incentives that will make MNCs invest in their market considering the dynamic nature of their environment.

One important piece of information to managers is that the research provides holistic or different business or marketing opportunities to resources seeking firms. They have to examine their specific advantages before internalizing them in emerging markets with abundant natural resources. Strong ownership advantages are the most important tools for resources seekers in emerging markets. It helps them to efficiently use the funding and resources at their disposal to gain a competitive advantage and aspire to achieve growth and sustainability.

7. Limitation and Direction for Further Studies

Despite the robustness of the qualitative analysis, this study has some noteworthy limitations. Qualitative research is rare in international business and the dominance of quantitative research is a limitation to the adoption of this research. There is also a limitation to the extent to which the findings can be generalized to the wider population.

Nonetheless, previous knowledge and ways of doing research may not be adequate to shed light on the activities of emerging multinationals operating in emerging markets. Qualitative research is a uniquely suited tool to identify and understand new phenomena that are rising rapidly within the research context. The research is also not aimed at testing pre-defined hypotheses. The research in this area is not exhaustive and there are promising avenues for future studies. Exploratory studies on the strategic motives of resources seeking Chinese multinationals as well as the outcome of internalizing the ownership advantages in other developing markets are further areas of study.

8. Conclusions

A total of five resources seeking Chinese firms' ownership advantages emerged from this present research. The analysis of each of the constructs demonstrated the importance of revisiting ownership advantages as demonstrated by John Dunning. The evidence from data collected and examined showed that Chinese technology, supporting network, size, monetary resources, government-firm relationship, and supporting infrastructures are specific attributes of Chinese firms seeking resources in an emerging market. The findings confirm that there were similarities and differences in Dunning's lists of Ownership advantages of capital, technology, access to markets, complementary assets and size, and negotiating strengths. These specific advantages enable the resources seeking firm to survive the business terrains in emerging and developing markets.

Author Contributions: Each author contributed in the following areas. Conceptualization, O.O.I. and A.G.; Methodology, O.O.I. and A.G.; Software, A.D.O.; Validation by O.O.I., A.G., J.A. and M.T.; Formal analysis by O.O.I. and J.A.; Investigation by O.O.I., A.G., J.A. and M.T.; Resources provided by H.K.I.; Data curation carried out by A.D.O., A.G., J.A. and M.T.; Writing—original draft preparation by O.O.I.; Writing—review and editing, J.A. and H.K.I.; Visualization by J.A.; Supervision, O.O.I.; Project administration, O.O.I.; Funding, by all the contributing authors: O.O.I., H.K.I., J.A., A.G., M.T. and A.D.O. All authors have read and agreed to the published version of the manuscript.

Funding: This research received no external funding.

Institutional Review Board Statement: Not applicable.

Informed Consent Statement: Not applicable.

Data Availability Statement: The data presented in this study are available on request from the corresponding author. The data are not publicly available due to the nature of the data collected. The majority of participants did not allow the use of audio and video. The interviews were handwritten, with the consent not to disclose the firms involved.

Conflicts of Interest: The authors declare no conflict of interest.

References

1. Brouthers, K.D.; Brouthers, L.E.; Werner, S. Dunning's eclectic theory and the smaller firm: The impact of ownership and locational advantages on the choice of entry-modes in the computer software industry. *Int. Bus. Rev.* **1996**, *5*, 377–394. [CrossRef]
2. Porter, M.E. *Competitive Strategy: Techniques for Analyzing Industries and Competitors*; Free Press: New York, NY, USA, 1980.
3. Dunning, J.H. *Multinational Enterprises and the Global Economy*; Addison-Wesley: New York, NY, USA, 2002.
4. Dunning, J.H. *Multinational Enterprises and the Global Economy*; Addison-Wesley: Essex, UK, 1993.
5. Fletcher, R.; Brown, L. *International Marketing: An Asia-Pacific Perspective*; Pearson Education Australia: Frenchs Forest, NSW, Australia, 2008.
6. Child, J.; Rodriguez, S.B. The Internationalization of Chinese Firms: A Case for Theoretical Extension? *Manag. Organ. Rev.* **2005**, *1*, 381–410. [CrossRef]
7. Mathews, J.A. Dragon Multinationals: New Players in 21st Century Globalization. *Asia Pac. J. Manag.* **2006**, *23*, 5–27.
8. Narula, R. Globalization, new ecologies, new zoologies, and the purported death of the eclectic paradigm. *Asia Pac. J. Manag.* **2006**, *23*, 143–151. [CrossRef]
9. Buckley, P.J. Internalisation Theory and Outward Direct Investment by Emerging Market Multinationals. *Manag. Int. Rev.* **2017**, *58*, 195–224. [CrossRef]
10. Hernandez, E.; Guillén, M.F. What's theoretically novel about emerging-market multinationals? *J. Int. Bus. Stud.* **2018**, *49*, 24–33. [CrossRef]

11. He, S.; Khan, Z.; Lew, Y.K.; Fallon, G. Technological innovation as a source of Chinese multinationals' firm-specific advantages and internationalization. *Int. J. Emerg. Mark.* **2019**, *14*, 115–133. [CrossRef]
12. Nambisan, S.; Zahra, S.A.; Luo, Y. Global platforms and ecosystems: Implications for international business theories. *J. Int. Bus. Stud.* **2019**, *50*, 1464–1486. [CrossRef]
13. Mathews, J.A. Dragon multinationals powered by linkage, leverage and learning: A review and development. *Asia Pac. J. Manag.* **2017**, *34*, 769–775. [CrossRef]
14. Luo, Y.; Zhang, H. Emerging Market MNEs: Qualitative Review and Theoretical Directions. *J. Int. Manag.* **2016**, *22*, 333–350. [CrossRef]
15. Dunning, J.H. Comment on Dragon multinationals: New players in 21st century globalization. *Asia Pac. J. Manag.* **2006**, *23*, 139–141. [CrossRef]
16. Narula, R. Do we need different frameworks to explain infant MNEs from developing countries? *Glob. Strat. J.* **2012**, *2*, 188–204. [CrossRef]
17. Peng, M.W. The global strategy of emerging multinationals from China. *Glob. Strat. J.* **2012**, *2*, 97–107. [CrossRef]
18. Athreye, S.; Kapur, S. Introduction: The Internationalization of Chinese and Indian Firms-Trends, Motivations and Strategy. *Ind. Corp. Chang.* **2009**, *18*, 209–221.
19. Shapiro, D.M.; Gedajlovic, E.; Erdener, C. The chinese family firm as a multinational enterprise. *Int. J. Organ. Anal.* **2003**, *11*, 105–122. [CrossRef]
20. Li, P.P. Toward a Geocentric Theory of Multinational Evolution: The Implications from the Asian MNEs as Latecomers. *Asia Pac. J. Manag.* **2003**, *20*, 217–242. [CrossRef]
21. Alden, C.; Davies, M. A profile of the operations of Chinese multinationals in Africa. *S. Afr. J. Int. Aff.* **2006**, *13*, 83–96. [CrossRef]
22. Dickson, M.A.; Zhang, L. Supplier-retailer relationships in China's distribution channel for foreign brand apparel. *J. Fash. Mark. Manag.* **2004**, *8*, 201–220. [CrossRef]
23. Liu, J.; Scott-Kennel, J. Asset-seeking investment by Chinese multinationals: Firm ownership, location, and entry mode. *Asia Pac. Glob. Rev.* **2011**, *1*, 16–36.
24. Morck, R.; Yeung, B.; Zhao, M. Perspectives on China's outward foreign direct investment. *J. Int. Bus. Stud.* **2008**, *39*, 337–350.
25. Chen, X.; Lee, C.-W.J.; Li, J. Chinese Tango: Government Assisted Earnings Management. Available online: https://ssrn.com/abstract=408800 (accessed on 19 May 2022).
26. Buckley, P.J.; Cross, A.R.; Tan, H.; Xin, L.; Voss, H. Historical and Emergent Trends in Chinese Foreign Direct Investment. *Manag. Int. Rev.* **2008**, *48*, 715–748. [CrossRef]
27. Wu, F. Corporate China goes Global. *World Econ.* **2005**, *6*, 171–181.
28. Santos, M.R.; Ruffin, C. Global village vs. small town: Understanding Networks at the Base of the Pyramid. *Int. Bus. Rev.* **2010**, *19*, 126–139. [CrossRef]
29. Lee, J.-W.; Abosag, I.; Kwak, J. The role of networking and commitment in foreign market entry process: Multinational corporations in the Chinese automobile industry. *Int. Bus. Rev.* **2012**, *21*, 27–39. [CrossRef]
30. Ajayi, S.B. Introduction: A general overview. In *Foreign Direct Investment in Sub-Saharan Africa: Origins, Targets, Impact and Potential*; Ajayi, S., Ed.; African Economic Research Consortium: Nairobi, Kenya, 2006; pp. 1–8.
31. Klossek, A.; Linke, B.M.; Nippa, M. Chinese enterprises in Germany: Establishment modes and strategies to mitigate the liability of foreignness. *J. World Bus.* **2012**, *47*, 35–44. [CrossRef]
32. Peng, M.W.; Luo, Y. Manageria ties and firm performance in a transition economy. The nature of micro macro link. *Acad. Manag. J.* **2000**, *43*, 486–501.
33. Chen, T.-J. Liability of foreignness and entry mode choice: Taiwanese firms in Europe. *J. Bus. Res.* **2006**, *59*, 288–294. [CrossRef]
34. Elango, B. Minimizing effects of 'liability of foreignness': Response strategies of foreign firms in the United States. *J. World Bus.* **2009**, *44*, 51–62. [CrossRef]
35. Hollensen, S. *Global Marketing: A Decision-Oriented Approach*, 3rd ed.; Prentice Hall: Upper Saddle River, NJ, USA, 2004.
36. Polsa, P. *Power and Distribution Network Structure in the People's Republic of China-The Case of an Inland City in Transition*; Svenska Handelshögskolan: Vaasa, Finland, 2002.
37. Cheng, Y.S.; Lo, D. Firm Size, Technical Efficiency and Productivity Growth in Chinese Industry. Department of Economics, University of London, Available from School of Oriental and African Studies. (No. 144). 2004. Available online: https://eprints.soas.ac.uk/105/1/econ144.pdf (accessed on 19 May 2022).
38. Dunning, J.H. The Eclectic Paradigm of International Production. A Restatement and some possible Extension. *J. Int. Bus.* **1988**, *19*, 1–33. [CrossRef]
39. David, B.; Hongyu, Z. International technology transfer: Perceptions and reality of quality and reliability. *J. Manuf. Technol. Manag.* **2004**, *15*, 410–415.
40. Von Zedtwitz, M.; Ikeda, T.; Li, G.; Carpenter, R.; Hämäläinen, S. Managing Foreign R&D in China. *Res. Technol. Manag.* **2007**, *50*, 19–27.
41. Paul, G.; Woetzel, J.R.; Wu, Y. Can Chinese brands make it abroad? *McKinsey Q.* **2003**, 54–65.
42. Kiley, D. Is America Ready for Cheap Chinese Cars? Available online: https://www.bloomberg.com/news/articles/2007-07-09/is-america-ready-for-cheap-chinese-cars-businessweek-business-news-stock-market-and-financial-advice (accessed on 19 May 2022).

43. Javorcik, B.S.; Saggi, K. Technological asymmetry among foreign investors and mode of entry. *Econ. Inq.* **2010**, *48*, 415–433. [CrossRef]
44. Wai-sum, S.; Carmen Hau-Ming Chan, P. Country-of-origin effects on product evaluations: The case of Chinese consumers in Hong Kong. *J. Int. Mark. Mark. Res.* **1997**, *22*, 115–122.
45. Shi, L. Is 'Made in China' still an indicator of cheap goods? *Am. Met. Mark.* **2010**, *119*, 38.
46. Rangasamy, L.; Swanepoel, J.A. China's impact on South African trade and inflation. *Dev. S. Afr.* **2011**, *28*, 141–156. [CrossRef]
47. Giovannetti, G.; Sanfilippo, M. Do Chinese Exports Crowd-out African Goods? An Econometric Analysis by Country and Sector. *Eur. J. Dev. Res.* **2009**, *21*, 506–530. [CrossRef]
48. Maxwell-Cook, P. Pain and Progress: Nigeria's Cement Industry. Online Forum Comment. May 2012. Available online: https://www.worldcement.com/africa-middle-east/24042012/cement_industry_nigeria_dangote_lafarge/ (accessed on 19 May 2022).
49. Doz, Y. Qualitative research for international business. *J. Int. Bus. Stud.* **2011**, *42*, 582–590. [CrossRef]
50. Piekkari, R.; Welch, C.; Paavilainen, E.; Tight, M. The Case Study as Disciplinary Convention: Evidence from International Business Journal. *Organ. Res. Methods* **2011**, *12*, 567–589. [CrossRef]
51. Chad, P. A structured approach for presenting theses. *Australas. Mark. J. AMJ* **1998**, *6*, 63–85.
52. Connell, A.; Farrington, D.P. Bullying among incarcerated young offenders: Developing an interview schedule and some preliminary results. *J. Adolesc.* **1996**, *19*, 75–93. [CrossRef] [PubMed]
53. Patton, M.Q. *Qualitative Research and Evaluation Methods*, 3rd ed.; Sage Publications: Thousand Oaks, CA, USA, 2002.
54. Denzin, N.; Lincoln, Y. *Collecting and Interpreting Qualitative Materials*; Sage: Thousand Oaks, CA, USA, 2003.
55. Parkhe, A. "Messy" research, methodological predispositions, and theory development in international joint ventures. *Acad. Manag. Rev.* **1993**, *18*, 227–268.
56. Yin, R. *Applications of Case Study Research*; Sage Publications: Thousand Oaks, CA, USA, 2012.
57. Gilroy, B.M.; Gries, T.; Naudé, W.A. (Eds.) *Multinational Enterprises, Foreign Direct Investment and Growth in Africa: South African Perspectives*; Springer Science & Business Media: Berlin/Heidelberg, Germany, 2004.
58. Luo, Y.; Xue, Q.; Han, B. How emerging market governments promote outward FDI: Experience from China. *J. World Bus.* **2010**, *45*, 68–79. [CrossRef]
59. McDonald, F.; Warhurst, S.; Allen, M. Autonomy, Embeddedness, and the Performance of Foreign Owned Subsidiaries. *Multinatl. Bus. Rev.* **2008**, *16*, 73–92. [CrossRef]
60. Schüler-Zhou, Y.; Schüller, M.; Sch, M. An empirical study of Chinese subsidiaries' decision-making autonomy in Germany. *Asian Bus. Manag.* **2013**, *12*, 321–350. [CrossRef]
61. Takeuchi, R.; Shay, J.P.; Jiatao, L. When Does Decision Autonomy Increase Expatriate Managers' Adjustment? An Empirical Test. *Acad. Manag. J.* **2008**, *51*, 45–60. [CrossRef]
62. Keilberger, C. Made in China. *Corp. Kn. Mag.* **2003**, *1*, 14–15.
63. Shi, J. Formal Institutional Distance and Innovation from OFDI: Evidence from China. *Sustainability* **2022**, *14*, 5368. [CrossRef]
64. Demirbag, M.; Tatoglu, E.; Glaister, K.W. Factors affecting perceptions of the choice between acquisition and greenfield entry: The case of Western FDI in an emerging market. *Manag. Int. Rev.* **2008**, *48*, 5–38. [CrossRef]
65. Kirkpatrick, C.; Parker, D.; Zhang, Y. Foreign direct investment in infrastructure in developing countries: Does regulation make a difference. *Transnatl. Corp.* **2006**, *15*, 144–171.
66. Luiz, J.M.; Stephan, H. Determinants of Foreign Direct Investment of South African Telecommunications Firms into Sub-Sahara Africa. *WITS Vol.* **2001**, *222*.
67. Lydon, R.; Williams, M. Communications networks and foreign direct investment in developing countries. *Commun. Strateg.* **2005**, *58*, 43–60.
68. Nwankwo, A. The Determinants of Foreign Direct Investment Inflows (FDI) in Nigeria. In Proceedings of the 6th Global Conference on Business and Economics at GUTMAN Conference Center, Cambridge, MA, USA, 15–17 October 2006.

sustainability

MDPI

Article

Corporate Nature, Financial Technology, and Corporate Innovation in China

Yuying Gao [1] and Shanyue Jin [2,*]

1 School of Economics and Management, Pingdingshan University, Pingdingshan 467000, China; gyy3990@outlook.com
2 College of Business, Gachon University, Seongnam 13120, Korea
* Correspondence: jsyrena0923@gachon.ac.kr

Abstract: Corporate innovation has become the main driving force for the long-term development of enterprises, but the characteristics of high risk, long cycle, and high capital demand of corporate innovation activities expose enterprises to high financial rejection. Financial technology, formed by combining digital technology with traditional financial services, is gradually changing the financial service model and providing new ideas for corporate investment and financing. In this study, using the data of non-financial and non-real estate listed companies in Shanghai and Shenzhen markets, A-shares from 2015 to 2020, we examine the effect of financial technology on corporate innovation through a fixed-effects model and investigate the influence of corporate characteristics on the relationship between financial technology and innovation through a moderating-effects model. The results show that financial technology enhances the ability to serve real enterprises by reshaping financial services, which in turn effectively drives an increase in corporate innovation, and the mechanism is conditionally heterogeneous. In addition, the moderating effect of the firm's nature is found to be more significant in non-state-owned firms, high-technology firms, and firms in the growth and maturity stages by life cycle. The policy implications of this study are to continuously promote theoretical research, to guide the development of fintech, and to improve the construction of financial technology infrastructure. Additionally, to deepen the integration of financial technology with real enterprises and establish differentiated financial technology support tools, so as to improve the precision of promoting enterprise innovation.

Keywords: financial technology; corporate innovation; state-owned enterprises; high-tech enterprises; life cycle

Citation: Gao, Y.; Jin, S. Corporate Nature, Financial Technology, and Corporate Innovation in China. *Sustainability* **2022**, *14*, 7162. https://doi.org/10.3390/su14127162

Academic Editors: Jeoung Yul Lee, Dilek Zamantili Nayir and Charles Chen

Received: 17 April 2022
Accepted: 9 June 2022
Published: 10 June 2022

1. Introduction

The endogenous driving effect of technological progress [1] argues that corporations can break the restriction of diminishing marginal benefits by improving their technological innovation ability. Technological innovation can effectively improve the production efficiency of enterprises by improving the three labor force factors, and it can also form a new innovative industry by relying on science and technology.

In recent years, science and technology globally have been developing rapidly and new breakthroughs have been made in key areas. Major economies around the world are accelerating the deployment of innovation development strategies, increasing innovation and R&D expenditures, and intensifying competition in the field of innovation [2]. As an important part of the innovation system, the increase in corporate innovation strongly supports the operation of the national innovation system and drives the global technological progress. Although the global spread of the epidemic has negatively impacted a large number of business operations, the overall level of corporate innovation continues to rise, and the number of patents and research investments continue to increase. Enterprises have become the most dynamic sector for global innovation development [3,4].

In China, corporate technological innovation mainly refers to the R&D, technological transformation, technology introduction, and technology promotion activities of enterprises, and the evaluation of corporate technological innovation includes two aspects: technological innovation activities and innovation output capacity; the former is mainly measured by the financial investment of enterprises in various aspects of technological innovation activities, and the latter is mainly measured by the number of corporate patents, which is the most direct and important index to evaluate the technological innovation capacity of enterprises [5]. By 2020, China's total research and development (R&D) investment exceeded CNY 2.4 trillion, an increase of CNY 224.95 billion or 10.2% over 2019; however, owing to the influence of the COVID-19 outbreak and other factors, the growth rate fell by 2.3% from 2019. The intensity of R&D expenditure (R&D expenditure as a share of GDP) reached 2.40%, an increase of 0.16 percentage points from 2019, a new high over the past 11 years. This indicates that China attaches more importance to the need for independent innovation [6]. By the end of 2020, China's participating R&D personnel had reached 7.5 million, and the total number of enterprises involved in R&D and innovation activities was 379,409, with a total of 346,491 domestic enterprises. Domestic firms are major players in R&D and innovation activities, accounting for 91.32% of the total number of innovative firms, with a share of over 90%, thus reflecting the strong innovation dynamics and willingness of Chinese firms [7]. In 2020, China's total R&D spending was approximately 54% of that of the United States and 2.1 times that of Japan, ranking second in the world.

In recent years, China's technological innovation achievements have grown rapidly, albeit "large quantity but low quality" and "strategic catering" characteristics exist in Chinese corporate technological innovation, which leads to the "low-end locking" dilemma of corporate innovation in the global technology chain [8]. From a financial perspective, the reasons for these are the adverse selection and moral hazard problems that are induced by the essential characteristics of innovation projects, such as high sunk costs, high uncertainty, long cycle time, and information asymmetry [9], which expose firms' innovation activities to serious external financing challenges and high internal financial risks [10,11]. Then, how to further strengthen the willingness and ability to promote technological innovation of individual micro enterprises in the market and crack the financing dilemma of enterprise innovation becomes an important issue.

Financial technology is a new financial services business model formed by the transformation of modern scientific and technological achievements to innovate the business model and business processes of financial products [12,13], which has great potential in terms of financial services industry profits, regulators' earnings, and consumers' welfare [14]. In recent years, with the development of advanced technologies such as big data, cloud computing, and blockchain, the emergence of "finance + technology" (fintech) has provided new ideas for corporate financing [15]. By integrating the abovementioned technological means and combining the business concept of sharing economy, fintech has developed two terminal application models, namely, fintech crowdfunding financing and financial technology lending financing, which present several advantages, such as wide funding channels, full range of financing, and high service quality [16–18], which have a profound impact on alleviating financing constraints and enhancing enterprises' financial stability. Financial technology can enable financial institutions to enhance information identification and screening of enterprises, provide financial support to enterprises with innovative potential, avoid financial mismatches, and improve the efficiency of credit fund usage. Moreover, a digital financial system can provide investors with more information about the current market conditions and industry prospects of investment projects, reducing the cost of information identification for investors and enhancing their willingness to invest [11,13]. As a new product formed by the way of traditional finance and technology enablement, digital finance supported by financial technology can effectively reduce financing costs, lower the financial risks of enterprises, and provide a sustainable and stable economic foundation for technological innovation of micro enterprises by continuously optimizing financial services, breaking down information barriers, and providing personalized products [19]. Digital finance supported by financial technology, as a new product formed by traditional finance through a technology-enabled approach, has a significant impact on the technological innovation of micro enterprises. The development of China's fintech industry started late. However, with its rapid development speed, China's financial technology development level has been ranked among the top in the world. According to the "2020 Global financial technology Index Report" published by Findexable, China ranks 21st in the world in overall financial technology strength, while the ranking of companies engaged in financial services as Internet companies shows that Chinese financial technology companies are ranked first in the world in terms of overall strength, with Ant Financial, Jingdong Digital, and Du Xiaoman Financial ranking 1st, 3rd, and 6th, respectively [20,21]. In view of China's leading position in the world's financial technology development scale and technology practice, under the general trend of the rapid development of big data, blockchain, artificial intelligence, and other technologies, an in-depth study on financial technology-driven corporate innovation has strong practical value and inspiring significance from a multidisciplinary-cum-intersectional research perspective.

Based on an analysis of the literature and real-world context, we construct a research sample with the data of non-financial non-real estate firms listed in A-shares in China's Shanghai and Shenzhen markets from 2015 to 2020, to empirically examine the driving role and structural differences of financial technology on corporate innovation. The results show that financial technology can effectively drive corporate innovation and has a stronger promotion effect on substantive innovation than non-substantive innovation. The study further explores the impact of financial technology on innovation of firms with different attributes and in different life cycles through the moderating effect model test, and finds that the nature of firms has a moderating effect in the above impact relationship, and the promotion effect of financial technology on firm innovation is more significant in non-SOEs, high-technology firms, and firms in the growth and maturity stages.

The possible marginal contributions of this study are as follows: first, the driving effect of financial technology on corporate innovation is empirically tested to reveal the differential impact of financial technology on different levels of corporate innovation. Second, the role of the firm's nature, such as ownership attributes, nature of technology, and stage of life cycle involved, in the relationship between financial technology and firm technological innovation is tested in economic practice. The heterogeneous effects of financial technology on corporate innovation performance are investigated along the lines of information economics theory, credit rationing theory, financial exclusion theory, technological innovation theory, and agency theory.

2. Theoretical Background and Hypotheses

2.1. Financial Technology and Corporate Innovation

Schumpeter [22] proposed a technological innovation theory wherein the optimal reorganization of production factors and conditions was first outlined as innovation and asserted that financial variables could affect economic growth by influencing corporate innovation. Later, Domar [23], Solow [24], and Hicks [25] further refined and developed the theory of economic growth, and they all concluded that the development of financial markets had a positive relationship with corporate technological innovation. The new growth theory of financial markets' influence on corporate innovation points out that the more mature the financial market development, the lower the possibility of moral hazard in enterprise financing, the smaller the external financing constraints faced by enterprises, and, consequently, the higher the level of firm technological innovation [26–28]. Originally proposed by Bettinger [29], financial technology means "combining the expertise of banks with modern management technology and computers", representing the fusion of finance and technology. The most evident feature that distinguishes it from traditional finance is "technologization", and the financial services it provides combine several emerging technologies, such as artificial intelligence, big data, blockchain, and cloud computing [10,12], which can significantly reduce the transaction costs of financial services, break the time and space limitations, make information transparent and networked, and effectively alleviate the information asymmetry problem [30]. However, at the same time, the new business form of financial technology has broken through traditional financial regulatory boundaries, increased the difficulty of regulation, and, to some extent, expanded financial risks. Fintech can provide diversified financing methods for enterprises, which can solve the problem of difficult and expensive financing by widening financing channels and accelerating capital flow, as well as effective financial support for enterprises to achieve technological upgrades. It can also enhance the risk tolerance of enterprises, encourage them to invest more effectively in high-risk and high-return projects, and improve their investment efficiency [31]. Finance is a core part of the micro-subject of technological innovation environment, and effective financial supply directly affects the development of technological innovation activities [32]. Based on information asymmetry theory and financial exclusion theory, financial technology uses information technology, such as big data, cloud computing, and artificial intelligence, to improve the problems of high risk premiums and high operating costs of traditional finance due to information asymmetry [14,30,33], provide stable technical support for finance to expand its services, reduce financial exclusion of innovative enterprises, and increase their availability of funds [34]. Based on the abovementioned analysis, this study proposes the following hypothesis:

Hypothesis 1 (H1). *Fintech can effectively improve corporate innovation performance.*

2.2. The Moderating Effect of Corporate Nature

Some structural mismatch problems exist in the traditional financial structure in economic activities, as mainly reflected in several aspects, including the nature of enterprise ownership, enterprise technology field, and enterprise life cycle. In the afore-stated analysis, financial technology can effectively promote corporate innovation activities, but its ability to effectively correct the target deviation problem existing in traditional finance and thus improve corporate innovation capacity deserves in-depth investigation. To further decompose the structural differences of enterprises, it is necessary to distinguish enterprises according to their individual characteristics. Many studies have also established that these natures are the main factors that influence corporate innovation activities [35–37].

2.2.1. Nature of Enterprise Ownership

The research on financial development, based on agency theory and the monitoring cost perspective, indicates that financial development is conducive to corporate innovation [31]. In the same financial environment, there may be differences in enterprise behavioral preferences and the performances of innovation output, and differences in enterprise ownership may affect the relationship between financial technology investment and innovation. State-owned enterprises (SOEs) have better economic strength and income, and they have national credit as support. Compared with non-SOEs, financial institutions can easily obtain financial support from financial institutions [38]. Moreover, SOEs assume more social responsibilities and undertake major issues of the national economy and people's livelihoods, and their innovation activities are more inclined toward the main areas of the country. According to agency theory, SOE operators are more interested in their economic or political goals [39], which leads to their preference for projects with short return cycles and reflected performance, while less attention is paid to innovative projects with long return cycles and high risks; their willingness to innovate and financial exclusion is also lower. In contrast, non-SOEs face greater financial exclusion in economic activities and are more active in innovation activities, where the rise of fintech has a greater impact. Based on the abovementioned analysis, this study proposes the following hypothesis:

Hypothesis 2 (H2). *Fintech plays a smaller role in promoting corporate innovation performance in SOEs than in non-SOEs.*

2.2.2. Nature of Enterprise Technology

The classification of firms into high-tech and non-high-tech firms when studying their innovation activities allows for a more accurate analysis of their influence mechanisms. The nature of enterprise technology is highly related to the development of innovation activities. The innovation of the high-tech industry is higher, the enterprise itself has a good foundation for innovation, and innovation activities are the main driving force to support the development of enterprises. Compared with non-high-tech enterprises, high-tech enterprises pay more attention to technological development and inherent innovation drive, while innovation itself is characterized by high uncertainty, high risk, and a long cycle, which require long-term sustainable financial support for high-tech enterprises, and the development of fintech can provide more convenient and low-cost financial support for high-tech enterprises. Aghion et al. [40] believe that venture capital institutions would help firms to solve the financing dilemma faced by technological innovation, thus promoting their growth. Han and Gu [41] empirically tested a panel model of data from high-technology industries by measuring the efficiency of innovation in different regions and show that fintech improves the efficiency of technological innovation. Canepa and Stoneman [42] point out that the technological innovation output of high-tech enterprises is more influenced by financial factors than in other industries, as well as the development of local banks [43]. Technological innovation theory considers financial variables as an important component of corporate innovation, and credit support is necessary for the development of corporate innovation [22]. In addition, the demand for innovation and the need for stable credit support is higher in high-technology firms than in non-high-technology firms, and the development of financial technology can meet this demand. Based on the above analysis, the following hypothesis is proposed:

Hypothesis 3 (H3). *Fintech plays a stronger role in promoting high-tech innovation performance than non-high-tech enterprises.*

2.2.3. Enterprise Life Cycle

It is difficult to obtain effective financing in the financial market, as it is an activity with both high risk and positive externality. This financing dilemma is more centrally reflected in some specific periods of the enterprise. Based on enterprise life cycle theory, the enterprise can be regarded as an organization with a life state; that is, the enterprise is bound to go through the development stage from germination, growth, and maturity to decline [44]. According to enterprise life cycle theory, in different stages of the life cycle, there are significant differences in various aspects of cash flow, financing constraints, and R&D innovation needs [45,46], and firms at different life cycle stages reflect different characteristics in terms of corporate governance, operations, and finance; thus, firms need to choose varying problem-solving approaches and strategies [47]. When enterprises are in different life cycle stages, the impact of fintech on corporate technological innovation may differ. From the perspective of financing demand and corporate innovation willingness and ability, firms in the growth and maturity stages have stronger willingness and potential to innovate and greater financing demand than firms in the decline stage, but firms in the decline stage have lower expansionary demand, less subjective motivation to innovate, as well as a better operating system and relatively lower external financing demand [48]. Based on financial exclusion and life cycle theory, financial institutions will reduce their support to declining stage firms, and effective financial support can have a great contribution to the development of corporate innovation for growth stage and mature stage firms with high innovation demand. Based on the above discussion, limiting the study of the relationship between fintech and technological innovation to the same cross-sectional time characteristics will result in biased research findings and blunted policy orientation. In view of this, drawing on Ling et al. [35] and Caggese [49], this study introduces a "life cycle" variable into the discussion of fintech promoting corporate innovation and proposes the following hypothesis:

Hypothesis 4 (H4). *Compared with companies in decline periods, fintech plays a stronger role in promoting corporate innovation performance in the growth and maturity periods.*

Figure 1 shows the model of this study.

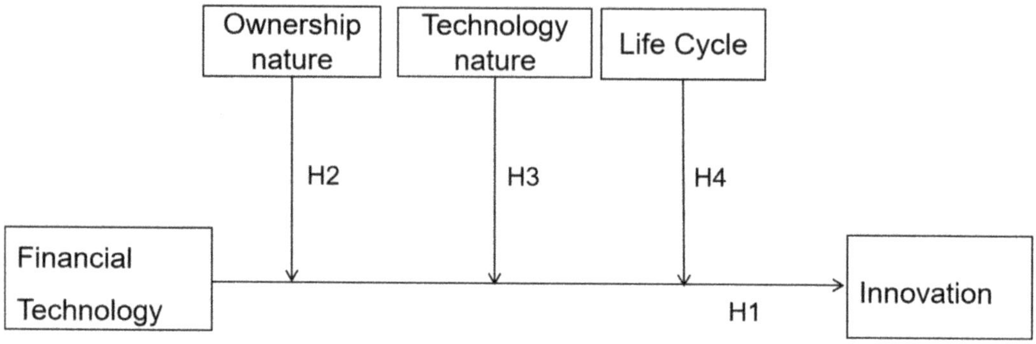

Figure 1. The Study Model.

3. Research Methods

3.1. Data and Samples

We constructed a panel dataset of 17,447 firm years from 2015 to 2020 using non-financial and non-real estate companies listed in Shanghai and Shenzhen as the research object. The enterprise-related data were obtained from the China Stock Market & Accounting Research (CSMAR) database. Enterprise patent data were obtained from the Chinese Research Data Services and Wind databases. The fintech proxy variable digital financial index was obtained from the Peking University Digital Inclusive Finance Index 2011–2020. To ensure the reliability of the research data, drawing on previous literature data processing, this study adopts the following data: (1) financial and real estate companies are excluded from the sample; (2) companies with ST, ST*, and PT during the study period were excluded; (3) variables in the data (excluding dummy variables) were winsorized to reduce the impact of outlier fluctuations; (4) samples with missing values were excluded; and (5) continuous variables were logarithmized to mitigate the interference of heteroskedasticity.

3.2. Definition and Measurement of Variables

3.2.1. The Explained Variable

The explanatory variable is firm innovation (Pat). Corporate innovation performance is generally represented by corporate R&D investment, share of intangible assets, and number of patent applications in the current year in previous studies [50,51]. However, due to the essential characteristics of long innovation activity cycles, high uncertainty, and the influence of data disclosure systems, enterprises have certain limitations as proxy variables of innovation performance [52]. Based on this, this study draws on Ling et al. [35] and Zhao et al. [53] to use patent innovation output data as a proxy variable to measure firms' technological innovation performance. We divide the number of enterprise patents into three levels according to the available enterprise patent application data: (1) the total number of patent applications by enterprise in the current period (*Patent*); (2) the number of invention patent applications by enterprise in the current period (*Pati*), to indicate the substantive technological innovation output performance of enterprises; and (3) the total number of utility model patent applications and design patent applications by enterprise in the current period (*Patud*), which is mainly the number of low-end patent applications, indicating the non-substantial innovation output of enterprises. The group of enterprise innovation variables, denoted by Pat, includes three measurement dimension indicators, Patent, Pati, and Patud. Due to the large variation in the degree of innovation among firms, they were normalized (*LnPatent*, *LnPati*, and *LnPatud*), and the measurements are shown in Table 1.

Table 1. Combination of the cash flow characteristics of companies in different life cycle periods.

Life Cycle		Net Cash Flow from Operations	Net Cash Flow from Investments	Net Cash Flow from Financing
Growth period	Start-up	−	−	+
	Growth	+	−	+
Maturity period	Maturity	+	−	−
Recession period	Decline	−	−	−
	Decline	+	+	+
	Decline	+	+	−
	Elimination	−	+	+
	Elimination	−	+	−

Note: When cash flows from financing are 0, depending on the characteristics of cash flows from operations and investments, they are included in the maturity, elimination, and decline periods. When the investment cash flow is 0, depending on the characteristics of operating and financing cash flows, the maturity, elimination, and recession periods are included.

3.2.2. The Explanatory Variable

The core explanatory variable is the fintech index (*Fintech*). This study draws on the variable design of Deng et al. [54], Liu et al. [55], and others to use the digital financial inclusion index as a proxy variable for *Fintech*.

3.2.3. The Moderating Variables

Different corporate natures have significant differences in various aspects of their business objectives, innovation areas, and capital needs. Drawing on the studies of Caggese [49], Guo et al. [56], and DeAngelo et al. [57], we selected here the natures of corporate ownership and technology, as well as the corporate life cycle as moderating variables.

The Nature of Corporate Ownership

Soe, the nature of enterprise ownership, is classified according to the nature of enterprise equity in the CSMAR database. A dummy variable is used, and it takes a value of 1 when the enterprise is state-owned; otherwise, it is 0.

The Nature of Enterprise Technology

The definition of "high technology industry", first proposed by the Organization for Economic Cooperation and Development to make high-technology industry research internationally comparable, is divided into six industries: aerospace manufacturing, pharmaceutical manufacturing, computer and office equipment manufacturing, electrical machinery manufacturing, scientific instruments and instruments manufacturing, and electronic and communication equipment manufacturing. To accurately reflect the development of high-tech industries and improve the statistical system of high-tech industries, China has released the "Classification of High-tech Industries (Manufacturing) (2017)", and added the information on chemical manufacturing industry to the "China High-tech Industries Statistical Yearbook." Meanwhile, the proportion of the tertiary industry in the national economy is gradually increasing, and several high-tech service industries, such as electronic information and professional and technical services, have developed rapidly in recent years, which has significantly altered the production and lifestyle of enterprises and residents. According to the "Classification of High-Technology Industries (Service Industry) (2018)" by the State Council of China, high-tech service industry is a collection of service activities using high-tech means for society, including information services, e-commerce services, inspection and testing services, high-tech services of professional and technical service industry, R&D and design services, science and technology achievement transformation services, intellectual property and related legal services, environmental monitoring and governance services and other high-tech services, and so on, in nine categories. This study draws on the treatment method of Lin et al. [58] on high-tech industry classification, and corresponding to the "Industry Classification Guidelines of Listed Companies (2012 Revision)", a total of 13 industries were selected as high-tech industries, with a value of 1, while other industries have a value of 0.

Enterprise Life Cycle

In the literature, with Chinese listed companies as the research sample, considering the strict requirements of the listing terms on enterprise profitability and establishment period, scholars generally believe that the sampled companies have passed the start-up period; thus, only the three divided stages of growth, maturity, and decline are retained. The academic circle has different definition standards regarding enterprise life cycle, but overall, they can be divided into the following three categories: single variable analysis, comprehensive financial index, and cash flow model methods. The cash flow method is more practical and exogenous than the single variable analysis and the financial composite index methods, and cash flow reflects the core vitality of the enterprise, which can comprehensively reflect the level of resource allocation, the strength to cope with risks, and the difference in the operating status of the enterprise in different growth stages [45]. This study adopts the cash flow-based classification method proposed by Dickinson [44] to judge the symbol of the life cycle proxy variable (*Lifecycle*) of the sample companies according to the requirements of Chinese listed companies (the specific results are detailed in Table 1). The start-up and growth periods are categorized as the growth period of the firm, and both the decline and elimination periods are categorized as the decline period of the firm. As the demand for external capital is higher in the growth and maturity periods than in the recession period, the demand for productivity improvement and increased innovation capacity is also higher in the growth and maturity periods than in the decline period. Therefore, the impact of fintech development on firms in the growth and maturity periods is significantly different from the impact on firms in decline. Based on the findings of Akcigit and Kerr [59], Chiang et al. [60], and Caggese [49] for fintech, digital finance, and the differences in firms' demand for external funding in different life cycles, dummy variables were set. The value is 1 for firms in the growth and maturity stages, and 0 for firms in the decline stage.

3.2.4. Control Variables

According to the relevant literature, this study has added a series of variables that can influence corporate innovation [61,62]. The variables include enterprise size (*Size*), year of enterprise (*Age*), asset-liability ratio (*Lev*), equity concentration (*SD*), net profit growth rate (*PG*), capital intensity (*CD*), and enterprise growth capacity (*Growth*). Owing to the large differences in enterprise technological innovation level between the different industries, we introduce the industry effect (*Industry*), a dummy variable that takes a value of 1 if the enterprise belongs to this industry and 0 otherwise. With the change in the macro environment and policy, the level of technological innovation may have a large difference in each year; therefore, we introduce the year effect (*Year*) to set a dummy variable; if the company is in the year, the value is 1, otherwise it is 0. Table 2 shows he variable names and definition of this study.

Table 2. Variable Names and Definition.

Variable	Symbol	Name	Definition
Explained variable	Lnpatent	Total number of enterprise patents	Ln (Total number of enterprise patents in the current period + 1)
	Lnpati	Substantial innovation performance	Ln (Total number of invention patents of enterprise in the current period + 1)
	Lnpatud	Non-substantial innovation performance	Ln (Current period number of utility model patent applications + number of design patent applications + 1)
Explanatory variable	Fintech	Digital finance index	The Digital Inclusive Finance Index of Peking University Digital Financial Research Center, 2011–2020
Moderating variable	Soe	Equity nature of the enterprise	1 = State-owned enterprise, and 0 = non-State-owned enterprise
	Tech	Technical nature of the enterprise	1 = High-tech enterprise 0 = Non-high-tech enterprise
	Life	Enterprise life cycle	Cash flow mode method to measure it
Controlled variable	Growth	Enterprise growth ability (%)	Main business income of this period/previous main business income of this period-1
	Age	The year of the establishment	(Study year—Establishment year) + 1
	Lev	Asset–liability ratio	Total liabilities/Total assets
	SD	Equity concentration	The largest shareholder holds the shareholding proportion
	Size	Total assets scale	Natural log of (millions of total assets disclosed in financial statements)
	PG	Net profit growth rate	(Current net profit-net profit of the previous period)/previous net profit of × 100%
	CD	Capital intensity	The ratio of total assets to operating income

3.3. Model Design

3.3.1. Benchmark Model

To analyze the impact of fintech on corporate innovation, based on the previous theoretical analysis and research hypotheses as well as with reference to the research of Makosa et al. [63], this study sets the following panel econometric model:

$$\text{LnPat}_{it} = \alpha_0 + \alpha_1 \text{Fintech}_{-1} + \Sigma\text{Control}_{it} + \mu_i + \gamma_t + \varepsilon_{it} \tag{1}$$

In the regression, Equation (1), subscripts i and t indicate the individual enterprise and year, respectively. The explained variable is the corporate innovation performance (*Pat*) of the enterprise; in the variable group *Pat*, three variables are included: overall innovation by enterprise (Patent), substantial innovation by enterprise (Pati), and non-substantial innovation by enterprise (Patud). The core explanatory variable is *Fintech*. To avoid endogeneity and reverse causality problems and to consider the lagged effect of Fintech on innovation activities, this study treats *Fintech* with a one-period lag ($Fintech_{-1}$)). *Control* indicates a series of control variables that affect corporate innovation. In addition, to reduce the impact of individual heterogeneity and year characteristics on corporate innovation performance, this study considers industry fixed effects μ_i and year fixed effects γ_t, in addition to individual effects, to eliminate the effects of time-invariant corporate characteristics and time-invariant macroeconomic environment. ε is the model's random error term.

3.3.2. Moderation Effect Model

To further verify the influence mechanism of heterogeneous enterprise nature on the role of fintech in promoting corporate innovation, the interaction term of enterprise nature variables and fintech was added to the benchmark regression model [55]. The following model was constructed:

$$\text{LnPat}_{it} = \beta_0+\beta_1\text{Fintech}_{-1}+\beta_2\text{Soe} + \Sigma\text{Control}_{it}+\mu_i+\gamma_t +\varepsilon_{it} \quad (2)$$

$$\text{LnPat}_{it}= \beta_0+\beta_1\text{Fintech}_{-1}+\beta_2\text{Soe} + \beta_3\text{Fintech}_{-1}*\text{Soe} +\Sigma\text{Control}_{it}+\mu_i+\gamma_t +\varepsilon_{it} \quad (3)$$

Model (2) indicates that, based on Model (1), the corporate ownership nature variable *Soe* is added, and Model (3) represents the interaction term $Fintech_{-1}*Soe$, with the nature of the firm's ownership based on Model (2). *Soe* takes a value of 1 when the firm is state-owned and 0 when it is non-state-owned. If the coefficient β3 of the interaction item ($Fintech_{-1}*Soe$) in Model (3) is negative and can pass the significance test, *Fintech* is less effective in promoting innovation in SOEs than in non-SOEs. Conversely, the role of *Fintech* in promoting firm innovation is considered to be stronger in SOEs.

$$\text{LnPat}_{it}= \varphi_0+\varphi_1\text{Fintech}_{-1}+\varphi_2\text{Tech} + \Sigma\text{Control}_{it}+\mu_i+\gamma_t +\varepsilon_{it} \quad (4)$$

$$\text{LnPat}_{it}= \varphi_0+\varphi_1\text{Fintech}_{-1}+\varphi_2\text{Tech} + \varphi_3\text{Fintech}_{-1}*\text{Tech} +\Sigma\text{Control}_{it}+\mu_i+\gamma_t +\varepsilon_{it} \quad (5)$$

Models (4) and (5) are based on Model (1), with the addition of the technology nature variable (*Tech*) and the interaction term ($Fintech_{-1}*Tech$) between fintech and firm technology nature, in turn. *Tech* takes the value of 1 when the sample firm is a high-technology firm and 0 when the sample firm is a non-high-technology firm. If the coefficient φ3 of $Fintech_{-1}*Tech$ in Model (5) is positive and passes the significance test, it indicates that compared to non-high-tech firms, fintech is a stronger contributor to corporate innovation in high-tech firms.

$$\text{LnPat}_{it}= \gamma_0+\gamma_1\text{Fintech}_{-1}+\gamma_2\text{Life} + \Sigma\text{Control}_{it}+\mu_i+\gamma_t +\varepsilon_{it} \quad (6)$$

$$\text{LnPat}_{it}= \gamma_0+\gamma_1\text{Fintech}_{-1}+\gamma_2\text{Life} + \gamma_3\text{Fintech}_{-1}*\text{Life} +\Sigma\text{Control}_{it}+\mu_i+\gamma_t +\varepsilon_{it} \quad (7)$$

Similarly, Models (6) and (7) add the enterprise life cycle variable (*Life*) and the interaction term between *Fintech* and enterprise life cycle ($Fintech_{-1}*Life$), respectively, based on Model (1). When *Life* takes a value of 1, it means that the firm is in the growth and maturity stages; when *Life* takes a value of 0, it means that the firm is in the decline stage. If the coefficient, γ3, of $Fintech_{-1}*Life$ in Model (7) is positive and can pass the significance test, it means that the greater the contribution of *Fintech* to the innovation performance of the firm in the growth and maturity stages relative to the declining-stage firms, and vice versa, the greater the contribution of *Fintech* to the innovation of the firm when it is in the declining stage.

4. Empirical Analysis Results

4.1. Descriptive Statistics and Correlations

Table 3 presents the descriptive statistics. The mean value of the overall innovation performance index (*Lnpatent*) is 2.478, the median value is 2.565, the standard deviation is 1.682, the maximum value is 6.650, and the minimum value is 0. This indicates that there is a significant difference in the overall level of innovation performance among the sample firms, and the fact that the median is higher than the mean also reflects to a certain extent that the level of innovation of the firms is more concentrated in the low-level stage. There are also significant differences between firms' substantive innovation (*Lnpati*) and firms' non-substantive innovation (*Lnpatud*), and the difference between firms' substantive innovation is slightly smaller than that of non-substantive innovation. The mean value of *Fintech* is 5.724, with a standard deviation of 0.192, which shows that the level of *Fintech* development varies greatly among provinces. For the enterprise nature variables, the mean value of *Soe* is 0.318, with a standard deviation of 0.466, the mean value of *Tech* is 0.425, with a standard deviation of 0.494, while the mean value of *Life* is 0.803, with a standard deviation of 0.398, indicating that there are significant differences in the individual characteristics of the sample companies. From the descriptive statistical results given above, the value range of the variables selected in this study is within reason, and there are no evident outliers or indicators that mainly violate the regression hypothesis, while the selected samples meet the requirements of the present study.

Table 3. Descriptive statistics.

Variable	*n*	Mean	*p* 50	SD	Min	Max
Lnpatent	17,447	2.478	2.565	1.682	0	6.650
Lnpati	17,447	1.811	1.792	1.493	0	5.969
Lnpatud	17,447	1.850	1.792	1.609	0	5.974
Fintech	17,447	5.724	5.739	0.192	5.325	6.068
Soe	17,447	0.318	0	0.466	0	1
Tech	17,447	0.425	0	0.494	0	1
Life	17,447	0.803	1	0.398	0	1
Size	17,447	8.411	8.251	1.249	6.228	12.29
CD	17,447	2.390	1.916	1.768	0.424	11.42
Lev	17,447	0.404	0.395	0.191	0.062	0.852
SD	17,447	33.67	31.49	14.51	8.540	73.56
PG	17,447	−0.251	0.050	3.557	−22.00	13.27
Growth	17,447	0.173	0.091	0.546	−0.790	3.735
Age	17,447	19.51	19	5.461	8	34

Before testing the impact of fintech on corporate innovation, the correlation among variables is preliminarily evaluated, judging whether there are multicollinearity problems and obtaining the Pearson correlation coefficient table (Table 4). In Table 4, the correlation coefficient of *Fintech* and the three dimensions of corporate innovation (*Lnpatent*, *Lnpati*, and *Lnpatud*) are 0.029, 0.031, and 0.0103, respectively, and pass the significance test, which can initially verify the correctness of the previous hypothesis. From the correlation analysis of the variables, the correlation coefficients between the variables are all below 0.8, indicating that the variables are relatively independent and there is no problem of multicollinearity, which has less influence on the errors arising from the subsequent regression analysis.

4.2. *Analysis of the Empirical Results*

4.2.1. Fintech and Corporate Innovation

According to the Hausman test results, the *p*-value is less than 0.05; therefore, this study chooses a fixed-effects model regression that controls for both year and industry fixed effects. Table 5 reports the results of the benchmark regression test for fintech and corporate innovation.

In Columns (1)–(3) of Table 5, the regression coefficients of $Fintech_{-1}$ are found to be significantly positive, regardless of the level of technological innovation activities of enterprises, thereby indicating that the development of *Fintech* has a significant contribution to the patent innovation performance of enterprises. However, the magnitude and significance of the coefficient of *Fintech* ($Fintech_{-1}$) in Column (3) are slightly lower than those of the previous two, indicating that the impact of the non-substantive patent innovation level on *Fintech* development enterprises is slightly weaker than that of substantive innovation. Second, the regression coefficients of $Fintech_{-1}$ on total corporate innovation and corporate substantive technological innovation in Columns (4)–(6) are 0.435 and 0.502, respectively, both of which are significantly positive at the 1% level, indicating that the development of fintech can significantly enhance the performance of corporate substantive technological innovation. However, the regression coefficients on the level of corporate non-substantive patent innovation (*Lnpatud*) regression coefficients are positive at the 10% level of significance, indicating that the impact of fintech development on firms' non-substantive innovation is slightly smaller than that of substantive innovation. The results indicate that the positive contribution of fintech to technological innovation activities in these three dimensions remains robust. This indicates that the increase in corporate innovation performance, especially the increase in firms' substantive creativity, can be effectively promoted through the development of fintech, thus supporting H1.

Table 4. Correlation matrix.

		1	2	3	4	5	6	7	8	9	10	11	12	13	14
1	Lnpatent	1													
2	Lnpati	0.903 ***	1												
3	Lnpatud	0.905 ***	0.701 ***	1											
4	Fintech	0.029 ***	0.031 ***	0.103 ***	1										
5	SOE	0.027 ***	0.052 ***	0.036 ***	−0.098 ***	1									
6	Tech	0.114 ***	0.174 ***	0.009 ***	0.054 ***	−0.157 ***	1								
7	Life	0.088 ***	0.080 ***	0.081 ***	−0.067 ***	−0.030 ***	0.015 **	1							
8	Size	0.347 ***	0.370 ***	0.324 ***	0.031 ***	0.385 ***	−0.205 ***	0.101 ***	1						
9	CD	−0.153 ***	−0.129 ***	−0.137 ***	−0.058 ***	0.029 ***	0.005 ***	−0.099 ***	0.018 ***	1					
10	Lev	0.161 ***	0.159 ***	0.182 ***	−0.012	0.266 ***	−0.209 ***	0.072 ***	0.516 ***	−0.097 ***	1				
11	SD	0.014 ***	−0.007 ***	0.048 ***	−0.032 ***	0.230 ***	−0.141 ***	0.039 ***	0.170 ***	−0.068 ***	0.034 ***	1			
12	PG	0.047 ***	0.042 ***	0.044 ***	−0.020 ***	−0.017 ***	0.008 ***	0.062 ***	0.043 ***	−0.080 ***	−0.080 ***	0.053 ***	1		
13	Growth	0.063 ***	0.057 ***	0.068 ***	−0.047 ***	−0.051 ***	0.025 ***	0.069 ***	0.077 ***	−0.099 ***	0.062 ***	0.001 ***	0.219 ***	1	
14	Age	−0.077 ***	−0.043 ***	−0.081 ***	0.161 ***	0.244 ***	−0.127 ***	−0.074 ***	0.153 ***	0.023 ***	0.134 ***	−0.051 ***	−0.025 ***	−0.038 ***	1

Note: $n = 17{,}447$; *** $p < 0.01$, ** $p < 0.05$.

4.2.2. The Moderating Effect of Corporate Nature on Fintech for Corporate Innovation

The operating objectives of enterprises with different natures are inconsistent. Facing the role of fintech under the same conditions, there may be differences in enterprise behavioral preference and its innovation output performance. Based on previous theoretical analysis and literature [6,64–66], enterprises are divided based on three different attributes—SOEs and non-SOEs (*Soe*), high-tech and non-high-tech enterprises (*Tech*), and enterprises with different life cycles (*Life*)—to identify the differential innovation-driven impact of *Fintech* on firms with different attributes.

Table 5. The impact of fintech on corporate innovation: fixed-effects regression.

	(1)	(2)	(3)	(4)	(5)	(6)
Variables	**Lnpatent**	**Lnpati**	**Lnpatud**	**Lnpatent**	**Lnpati**	**Lnpatud**
$Fintech_{-1}$	0.572 *** (4.20)	0.606 *** (4.80)	0.295 ** (2.32)	0.435 *** (3.75)	0.502 *** (4.66)	0.191 * (1.70)
Size				0.711 *** (66.55)	0.667 *** (67.23)	0.586 *** (56.70)
CD				−0.100 *** (−14.51)	−0.074 *** (−11.58)	−0.092 *** (−13.79)
Lev				−0.329 *** (−4.72)	−0.369 *** (−5.69)	−0.089 (−1.32)
SD				−0.001 * (−1.92)	−0.002 ** (−2.52)	0.000 (0.19)
PG				0.003 (1.05)	0.002 (0.56)	0.003 (1.05)
Growth				−0.089 *** (−3.57)	−0.067 *** (−2.91)	−0.080 *** (−3.32)
Age				−0.009 *** (−4.46)	−0.005 ** (−2.57)	−0.008 *** (−4.19)
Constant	−0.734 (−0.95)	−1.580 ** (−2.20)	0.188 (0.26)	−5.377 *** (−8.06)	−6.162 *** (−9.95)	−3.769 *** (−5.84)
Year FX	Yes	Yes	Yes	Yes	Yes	Yes
Industry FX	Yes	Yes	Yes	Yes	Yes	Yes
Obs	13,947	13,947	13,947	13,947	13,947	13,947
R-squared	0.267	0.206	0.302	0.478	0.434	0.468
Adj. R^2	0.263	0.202	0.298	0.475	0.430	0.465

Notes: t-statistics in parentheses; *** $p < 0.01$, ** $p < 0.05$, * $p < 0.1$.

Nature of Corporate Ownership

Table 6 reports the regression results of the moderating role of heterogeneous firm ownership attributes in the promotion of firm innovation by *Fintech*. The results in the table show that in the regression of the total number of corporate innovations (*Lnpatent*), the coefficient of $Fintech_{-1}$ in Model (3) is 0.499, while the coefficient of the interaction term between fintech and firm equity attributes ($Fintech_{-1}$*Soe*) is −0.504, and both pass the significance test at the 1% level. The adjusted R^2 of Model (3) increases from 0.4777 in Model (2) to 0.4783 after adding the interaction term, indicating that the moderating effect of the nature of corporate ownership on the promotion of corporate innovation by fintech is significant; that is, the promotion of fintech on the overall innovation performance of firms is weaker in SOEs compared to non-SOEs. In the regression of substantive corporate innovation (*Lnpati*), the coefficient of $Fintech_{-1}$ in Model (3) is 0.547, while the coefficient of the interaction term ($Fintech_{-1}$*Soe*) between fintech and corporate equity attributes is −0.507, and they both pass the significance test at the 1% level. The adjusted R^2 of Model (3) after adding the interaction term increases from 0.4375 in Model (2) to 0.4382, indicating that the moderating effect of corporate ownership nature on the promotion of substantive innovation by *Fintech* is significant; that is, the promotion of substantive innovation by *Fintech* in SOEs is weaker in SOEs compared to non-SOEs. In the regression of corporate non-substantial innovation (*Lnpatud*), the coefficient of the *Fintech* index ($Fintech_{-1}$) in Model (3) is 0.253, which passes the 5% significance test, and the coefficient of the interaction term $Fintech_{-1}$*Soe* between the *Fintech* index and corporate equity attributes is −0.417, and it passes the significance test at the 1% level; after adding the interaction term, the adjusted R^2 of Model (3) increases from 0.4658 in Model (2) to 0.4662, indicating that the moderating effect of corporate equity properties on the promotion of corporate non-substantive innovation by *Fintech* is significant; that is, the promotion of corporate non-substantive innovation by *Fintech* is weaker in SOEs compared to non-SOEs.

Table 6. The regulating role of the ownership nature of enterprises.

	(2)	(3)	(2)	(3)	(2)	(3)
Variables	Lnpatent	Lnpatent	Lnpati	Lnpati	Lnpatud	Lnpatud
$Fintech_{-1}$	0.529 ***	0.499 ***	0.578 ***	0.547 ***	0.278 **	0.253 **
	(4.53)	(4.26)	(5.32)	(5.03)	(2.46)	(2.24)
Soe	−0.120 ***	−0.151 ***	−0.165 ***	−0.197 ***	−0.062 **	−0.088 ***
	(−4.41)	(−5.36)	(−6.55)	(−7.50)	(−2.34)	(−3.21)
$Fintech_{-1}$*Soe		−0.504 ***		−0.507 ***		−0.417 ***
		(−4.03)		(−4.37)		(−3.44)
Constant	−6.023 ***	−5.790 ***	−6.582 ***	−6.348 ***	−4.462 ***	−4.269 ***
	(−9.04)	(−8.66)	(−10.63)	(−10.22)	(−6.92)	(−6.60)
Control	Yes	Yes	Yes	Yes	Yes	Yes
Year FX	Yes	Yes	Yes	Yes	Yes	Yes
Industry FX	Yes	Yes	Yes	Yes	Yes	Yes
Obs	13,947	13,947	13,947	13,947	13,947	13,947
R-squared	0.4810	0.4816	0.4410	0.4418	0.4692	0.4696
Adj. R^2	0.4777	0.4783	0.4375	0.4382	0.4658	0.4662

Notes: t-statistics in parentheses; *** $p < 0.01$, ** $p < 0.05$.

The regression results presented above show that the nature of enterprise ownership has a significant moderating effect on the promotion of corporate innovation performance at all three levels of fintech; that is, the promotion of corporate innovation by fintech is weaker in SOEs than in non-SOEs, thus supporting H2.

Technical Nature of the Enterprise

Table 7 reports the regression results on the moderating role of heterogeneous firm technology properties in fintech-driven corporate innovation. The results show that in the regression of the total number of corporate innovations (*Lnpatent*), the coefficient of *Fintech* index (*Fintech*$_{-1}$) in Model (5) is 0.475, and the coefficient of the interaction term (*Fintech*$_{-1}$**Tech*) between *Fintech* and firm technology nature is 0.742, and they both pass the significance test at the 1% level. Then, the adjusted R^2 value increases from 0.4678 in Model (4) to 0.4693 in Model (5) after the inclusion of the interaction term, indicating that the moderating effect of the nature of firm technology on the promotion of corporate innovation by fintech is significant; that is, compared with non-high-tech enterprises, high-tech enterprise fintech plays a stronger role in promoting the overall innovation performance of enterprises. In the regression on firm substantive innovation (*Lnpati*), the coefficient of the fintech index (*Fintech*$_{-1}$) in Model (5) is 0.526, while the coefficient of the interaction term (*Fintech*$_{-1}$**Tech*) between fintech and firm equity attributes is 0.622, and they both pass the significance test at the 1% level. The adjusted R^2 value increases from 0.4215 in Model (4) to 0.4228 in Model (5) after adding the interaction term, indicating that the moderating effect of the nature of firm technology on the promotion of substantive innovation by *Fintech* is significant; that is, compared to non-high-tech firms, the promotion of substantive innovation performance by *Fintech* in high-tech firms is stronger. In the regression of firms' non-substantial innovation (*Lnpatud*), the coefficient of the fintech index (*Fintech*$_{-1}$) in Model (5) is 0.235, which passes the 5% significance test, while the coefficient of the interaction term (*Fintech*$_{-1}$**Tech*) is 0.814 and passes the significance test at the 1% level, and the value of R^2 increases from 0.4591 in Model (4) to 0.4661 in Model (5) after adding the interaction term. The value of R^2 increases from 0.4591 in Model (4) to 0.4661 in Model (5) after adding the interaction term, indicating that the moderating effect of the nature of firm technology on the promotion of non-substantial innovation by fintech is significant, meaning that the contribution of fintech to the non-substantial innovation performance of firms is stronger in high-tech firms compared to non-high-tech firms.

Table 7. The moderating effect of the nature of the firm's technology.

	(4)	(5)	(4)	(5)	(4)	(5)
Variables	**Lnpatent**	**Lnpatent**	**Lnpati**	**Lnpati**	**Lnpatud**	**Lnpatud**
$Fintech_{-1}$	0.468 *** (4.08)	0.475 *** (4.15)	0.521 *** (4.91)	0.526 *** (4.97)	0.227 ** (2.05)	0.235 ** (2.12)
Tech	−1.246 *** (−6.66)	−1.198 *** (−6.41)	−0.957 *** (−5.54)	−0.917 *** (−5.31)	−1.315 *** (−7.29)	−1.263 *** (−7.01)
$Fintech_{-1}$*Tech		0.742 *** (6.25)		0.622 *** (5.67)		0.814 *** (7.11)
Constant	−4.790 *** (−7.37)	−4.816 *** (−7.42)	−5.622 *** (−9.36)	−5.645 *** (−9.41)	−3.176 *** (−5.06)	−3.205 *** (−5.12)
Control	Yes	Yes	Yes	Yes	Yes	Yes
Year FX	Yes	Yes	Yes	Yes	Yes	Yes
Industry FX	Yes	Yes	Yes	Yes	Yes	Yes
Obs	13,947	13,947	13,947	13,947	13,947	13,947
R-squared	0.4711	0.4726	0.4251	0.4264	0.4625	0.4645
Adj. R^2	0.4678	0.4693	0.4215	0.4228	0.4591	0.4611

Notes: t-statistics in parentheses; *** $p < 0.01$, ** $p < 0.05$.

The regression results presented above show that, regardless of the level of innovation performance of the explained variables, the promotion effect in high-tech enterprises is stronger than that in non-high-tech enterprises; that is, compared to non-high-tech firms, the contribution of fintech in high-tech firms to firms' innovation performance is stronger, thus supporting H3.

Enterprise Life Cycle

When an enterprise is in different life cycle stages, its investment, financing, and operational funds show significant differences, and the business purpose of the enterprise is also different. Innovation activities indicate different aspects for each stage of the firm. Table 8 reports the regression results for the moderating role of heterogeneous corporate life cycle attributes in fintech-driven corporate innovation. The results show that in the regression of the total number of corporate innovations (*Lnpatent*), the coefficient of the fintech index (*$Fintech_{-1}$*) in Model (7) is 0.400, while the coefficient of the interaction term (*$Fintech_{-1}$*Life*) is 0.387, and they all pass the significance test at the 1% level. Then, the adjusted R^2 value increases from 0.4773 in Model (6) to 0.4776 in Model (7) after adding the interaction term, indicating that the moderating effect of the nature of the firm's technology on the contribution of fintech to the overall innovation of the firm is significant; that is, compared to the declining period firms, the contribution of fintech to the overall innovation performance of the firm is stronger in the growing and maturing period firms. In the regression of substantial corporate innovation (*Lnpati*), the coefficient of the fintech index (*$Fintech_{-1}$*) in Model (7) is 0.454, while the coefficient of the interaction term (*$Fintech_{-1}$*Life*) between fintech and the corporate life cycle is 0.294, and they pass the significance test at the 5% level. The adjusted R^2 value after adding the interaction term increases from 0.4360 in Model (6) to 0.4361 in Model (7), indicating that the moderating effect of the nature of the firm's technology on the promotion of substantive innovation by *Fintech* is significant, which means that the contribution of *Fintech* to the substantive innovation performance of firms in the growth and maturity periods is stronger than that of firms in the decline period. In the return to corporate non-substantial innovation (*Lnpatud*), the coefficient of the fintech index (*$Fintech_{-1}$*) in Model (7) was 0.166, but it failed the significance test. The coefficient of the interaction term *$Fintech_{-1}$*Life* between fintech and corporate life cycle is 0.407, and it passes the significance test at the 1% level, while the adjusted R^2 value after adding the interaction term value increases from 0.4657 in Model (6) to 0.4660 in Model (7), indicating that the moderating effect of the nature of firm technology on the promotion of non-substantial innovation by fintech is significant; that is, compared to firms in decline, fintech has a stronger contribution to the non-substantial innovation performance of firms in growth and maturity periods.

Table 8. The moderating effect of the enterprise life cycle.

	(6)	(7)	(6)	(7)	(6)	(7)
Variables	Lnpatent	Lnpatent	Lnpati	Lnpati	Lnpatud	Lnpatud
$Fintech_{-1}$	0.486 ***	0.400 ***	0.519 ***	0.454 ***	0.256 **	0.166
	(4.18)	(3.32)	(4.79)	(4.04)	(2.27)	(1.42)
Life	−0.077 ***	−2.276 ***	−0.058 **	−1.729 **	−0.049 *	−2.361 ***
	(−2.93)	(−2.80)	(−2.39)	(−2.29)	(−1.92)	(−3.01)
$Fintech_{-1}$*Life		0.387 ***		0.294 **		0.407 ***
		(2.71)		(2.21)		(2.94)
Constant	−5.966 ***	−5.480 ***	−6.531 ***	−6.161 ***	−4.428 ***	−3.917 ***
	(−8.95)	(−7.94)	(−10.53)	(−9.59)	(−6.86)	(−5.86)
Control	Yes	Yes	Yes	Yes	Yes	Yes
Year FX	Yes	Yes	Yes	Yes	Yes	Yes
Industry FX	Yes	Yes	Yes	Yes	Yes	Yes
Obs	13,947	13,947	13,947	13,947	13,947	13,947
R-squared	0.4806	0.4809	0.4395	0.4397	0.4691	0.4694
Adj. R^2	0.4773	0.4776	0.4360	0.4361	0.4657	0.4660

Notes: t-statistics in parentheses; *** $p < 0.01$, ** $p < 0.05$, * $p < 0.1$.

Based on the results presented above, it can be seen that regardless of the dimension of patent innovation activities for enterprises, the effect of fintech in promoting corporate innovation in the growth and maturity periods is higher than that of enterprises in the decline period, thus supporting H4.

4.3. Robustness Test

To further verify the robustness of this study's findings related to the promotion of corporate innovation performance via fintech, the main effects regression of this study is tested for robustness by varying the sample interval and 2SLS.

4.3.1. Test Based on Sample Interval Adjustment

The global COVID-19 outbreak in late 2019 has had a huge impact on social and economic growth in all countries. With the implementation of various restrictive epidemic prevention policies, the operation of enterprises has been greatly restricted. Big data information, contactless service models, and online Internet products have developed rapidly during the COVID-19 pandemic. Fintech can use its Internet technology to provide more diversified financial products and services to demanders without contact. Therefore, in 2020, an important period after the COVID-19 outbreak, notable differences in the production, operation, and technological innovation of enterprises as well as the development of fintech were evident. The sample observation value may lead to bias in the study findings; therefore, this study uses sample firms excluding 2020 to conduct robustness tests to verify the reliability of the abovementioned empirical analysis findings.

Table 9 reports the regression analysis results of fintech promoting corporate innovation after excluding the sample of enterprises in 2020. As can be seen from the results of Columns (1)–(3), the regression coefficients of fintech on the overall innovation level, substantive innovation, and non-substantive innovation are 0.517, 0.521, and 0.288, respectively, all of which pass the significance test, indicating that fintech has a significant promoting effect on firm innovation, which is consistent with the results of the previous regression analysis.

Table 9. Robustness test: the regression results of the adjusted sample interval.

	(1)	(2)	(3)
Variables	**Lnpatent**	**Lnpati**	**Lnpatud**
$Fintech_{-1}$	0.517 *** (3.86)	0.521 *** (4.23)	0.288 ** (2.22)
Size	0.715 *** (56.28)	0.666 *** (57.12)	0.594 *** (48.33)
CD	−0.122 *** (−13.66)	−0.093 *** (−11.33)	−0.114 *** (−13.09)
Lev	−0.338 *** (−4.15)	−0.391 *** (−5.25)	−0.064 (−0.82)
Share	−0.002 *** (−2.65)	−0.003 *** (−3.22)	−0.000 (−0.45)
PG	0.004 (0.69)	0.000 (0.10)	0.006 (1.18)
Growth	−0.085 ** (−2.44)	−0.067 ** (−2.10)	−0.083 ** (−2.48)
Age	−0.011 *** (−4.58)	−0.007 *** (−3.08)	−0.009 *** (−4.00)
Constant	−5.667 *** (−7.42)	−6.095 *** (−8.69)	−4.199 *** (−5.68)
Year FX	yes	yes	yes
Industry FX	yes	yes	yes
Obs	10,813	10,813	10,813
R-squared	0.481	0.433	0.477
Adj. R^2	0.476	0.429	0.473

Notes: t-statistics in parentheses; *** $p < 0.01$, ** $p < 0.05$.

4.3.2. Test Based on a Two-Stage Least Squares Model

In this study, when benchmark regressions are used to study the impact of fintech on corporate innovation performance, endogeneity problems may arise due to differences in the selection of control variables, omitted variables, and reciprocal causality. According to previous research, fintech development can effectively enhance firms' innovation performance, but the enhancement of firm innovation may also affect the level of fintech development. To avoid the reverse causality problem, this study uses the lags of fintech as explanatory variables for fixed effects regression, but it is necessary to conduct further endogeneity tests on the model to make the research results more credible. Therefore, this study uses 2SLS regression with a lagged second period of *Fintech* (*Fintech-t-2*) as the instrumental variable. The 2SLS regression is conducted using the same test for the identifiability of instrumental variables and the presence of weak instrumental variables.

Table 10 presents the 2SLS regression results. The results show that at a significance level of 1%, the regression coefficient of $Fintech_{-1}$ on the overall innovation performance of enterprises is 9.752, and the regression coefficient increases after solving the endogenous nature of variables, indicating that the development of fintech has a significant effect on promoting corporate innovation performance. At the 5% significance level, the regression coefficient of fintech on firms' substantive innovation is 8.676, and the regression coefficient of fintech on firms' non-substantive innovation is 8.576; that is, fintech significantly contributes to corporate innovation, and its contribution to firms' substantive innovation is stronger than that of non-substantive innovation. The benchmark regression results with the inclusion of instrumental variables are generally consistent, further indicating the reliability of the results. Moreover, in Table 10, the Kleibergen–Paap rk LM statistic for Models (1)–(4) is 259.802, which corresponds to a p-value of 0, indicating that the instrumental variables are identifiable. Meanwhile, the Cragg–Donald Wald F statistic of 387.686 is much larger than the Stock–Yogo weak ID test critical values at the 10% level of judgment of 16.38; thus, there is no weak instrumental variable problem.

Table 10. Robustness test: two-stage least squares regression results.

	First Stage	Second Stage		
	(1)	(2)	(3)	(4)
Variables	$Fintech_{-1}$	Lnpatent	Lnpati	Lnpatud
$Fintech_{-2}$	0.077 *** (12.042)			
$Fintech_{-1}$		9.752 *** (2.62)	8.676 ** (2.53)	8.576 ** (2.18)
Size	0.001 (1.001)	0.450 *** (7.81)	0.429 *** (8.10)	0.329 *** (5.79)
CD	−0.000 (−1.19)	−0.029 (−1.53)	−0.020 (−1.23)	−0.015 (−0.82)
Lev	0.002 (1.0204)	−0.273 * (−1.68)	−0.282 * (−1.93)	−0.075 (−0.45)
SD	0.000 (0.61)	0.006 ** (2.16)	0.003 (1.33)	0.006 ** (2.01)
PG	0.000 *** (5.05)	−0.018 *** (−3.51)	−0.015 *** (−3.25)	−0.010 * (−1.82)
Growth	−0.000 (−1.160)	0.002 (0.05)	−0.012 (−0.35)	0.021 (0.50)
Age	−0.008 ** (−2.31)	0.015 (0.38)	−0.007 (−0.21)	−0.004 (−0.10)
Year FX	yes	yes	yes	yes
Industry FX	yes	yes	yes	yes
Obs	10,582	10,582	10,582	10,582
R-squared		0.212	0.065	0.313
Kleibergen–Paap rk LM statistic	259.802 (Chi-sq(1) p-value = 0.0000)			
Cragg–Donald F statistic	387.686			
Kleibergen–Paap rk Wald F statistic	237.755			
10% maximal IV size	16.38			

Notes: t-statistics in parentheses; *** $p < 0.01$, ** $p < 0.05$, * $p < 0.1$.

5. Discussion and Conclusions

5.1. Discussion

The rapid development of digital technology has promoted the integration of finance and technology, giving rise to a series of new financial business models. The study found that the development of fintech has reduced the financing dilemma faced by innovative subjects, further enhanced enterprises' willingness to innovate technology, and enabled technological innovation. We argue that, first, fintech fills the gaps in traditional financial services. Financial institutions can provide more diversified and personalized financial services for enterprises, enabling them to obtain a more stable flow of funds to support their innovation projects and achieve the optimal allocation of financial resources [18]. Second, the development of financial technology can effectively crack the information asymmetry within enterprises, between enterprises, and between enterprises and financial institutions. It enhances the information recognition ability of enterprises, helps them judge the innovation direction and market potential, as well as maintain customers, etc., and improves the efficiency of enterprise innovation decisions [19,33]. Furthermore, due to the profit-seeking nature of capital, firms will pay more attention to the improvement of core innovation competitiveness and focus their resources on these innovation activities, with little impact on those non-substantial innovations with less economic potential (e.g., utility model patents and design patents) [30].

Differences in corporate nature lead to large differences in business goals, innovation motivation, and innovation behavior, and such differences can similarly affect the role of fintech in driving corporate innovation [6,65]. We argue that SOEs are more likely to receive policy support than non-SOEs, and that the incentives they receive from fiscal, tax, and subsidy sources expose them to lower financial exclusion from traditional financial services [36]. Therefore, the impact of fintech on SOEs' economic activities has clear boundary limits [38,39]. In terms of technological nature, high-tech enterprises face fiercer competition than non-high-tech enterprises, have stronger technology development requirements and an intrinsic innovation drive, and pay more attention to the improvement of innovation capability, which makes high-tech enterprises have higher requirements for long-term sustainable funding, and the development of fintech effectively meets this demand [42]. From the perspective of enterprise life cycle, enterprises in the growth stage develop rapidly and have high innovation creativity, but lack sufficient funds to transform into real innovation results. Firms at this stage have higher technological and operational risks, growth in earnings lags behind revenue growth, and external investors are more cautious or require higher risk premiums, limiting the possibility of obtaining funding. Therefore, firms in the growth stage have a higher degree of demand for financial resources, and the development of financial technology enables investors to more accurately identify the development capabilities of firms and increase the availability of capital [44,47]. Upon entering the maturity stage, the internal organizational structure of enterprises tends to be perfected, management is gradually standardized, market share reaches its highest level, the trend of capital expansion gradually slows down, and the innovation capacity of enterprises reaches its highest level at this stage, where fintech can play its facilitating role more effectively [45]. The differences in the nature of enterprises prompt the development of fintech to consider the differences in the nature of innovation subjects, and through personalized services can effectively play its promotional role, which is of great practical significance for the study of how fintech can promote enterprise innovation.

5.2. Conclusions, Implications, and Limitations Section

This study empirically examines the promoting effect of fintech on corporate innovation and the moderating effect of corporate characteristics by using Chinese A-share non-financial and non-real estate listed companies from 2015 to 2020. The study finds that fintech has a significant facilitative effect on corporate innovation, supporting hypothesis 1. In-depth comparisons reveal that this facilitative effect reflects structural differences, with fintech having a stronger facilitative effect on corporate substantive innovation than non-substantive innovation, extending previous studies in the literature. Further research finds that corporate nature has a moderating effect on the promotion of corporate innovation by fintech. The difference in firm ownership makes the role of fintech in promoting firm innovation weaker in SOEs than in non-SOEs. Differences in technology nature result in differences in firms' willingness to innovate and financial needs, making the promotion effect stronger for high-tech firms than for non-high-tech firms. Similarly, the promotion effect of financial technology on firm innovation is stronger in firms in the growth and maturity stages than in firms in the decline stage. Hypotheses H2, H3, and H4 are supported.

The findings of this study provide the following theoretical and practical implications for promoting fintech development and enabling corporate innovation. First, it is imperative to accelerate theoretical research on fintech and provide constructive guidance for macro-policy formulation to promote the reform and development of the financial industry. Second, we actively promote the development of financial technology and build a healthy fintech ecosystem to promote the innovation performance of enterprises [67]. The key to the development of financial technology lies in the effective combination of finance and technology, and technology companies and financial institutions should target frontier areas, actively participate in the research of emerging technologies, establish specialized technology research teams, and increase investment in talents and funds, especially strategic resources such as global financial technology talents, patents, and standards. Third, from a life cycle perspective, growing firms need to make full use of fintech to obtain diversified financing channels through new fintech products and services, such as equity and accounts receivable financing [48,66]. Enterprises in the mature stage should face up to their technological shortcomings, promote the integration of financial technology innovation and enterprise technological innovation, and mobilize their innovative energy [68]. For enterprises in decline, we should strengthen the identification function of financial technology for declining enterprises, encourage financial institutions to provide targeted financial support for innovation, and encourage enterprises to actively explore new R&D fields to achieve sustainable development.

There are limitations in the research on the moderating effect of corporate nature in this study, as there are other micro and macro factors on corporate innovation performance, such as financial regulation, regional capital market development level, and regional capital market development level, in the previous literature, which are not fully incorporated in this study and can be explored more deeply and extensively in future research.

Author Contributions: Data curation and draft, Y.G.; methodology, review, and editing, S.J. All authors have read and agreed to the published version of the manuscript.

Funding: This study received no external funding.

Institutional Review Board Statement: Not applicable.

Informed Consent Statement: Not applicable.

Data Availability Statement: Not applicable.

Conflicts of Interest: The authors declare no conflict of interest.

References

1. Romer, P.M. Endogenous Technological Change. *J. Political Econ.* **1990**, *98*, S71–S102. [CrossRef]
2. Csedo, Z.; Magyari, J.; Zavarko, M. Dynamic Corporate Governance, Innovation, and Sustainability: Post-COVID Period. *Sustainbility* **2022**, *14*, 3189. [CrossRef]
3. Ma, D.; Yu, Q.; Li, J.; Ge, M. Innovation diffusion enabler or barrier: An investigation of international patenting based on temporal exponential random graph models. *Technol. Soc.* **2021**, *64*, 101456. [CrossRef]
4. Arifin, M.R.; Raharja, B.S.; Nugroho, A.; Aligarh, F. The Relationship Between Corporate Innovation and Corporate Governance: Empirical Evidence from Indonesia. *J. Asian Financ. Econ. Bus.* **2022**, *9*, 105–112.
5. Chen, S.S.; Huang, C.W.; Hwang, C.Y.; Wang, Y.Z. Voluntary disclosure and corporate innovation. *Rev. Quant. Financ. Account.* **2022**, *58*, 1081–1115. [CrossRef]
6. Yang, D.; Wang, J.; Chen, H. Earnings guidance: Market pressure or corporate governance? Evidence from corporate innovation in China. *Nankai Bus. Rev. Int.* **2021**, *12*, 409–433. [CrossRef]
7. Gao, Y.; Lin, R.; Lu, Y. A visualized analysis of the research current hotspots and trends on innovation chain based on the knowledge map. *Sustainbility* **2022**, *14*, 1708. [CrossRef]
8. Guan, J.; Xu, H.; Huo, D.; Hua, Y.; Wang, Y. Economic policy uncertainty and corporate innovation: Evidence from China. *Pac.-Basin Financ. J.* **2021**, *67*, 101542. [CrossRef]
9. Haddad, C.; Hornuf, L. The emergence of the global fintech market: Economic and technological determinants. *Small Bus. Econ.* **2019**, *53*, 81–105. [CrossRef]
10. Leong, K.; Sung, A. Fin tech (Financial technology): What is it and how to use technologies to create business value in fintech way? *Int. J. Innov. Manag. Technol.* **2018**, *9*, 74–78. [CrossRef]
11. Alkhazaleh, A.M.K.; Haddad, H. How does the fintech services delivery affect customer satisfaction: A scenario of jordanian banking sector. *Strateg. Change* **2021**, *30*, 405–413. [CrossRef]
12. Schueffel, P. Taming the beast: A scientific definition of fintech. *J. Innov. Manag.* **2016**, *4*, 32–54. [CrossRef]
13. Lee, I.; Shin, Y.J. Fintech: Ecosystem, business models, investment decisions, and challenges. *Bus. Horiz.* **2018**, *61*, 35–46. [CrossRef]
14. Anagnostopoulos, I. Fintech and regtech: Impact on regulators and banks. *J. Econ. Bus.* **2018**, *100*, 7–25. [CrossRef]
15. Gimpel, H.; Rau, D.; Röglinger, M. Fintech-geschäftsmodelle im visier. *Wirtsch. Manag.* **2016**, *8*, 38–47. [CrossRef]
16. Zavolokina, L.; Dolata, M.; Schwabe, G. The fintech phenomenon: Antecedents of financial innovation perceived by the popular press. *Financ. Innov.* **2016**, *2*, 16. [CrossRef]
17. Cristina, C.V.; Luis, F.A. Fintech and sustainability: Do they affect each other? *Sustainbility* **2021**, *13*, 7012.
18. Valentin, B.; Ana, G.; Manju, P. On the rise of fintechs: Credit scoring using digital footprints. *Rev. Financ. Stud.* **2019**, *32*, 3401–3450.
19. Li, J.W.; Li, N.; Cheng, X. The Impact of Fintech on Corporate Technology Innovation Based on Driving Effects, Mechanism Identification, and Heterogeneity Analysis. *Discret. Dyn. Nat. Soc.* **2021**, *2021*, 7825120. [CrossRef]

20. Chorzempa, M.; Huang, Y. Chinese fintech innovation and regulation. *Asian Econ. Policy Rev.* **2022**, *7*, 1–19. [CrossRef]
21. Takeda, A.; Ito, Y. A review of fintech research. *Int. J. Technol. Manag.* **2021**, *86*, 67. [CrossRef]
22. Schumpeter, J.A. The theory of economics development. *J. Political Econ.* **1934**, *1*, 170–172.
23. Domar, E.D. Capital expansion, rate of growth, and employment. *Econometrica* **1946**, *14*, 137–147. [CrossRef]
24. Solow, R.M. A contribution to the theory of economic growth. *Q. J. Econ.* **1956**, *70*, 86–94. [CrossRef]
25. Hicks, J.R. *A Theory of Economic History*; OUP Catalogue: Oxford, UK, 1969.
26. Blackburn, K.; Hung, V. A theory of growth, financial development and trade. *Economica* **1998**, *65*, 107–124. [CrossRef]
27. Wamda; PAYFORT. Fintech in MENA: Unbundling the Financial Services Industry. *Findevgateway*. Available online: https://www.wamda.com/research/fintech-mena-unbundling-financial-services-industry (accessed on 16 March 2017).
28. Gomber, P.; Kauffman, R.J.; Parker, C. On the fintech revolution: Interpreting the forces of innovation, disruption and transformation in financial services. *J. Manag. Inf. Syst.* **2018**, *35*, 220–265. [CrossRef]
29. Bettinger, A. Fintech: A series of 40time shared models used at manufacturers handover trust company. *Interfaces* **1972**, *2*, 62–63.
30. Chowdhury, R.H.; Min, M. Financial market development and the effectiveness of r&d investment: Evidence from developed and emerging countries. *Res. Int. Bus. Financ.* **2012**, *26*, 258–272.
31. Morales, M.F. Financial intermediation in a model of growth through creative destruction. *Macroecon. Dyn.* **2003**, *7*, 363–393. [CrossRef]
32. He, J.; Tian, X. Finance and corporate innovation: A survey. *Asia-Pac. J. Financ. Stud.* **2018**, *47*, 165–212. [CrossRef]
33. Grennan, J.; Michaely, R. Fintechs and the market for financial analysis. *J. Financ. Quant. Anal.* **2021**, *56*, 1877–1907. [CrossRef]
34. Blach, J.; Klimontowicz, M. The determinants of paytech's success in the mobile payment market: The case of BLIK. *J. Risk Financ. Manag.* **2021**, *14*, 422. [CrossRef]
35. Ling, S.X.; Han, G.S.; An, D.; Akhmedov, A.; Wang, H.; Li, H.; Hunter, W.C. The effects of financing channels on corporate innovation and life cycle in chinese a-share listed companies: An empirical analysis. *Sustainbility* **2020**, *12*, 6704. [CrossRef]
36. Aghion, P.; Van Reenen, J.; Zingales, L. Innovation and Institutional Ownership. *Am. Econ. Rev.* **2013**, *103*, 277–304. [CrossRef]
37. Chi, J.; Liao, J.; Yang, J. Institutional stock ownership and firm innovation: Evidence from China. *J. Multinatl. Financ. Manag.* **2019**, *50*, 44–57. [CrossRef]
38. Borisova, G.; Brockman, P.; Salas, J.M.; Zagorchev, A. Government ownership and corporate governance: Evidence from the eu. *J. Bank. Financ.* **2012**, *36*, 2917–2934. [CrossRef]
39. Shleifer, A.; Vishny, R.W. A survey of corporate governance. *J. Financ.* **1997**, *52*, 737–783. [CrossRef]
40. Aghion, P.; Howitt, P. Some thoughts on capital accumulation, innovation, and growth. *Ann. Econ. Stat.* **2017**, *125/126*, 57–78. [CrossRef]
41. Han, H.Y.; Gu, X.M. Linkage between inclusive digital finance and high-tech corporate innovation performance: Role of debt and equity financing. *Front. Psychol.* **2021**, *12*, 4408. [CrossRef]
42. Canepa, A.; Stoneman, P. Financial constraints to innovation in the uk: Evidence from cis2 and cis3. *Oxf. Econ. Pap.* **2008**, *60*, 394–398. [CrossRef]
43. Benfratello, L.; Schiantarelli, F.; Sembenelli, A. Banks and innovation: Microeconometric evidence on italian firms. *Boston Coll. Work. Pap. Econ.* **2007**, *90*, 197–217.
44. Dickinson, V. Cash flow patterns as a proxy for firm life cycle. *Account. Rev.* **2011**, *86*, 1969–1994. [CrossRef]
45. Chang, J. The economics of crowdfunding. *Am. Econ. J. Microecon* **2020**, *12*, 257–280. [CrossRef]
46. Mclean, R.D.; Zhao, M.X. The Business Cycle, Investor Sentiment, and Costly External Finance. *J. Financ.* **2014**, *69*, 1377–1409. [CrossRef]
47. Greiner, L.E. Evolution and revolution as organizations grow. *Harv. Bus. Rev.* **1998**, *76*, 55–64. [PubMed]
48. Yang, C.; Hua, Y.; Hua, Z. R&D investment along the firm life-cycle: New evidence from high-tech industries. *Int. J. Technol. Manag.* **2022**, *88*, 353–388.
49. Caggese, A. Financing constraints, radical versus incremental innovation, and aggregate productivity. *Am. Econ. J. Macroecon.* **2019**, *11*, 275–309. [CrossRef]
50. Acharya, V.; Xu, Z. Financial dependence and innovation: The case of public versus private firms. *J. Financ. Econ.* **2016**, *124*, 223–243. [CrossRef]
51. Zu, Y.; Zhang, R. Supplier change, market competition and corporate innovation. *Eur. J. Innov. Manag.* **2022**. *ahead-of-print*. [CrossRef]
52. Kleinknecht, A.; Montfort, V.; Brouwer, K. The non-trivial choice between innovation indicators. *Econ. Innov. New Technol.* **2002**, *1*, 109–121. [CrossRef]
53. Zhao, J.S.; Li, X.H.; Yu, C.H.; Chen, S.; Lee, C.C. Riding the fintech innovation wave: FinTech, patents and bank performance. *J. Int. Money Financ.* **2022**, *122*, 102552. [CrossRef]
54. Deng, L.R.; Lv, Y.B.; Liu, Y.; Zhao, Y.W. Impact of fintech on bank risk-taking: Evidence from China. *Risks* **2021**, *9*, 27. [CrossRef]
55. Guo, H.; Pan, Z.; Tian, G.G. State ownership and the risk-reducing effect of corporate derivative use: Evidence from China. *J. Bus. Financ. Account.* **2021**, *48*, 1092–1133. [CrossRef]
56. Liu, H.M.; Wu, S.; Zhong, C.W.; Liu, Y. The sustainable effect of operational performance on financial benefits: Evidence from chinese quality awards winners. *Sustainbility* **2020**, *12*, 1966. [CrossRef]

57. DeAngelo, H.; DeAngelo, L.; Stulz, R.M. Seasoned equity offerings, market timing, and the corporate lifecycle. *J. Financ. Econ.* **2010**, *95*, 275–295. [CrossRef]
58. Lin, R.H.; Xie, Z.Y.; Hao, Y.H.; Wang, H.J. Improving high-tech corporate innovation in big data environment: A combinative view of internal and external governance. *Int. J. Inf. Manag.* **2020**, *50*, 575–585. [CrossRef]
59. Akcigit, U.; Kerr, W.R. Growth through heterogeneous innovations. *J. Political Econ. Univ. Chic. Press* **2018**, *126*, 1374–1443. [CrossRef]
60. Chiang, S.; Lee, P.; Anandarajan, A. Corporate governance and innovative success: An examination of the moderating influence of a firm's life cycle stage. *Innov. Manag. Policy Pract.* **2013**, *15*, 500–514. [CrossRef]
61. Hasan, I.; Hoi, C.K.S.; Wu, Q.; Zhang, H. Is social capital associated with corporate innovation? Evidence from publicly listed firms in the US. *J. Corp. Financ.* **2020**, *62*, 101623. [CrossRef]
62. Jin, S.; Gao, Y.Y.; Xiao, S. Corporate governance structure and performance in the tourism industry in the COVID-19 pandemic: An empirical study of Chinese listed companies in China. *Sustainbility* **2021**, *13*, 11722. [CrossRef]
63. Makosa, L.; Sun, J.; Bonga, W.G.; Jachi, M.; Sitsha, L. Does economic policy uncertainty aggravate financial constraints? *S. Afr. J. Account. Res.* **2021**, *35*, 151–166. [CrossRef]
64. Wang, R.; Ma, S.; Xu, X.; Song, P. Heterogeneous shareholders participation, COVID-19 impact, and innovation decisions of state-owned firms: Evidence from China. *Sustainbility* **2021**, *13*, 4406. [CrossRef]
65. Wang, S. How does stock market liberalization influence corporate innovation? Evidence from stock connect scheme in China. *Emerg. Mark. Rev.* **2020**, *47*, 100762. [CrossRef]
66. Shahzad, F.; Ahmad, M.; Fareed, Z.; Wang, Z. Innovation decisions through firm life cycle: A new evidence from emerging markets. *Int. Rev. Econ. Financ.* **2022**, *78*, 51–67. [CrossRef]
67. Castro, P.; Rodrigues, J.P.; Teixeira, J.G. Understanding FinTech ecosystem evolution through service innovation and socio-technical system perspective. In *International Conference on Exploring Services Science*; Springer: Cham, Switzerland, 2020; pp. 187–201.
68. Ryu, S.L.; Won, J. The Value Relevance of Operational Innovation: Insights from the Perspective of Firm Life Cycle. *Sustainability* **2022**, *14*, 2058. [CrossRef]

sustainability

MDPI

Article

The Mexican Ecological Conscience: A Predictive Model

Jessica Müller-Pérez [1], Ángel Acevedo-Duque [2,*], Gonzalo R. Llanos-Herrera [3], Elizabeth Emperatriz García-Salirrosas [4], Luiz Vicente Ovalles-Toledo [5], Lidyeth Azucena Sandoval Barraza [5,6] and Rina Álvarez-Becerra [6]

1 Faculty of Commerce and Administration, Universidad Autónoma de Tamaulipas, Matamoros SN, Zona Centro, Ciudad Victoria 87000, Mexico; jsmuller@docentes.uat.edu.mx
2 Programa Doctorado Ciencias Sociales, Universidad Autónoma de Chile, Santiago 7500912, Chile
3 School of Economics and Business, Universidad Finis Terrae, Santiago 7501015, Chile; gllanos@uft.cl
4 Faculty of Management Science, Universidad Autónoma del Perú, Lima 15842, Peru; egarciasa@autonoma.edu.pe
5 Faculty of Accounting and Administration, Autonomous University of Sinaloa, Culiacán 80020, Mexico; luiz.ovalles@uas.edu.mx (L.V.O.-T.); azucena_sandoval@uas.edu.mx (L.A.S.B.)
6 Graduate School, Universidad Nacional Jorge Basadre Grohmann, Tacna 23001, Peru; ralvarezb@unjbg.edu.pe
* Correspondence: angel.acevedo@uautonoma.cl

Citation: Müller-Pérez, J.; Acevedo-Duque, Á.; Llanos-Herrera, G.R.; García-Salirrosas, E.E.; Ovalles-Toledo, L.V.; Sandoval Barraza, L.A.; Álvarez-Becerra, R. The Mexican Ecological Conscience: A Predictive Model. *Sustainability* **2022**, *14*, 7050. https://doi.org/10.3390/su14127050

Academic Editors: Jeoung Yul Lee, Dilek Zamantili Nayir, Charles Chen and Ioannis Nikolaou

Received: 9 April 2022
Accepted: 31 May 2022
Published: 9 June 2022

Publisher's Note: MDPI stays neutral with regard to jurisdictional claims in published maps and institutional affiliations.

Abstract: Recently, the number of Mexicans who buy sustainable products has been increasing, which has led to sustainable trade. Therefore, the objective of this study is to determine which variables have a greater effect on Mexicans' intention to buy green products, their ecological awareness, or moral obligation, and, in turn, to determine the degree to which moral obligation is affected by ecological awareness. A sample of 690 Mexicans was obtained, and a PLS–SEM model was applied for data analysis. The results confirmed that both a moral obligation and ecological awareness explain the intention to purchase green products, with ecological awareness contributing the most to the intention. Furthermore, the findings showed that moral obligation is affected by ecological awareness. The originality of the article is that it contributes to the consumer behavior literature by providing an insight for companies that manufacture sustainable products to understand and promote environmentally conscious consumer behavior. However, there are some limitations that can be addressed in future research.

Keywords: sustainability; ecological awareness; moral obligation; purchase intention

1. Introduction

Recent consumer behavior towards eco-friendly or green products is a prominent issue for governments and companies [1]. Today, companies apply sustainable marketing strategies to gain a competitive advantage by creating ecological awareness among consumers [2], focusing on economic, social, and environmental values to achieve a balance between people, profit, and planet [2]. The Brundtland report describes sustainability as the process of meeting today's needs without compromising tomorrow's resources [3]. According to [4], awareness of green consumption is necessary regarding concern for the health of the planet. Indeed, the Earth is considered a system that connects space and time, so it is important to promote and support sustainable development in Mexico so that the rest of the world can follow [5].

Many studies describe a person's motivation through extrinsic means, i.e., perceived behavioral control, subjective norms, and attitude, and subsequently study their effect on green purchasing behavior [4,5]. However, a consumer may be willing to buy green products due to their interest in environmental care (intrinsic motivation), because they realize how important it is to consume green products (identified motivation), because they feel uncomfortable not buying them (introjected motivation), or because their partner wants them to buy green products (external motivation) [6,7].

According to Vargas-Hernández and Cervantes-Guzmán (2019) [8], "eco-conscious" consumers are a fast-growing niche in Mexico; moreover, there is also some research on green products in Mexican academia, such as the TNS Research Green Study (2010) [9], which notes that almost 50% of Mexicans are more willing to buy green products, so further research on Mexican consumers and their sustainability intentions is needed. In a previous study, the variables considered predictors of intention—attitudes, subjective norms, and perceived purchase control—which, according to Ajzen (2011) [10], did not have a significant effect on intention; however, environmental awareness was an additional variable in ongoing behavioral studies [11,12], while moral obligations have been shown to be the opposite [13].Therefore, the study aims to find out the extent to which environmental awareness and moral obligation influence the purchase decision of Mexican consumers to buy green products, and whether environmental awareness influences consumers' moral obligation. The study contributes in two ways: firstly, by contributing to the literature on Mexican consumer behavior in the sustainable context, and, secondly, by providing an overview for companies that manufacture sustainable products on consumer behavior for them to understand and promote such environmentally conscious behavior in their sales strategies.

2. Background

2.1. *Mexican Consumers and Their Purchase Intention*

Over the last decade, several studies have been conducted to understand how consumers react when given the opportunity to purchase green or sustainable products, and what aspects consumers consider important for purchasing these products [3]. Consumer behavior is seen as an activity that enables consumers to purchase, consume, and acquire products and services, including the decision-making stages before and after a purchase [14]. The above reflects the interesting analysis presented by the World Bank concerning consumer price inflation (annual %) in Mexico [15]. Inflation is a phenomenon observed in the economy of a country related to the disorderly increase in the prices of most of the products in a market that can be fixed or variable at given intervals, e.g., annually (See Figure 1). The Laspeyres formula is generally used.

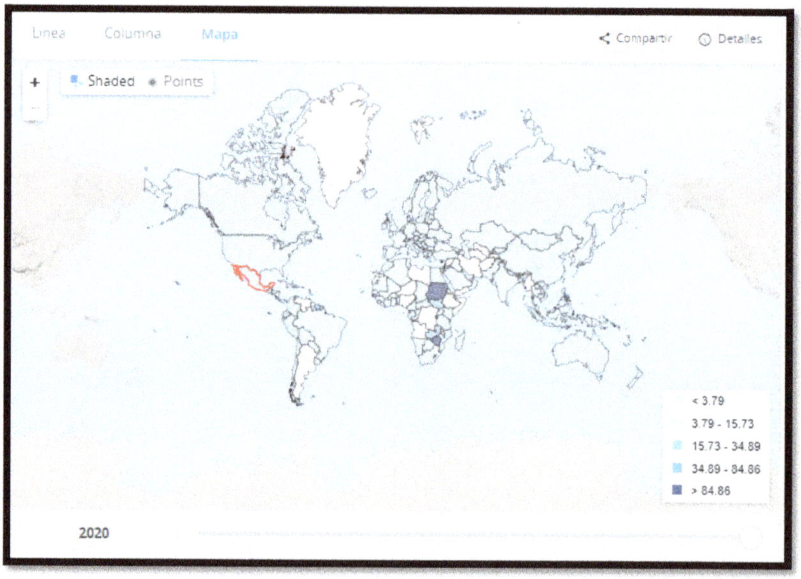

Figure 1. Inflation, consumer prices (annual %) in Mexico. Source: World Bank data 2022.

Green consumer behavior refers to the purchase of environmentally friendly products, the conservation of natural resources, and the shift towards recycled products [7]. According to Ghose and Chandra (2020), a green product is beneficial for human beings, and does not harm the environment; furthermore, it can be perceived when some of these are made of recyclable materials or if their packaging is made of biodegradable materials. For example, LUSH cosmetics replaced standard wrapping paper with reusable fabric wrapping, and when they ship some products that are sold online, they send them in biodegradable bags cushioned by compostable renatured peanuts, packaged in 100% recyclable cardboard boxes [8]. On the other hand, an example of products that do not harm the environment is energy efficient appliances (EEAs) since they promote energy efficiency to cut total greenhouse gas emissions globally [9]. For example, LG India launched an LED E60 and E90 series of monitors that consume 40% less energy than conventional LED monitors [10]. At the same time, in the fashion industry, clothing made of cotton, linen, silk, or wool can be recycled into fibers or resold, donated, repaired, adapted, or redesigned [11]. For example, the company "Indi-green" in India use 100% eco-friendly cotton, bamboo material, and hand-woven khadi in their products [12–15]. Furthermore, the purchase intention for these products indicates the extent to which consumers are willing or prepared to buy environmentally friendly products, or at least adopt greener practices [16]. Additionally, in the construction, textile, gardening, landscape architecture, and energy sectors, bamboo is used to replace conventional materials, since it has a positive environmental impact, as well as economic benefits, playing a key role in economic development from environmental protection as a key green material.

In this sense, refs. [17] mentioned that purchase intention for environmentally friendly products is considered as the desire to buy environmentally friendly products, rather than conventional products. Furthermore, ref. [18] pointed out that intention is the most important predictor of human behaviour, and that humans are rational in their systematic use of available information.

Furthermore, purchase intention for these products indicates the extent to which consumers are willing or prepared to buy environmentally friendly products or, at least, to adopt greener choice practices [16]. Therefore for, refs. [17–19] mention that purchase intention for green products is considered as the desire to buy green products, rather than conventional products. Furthermore, refs. [20–22] point out that intention is the most important predictor of human behaviour and that humans are rational in their systematic use of available information.

2.2. Moral Obligation

According to Fu et al. (2019) [23], moral obligation refers to a person's sense of pride or guilt in performing a particular action. Furthermore, moral obligation is an important variable for measuring intention, especially in terms of environmental protection and green consumption behavior [24]. For example, consumers may feel that they should use products and services in a sustainable way because they may feel guilty if they do not [25]. However, Schwartz (1977) [26] was one of the first to propose the concept of personal duty, defining it as a moral feeling that manifests itself to enforce some form of pro-social acceptance. Schwartz (1977) [25] emphasized its effect on an individual's tendency to help others. Generally, ethical or green consumers tend to be conscientious, and tend to buy green products to contribute to caring for the environment [24]. Similarly, Chen (2016) [27] described moral obligation as an important variable in understanding a person who has the intention to take care of the environment and consume green products. Similarly, Bergquist (2020) [28] mentions that people have a positive moral self but, to maintain it, they face social and ethical dilemmas, which motivate them to take pro-social actions when their moral self is threatened. Generally, ethical or green consumers are looking to buy green products or other products that do not cause much harm to the environment or society [24]. Furthermore, ref. [24] mentions that previous studies have found that moral obligation can greatly enhance the explanatory or predictive power of consumer intentions. This was demonstrated in a study conducted by Si et al. (2020) [25] in China, where moral obligation was one of the most important elements that increase intention.

However, Chan and Bishop (2013) [29] highlighted that morality is of paramount importance in the study of consumer behavior, as the lack of mitigation response is believed to be the result of not perceiving climate change as a moral issue, thereby failing to stimulate an effective response that would otherwise motivate more people to act. Therefore, the following hypothesis is developed:

H1. *Moral obligation positively affects purchase intention for green products.*

2.3. Environmental Awareness

Landry et al. (2018) [30] stated that environmental concerns are widespread, but many are reluctant to take environmental action. Other studies have found a correlation between environmental awareness and green purchasing behavior, which increases consumers' willingness to spend [31]. Environmental awareness lies in understanding that environmental problems exist, and that these problems can significantly influence individual behavior to be more environmentally friendly [32]. According to Taufique and Vaithianathan (2018) [33], the environmental impact of products and services purchased by environmentally conscious consumers is positive (or negative). Similarly, Han et al. (2017) [34] demonstrated that environmental awareness indirectly affects behavioral intention through three fundamental variables: attitudes, subjective norms, and perceived purchase perception. Similarly, Paul et al., (2016) [35] mentioned that when consumers know about the environmental and health benefits of consuming green products, they exhibit higher purchase intentions. Furthermore, Saleki et al., (2019) [36] showed that environmental awareness impacts purchase intention for organic products.

Finally, Paul et al., (2016) [35] reveal that there are more and more studies related to the effect of consumers' environmental awareness concerning various issues and, above all, the direct and indirect effect of environmental awareness on other variables considered predictors of intention (See Figure 2). Therefore, the following hypotheses are formulated:

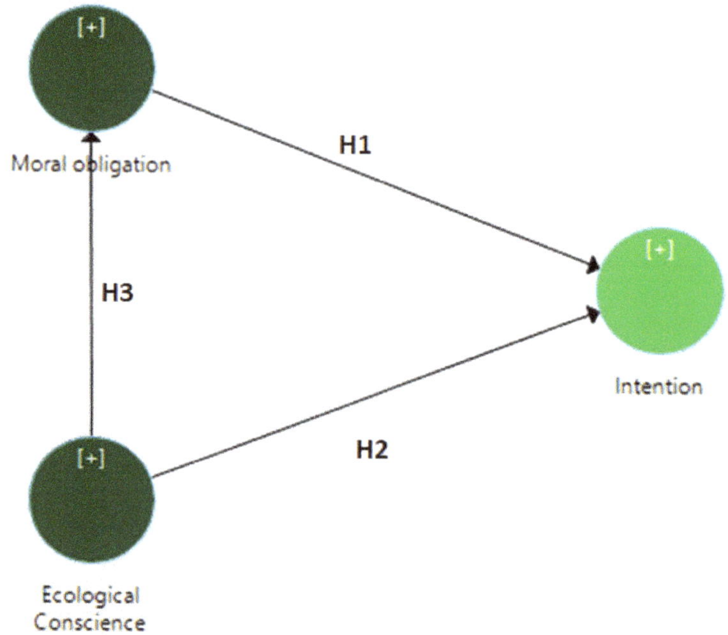

Figure 2. Conceptual model. Source: Own elaboration.

H2. *Environmental awareness positively affects purchase intention for green products.*

H3. *Ecological awareness is positively related to the moral obligation in the intention to purchase green products.*

3. Materials and Methods

Data were collected online, since it allowed for replicability and strengthened the statistical power [37,38]. Data collection was carried out between 4 January 2021 and 2 February 2021. All measurement items were adopted from related studies, which were previously validated.

In the first part of the questionnaire, the items of ecological awareness, moral obligation, and purchase intention were taken, where a six-point Likert scale was implemented, where 1 = "Strongly disagree" and 6 = "Strongly agree". Regarding the ecological awareness variable, it was based on items used by [12,33,35,39]; in the moral obligation variable, items used by Diddi y Niehm (2017) [40], Wang et al., (2016) [41], and Yadav y Pathak (2016) [42] were used; for the purchase intention variable, the statements used by Paul et al., (2016) and Nystrand and Olsen (2020) [35–43], and Huang and Ge (2019) [44] formed a basis (see Table in appendix). Finally, some demographic data, such as age, educational level, and gender, were requested. Non-probability sampling was employed, applying the convenience technique [45]. Convenience sampling has several advantages in terms of variables of access, territory, time, and participation [21,46–48]. The sample involved 690 consumers, mostly residing in the states of Tamaulipas, Nuevo Léon, and Coahuila.

The objective of the study was to predict which variables most influence purchase intention for green products in Mexico, and to determine the degree to which moral obligation is affected by ecological awareness (see Figure 3. Therefore, it was decided to use partial least squares–structural equation modeling (PLS–SEM) for the analysis [49,50].

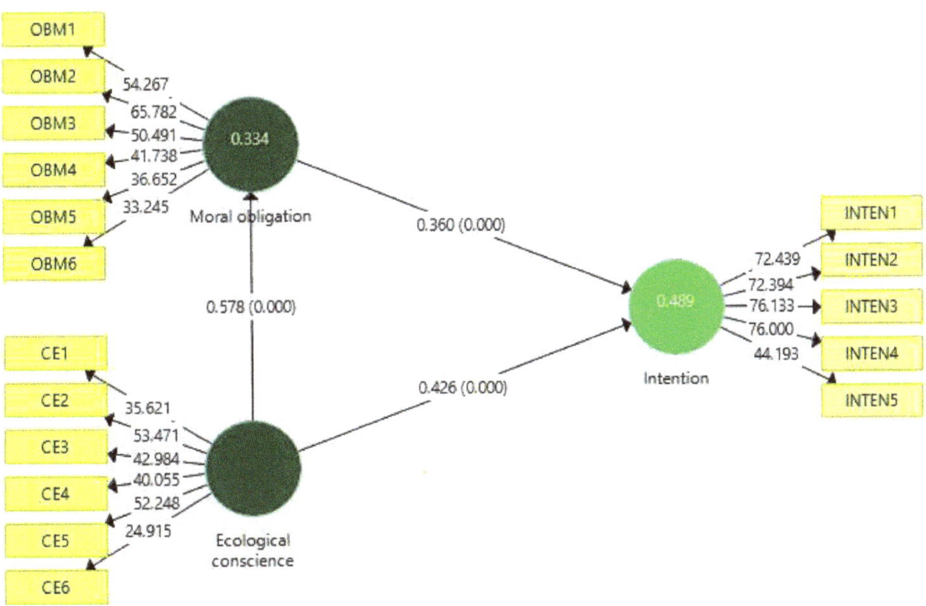

Figure 3. Results of the structural model. Source: Own elaboration in SmartPLS3.

First, the reliability of the constructs (internal and composite) was measured, as well as the structural model [50]. Subsequently, the predictive power of the model was analyzed: in the adjusted R2, values of 0.25, 0.50, and 0.75 are considered weak, moderate, and significant, respectively, according to Hair Jr. et al., (2019) [50]; this is similar to the effect size of f2 [51] Finally, the predictive relevance was examined using the Q2 indicator and the q2 effect of each construct [50].

4. Results

In the respondent group (n = 690), 59.6% were female and 40.1% were male. A total of 31.4% were aged 18–21, 12.9% were aged 22–25, 8.3% were aged 26–29, 7.7% were aged 30–33, 14.2% were aged 34–41, 11.3% were aged 42–49 and over 60 (1.9%), and 14.2% were over 50. In addition, 69.6% had a bachelor's degree, 28.6% had a postgraduate degree, and 1.9% had a high school education. In terms of occupation, 49.4% were students, 34.2% were employed in public or private companies, 8.3% were entrepreneurs, 4.6% were homemakers, and 3.5% were unemployed. Finally, 84.9% were from the state of Tamaulipas, 11.45% from the state of Nuevo León, and 3.52% from the state of Coahuila (see Table 1).

Table 1. Demographics of participants.

Characteristics	Frequency	Percentage (%)
Age (years)		
18 to21	206	65.4
22 to 25	49	15.6
26 to 29	14	4.4
30 to 33	7	2.2
34 to 37	6	1.9
38 to 41	5	1.6
42 to 45	9	2.9
46 to 49	13	4.1
Over the 50 s	6	1.9
Sex		
Female	411	58.1
Male	277	41.9
Educational level		
Secondary	2	0.6
High school	1	0.3
Bachelor's degree/ Engineering	285	90.5
Postgraduate	27	8.6
Occupation	267	84.8
Student	22	7.0
Employee of a public/private company		
Self-employed	19	6.0
Homemaker	5	1.6
Unemployed	2	0.6
State of residence		
Tamaulipas	586	84.9%
Coahuila	25	3.52%
Nuevo Leon	79	11.45%

Source: Own elaboration.

4.1. Analysis of Results, Validation of Constructs

Internal data reliability and composite reliability analyses were conducted, which confirmed the robustness of the data. The composite reliability values are between the ranges of 0.912 and 0.953, which exceed the recommended threshold of 0.70 [52,53]. Similarly, Cronbach's alpha and convergent validity values agree with the values recommended by Hair Jr. et al., (2019) [50] (see Table 2). Finally, discriminant validity (HTMT) was determined, and the results indicated good discriminant validity (See Table 2) [54].

Table 2. Convergent and discriminant validity of constructs.

Variable		Convergent Validity				Discriminant Validity (HTMT Criterion)		
	Loads	AVE	FC	Alpha		CE	INTEN	OBM
CE1	0.759							
CE2	0.808							
CE3	0.818	0.637	0.913	0.886	**CE**	-		
CE4	0.804							
CE5	0.842							
CE6	0.753							
INTEN1	0.895							
INTEN2	0.899							
INTEN3	0.913		0.953	0.938	**INTEN**	0.694	-	
INTEN4	0.909							
INTEN5	0.860							
OBM1	0.806							
OBM2	0.850							
OBM3	0.816	0.633	0.912	0.885	**OBM**	0.640	0.651	-
OBM4	0.774							
OBM5	0.779							
OBM6	0.746							

Source: Own elaboration based on data analysis in SMART PLS3.

4.2. Validity of the Structural Model

Figure 3 shows the results of the structural model, where the relationship between the constructs was determined and the path coefficients. In the hypothesis testing results, environmental awareness is the variable that most influences the intention to purchase green products (0.426), compared to moral obligation (0.360). Furthermore, all hypotheses were significant at a p-value < 0.05 (see Table 3).

Table 3. Hypothesis test results.

Hypothesis	Coefficient Path	p-Value	f^2	Accepted/Not Accepted
H1 CE → ICPV	0.426	0.000	0.270	Accepted
H2 CE → OBM	0.578	0.000	0.334	Accepted
H3 OBM → ICPV	0.360	0.000	0.218	Accepted

Source: Own elaboration in SmartPLS3.

Regarding the predictive power of ecological awareness and moral obligation, the results show that it is moderate (R^2 of 0.489), and the effect size of the construct of ecological awareness and moràl obligation is moderate (f^2 of 0.270 and 0.218, respectively). In addition, the predictive relevance is greater than zero ($Q^2 = 0.386$). Furthermore, concerning the predictive power of ecological awareness on moral obligation, the results show that it is weak (R^2 of 0.334); similarly, the model presents a predictive relevance, since the Q^2 is greater than zero (0.206). Therefore, it is confirmed that ecological awareness influences moral obligation; however, this influence is weak.

5. Discussion

As previously mentioned, this study aimed to explore the extent to which environmental awareness and moral obligation positively affect Mexicans' intention to purchase green products, and whether environmental awareness influences consumers' moral obligation. The results revealed that environmental awareness and moral obligation affect the intention to purchase green products positively and directly; therefore, hypotheses 1 and 2 are accepted. However, ecological awareness has the most significant influence on intention, which means that if people are more oriented toward preservation and concern for the environment, they will be more likely to engage in activities that encourage such actions [55], reflecting their commitment to the environment [12].

In addition, environmental awareness guides consumers to perform environmentally beneficial behaviors, reflecting loyalty and a strong sense of commitment to sustainability [56]. Regarding hypothesis 3, the results show that moral obligation positively affects the intention to purchase green products; therefore, this hypothesis is accepted, which is consistent with the results presented by Spielmann (2020) [57–59], where he mentions that 70% of consumers feel it is their moral responsibility to engage in greener behaviors. Similarly, Bergquist (2020) [28] comments on moral–ethical behavior.

Furthermore, the results show that the relationship between environmental awareness and moral obligation is positive and significant, which confirms the view of Paul et al., (2016) [35], who reported the effect of environmental awareness on other important predictors of intention. This means that Mexican consumers must first take responsibility for environmental problems before they feel obliged to buy green products [60–62]. In terms of theoretical implications, the proposed model helps to confirm the role of the studied variables in understanding and comprehending green purchase intentions. The proposed model helped to explain 52% of the variance in organic purchase intention (R^2 = 0.489), thereby providing a basis for future research. Furthermore, the present study provides empirical foundations that companies can use when displaying advertising messages regarding how the consumption of green products by environmentally concerned consumers can potentially reduce environmental problems. In other words, both governments and non-profit organizations should raise awareness of the benefits of recycling or buying green products for the conservation of natural resources through green campaigns. In addition, in order to increase moral obligation, consumers should be told that their green actions can reduce energy waste, water waste, product reuse, recycling, etc., to improve their understanding of environmental value. Finally, companies should improve the quality of the green products that they manufacture so that consumers will consider switching from a conventional product to a sustainable one, and, at the same time, feel that they are contributing to the conservation of the planet.

6. Conclusions

As part of resilience practices following COVID-19, companies have had to look for new alternatives to offer good products to the customers and friendly to the environment at the same time. This is why this study provides an overview of the new green consumer behavior, as well as offering insight for companies that manufacture sustainable products to understand and promote environmentally-conscious consumer behavior. Companies are interested in making their products and services more sustainable. In this sense, the results can help stakeholders to create new business strategies based on the studied variables. However, there are some theoretical implications in the field of business and company adoption related to environmental awareness.

First, a theoretical and conceptual framework was developed regarding the individuals' intention to adopt the use of good practices contributing to the well-being of the surrounding world in their daily activities based on the existing literature on behavioral intention theory. Secondly, this study provides the basis for further research in emerging countries that are facing environmental problems in order to change the way in which customers buy products, presented as a new opportunity to predict their purchase intentions.

Limitations and Future Research

One of the limitations of this study is that it was conducted with a focus on green products in general. As such, future research can test the model on other product categories such as organic foods, visiting green hotels where they use products and services that minimize water and energy consumption, and recyclable products. Another limitation is the measurement of the relationship between environmental awareness and moral obligation, which could be extended by applying it to other variables, such as environmental attitude, willingness to pay, brand perception, green packaging, or customer value. Therefore, a qualitative study could help to identify the variables that could be most relevant for the consumer of green products. In addition, the study focused on predicting purchase intention. As such, future research could consider actual purchase behavior. Finally, it is important to be cautious in generalizing the results, as the sample was collected mainly in the northeast of Mexico. Future studies could apply this method equally to the rest of the country, and make a cross-country comparison.

Author Contributions: Conceptualization, J.M.-P. and Á.A.-D.; methodology, J.M.-P., Á.A.-D. and G.R.L.-H.; software, J.M.-P., Á.A.-D. and E.E.G.-S.; validation, J.M.-P., Á.A.-D., L.V.O.-T., L.A.S.B. and R.Á.-B.; formal analysis, J.M.-P. and Á.A.-D.; investigation, J.M.-P. and Á.A.-D.; resources, J.M.-P. and Á.A.-D.; data curation, J.M.-P. and Á.A.-D.; writing—original draft preparation, J.M.-P., Á.A.-D., G.R.L.-H., E.E.G.-S., L.V.O.-T., L.A.S.B. and R.Á.-B.; writing—review and editing, J.M.-P., Á.A.-D., G.R.L.-H., E.E.G.-S., L.V.O.-T., L.A.S.B. and R.Á.-B.; visualization, J.M.-P., Á.A.-D., G.R.L.-H., E.E.G.-S., L.V.O.-T., L.A.S.B. and R.Á.-B.; supervision, J.M.-P. and Á.A.-D. Project administration, J.M.-P. and Á.A.-D.; funding acquisition, J.M.-P., Á.A.-D., G.R.L.-H., E.E.G.-S., L.V.O.-T., L.A.S.B. and R.Á.-B. All authors have read and agreed to the published version of the manuscript.

Funding: This research received no external funding.

Institutional Review Board Statement: Not applicable.

Informed Consent Statement: Not applicable.

Data Availability Statement: Data are available upon request from the authors.

Conflicts of Interest: The authors declare no conflict of interest.

References

1. Zou, L.W.; Chan, R.Y.K. Why and when do consumers perform green behaviors? An examination of regulatory focus and ethical ideology. *J. Bus. Res.* **2019**, *94*, 113–127. [CrossRef]
2. Szabo, S.; Webster, J. Perceived Greenwashing: The Effects of Green Marketing on Environmental and Product Perceptions. *J. Bus. Ethics* **2020**, *162*, 719–739. [CrossRef]
3. Brundtland, G.H.; Comum, N.F.; Brundtland, R. Our Common Future: United Nations.Butlin, J. Our common future. By World commission on environment and development. (London, Oxford University Press, 1987, pp.383 £5.95). *J. Int. Dev.* **1989**, *1*, 284–287. [CrossRef]
4. Choi, D.; Johnson, K.K. Influences of environmental and hedonic motivations on intention to purchase green products: An extension of the theory of planned behavior. *Sustain. Prod. Consum.* **2019**, *18*, 145–155. [CrossRef]
5. Borowski, P.F.; Patuk, I. Environmental, social and economic factors in sustainable development with food, energy and eco-space aspect security. *Present Environ. Sustain. Dev.* **2021**, *15*, 153–169. [CrossRef]
6. Gilal, F.G.; Chandani, K.; Gilal, R.G.; Channa, N.A. Towards a new model for green consumer behaviour: A self-determination theory perspective. *Sustain. Dev.* **2019**, *28*, 711–722. [CrossRef]
7. Ghose, A.; Chandra, B. Models for Predicting Sustainable Durable Products Consumption Behaviour: A Review Article. *Vis. J. Bus. Perspect.* **2019**, *24*, 81–89. [CrossRef]
8. Vargas-Hernández, J.G.; Cervantes-Guzmán, J.N. Consumer Behavior. In *Advanced Integrated Approaches to Environmental Economics and Policy: Emerging Research and Opportunities*; Business Science Reference: Hershey, PA, USA, 2020; pp. 141–174. [CrossRef]
9. Nguyen, T.N.; Lobo, A.; Nguyen, B.K. Young consumers' green purchase behaviour in an emerging market. *J. Strat. Mark.* **2017**, *26*, 583–600. [CrossRef]
10. Ajzen, I. Perceived Behavioral Control, Self-Efficacy, Locus of Control, and the Theory of Planned Behavior. *J. Appl. Soc. Psychol.* **2002**, *32*, 665–683. [CrossRef]
11. Lai, C.-C.; Chang, C.-E. A Study on Sustainable Design for Indigo Dyeing Color in the Visual Aspect of Clothing. *Sustainability* **2021**, *13*, 3686. [CrossRef]
12. Kumar, A.; Prakash, G.; Kumar, G. Does environmentally responsible purchase intention matter for consumers? A predictive sustainable model developed through an empirical study. *J. Retail. Consum. Serv.* **2020**, *58*, 102270. [CrossRef]
13. Müller, J.; Acevedo-Duque, Á.; Müller, S.; Kalia, P.; Mehmood, K. Predictive Sustainability Model Based on the Theory of Planned Behavior Incorporating Ecological Conscience and Moral Obligation. *Sustainability* **2021**, *13*, 4248. [CrossRef]
14. Blackwell, R.D.; Miniard, P.W.; Engel, J.F. *Consumer Behavior*, 9th ed.; South-Western Thomas Learning: Mason, OH, USA, 2001.
15. World Bank data 2022 Inflation, Consumer Prices (Annual %)–Mexico. Available online: https://datos.bancomundial.org/indicator/FP.CPI.TOTL.ZG?end=2020&locations=MX&start=2010&view=map (accessed on 5 April 2022).

16. García-Salirrosas, E.E.; Acevedo-Duque, Á. PERVAINCONSA Scale to Measure the Consumer Behavior of Online Stores of MSMEs Engaged in the Sale of Clothing. *Sustainability* **2022**, *14*, 2638. [CrossRef]
17. Rashid, N.R.N.A. Awareness of Eco-label in Malaysia's Green Marketing Initiative. *Int. J. Bus. Manag.* **2009**, *4*, 132. [CrossRef]
18. Zhikun, D.; Fungfai, N. Knowledge sharing among architects in a project design team. *Chin. Manag. Stud.* **2009**, *3*, 130–142. [CrossRef]
19. Nguyen, T.N.; Lobo, A.; Nguyen, H.L.; Phan, T.T.H.; Cao, T.K. Determinants influencing conservation behaviour: Perceptions of Vietnamese consumers. *J. Consum. Behav.* **2016**, *15*, 560–570. [CrossRef]
20. Notimex. *Mexicanos Consumen Cada Vez Más Productos Amigables Con el Medio Ambiente*; 20 Minutos: Madrid, Spain, 2017; Available online: https://www.20minutos.com.mx/noticia/203141/0/mexicanos-consumen-cada-vez-mas-productos-amigables-con-el-medio-ambiente/ (accessed on 25 March 2022).
21. Larios-Gómez, E. Relation among ecological affect, concern and knowledge and purchase behavior: A study regarding Mexican Consumers. *Rev. Bras. Mark.* **2019**, *18*, 73–100. [CrossRef]
22. Adrián, A. *Más Mexicanos Toman Acciones Para Cuidar Medio Ambiente*; Kantar World Panel: London, UK, 2020; Available online: https://www.kantarworldpanel.com/mx/Noticias-/Mas-mexicanos-toman-acciones-para-cuidar-medio-ambiente (accessed on 4 May 2022).
23. Fu, B.; Kurisu, K.; Hanaki, K.; Che, Y. Influential factors of public intention to improve the air quality in China. *J. Clean. Prod.* **2018**, *209*, 595–607. [CrossRef]
24. Chen, M. The impacts of perceived moral obligation and sustainability self-identity on sustainability development: A theory of planned behavior purchase intention model of sustainability-labeled coffee and the moderating effect of climate change skepticism. *Bus. Strat. Environ.* **2020**, *29*, 2404–2417. [CrossRef]
25. Si, H.; Shi, J.-G.; Tang, D.; Wu, G.; Lan, J. Understanding intention and behavior toward sustainable usage of bike sharing by extending the theory of planned behavior. *Resour. Conserv. Recycl.* **2020**, *152*, 104513. [CrossRef]
26. Schwartz, S.H. Normative influences on altruism. *Adv. Exp. Soc. Psychol.* **1977**, *10*, 221–279.
27. Chen, M.-F. Extending the theory of planned behavior model to explain people's energy savings and carbon reduction behavioral intentions to mitigate climate change in Taiwan—Moral obligation matters. *J. Clean. Prod.* **2016**, *112*, 1746–1753. [CrossRef]
28. Bergquist, M. Most People Think They Are More Pro-Environmental than Others: A Demonstration of the Better-than-Average Effect in Perceived Pro-Environmental Behavioral Engagement. *Basic Appl. Soc. Psychol.* **2019**, *42*, 50–61. [CrossRef]
29. Chan, L.; Bishop, B. A moral basis for recycling: Extending the theory of planned behaviour. *J. Environ. Psychol.* **2013**, *36*, 96–102. [CrossRef]
30. Landry, N.; Gifford, R.; Milfont, T.L.; Weeks, A.; Arnocky, S. Learned helplessness moderates the relationship between environmental concern and behavior. *J. Environ. Psychol.* **2018**, *55*, 18–22. [CrossRef]
31. Xu, X.; Wang, S.; Yu, Y. Consumer's intention to purchase green furniture: Do health consciousness and environmental awareness matter? *Sci. Total Environ.* **2019**, *704*, 135275. [CrossRef]
32. Wang, S.; Li, J.; Zhao, D. Institutional Pressures and Environmental Management Practices: The Moderating Effects of Environmental Commitment and Resource Availability. *Bus. Strat. Environ.* **2017**, *27*, 52–69. [CrossRef]
33. Taufique, K.M.R.; Vaithianathan, S. A fresh look at understanding Green consumer behavior among young urban Indian consumers through the lens of Theory of Planned Behavior. *J. Clean. Prod.* **2018**, *183*, 46–55. [CrossRef]
34. Han, H.; Meng, B.; Kim, W. Emerging bicycle tourism and the theory of planned behavior. *J. Sustain. Tour.* **2016**, *25*, 292–309. [CrossRef]
35. Paul, J.; Modi, A.; Patel, J. Predicting green product consumption using theory of planned behavior and reasoned action. *J. Retail. Consum. Serv.* **2016**, *29*, 123–134. [CrossRef]
36. Saleki, R.; Quoquab, F.; Mohammad, J. What drives Malaysian consumers' organic food purchase intention? The role of moral norm, self-identity, environmental concern and price consciousness. *J. Agribus. Dev. Emerg. Econ.* **2019**, *9*, 584–603. [CrossRef]
37. Rahim, R.A.; Sulaiman, Z.; Chin, T.A.; Arif, M.S.M.; Hamid, M.H.A. E-WOM Review Adoption: Consumers' Demographic Profile Influence on Green Purchase Intention. *IOP Conf. Ser. Mater. Sci. Eng.* **2017**, *215*, 012020. [CrossRef]
38. Zanetta, L.D.; Umebara, M.T.C.; Costa, J.P.; Takeda, D.K.; Da Cunha, D.T. Hedonic, emotional and willingness-to-pay response to beers of a different type in Brazil. *Br. Food J.* **2020**, *123*, 87–107. [CrossRef]
39. Koenig-Lewis, N.; Palmer, A.; Dermody, J.; Urbye, A. Consumers' evaluations of ecological packaging–Rational and emotional approaches. *J. Environ. Psychol.* **2014**, *37*, 94–105. [CrossRef]
40. Diddi, S.; Niehm, L.S. Exploring the role of values and norms towards consumers' intentions to patronize retail apparel brands engaged in corporate social responsibility (CSR). *Fash. Text.* **2017**, *4*, 179. [CrossRef]
41. Wang, S.; Fan, J.; Zhao, D.; Yang, S.; Fu, Y. Predicting consumers' intention to adopt hybrid electric vehicles: Using an extended version of the theory of planned behavior model. *Transportation* **2016**, *43*, 123–143. [CrossRef]
42. Yadav, R.; Pathak, G.S. Intention to purchase organic food among young consumers: Evidences from a developing nation. *Appetite* **2016**, *96*, 122–128. [CrossRef]
43. Nystrand, B.T.; Olsen, S.O. Consumers' attitudes and intentions toward consuming functional foods in Norway. *Food Qual. Prefer.* **2019**, *80*, 103827. [CrossRef]
44. Huang, X.; Ge, J. Electric vehicle development in Beijing: An analysis of consumer purchase intention. *J. Clean. Prod.* **2019**, *216*, 361–372. [CrossRef]

45. Giampietri, E.; Verneau, F.; Del Giudice, T.; Carfora, V.; Finco, A. A Theory of Planned behaviour perspective for investigating the role of trust in consumer purchasing decision related to short food supply chains. *Food Qual. Prefer.* **2018**, *64*, 160–166. [CrossRef]
46. Jánská, M.; Kollar, P.; Celer, Č. Factors Influencing Purchases of Organic Food. *Zagreb Int. Rev. Econ. Bus.* **2020**, *23*, 81–94. [CrossRef]
47. Simon, L.; Moraes, C.A.; Modolo, R.C.; Vargas, M.; Calheiro, D.; Brehm, F.A. Recycling of contaminated metallic chip based on eco-efficiency and eco-effectiveness approaches. *J. Clean. Prod.* **2017**, *153*, 417–424. [CrossRef]
48. Sun, Y.; Luo, B.; Wang, S.; Fang, W. What you see is meaningful: Does green advertising change the intentions of consumers to purchase eco-labeled products? *Bus. Strat. Environ.* **2020**, *30*, 694–704. [CrossRef]
49. Bhutto, M.H.; Tariq, B.; Azhar, S.; Ahmed, K.; Khuwaja, F.M.; Han, H. Predicting consumer purchase intention toward hybrid vehicles: Testing the moderating role of price sensitivity. *Eur. Bus. Rev.* **2020**, *34*, 62–84. [CrossRef]
50. Hair, J.F., Jr.; Hult, G.T.M.; Ringle, C.M.; Sarstedt, M.; Apraiz, J.C.; Carrión, G.A.C.; Roldán, J.L. *Manual de Partial Least Squares Structural Equation Modeling (PLS-SEM)*, 2nd ed.; SAGE Publishing: Thousand Oaks, CA, USA, 2019.
51. Cohen, J. Statistical power analysis. *Curr. Dir. Psychol. Sci.* **1992**, *1*, 98–101. [CrossRef]
52. Chin, W.W. How to Write Up and Report PLS Analyses. In *Handbook of Partial Least Squares*; Esposito, V.V., Chin, W.W., Henseler, J., Wang, H., Eds.; Springer: Berlin/Heidelberg, Germany, 2010; pp. 655–690.
53. Gefen, D.; Straub, D.; Boudreau, M.-C. Structural equation modeling and regression: Guidelines for research practice. *Commun. Assoc. Inf. Syst.* **2000**, *4*, 1–70. [CrossRef]
54. Henseler, J.; Hubona, G.; Ray, P.A. Using PLS path modeling in new technology research: Updated guidelines. *Ind. Manag. Data Syst.* **2016**, *116*, 2–20. [CrossRef]
55. Zhao, H.-H.; Gao, Q.; Wu, Y.-P.; Wang, Y.; Zhu, X.-D. What affects green consumer behavior in China? A case study from Qingdao. *J. Clean. Prod.* **2014**, *63*, 143–151. [CrossRef]
56. Lin, S.-T.; Niu, H.-J. Green consumption: Environmental knowledge, environmental consciousness, social norms, and purchasing behavior. *Bus. Strat. Environ.* **2018**, *27*, 1679–1688. [CrossRef]
57. Spielmann, N. Green is the New White: How Virtue Motivates Green Product Purchase. *J. Bus. Ethics* **2020**, *173*, 759–776. [CrossRef]
58. Pérez, J.M.; Núñez, J.B.A.; Pérez, S.M. Intención de compra de productos verdes de acuerdo con la Teoría del Comportamiento Planeado: Incorporación de la obligación moral al modelo. *RAN Rev. Acad. Negocios* **2021**, *7*, 15–30. [CrossRef]
59. Yue, B.; Sheng, G.; She, S.; Xu, J. Impact of Consumer Envir onmental Responsibility on Green Consumption Behavior in China: The Role of Environmental Concern and Price Sensitivity. *Sustainability* **2020**, *12*, 2074. [CrossRef]
60. Kalia, P.; Dwivedi, Y.K.; Acevedo-Duque, Á. Cellulographics©: A novel smartphone user classification metrics. *J. Innov. Knowl.* **2022**, *7*, 100179. [CrossRef]
61. García-Salirrosas, E.E.; Acevedo-Duque, Á.; Marin Chaves, V.; Mejía Henao, P.A.; Olaya Molano, J.C. Purchase Intention and Satisfaction of Online Shop Users in Developing Countries during the COVID-19 Pandemic. *Sustainability* **2022**, *14*, 6302. [CrossRef]
62. Wen, C.; Akram, R.; Irfan, M.; Iqbal, W.; Dagar, V.; Acevedo-Duqued, Á.; Saydaliev, H.B. The asymmetric nexus between air pollution and COVID-19: Evidence from a non-linear panel autoregressive distributed lag model. *Environ. Res.* **2022**, *209*, 112848. [CrossRef]

sustainability

MDPI

Article

The Environmental Cost of Attracting FDI: An Empirical Investigation in Brazil

Eduardo Polloni-Silva [1,*], Guilherme Augusto Roiz [2], Enzo Barberio Mariano [3], Herick Fernando Moralles [1] and Daisy Aparecida Nascimento Rebelatto [2]

1 Department of Production Engineering (DEP), Federal University of São Carlos (UFSCar), São Carlos 13565-905, Brazil; herickmoralles@dep.ufscar.br
2 Department of Production Engineering, Escola de Engenharia de São Carlos (EESC), University of São Paulo (USP), São Carlos 05508-270, Brazil; guilhermeroiz@gmail.com (G.A.R.); daisy@usp.br (D.A.N.R.)
3 Department of Production Engineering, School of Engineering of Bauru, Campus Bauru, São Paulo State University (UNESP), Bauru 14800-903, Brazil; enzo.mariano@unesp.br
* Correspondence: eduardopolloni1@gmail.com; Tel.: +55-16-3351-9509

Abstract: Many emerging economies seek to increase their Foreign Direct Investment (FDI) inflows to achieve some promised benefits, such as economic growth and advanced technologies. Nevertheless, FDI does not represent a random investment decision, and international literature demonstrates that foreign investors are mostly interested in fast-growing regions. Therefore, this study uses traditional panel data econometrics coupled with Data Envelopment Analysis (DEA) to investigate the environmental impact in regions with great potential to attract foreign investments (e.g., more advanced regions with growing infrastructure), therefore analyzing the environmental cost of attracting FDI. Additionally, this study employs regional data from the 'Atlas of FDI in the State of São Paulo' to investigate the environmental effects of FDI in the periphery, where attractiveness levels are low. The results indicate that regions with higher attractiveness levels prepare a pollutant development strategy and that FDI in less-developed regions is harmful to the environment. The results point to new perspectives on the FDI–environment debate and suggest that attracting FDI is environmentally costly. Also, FDI is heterogeneous, with its presence in peripheral areas being harmful to the environment. To conclude, we discuss these results and present an agenda for future research.

Keywords: environment; CO_2; Foreign Direct Investment (FDI); econometrics; Data Envelopment Analysis (DEA); Brazil; Latin America

Citation: Polloni-Silva, E.; Roiz, G.A.; Mariano, E.B.; Moralles, H.F.; Rebelatto, D.A.N. The Environmental Cost of Attracting FDI: An Empirical Investigation in Brazil. *Sustainability* **2022**, *14*, 4490. https://doi.org/10.3390/su14084490

Academic Editors: Jeoung Yul Lee, Dilek Zamantili Nayir and Charles Chen

Received: 7 February 2022
Accepted: 5 April 2022
Published: 9 April 2022

1. Introduction

According to international business literature, Foreign Direct Investment (FDI) is recognized by many scholars as a valuable tool to boost development [1–3]. Accordingly, many countries (particularly in emerging regions) aim to increase their incoming FDI stock. Historical data show that many fast-growing countries in Latin America (e.g., Brazil, Chile, Colombia, Peru, Panama) presented a growing incoming FDI stock in more recent years [4]. From a regional perspective, another interesting example is the State of São Paulo, the richest and most developed region in Brazil, which hosts approximately 40% of all FDI in the country [5]. Potentially, these regions use foreign investments, among other tools, to advance their developmental process.

Here, it is important to note that the debate on the effects of FDI on the host presents no consensus [3,6], and some of the literature argues that FDI could be harmful to the host's development [7–9]. Still, considering the promised benefits of FDI (e.g., economic growth) and some positive empirical findings, policymakers are interested in understanding the FDI attraction process, as well as the foreign investors' location choices. In reality, FDI does not represent random investment decisions [10,11]. Although there are still discussions about the location choice of foreign investments, aspects such as infrastructure, market size, and industrialization, among others, are known to increase the inflow of foreign investments [12–14]. However, fast-growing regions may also display an environmentally costly development strategy [15]. As such, although previous evidence shows that FDI may bring environmental benefits (e.g., cleaner technologies, higher productivity, and green products) [16–18], FDI is arguably investing in polluted regions. In other words, to attract FDI, regions could look into boosting industrialization, services, and creating infrastructure to accelerate their growth process, which will result in greater environmental impacts.

Even so, the current international literature and its empirical studies are either interested in understanding how foreign investors choose their new investments' locations or in exploring the direct impacts of FDI. Accordingly, the literature presents interesting findings on the location choices of Multinational Companies (MNCs) [10,13], as well as on the effects of FDI on employment, economic growth, and the host's environment [1,19,20]. Yet to our knowledge, there is a gap in the literature concerning the level of 'FDI attractiveness' (i.e., the potential to attract FDI) and its effects on the environment. This is particularly worrisome for emerging economies such as Brazil, as FDI-related studies are limited [21]. To sum up, FDI can be beneficial, but if foreign investors are mainly attracted to polluted regions, the possible environmental benefits of FDI may be offset by these regions' accelerated development. Therefore, this study aims to investigate whether higher attractiveness levels indeed increase CO_2 levels.

This absence of studies linking attractiveness (and the potential to attract new foreign investments) and environmental impacts may be the result of a current lack of regional FDI data in Latin America [11]. Indeed, an analysis of FDI attractiveness will arguably demand that regional-level data and heterogeneity be considered, which is limited in country-level studies. To tackle this issue, this study will use a unique and new FDI dataset and mix both parametric and nonparametric techniques to investigate FDI attraction in Brazil, along with its environmental impacts. This novel dataset contains information on FDI in all municipalities (i.e., cities) of the State of São Paulo, Brazil, and its use will facilitate the development of a more in-depth analysis of FDI.

Particularly, this study's goals regarding the FDI-regional attractiveness nexus are twofold. Initially, this study will revisit the issue of the determinants of FDI to define which regional characteristics are significantly influencing the FDI agglomeration (i.e., intensity) in the municipalities of the State of São Paulo.

Second, with these results, the Data Envelopment Analysis (DEA) technique will be used to create two distinct composite indexes regarding the attraction of FDI. First, an 'FDI attractiveness' index will be calculated for each municipality and each year. As previously commented, we expect some of these regions' features (e.g., richness, productivity, infrastructure) to influence the location of FDI, while also affecting the environment. With this index, this study will then evaluate the environmental impact of regions with the increasing potential to attract FDI. The creation of a composite index of FDI attractiveness provides a different perspective of analysis, which the simple use of isolated variables cannot provide. With the composite index, we can verify whether the attractiveness of FDI, seen in aggregate, affects the environment.

Third, we advance this discussion by investigating the environmental effects of FDI in less-developed regions. As commented earlier, many scholars consider FDI as a driver of development for the host. However, FDI is not free of criticism from international literature. Another part of this debate argues that FDI could be particularly interested in regions with lower attractiveness levels (i.e., peripheral areas with lower development levels) to take advantage of natural resources, a cheaper workforce, and tax incentives [7,8,22,23]. As a result, some of the literature claims that FDI can be detrimental to the host's environment, and some empirical literature also supports this claim [24–26].

Considering this perspective, the employed FDI dataset (see Section 2 for more details) presents an interesting discovery. As shown in Figure 1, the MNCs coming to Brazil are spreading out to peripheral regions in the State of São Paulo.

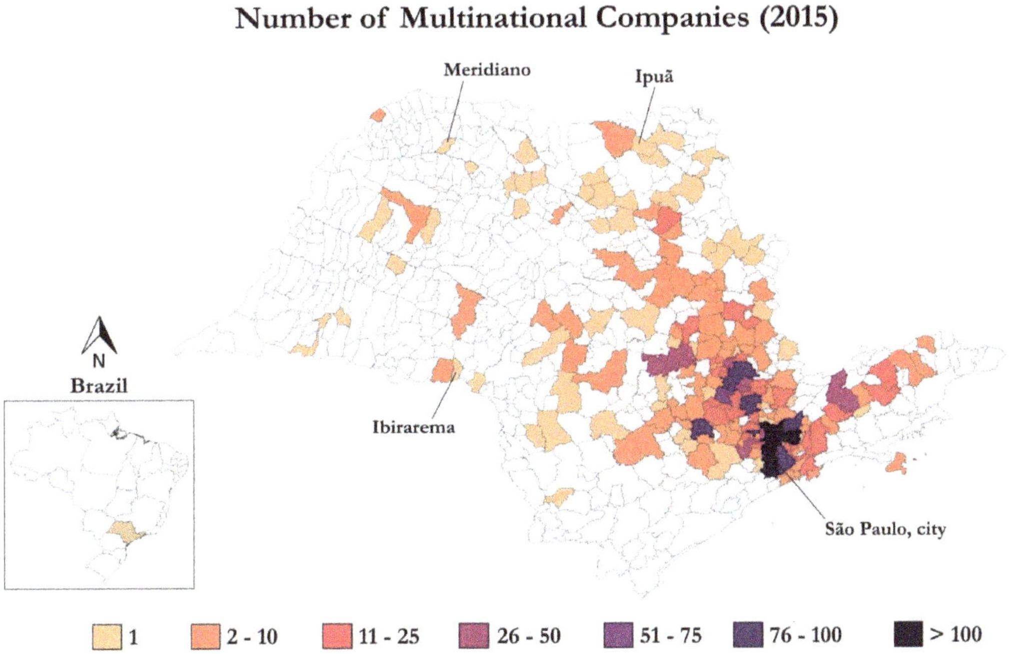

Figure 1. Number of Multinational Companies (MNCs) in each municipality in the State of São Paulo for the year 2015 (data from the 'Atlas of FDI in the State of São Paulo'—see Section 2).

Although the region close to the city of São Paulo still hosts the majority of foreign investments, smaller and less-developed regions are also hosting MNCs. These regions present lower levels of development, richness, and infrastructure, among other possible drivers of FDI. In many cases, although only a few MNCs operate in a specific municipality, they are of great importance for the regions' economies. To exemplify, the municipalities of Meridiano (approximately 3000 inhabitants), Ibirarema (approximately 7000 inhabitants), and Ipuã (approximately 16,000 inhabitants) all host one MNC each, despite presenting relatively less-developed characteristics. Arguably, the economic impact of these companies is significant for these developing regions.

Yet, these MNCs do not operate in sophisticated sectors and represent investments in farming and other agribusiness-related activities (e.g., producing fuel from sugarcane). In other words, these regions present a less-developed business environment and industrial network but could still be able to offer cheap labor and natural resources for MNCs. Thus, it is important to evaluate the impact of FDI in peripheral regions on the environment, as the results may differ from previous and more generalized FDI studies. Here, we argue that the environmental cost of attracting FDI to lagging regions could be significant.

Appropriately, we expand the attractiveness-environment discussion by creating a Low-Attractiveness-High-Intensity index, and by including this index in the environmental model. Both indexes presented in this paper (and further discussed in the next section) will expand the discussion of FDI in Brazil, as well as influence future developmental policies, particularly concerning less-developed regions. Moreover, the presented approach fills a gap in the literature by using more micro-level data and by considering the possible heterogeneous effects of hosting FDI in the periphery.

The remainder of this paper is organized as follows: Section 2 presents the data and the parametric and nonparametric techniques employed in this study; Section 3 presents the results and discusses their implications; Section 4 concludes the presented discussion and introduces an agenda for future scholars.

2. Data and Method

To facilitate the reader's experience, this section is divided into four topics to present an orderly description of all the steps involved in this research. In short, we employ data regarding the municipalities in the State of São Paulo, Brazil, for the 2010–2016 period. Details on variables and data sources are presented in Appendix A, and the descriptive statistics are presented in Appendix B. Also, the State of São Paulo presents 645 municipalities but some regions were excluded due to a lack of regional data in both the FDI and environmental models presented in the remainder of this section.

2.1. The FDI Model

We start our empirical investigation by verifying which variables should be included in the DEA model regarding FDI attractiveness (see Section 2.2). To define which regional variables (e.g., infrastructure, market size) influence FDI concentration in specific regions in the State of São Paulo, we use FDI as the dependent variable. Accordingly, it is important to choose a measure for regional FDI. Figure 1 was built using the number of MNCs for each municipality, as it is an accessible way to visualize the distribution of FDI in the region. However, the number of MNCs is not an appropriate measure for this study, as it does not represent the relative importance of FDI for a given region's economy. Moreover, this measure would only demonstrate that São Paulo city still holds the majority of MNCs in the sample.

To deal with this issue, this study uses a measure for the 'intensity of FDI' for each municipality. Here, we use the 'Atlas of FDI in the State of São Paulo', a manually built unique dataset using information from the Brazilian Integrated System of Foreign Trade (SISCOMEX). As a result, we employ an export-related proxy for FDI in Brazil, as utilized by Moralles and Moreno [21]. In sum, SISCOMEX presented a list containing over 20,000 export companies operating in the State of São Paulo, and a research team manually verified the origins of these companies (i.e., domestic or foreign). With this, this Atlas presents information on all exporting MNCs' origins, size (i.e., export band value), and address.

Following previous regional studies [19,21], the intensity of FDI (*IFDI*) can be calculated as:

$$IFDI_{jt} = W_{jt} \times \left(\frac{MNC_{jt}}{TC_{jt}} \right) \quad (1)$$

and,

$$W_{jt} = \frac{SFE_{jt}}{STE_{jt}} \quad (2)$$

where W is the adjustment weight regarding exports from foreign companies in region j at time t, MNC is the number of MNCs, TC is the total number of export companies (national and foreign companies), SFE is the sum of foreign exports, and STE is the sum of all exports (regarding national and foreign companies). Similar to Moralles and Moreno [21], we used each company's export band value to calculate SFE and STE.

This FDI measure varies between 0 and 1. *IFDI* is equal to 0 in the absence of foreign companies and is equal to 1 when all exports are dependent upon foreign companies. As such, this measure demonstrates how important FDI is for a given region (i.e., municipality), which is particularly useful for this study's goals. In other words, this measure facilitates an understanding of the concentration and growth of FDI in a region's economy through time, and will not overestimate large cities' indexes (e.g., São Paulo city).

It is important to note that this dataset only includes export companies, yet this limitation does not diminish our findings. Scholars have commented that MNCs use Brazil as an base for export to other Mercosul (*Mercado Comum do Sul*) countries [19,27], which justifies the use of this list of export companies to study FDI in Brazil. Also, the data show that many Latin American countries receive a large porting of their imports from Brazil, such as Argentina (20%) and Paraguay (23%), including a variety of products (e.g., cars, chemical products, metals, polymers, produce) [28]. As a result, the employed dataset arguably presents a unique opportunity to study regional FDI-related issues.

Following this, we revisited previous studies [12,14,29–31] to identify possible drivers of FDI to be tested econometrically. Namely, we included each municipality's population density (*DEN*), GDP per capita (*GDPPC*), industry share of GDP (*IND*), service's share of GDP (*SERV*), education level (*EDU*), productivity (*PROD*), and infrastructure, which was represented by the construction (*CONSTR*) and transport (*TRANSP*) sectors. All explanatory variables were employed in their natural log form. Again, details about the variables are presented in Appendix A. The model can be expressed as:

$$IFDI_{jt} = \beta_0 + \beta_1 \mathbf{X}'_{j,t-1} + \alpha_j + e_{jt} \tag{3}$$

where β_0 is the intercept, β_1 represents the parameters to be estimated, $\mathbf{X}'$ is the set of explanatory variables included in this model, α_j is the regional fixed-effect, and e is the error term. It should be noted that all explanatory variables were lagged to ensure theoretical consistency.

We first verified if collinearity was an issue using the Variance Inflammation Factor (VIF) to estimate such a model. Furthermore, we used the Wooldridge test for autocorrelation [32], the modified Wald test for heteroscedasticity [33], and the Pesaran test for cross-sectional dependence [34]. The results suggest that all these non-spherical disturbances should be treated. Thus, we employed the fixed-effects Driscoll–Kraay (DK) estimator, as used in previous regional studies [19,35,36]. The results, which will be displayed in Section 3, will be used to build an 'FDI attractiveness' index, as explained in the next section.

2.2. The FDI Attractiveness Index (FAI)

The first index built in this study is called the "FDI Attractiveness Index" (*FAI*). The *FAI* is a composite index (CI) in which the main goal is to quantify the municipalities' potential to attract foreign investments or FDI. It is noteworthy that this potential is defined by the municipal characteristics that were considered significant determinants of FDI, according to the results of the regression carried out in Equation (3) (see Table 1). With the *FAI*, it will be possible to verify how much the most attractive characteristics of foreign capital can penalize the environment.

In the construction of this first index, the Benefit of Doubt (BoD) method was employed. The BoD was presented in Cherchye et al. [37] and detailed and expanded by Mariano et al. [38]. In short, the traditional BoD method is derived from the input-oriented CCR model of Data Envelopment Analysis (DEA) [39]. In BoD, however, a single constant input equal to 1 is adopted for all units, which makes the DEA result a CI and not an efficiency index.

Using the BoD method, each compared municipality will assign the weights that are most advantageous to them for the aggregated indicators in the index. This approach makes it possible to build an indicator in which the unit's strengths are taken more into account and the weaknesses are taken less into account. This is an interesting and nonarbitrary way of assigning weights to an FDI attractiveness index, in which there is no theoretical prioritization among the indicators to be aggregated.

Each municipality usually specializes in a specific set of characteristics to attract FDI (which can be considered heterogeneous investment decisions), so it is coherent that the *FAI* allows municipalities to assign more weights to these characteristics. Furthermore, an investor may consider different combinations of factors in his decision, placing more emphasis on one aspect or another and these combinations will be different for different investors. Given the uncertainty present in the decision process of a foreign investor, the use of BoD becomes a very interesting alternative to building FDI Attractiveness. In fact, Gong et al. [40] argue that in a setting in which objective knowledge of the true policy weights is usually lacking or incomplete, the BoD model derives for each object a set of optimal weights from the observed subindicator values themselves.

Table 1. The potential drivers of FDI.

Variables	Dependent: Intensity of FDI
	(1)
$LN\_DEN_{t\text{-}1}$	0.0628 ***
	(0.0095)
$LN\_GDPPC_{t\text{-}1}$	0.0104 **
	(0.0049)
$LN\_IND_{t\text{-}1}$	−0.0022
	(0.0031)
$LN\_SERV_{t\text{-}1}$	0.0339 **
	(0.0151)
$LN\_EDU_{t\text{-}1}$	0.0136
	(0.0090)
$LN\_PROD_{t\text{-}1}$	0.0050 ***
	(0.0009)
$CONSTR_{t\text{-}1}$	0.0001 **
	(7.75×10^{-5})
$TRANSP_{t\text{-}1}$	−0.0001
	(0.0004)
Constant	−0.426 ***
	(0.0232)
F	7535.20 ***
Wooldridge (Autocorrelation)	6.65 **
Mod. Wald (Heteroskedasticity)	1.60×10^{9} ***
Pesaran CD	322.41 ***
Mean VIF	1.73
Observations	3549
Number of municipalities	592

Standard errors in parentheses. *** $p < 0.01$, ** $p < 0.05$.

2.3. *The Low-Attractiveness-High-Intensity Index (LAHI)*

The second index built in this study, also with the help of DEA, is called the Low-Attractiveness-High-Intensity Index (*LAHI*). This index, unlike the previous one (which was an IC), measures the efficiency of a municipality, that is, its ability to convert inputs into outputs. *LAHI*, specifically, seeks to verify which municipalities most efficiently convert their FDI (input) attractiveness into effective foreign investment (output). Thus, regions that, despite having a low attractiveness, still manage to attract FDI will stand out with this indicator. Similar to the econometric FDI model, the 'intensity of FDI' (see Equations (1) and (2)) is used to check the relative importance of FDI for each municipality's economy, while avoiding overestimating indexes for large regions such as São Paulo, city.

The *LAHI* was built from the output-oriented BCC model [41] of the DEA. The reason the output orientation was chosen is the fact that the interest was in maximizing the FDI and not in reducing the attractiveness of the municipalities. Also, the use of the BCC model occurred because it adopts the assumption of variable returns to scale, considered the most representative of reality since an increase in the attractiveness of the municipality will not necessarily generate a proportional increase in attracted FDI (the use of logarithms in the regression of Equation (3) supports this hypothesis).

Accordingly, the *LAHI* was constructed using a single output, which is the effective amount of FDI attracted by the municipality and inputs the same as the outputs used to construct the *FAI* indicator in the previous section. A point that deserves to be highlighted is that many municipalities had FDI equal to zero, which hinders the construction of the index since the DEA does not deal well with this type of data. To avoid this problem, and to be able to discriminate between municipalities with zero FDI, as a municipality with zero FDI and high attractiveness is considered less efficient than one with zero FDI and low attractiveness, the zeros in the inputs were replaced by 1×10^{-5}, as suggested by

Thompson et al. [42]. It should be noted that 1×10^{-5} is an arbitrary number, but low enough to bring consistent results.

With *LAHI*, it is possible to verify whether the presence of FDI in municipalities with low attractiveness, and which are therefore highly efficient (inland municipalities, for example), has a more positive or negative effect on the environment. The hypothesis for this analysis is that the FDI attracted to unattractive places could be of worse quality in terms of sustainability.

2.4. The Environmental Model

To evaluate the environmental cost of attracting FDI, as well as the environmental impact of FDI increases in less-developed areas, an environmental model is employed. For this model, the dependent variable is the energy-related CO_2 per capita for each municipality and year. It is important to note that other variables could lead to interesting findings (e.g., waste, water footprint, agricultural burning) but Brazil is currently lacking a detailed dataset containing firm-specific and region-specific information on such issues. Also, studies focusing on these variables would arguably demand a case-study framework. Furthermore, CO_2 is widely recognized as a major pollution variable as it causes issues worldwide (i.e., global warming) and has been widely used in developmental studies including research regarding the effects of FDI. Hence, this study focuses on CO_2 and a more generalized discussion.

Following the protocol presented by previous environmental studies [19,42,43], the CO_2 emissions were calculated using the energy consumption from electricity and fossil fuels (gasoline, diesel, liquefied petroleum gas, fuel oil, aviation gasoline, and aviation kerosene). Also, the guidelines of the Intergovernmental Panel on Climate Change (IPCC) [44] were considered, and a more detailed discussion of Brazilian legislation is presented by Polloni-Silva et al. [19].

For this model, the previously presented indexes (*FAI* and *LAHF*) are employed as the main explanatory variables. Additionally, the literature was revisited to include alternative control variables. As a result, the environmental model can be expressed as:

$$EE_{jt} = \beta_0 + \beta_1 \text{FAI}_{jt} + \beta_2 \text{LAHF}_{jt} + \beta_3 \mathbf{Z}'_{jt} + \alpha_j + e_{jt} \tag{4}$$

where *EE* represents the energy-related CO_2 emissions per capita, *FAI* and *LAHF* are the indexes generated by DEA, and $\beta_{1\text{-}3}$ and $\mathbf{Z}'$ represent the set of alternative control variables, namely urbanization (*URB*), population growth (*POPGROWTH*), and employment levels (*EMPLOY*).

As this model presents disturbances similar to the FDI model (i.e., autocorrelation, heteroscedasticity, and cross-sectional dependence), the fixed-effects Driscoll–Kraay estimator [45] was used again. By using the DK estimator and alternative control variables, we ensure the consistency of our results.

3. Results and Discussion

Initially, we selected the possible drivers of FDI from international literature. With these drivers, we built a model using the intensity of FDI (*IFDI*) as the dependent variable, and the results are displayed in Table 1. As previously explained, Table 1 was estimated using the Driscoll–Kraay (DK) technique to avoid biased results.

In sum, the majority of the employed variables returned significant and positive coefficients. According to the results, population density (*DENS*), GDP per capita (*GDPPC*), the service sector (*SERV*), labor productivity (*PROD*), and the construction sector (*CONSTR*), representing infrastructure, are significant predictors of the intensity of FDI, meaning that FDI gains relative importance (i.e., participation in the regions' economies) in fast-growing areas.

As such, these results are aligned with the literature on this topic. As commented by previous scholars [10,11,13], FDI does not seem to be a random investment decision, and foreign investors search for regions with the potential for growth. Still, this potential could represent major increases in these regions' environmental impacts. Hence, using these results, the FIA index can be calculated using DEA.

Yet, before calculating and using an attractiveness index to check the effects on CO_2, we validate the use of these variables in an environmental model. In other words, we validate these variables by including them in a model with CO_2 as the dependent variable. The results in Table 2 demonstrate that many of our selected variables are in fact significant predictors of CO_2. Although model 2 displays the results for all variables, model 3 uses only the significant predictors of FDI (see Table 1). In both cases, the Brazilian regions' development seems to be having a significant effect on the environment.

Table 2. The effects of regional development on CO_2 levels.

Variables	Dependent: Energy-Related CO_2 Emissions per Capita	
	(2)	(3)
LN_DEN	1.658 *	0.982
	(0.893)	(1.162)
LN_GDPPC	1.250 ***	1.181 ***
	(0.0840)	(0.0895)
LN_IND	0.284 ***	
	(0.0633)	
LN_SERV	1.825 ***	1.427 ***
	(0.180)	(0.171)
LN_EDU	−0.314 ***	
	(0.0648)	
LN_PROD	−0.133 ***	−0.103 ***
	(0.0390)	(0.0373)
CONSTR	−0.0012	0.0020
	(0.0019)	(0.0019)
TRANSP	0.0415 ***	
	(0.0102)	
Constant	−5.27 ***	−10.65 **
	(4.182)	(4.938)
F	33.42 ***	84.56 ***
Wooldridge (Autocorrelation)	85.84 ***	82.69 ***
Mod. Wald (Heteroskedasticity)	1.00×10^7 ***	2.30×10^7 ***
Pesaran CD	94.73 ***	159.86 ***
Mean VIF	1.72	1.53
Observations	3927	3927
Number of groups	561	561

Standard errors in parentheses. *** $p < 0.01$, ** $p < 0.05$, * $p < 0.1$.

Here, it is interesting to note that some factors (e.g., higher education levels, higher productivity) are negatively associated with CO_2 levels, which is positive for the environment. However, many previous environmental studies (e.g., studies using the STIRPAT model) have discussed the isolated effect of such variables on the environment. Accordingly, this study will not further develop the discussion of individual variables. Indeed, the novelty of this paper is to check whether the overall attractiveness of foreign investments is negatively associated with CO_2. Arguably, creating an attractiveness index and including it in an environmental model represent a new perspective within the debate about FDI and its effects on the host.

Finally, Table 3 displays the results regarding the relationship between the calculated *FAI* and *LAHI* indexes and the environment. In other words, Table 3 shows the environmental impact of regions with increasing potential to attract FDI, along with the effects of FDI in peripheral regions.

Table 3. The effects of the *FAI* and the *LAHI* indexes on CO_2 emissions.

Variables	Dependent: Energy-Related CO_2 Emissions per Capita			
	(4)	(5)	(6)	(7)
FAI	0.910 *	0.755 **		
	(0.529)	(0.339)		
LAHI			2.446 *	1.840 *
			(1.458)	(1.073)
LN_URB		4.822 ***		5.069 ***
		(1.827)		(1.903)
POPGROWTH		0.0148 *		0.0150 *
		(0.0078)		(0.0079)
LN_EMPLOY		1.192 ***		1.171 ***
		(0.163)		(0.160)
Constant	1.506 ***	−23.44 ***	0.0636	−25.51 ***
	(0.377)	(8.407)	(1.252)	(9.307)
F	2.81 *	82.21 ***	2.81 *	220.16 ***
Wooldridge (Autocorrelation)	75.21 ***	82.41 ***	75.97 ***	82.78 ***
Mod. Wald (Heteroskedasticity)	2.50×10^7 ***	2.20×10^7 ***	1.70×10^7 ***	9.60×10^6 ***
Pesaran CD	320.46 ***	158.09 ***	324.65 ***	159.18 ***
Mean VIF	1	1.09	1	1.07
Observations	3913	3913	3913	3913
Number of municipalities	559	559	559	559

Standard errors in parentheses. *** $p < 0.01$, ** $p < 0.05$, * $p < 0.1$.

The *FAI* index, which was used to investigate how the potential to attract foreign investments could impact the environment, demonstrates that this potential attractiveness is environmentally costly. Here, the results suggest that this growth process significantly increases the energy-related CO_2 emissions. Thus, FDI targets polluted regions.

This is an interesting finding, as previous scholars have commented on the possible environmental benefits of FDI. Even some recent discoveries in Latin America suggest that FDI could benefit the environment, as demonstrated by Polloni-Silva et al. [19] and Xu et al. [46]. Part of the literature defends the idea that FDI brings innovation, green technologies, and higher productivity levels to emerging economies [16–18]. Our results do not contradict these claims but demonstrate that these companies—despite bringing new technologies—invest in increasingly polluted regions. As such, more traditional growth policies aiming to simply increase the FDI inflows might not be in the host regions' best interest, at least from an environmental standpoint.

Still, on the technological benefits of hosting FDI, and therefore benefiting from cleaner and more productive technological solutions, the results suggest that the impact of FDI is limited. As previously commented, the State of São Paulo hosts the majority of foreign investments in the country. Yet recent studies suggest that the promised environmental benefits of São Paulo's development (e.g., sophistication, higher productivity) were not achieved. Gandhi et al. [47] and Geller et al. [48] comment that the energy intensity (i.e., the energy needed to produce one unit of GDP) did not fulfill the optimism predictions. In reality, São Paulo is arguably a development benchmark for Brazil, but the region still presents an energy trend unlike those in developed economies [47]. As such, any positive effects coming from the presence of MNCs in these regions may be neutralized due to the regions' growth.

In short, this growth process is environmentally costly. Considering these results, local policymakers should revisit their economic growth process. Arguably, bringing FDI to these regions might not be enough to genuinely boost economic sophistication and reduce emissions. The results of the *FAI* index, along with the control variables, suggest that the growth process of the municipalities in the State of São Paulo has a great impact on the environment. Urbanization levels, for example, represent a great source of CO_2, along with employment levels.

Consequently, when discussing how to attract FDI to a region to modernize its economy, the debate should include the regions' history and economic growth to evaluate what other measures should be accounted for. As discussed by Adeel-Farooq et al. [49], local policymakers should stop blaming foreign investors and foreign governments for their environmental issues and instead take an active role in their energy-related policies. It implies that the policymakers should also pay attention to clean energy technologies such as solar, photovoltaic, biomass, and wind in peripheral areas since their current development path tends to be environmentally harmful.

In addition, Table 3 displays the results regarding the relationship between the *LAHI* index and the environment, with *LAHI* representing the FDI in less-developed areas. Here, *LAHI* represents an efficiency-type of measure calculated using DEA, as previously explained. The results suggest that less-developed regions with greater participation of FDI in their economies (i.e., regions in which the MNCs have a prominent role in the economy, at least concerning the regions' exports) present an environmentally costly development. In other words, when these peripheral regions host MNCs, the effect on the environment is negative, as the estimated coefficient for the *LAHI* index is significant and positive to the energy-related CO_2 emissions.

This is an interesting finding as several scholars have commented on the environmental benefits of hosting FDI, even in the case of Latin America [19]. However, more recent scholars point to FDI being heterogeneous in many aspects, including technologically [3,50]. As a result, many results coming from generalized datasets (e.g., country-level studies) or studying the general effect of FDI on emissions may result in an incomplete analysis of FDI on the environment.

Our results suggest a distinction between FDI in larger and better-developed areas, which arguably involves a large number of MNCs in distinct areas including high-technology sectors, and the FDI choosing the periphery. As commented earlier, many regions in the countryside can be seen as a valuable source of natural resources and workforce. Indeed, the FDI in regions that are not considered the benchmark for fast growth, along with other desirable aspects (e.g., infrastructure), may not represent an environmentally friendly investment decision.

On this heterogeneity, several regions with high levels for the *LAHI* index are home to agribusiness-related MNCs. According to the employed Atlas, these companies represent activities regarding cereal cultivation, seeds, sugarcane, poultry, corn, and vegetable oils, among others. This is the case for municipalities in the countryside of São Paulo, such as Santa Cruz das Palmeiras, Meridiano, Ibirarema, Itaí, Ipuã, and Palmital. Accordingly, these companies represent a segment of FDI that differs from the traditional 'technologically advanced multinationals' constantly discussed in the literature.

Nevertheless, it is important to declare that our results do not conflict with previous findings. Alternatively, we argue that it is necessary to include technological heterogeneity and variables such as sector in FDI studies. In sum, the 'one size fits all' approach regarding FDI seems to limit many empirical studies. For example, some recent investigations have started to include the quality of FDI and these investments' sectors in the econometric models to further investigate how heterogeneity may influence the effect of FDI on the host [3,50,51]. Our results are aligned with these scholars' claims.

To sum up, local policymakers in the 'FDI tournament' [52] should analyze the type of investments their regions host, and arguably seek high-technology MNCs to benefit from higher productivity levels, more frequent knowledge, and technology spillovers, whilst also reducing the energy intensity and the local CO_2 emissions.

4. Conclusions

This study investigates the environmental cost of attracting FDI through two distinct perspectives. First, as FDI is not represented by random investment decisions, this study analyzed how the attractiveness levels (i.e., the potential to attract FDI) of the municipalities in the State of São Paulo impact the environment. Following, considering that the literature presents no consensus on the effects of FDI, and recent investigations point to the heterogeneous qualities of FDI, we investigate the environmental effects of the FDI in the periphery of the State of São Paulo. In short, this study employed robust panel data techniques coupled with Data Envelopment Analysis to contribute to the literature on growth strategy and the role of FDI in emerging regions.

Our results suggest that FDI mostly concentrate in fast-growing areas and that these regions' recent development strategies are environmentally costly. Also, the FDI in peripheral regions (e.g., the countryside of the State of São Paulo) does not present the technological capabilities to benefit the host regions' environments, as predicted by previous studies. FDI in the periphery seems to be concentrated in agriculture. Although these regions present lower levels of attractiveness (e.g., smaller economies, weaker infrastructure), they still host MNCs. Yet the presence of these MNCs is not capable of positively influencing the environment.

Previous studies have commented on how Brazilian growth is highly polluting [19,47,53,54]. Therefore, policymakers should revisit their growth strategies. Moreover, as the periphery might represent unique investment opportunities where foreign investors can access cheap labor and natural resources, local policymakers should create ways to attract MNCs to more developed areas. For example, some empirical evidence shows that FDI in dirty sectors is harmful to the host [55], whereas investments in high-technology sectors could be advantageous [56,57]. Thus, following this idea, policymakers may incentivize more environmentally friendly sectors, especially in high LAHI areas, since modern and technology-intensive FDI will concentrate on developed regions.

Conclusively, future research should consider these possible heterogeneous effects of FDI and include sector-specific data in econometric models. Also, alternative econometric techniques (e.g., threshold regression, quantile regression) could facilitate an understanding of the effects of FDI under distinct development levels. Alternatively, the use of regional heterogeneity and cluster analysis could advance the discussion on regional heterogeneity and FDI/growth. To sum up, Brazil and other Latin American countries could benefit from a larger dataset and a longer timeframe.

Finally, as commented earlier, future case studies could use other measures of pollution, including more local measures (e.g., water footprint), to better compare foreign and Brazilian companies.

Author Contributions: Conceptualization, E.P.-S., E.B.M., H.F.M. and D.A.N.R.; Writing—original draft preparation, E.P.-S., G.A.R. and E.B.M.; Methodology and software H.F.M., E.P.-S. and E.B.M.; Writing—review and editing, H.F.M. and G.A.R.; Project administration, D.A.N.R. All authors have read and agreed to the published version of the manuscript.

Funding: The authors acknowledge the support from the Coordenação de Aperfeiçoamento de Pessoal de Nível Superior—Brasil (CAPES) and the São Paulo Research Foundation (FAPESP) (Process no. #2019/19905-0 and #2020/06473-1).

Institutional Review Board Statement: Not applicable.

Informed Consent Statement: Not applicable.

Data Availability Statement: Data will be made available upon reasonable request, following the embargo period on the FDI-related dataset, which will make the dataset publicly available on 30 November 2023.

Conflicts of Interest: The authors declare no conflict of interest.

Appendix A

Table A1. Variables and sources.

Variable	Description	Source
IFDI	Intensity of FDI	Calculated with data from the Atlas of FDI in the State of São Paulo
EE	Energy-related CO_2 emissions per capita	Calculated with data from the Ministry of Science, Technology, Innovation, and Communications (MCTIC), the National Agency for Petroleum, Natural Gas and Biofuels (ANP), and the Brazilian Energy Research Office (EPE).
FAI	FDI Attractiveness Index	Calculated with Data Envelopment Analysis (DEA)
LAHI	Low-Attractiveness-High-Intensity Index	Calculated with Data Envelopment Analysis (DEA)
DEN	Population density (inhabitants per square kilometer)	Brazilian Institute of Geography and Statistics (IBGE)
GDPPC	Real GDP per capita	IBGE
IND	Industry's share of GDP (%)	IBGE
SERV	Services' share of GDP (%)	IBGE
PROD	Manufacturing labor productivity (value added by manufacturing/total jobs in manufacturing)	Calculated with data from IBGE and the Annual Social Information Report (RAIS)
CONSTR	Jobs in the construction sector (% of total jobs)	RAIS
TRANSP	Jobs in the transport sector (% of total jobs)	RAIS
URB	Urbanization rate (%)	IBGE
POPGROWTH	Population growth (%)	IBGE
EMPLOY	Employment rate (%)	RAIS

Appendix B

Table A2. Descriptive statistics.

Variable	Mean	Std. Dev.	Min	Max
IFDI	0.047	0.144	0.000	1.000
EE *	2.127	2.587	0.105	34.413
FAI	0.672	0.138	0.265	1.000
LAHI	0.841	0.054	0.630	1.000
DENS *	4.118	1.446	1.650	9.470
GDPPC *	2.861	0.546	1.580	5.691
IND *	2.739	0.725	0.992	4.454
SERV *	4.010	0.257	2.460	4.479
EDU *	2.516	0.337	1.015	4.120
PROD *	4.372	1.045	0.486	13.645
CONSTR	2.883	4.167	0.000	75.934
TRANSP	3.554	3.388	0.000	30.048
POPGROWTH	1.024	2.605	−23.724	31.754
URB *	4.438	0.196	3.216	4.605
EMPLOY *	3.020	0.473	1.685	5.395

* Presented in the natural-log form.

References

1. Gherghina, Ş.C.; Simionescu, L.N.; Hudea, O.S. Exploring Foreign Direct Investment—Economic Growth Nexus—Empirical Evidence from Central and Eastern European Countries. *Sustainability* **2019**, *11*, 5421. [CrossRef]
2. Yue, S.; Yang, Y.; Hu, Y. Does Foreign Direct Investment Affect Green Growth? Evidence from China's Experience. *Sustainability* **2016**, *8*, 158. [CrossRef]
3. Gönel, F.; Aksoy, T. Revisiting FDI-led growth hypothesis: The role of sector characteristics. *J. Int. Trade Econ. Dev.* **2016**, *25*, 1144–1166. [CrossRef]
4. World Bank. World Bank Open Data. Available online: https://data.worldbank.org/ (accessed on 15 January 2022).
5. BCB. *Foreign Direct Investment in Brazil Report—2018*; Banco Central do Brasil: Brasilia, Brasil, 2018.
6. Rafique, M.Z.; Fareed, Z.; Ferraz, D.; Ikram, M.; Huang, S. Exploring the heterogenous impacts of environmental taxes on environmental footprints: An empirical assessment from developed economies. *Energy* **2022**, *238*, 121753. [CrossRef]
7. Aleksynska, M.; Havrylchyk, O. FDI from the south: The role of institutional distance and natural resources. *Eur. J. Political Econ.* **2013**, *29*, 38–53. [CrossRef]
8. Feng, Y.; Gao, Z.; Jiang, W. What attracts China's contracts to Latin America and the Caribbean? An empirical study of the determinants of Chinese contracts. *Econ. Polit. Stud.* **2018**, *6*, 91–117. [CrossRef]
9. Veltmeyer, H. The political economy of natural resource extraction: A new model or extractive imperialism? *Can. J. Dev. Stud.* **2013**, *34*, 79–95. [CrossRef]
10. Li, X.; Quan, R.; Stoian, M.-C.; Azar, G. Do MNEs from developed and emerging economies differ in their location choice of FDI? A 36-year review. *Int. Bus. Rev.* **2018**, *27*, 1089–1103. [CrossRef]
11. Polloni-Silva, E.; Moralles, H.F.; Rebelatto, D.A.d.N.; Hartmann, D. Are foreign companies a blessing or a curse for local development in Brazil? It depends on the home country and host region's institutions. *Growth Change* **2021**, *52*, 933–962. [CrossRef]
12. Villaverde, J.; Maza, A. Foreign direct investment in Spain: Regional distribution and determinants. *Int. Bus. Rev.* **2012**, *21*, 722–733. [CrossRef]
13. De Beule, F.; Somers, D.; Zhang, H. Who Follows Whom? A Location Study of Chinese Private and State-Owned Companies in the European Union. *MIR Manag. Int. Rev.* **2018**, *58*, 43–84. [CrossRef]
14. Hoang, H.H.; Huynh, C.M.; Duong, N.M.H.; Chau, N.H. Determinants of foreign direct investment in Southern Central Coast of Vietnam: A spatial econometric analysis. *Econ. Change Restruct.* **2021**, *55*, 285–310. [CrossRef]
15. Hafeez, M.; Yuan, C.; Yuan, Q.; Zhuo, Z.; Stromaier, D.; Musaad, O.A.S. A global prospective of environmental degradations: Economy and finance. *Environ. Sci. Pollut. Res.* **2019**, *26*, 25898–25915. [CrossRef] [PubMed]
16. Bakhsh, K.; Rose, S.; Ali, M.F.; Ahmad, N.; Shahbaz, M. Economic growth, CO_2 emissions, renewable waste and FDI relation in Pakistan: New evidences from 3SLS. *J. Environ. Manag.* **2017**, *196*, 627–632. [CrossRef]
17. Zafar, M.W.; Zaidi, S.A.H.; Khan, N.R.; Mirza, F.M.; Hou, F.; Kirmani, S.A.A. The impact of natural resources, human capital, and foreign direct investment on the ecological footprint: The case of the United States. *Resour. Policy* **2019**, *63*, 101428. [CrossRef]
18. Ferraz, D.; Costa, N.J.d.; Fernandes, B.; Silva, E.P.; Marques, P.H.M.; Moralles, H.F.; Rebelatto, D. Analysis of absorptive capacity and foreign direct investment in the productivity of Brazilian municipalities. *Production* **2018**, *28*. [CrossRef]
19. Polloni-Silva, E.; Ferraz, D.; Camioto, F.d.C.; Rebelatto, D.A.d.N.; Moralles, H.F. Environmental Kuznets Curve and the Pollution-Halo/Haven Hypotheses: An Investigation in Brazilian Municipalities. *Sustainibility* **2021**, *13*, 4114. [CrossRef]
20. Abor, J.; Harvey, S.K. Foreign direct investment and employment: Host country experience. *Macroecon. Financ. Emerg. Mark. Econ.* **2008**, *1*, 213–225. [CrossRef]
21. Moralles, H.F.; Moreno, R. FDI productivity spillovers and absorptive capacity in Brazilian firms: A threshold regression analysis. *Int. Rev. Econ. Financ.* **2020**, *70*, 257–272. [CrossRef]
22. Haleem, F.; Farooq, S.; Boer, H. The impact of country of origin and operation on sustainability practices and performance. *J. Clean. Prod.* **2021**, *304*, 127097. [CrossRef]
23. Hsu, M.; Lee, J.; Leon-Gonzalez, R.; Zhao, Y. Tax incentives and foreign direct investment in China. *Appl. Econ. Lett.* **2019**, *26*, 777–780. [CrossRef]
24. Jiang, Y. Foreign Direct Investment, Pollution, and the Environmental Quality: A Model with Empirical Evidence from the Chinese Regions. *Int. Trade J.* **2015**, *29*, 212–227. [CrossRef]
25. Opoku, E.E.O.; Boachie, M.K. The environmental impact of industrialization and foreign direct investment. *Energy Policy* **2020**, *137*, 111178. [CrossRef]
26. Shahbaz, M.; Nasreen, S.; Abbas, F.; Anis, O. Does foreign direct investment impede environmental quality in high-, middle-, and low-income countries? *Energy Econ.* **2015**, *51*, 275–287. [CrossRef]
27. Castilho, M.; Zignago, S. Foreign Direct Investment, Trade and Regional Integration in Mercosur. In *Multinationals and Foreign Investment in Economic Development*; Graham, E.M., Ed.; Palgrave Macmillan: London, UK, 2005; pp. 145–162.
28. OEC. Observatory of Economic Complexity. Available online: https://oec.world (accessed on 15 January 2022).
29. Kayam, S.S.; Yabrukov, A.; Hisarciklilar, M. What Causes the Regional Disparity of FDI in Russia? A Spatial Analysis. *Transit. Stud. Rev.* **2013**, *20*, 63–78. [CrossRef]
30. Liu, K.; Daly, K.; Varua, M.E. Determinants of Regional Distribution of FDI Inflows across China's Four Regions. *Int. Bus. Res.* **2012**, *5*. [CrossRef]

31. Boermans, M.A.; Roelfsema, H.; Zhang, Y. Regional determinants of FDI in China: A factor-based approach. *J. Chin. Econ. Bus. Stud.* **2011**, *9*, 23–42. [CrossRef]
32. Wooldridge, J.M. *Econometric Analysis of Cross Section and Panel Data*; MIT Press: Cambridge, MA, USA, 2010.
33. Greene, W.H. *Econometric Analysis*, 5th ed.; Pearson Education: Hoboken, NJ, USA, 2002.
34. Pesaran, M.H. *General Diagnostic Tests for Cross Section Dependence in Panels*; Faculty of Economics, University of Cambridge: Cambridge, UK, 2004.
35. Wang, J.; Li, J. Exploring the Impact of International Trade on Carbon Emissions: New Evidence from China's 282 Cities. *Sustainability* **2021**, *13*, 8968. [CrossRef]
36. Ma, B.; Yu, Y. Industrial structure, energy-saving regulations and energy intensity: Evidence from Chinese cities. *J. Clean. Prod.* **2017**, *141*, 1539–1547. [CrossRef]
37. Cherchye, L.; Moesen, W.; Rogge, N.; Puyenbroeck, T.V. An Introduction to 'Benefit of the Doubt' Composite Indicators. *Soc. Indic. Res.* **2007**, *82*, 111–145. [CrossRef]
38. Mariano, E.B.; Ferraz, D.; Gobbo, S.C.d.O. The Human Development Index with Multiple Data Envelopment Analysis Approaches: A Comparative Evaluation Using Social Network Analysis. *Soc. Indic. Res.* **2021**, *157*, 443–500. [CrossRef]
39. Charnes, A.; Cooper, W.W.; Rhodes, E. Measuring the efficiency of decision making units. *Eur. J. Oper. Res.* **1978**, *2*, 429–444. [CrossRef]
40. Gong, C.; Gong, N.; Qi, R.; Yu, S. Assessment of natural gas supply security in Asia Pacific: Composite indicators with compromise Benefit-of-the-Doubt weights. *Resour. Policy* **2020**, *67*, 101671. [CrossRef]
41. Banker, R.D.; Charnes, A.; Cooper, W.W. Some Models for Estimating Technical and Scale Inefficiencies in Data Envelopment Analysis. *Manag. Sci.* **1984**, *30*, 1078–1092. [CrossRef]
42. Thompson, R.G.; Dharmapala, P.S.; Thrall, R.M. Importance for DEA of zeros in data, multipliers, and solutions. *J. Product. Anal.* **1993**, *4*, 379–390. [CrossRef]
43. Wen, L.; Li, Z. Provincial-level industrial CO_2 emission drivers and emission reduction strategies in China: Combining two-layer LMDI method with spectral clustering. *Sci. Total Environ.* **2020**, *700*, 134374. [CrossRef]
44. IPCC. 2006 IPCC Guidelines for National Greenhouse Gas Inventories. Available online: https://www.ipcc-nggip.iges.or.jp/public/2006gl/ (accessed on 17 May 2020).
45. Driscoll, J.C.; Kraay, A.C. Consistent Covariance Matrix Estimation with Spatially Dependent Panel Data. *Rev. Econ. Stat.* **1998**, *80*, 549–560. [CrossRef]
46. Xu, C.; Zhao, W.; Zhang, M.; Cheng, B. Pollution haven or halo? The role of the energy transition in the impact of FDI on SO_2 emissions. *Sci. Total Environ.* **2021**, *763*, 143002. [CrossRef]
47. Gandhi, O.; Oshiro, A.H.; Costa, H.K.d.M.; Santos, E.M. Energy intensity trend explained for Sao Paulo state. *Renew. Sustain. Energy Rev.* **2017**, *77*, 1046–1054. [CrossRef]
48. Geller, H.; Schaeffer, R.; Szklo, A.; Tolmasquim, M. Policies for advancing energy efficiency and renewable energy use in Brazil. *Energy Policy* **2004**, *32*, 1437–1450. [CrossRef]
49. Adeel-Farooq, R.M.; Riaz, M.F.; Ali, T. Improving the environment begins at home: Revisiting the links between FDI and environment. *Energy* **2021**, *215*, 119150. [CrossRef]
50. Hanafy, S.a.; Marktanner, M. Sectoral FDI, absorptive capacity and economic growth—Empirical evidence from Egyptian governorates. *J. Int. Trade Econ. Dev.* **2019**, *28*, 57–81. [CrossRef]
51. Doytch, N.; Uctum, M. Globalization and the environmental impact of sectoral FDI. *Econ. Syst.* **2016**, *40*, 582–594. [CrossRef]
52. Pao, H.-T.; Tsai, C.-M. Multivariate Granger causality between CO_2 emissions, energy consumption, FDI (foreign direct investment) and GDP (gross domestic product): Evidence from a panel of BRIC (Brazil, Russian Federation, India, and China) countries. *Energy* **2011**, *36*, 685–693. [CrossRef]
53. Polloni-Silva, E.; Silveira, N.; Ferraz, D.; de Mello, D.S.; Moralles, H.F. The drivers of energy-related CO_2 emissions in Brazil: A regional application of the STIRPAT model. *Environ. Sci. Pollut. Res.* **2021**, *28*, 51745–51762. [CrossRef]
54. Lima, M.A.; Mendes, L.F.R.; Mothé, G.A.; Linhares, F.G.; de Castro, M.P.P.; da Silva, M.G.; Sthel, M.S. Renewable energy in reducing greenhouse gas emissions: Reaching the goals of the Paris agreement in Brazil. *Environ. Dev.* **2020**, *33*, 100504. [CrossRef]
55. Adom, P.K.; Opoku, E.E.O.; Yan, I.K.-M. Energy demand–FDI nexus in Africa: Do FDIs induce dichotomous paths? *Energy Econ.* **2019**, *81*, 928–941. [CrossRef]
56. Li, C.; Li, M.; Zhang, L.; Li, T.; Ouyang, H.; Na, S. Has the High-Tech Industry along the Belt and Road in China Achieved Green Growth with Technological Innovation Efficiency and Environmental Sustainability? *Int. J. Environ. Res. Public Health* **2019**, *16*, 3117. [CrossRef]
57. Gu, W.; Liu, D.; Wang, C.; Dai, S.; Zhang, D. Direct and indirect impacts of high-tech industry development on CO_2 emissions: Empirical evidence from China. *Environ. Sci. Pollut. Res.* **2020**, *27*, 27093–27110. [CrossRef]

sustainability

MDPI

Article

Determinants of Staff Localization in Headquarters-Subsidiary-Subsidiary Relationships

Chan Bok Kim, Seong-Jin Choi * and Luyao Zhang

School of Business, Hanyang University, 222 Wangsimni-ro, Seongdong-gu, Seoul 04763, Korea; speed5733@hanyang.ac.kr (C.B.K.); 17864271171@163.com (L.Z.)
* Correspondence: seongjin@hanyang.ac.kr

Abstract: This paper investigates how cultural distance, the local experience of a foreign subsidiary, and the intensity of local competition jointly affect the staff localization of MNEs' subsidiaries. While previous studies on the effects of cultural distance have mainly focused on the gap between home and host countries, we extend the existing "home-host" country perspective to the home-intermediary-host country relationship. This study regards Korea as an intermediary country and utilizes 520 observations from a unique survey conducted by the Export-Import Bank of Korea from 2006 to 2013. The results suggest that the impact of cultural distance on staff localization is a function of local experience and competitive environment in the home-intermediate-host relationship structure. This paper makes a theoretical contribution to our understanding of the behavior of multinational corporations by expanding the cultural distance perspective between the home and host countries explored in previous research to the home-subsidiary-subsidiary structure.

Keywords: multinational enterprises (MNEs); staff localization; cultural distance; local experience; competition intensity

Citation: Kim, C.B.; Choi, S.-J.; Zhang, L. Determinants of Staff Localization in Headquarters-Subsidiary-Subsidiary Relationships. *Sustainability* **2022**, *14*, 249. https://doi.org/10.3390/su14010249

Academic Editor: Anna Visvizi

Received: 26 November 2021
Accepted: 24 December 2021
Published: 27 December 2021

1. Introduction

The impact of distance between home and host countries on strategies adopted by multinational enterprises (MNEs) is well established in international business literature [1,2]. Distance has been found to affect organizational processes and consequences [3], including location choice [4,5], entry choice [6], corporate political activities [7,8], transfer of knowledge [9], and firm performance [10]. Although previous studies have focused primarily on the distance between home and host countries [11,12], the investment situation of MNEs is more complicated. When expanding into rather "distant" host countries, understanding the impact of cultural differences is vital for corporate sustainability [13], and the invariable international norms and practices do not necessarily suit each subsidiary. Researchers suggest that attempts to across national borders are likely to be more successful, with senior managers often leaving scope for local interpretation to tackle challenges they face in host countries [14]. And in practice, an MNE can invest indirectly in its foreign subsidiary in a host country through another foreign subsidiary in a third (neither home nor host) country, termed an intermediate country. While this home-ubsidiary-subsidiary investment (illustrated in Figure 1) by MNE is frequently observed [15], it has been largely understudied in the literature.

To address this research gap, we developed an integrated model that considers the effects of cultural distance between home and intermediate countries on the local responsiveness of MNEs. Our research question is to study the impact of cultural distance on staff localization and the contingent relationship of local experience and competitive environment in the home-intermediate-host relationship structure. We propose that cultural distance is a determinant of localization even in the parent-subsidiary-subsidiary context. Specifically, we focus on localization in human resource management in multinational subsidiaries. In addition, we explore whether or not the impact of cultural distance on staff localization is contingent on subsidiary capabilities and the competitive environment.

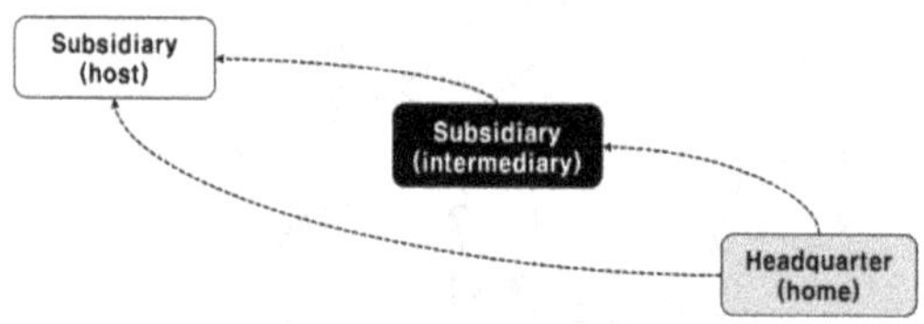

Figure 1. Illustration of "home-subsidiary-subsidiary" investment.

This study makes both theoretical and practical contributions. First, it builds on previous research that focused on the cultural distance between home and host countries. We broaden the scope of discussion by exploring the cultural distance between intermediate and home countries, providing a theoretical contribution in opening the black box of MNEs' investment options. Second, we examine the foreign subsidiary itself as a unit of analysis by addressing the impact of subsidiary-level conditions on localization. While many studies of MNE subsidiaries deal with institutional differences, only a few address subsidiary-level constructs [16]. Thus, our findings deepen extant understanding of MNE localization and their subsidiaries' entrepreneurial actions.

Our conclusions should be of interest to multinational parent firms interested in employing expatriates, granting autonomy to their subsidiaries, and developing market strategies. Because MNE subsidiaries often lack knowledge of local market conditions, they are likely to employ local employees to improve their local competitiveness. In addition, organizational experience over time can improve a subsidiary's market knowledge, which results in parent firms' granting more autonomy [17]. In contrast, increased competition in culturally dissimilar markets can cause subsidiaries to orient toward a globally integrated strategy using expatriate employees [18,19]. We suggest that the impact of cultural distance on staff localization depends on the MNE subsidiary's local experience and the intensity of competition in the host country. Specifically, we argue that while a subsidiary's local experience can be a positive moderating factor, the intensity of competition in the host market negatively moderates the effect of cultural distance on localization of staffing. Panel data of 520 MNE subsidiaries over five years provides general support for our hypotheses.

2. Background and Hypothesis Development

2.1. Local Responsiveness and Staff Localization of MNEs

Multinational corporations must choose between globally integrated or locally responsive strategic orientations. The former involves control of foreign subsidiaries within the parent firm, while the latter separates them from domestic operations and requires adaptation to local conditions [20–24]. Most MNEs attempt to improve their global competence by establishing networks with overseas subsidiaries while dealing with institutional obstacles associated with local market heterogeneity. Whether an MNE succeeds depends mainly on the extent to which it responds to local conditions [25,26].

Many previous studies examined the determinants of a global integration strategy [27,28]. However, some investigated the determinants of local responsiveness by shedding new light on subsidiary roles and explaining subsidiary autonomy from headquarters [29–32]. In practice, most MNE subsidiaries respond to local adaptation by hiring a local chief executive officer or employees, creating a joint venture with local firms, and using local embedded marketing [33]. Subsidiaries with local experience tend to cope effectively with problems specific to the location, which leads to superior performance [34,35], but acquiring local market knowledge through market transactions can be challenging [36]. For example, local employees can provide unique knowledge about social customs, local business practices and customer orientation [37]. Likewise, MNEs are more likely to use host-country nationals (HCNs) rather than parent-country national (PCN) expatriates or third-country national (TCN) expatriates to respond to local pressures [38].

Subsidiaries' motivations for staff localization vary. For example, MNE subsidiaries in China conform to government pressures such as legal restrictions [39]. In addition, they must deal with socio-cultural differences, particularly when operating in culturally dissimilar markets such as emerging economies. For instance, "guanxi" is a locally accepted practice that fosters connections that build formal institutional support in China [40,41]. Also, MNEs are often aware of the considerable cost of using expatriates rather than local employees [41]. In addition, the effectiveness of expatriates relies on contextual variables, including cultural distance [42], which can also encourage the hiring of local staff.

2.2. Cultural Distance

International business (IB) scholars have introduced the concept of distance between countries in the form of cultural, institutional, and psychological dimensions to explain the relationship between MNEs and their subsidiaries [42]. Cultural distance refers to the differences that individuals from different countries may have in observing certain behaviors, affecting the transfer of work practices and methods from one country to another [43]. This may increase the costs of obtaining information and interrupt communications, making it difficult for local subsidiaries to integrate, apply their own routines, and adjust products [7].

For organizations engaged in international activities, the cultural distance may be crucial. For example, it is commonly believed that a greater cultural distance means a larger cultural difference, which explains why a foreign firm in culturally dissimilar markets deals with institutional obstacles attributable to the liability of foreignness [44]. Hofstede et al. [43] argued that this is because culture is the basis of institutional arrangements. More precisely, culture can be regarded as a part of the informal system of an environment, which is the basis of formal systems [45]. When multinational companies enter an institutional setting with different rules, they must meet social expectations, show social responsibility in the host country, and establish social legitimacy. Difficulty obtaining social legitimacy is a function of the cultural distance between the country of origin and the host country [46]. This makes multinational companies more inclined to invest in countries with cultures similar to those of their home countries [47]. Many researchers have analyzed the effects of cultural distance on strategic decisions such as location choice [48], degree of ownership [49], entry mode [1,6], transfer of practices [10,50], and even performance [51].

2.3. Hypothesis Development

Once a host country has been targeted, entry strategies must be matched with the cultural distance to that country to enhance competitive advantages resulting either from a small cultural distance or the ability to mitigate the negative impact of a large distance. The existing cultural distance is a measure of the difference between home and host countries, and heterogeneity is assumed due to characteristic differences of the countries. However, the investment situation of MNEs can be complicated. In practice, there are many foreign subsidiaries in a host country in which their individual parent firms indirectly invest through a subsidiary in another country, requiring us to define this third country as an intermediate country. A subsidiary in an intermediate country mediates between its headquarters in the home country and the subsidiary in the host country. Therefore, the subsidiary in the host country faces pressure from two sides: one from the intermediate subsidiary and the other from the parent firm [16]. The home and host country effects still affect staff localization even when the subsidiary in the host country receives investments from the intermediate firm rather than the parent firm.

Facing the dual pressures of globalization and local response, multinational companies may choose a competitive strategy, such as a global strategy or multi-domestic strategy, and then select staffing practices for their subsidiaries appropriate to the strategy [52]. An MNE often balances its strategic needs by responding to both global integration and local responsiveness. In terms of global integration, greater cultural distance leads to greater use of PCN expatriates because different cultures result in uncertainty, risk, and information asymmetry between the headquarters and its subsidiaries [53,54]. In terms of local responsiveness, greater cultural distance leads to more employment of local staff [41,54].

In the former case, because the subsidiary makes decisions and conducts management operations under the control of headquarters and therefore benefits from the competency of the resource-rich headquarters as a member of a multinational company, how the competency of headquarters is applied at the local level is essential. In the latter case, because it is a foreign company operating at a local level, exploration competency, which manages competition with local companies and relationships with governments and develops local competency that headquarters do not have, is also important. Subsidiaries in mediating countries, which are under pressure to use both competencies, can go abroad to reduce costs or explore global markets, regardless of resource utilization at headquarters or independent exploration activities of subsidiaries [23]. Although the subsidiary makes local investment decisions on its own, the subsidiary cannot ignore the influence of headquarters because it operates within the management system and culture of headquarters. If headquarters invests in the host country through a subsidiary in a mediating country-a bypass strategy-the influence of headquarters cannot be ignored [16]. Regardless of the presence of a subsidiary in the mediating country or the level of autonomy of the subsidiary, the cultural distance between home and host countries can affect the localization of the subsidiary in the host country. We can therefore expect that:

Hypothesis 1 (H1). *Cultural distance between home and host country is positively related to the employment of local managerial staff.*

Foreign subsidiaries are embedded in the local environment, which requires responsiveness to the local context, as a bypass strategy to overcome heterogeneity between the home and host country [55]. However, if the cultural distance between the home and intermediate countries is considerable, a subsidiary in the intermediate country also has to overcome the liability of foreignness [16]. As a result, headquarters may apply new institutions through localization. When a country such as China has undeveloped systems or relies heavily on informal transactions, a coercive isomorphism can motivate to increase localization [40].

Previous research has explored the importance of congruence between mitigating cultural conflicts in MNEs and staff localization strategies [52]. The unique Chinese social culture and internal labor market have been identified as the core factors determining Chinese human resource management practices [56]. Successful MNEs are likely to mitigate cultural conflicts between home and target countries by developing staff localization strategies that accurately interpret the highly heterogeneous environment and lead to appropriate actions [5]. To avoid cultural friction between local norms and a company's practices, many firms, and those from western countries, in particular, will tend to invest temporarily where the culture and social norms are similar (and the cultural distance is relatively smaller), as is the case in Korea and Japan [3,57]. Drawing on staff localization strategies identified in previous research [58], we hypothesized that cultural distance between home and intermediate countries would be positively related to employment for local managerial staff:

Hypothesis 2 (H2). *Cultural distance between home and the intermediate country is positively related to the employment of local managerial staff.*

Foreignness is a burden because foreign companies are less familiar with the local market and business environment than their local counterparts [2]. As far as China is concerned, foreign companies need to employ more than a certain proportion of local employees. If they have local managers or invest in local companies or state-owned companies, it is usually easier to set up companies in the registration process. If the cultural distance between home and host countries is large and there is great heterogeneity, it may be challenging to overcome external responsibility. Subsidiaries can use their experience, ability and understanding of the local business environment to offset external responsibilities. With the expansion of cultural distance, the ability of relatively independent subsidiaries will have a greater offset effect. If local subsidiaries can avoid relying on the headquarters or subsidiaries of intermediary countries, the headquarters can accept greater localization [59,60]. Therefore, if the cultural distance is large, the subsidiary will actively hire local people, and with the improvement of the subsidiary's experience and ability, the company will be more likely to hire local managers who can make crucial decisions.

Because a subsidiary can gain internal competency through operational experiences by connecting local customers, the subsidiary can make decisions based on its experiences rather than the guidelines of headquarters when those guidelines are a poor fit for local conditions. It has superior alternatives, even if a subsidiary follows unilateral guidelines established by headquarters in the early stages of business development. This will give a subsidiary an independent role in the local market rather than one that depends on the direction from headquarters [22,28]. Local business experiences can allow a subsidiary to exercise its absorptive capacity to capture new business opportunities and introduce new management activities and performance standards. Therefore, the empirical capacity of a subsidiary can be a factor in its ability to increase localization.

Hypothesis 3 (H3). *A subsidiary's local experience positively moderates the impact of the cultural distance between home and host country on the employment of local managerial staff.*

From two perspectives, the local competitive environment may be seen as an external responsibility. First, if competition in a local market is fierce, and overseas subsidiaries compete aggressively with local companies, performance may suffer directly. From an uncertainty perspective, the competitive strategies in the home country may not be effective in the local country, and it is possible to spend additional resources on developing new competition strategies such as analyzing competition structure and conducting marketing [61]. These factors may make it challenging to achieve high levels of performance [62]. However, intense competition is not necessarily a negative factor as it could positively affect innovation in the local country. Cultural distance and local competitive environment may promote localization, and both aspects are based on the characteristics of the local market. However, a combination of the two could raise the pressure from global integration rather than generate a local response.

The existing competition environment is regarded as a foreignness liability comparable to cultural distance. To address it, a foreign company can improve connections with local customers by hiring local employees and seeking guanxi relationships with governments or suppliers by localizing managerial positions [40]. The cultural distance at the national level and the intense competition at the industrial level can be understood through the liability of foreignness [16]. As foreign companies feel their limitations as a foreign company, the stronger the competition, the more prominent localization becomes.

This paper deals with the control of subsidiaries, which receive knowledge and competence from headquarters (illustrated in Figure 2). Companies operating in an intermediate country can utilize the subsidiary's capabilities in that country. When competition with local companies is intense, foreign companies can acquire local knowledge and build competency by hiring local staff. This can involve simply imitating the competitive strategies used by local competitors. Multinational companies can also increase the number of expatriates to transplant their management methods because, as a first-mover, they can develop innovative marketing and effective management strategies that differ from local competitors [63].

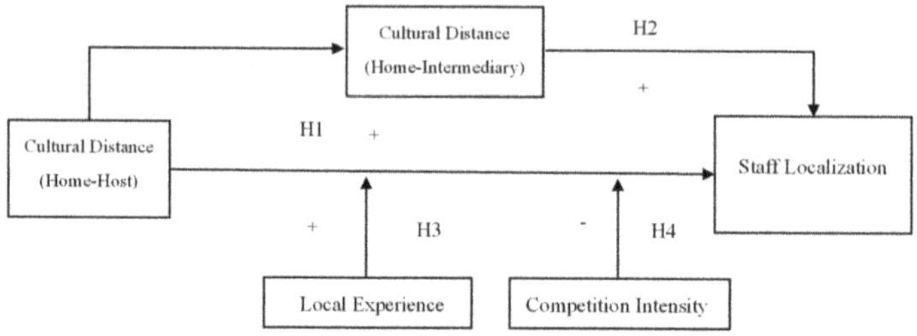

Figure 2. Conceptual model of "home-subsidiary-subsidiary" investment.

Hypothesis 4 (H4). *The intensity of local competition negatively moderates the impact of cultural distance between home and host country on the employment of local managerial staff.*

3. Sample and Methods

3.1. Data Source

We utilized 11,002 observations made by the Export-Import Bank of Korea from 2006 to 2013 of the investment statuses of Korean companies operating in China. Focusing only on companies that placed their headquarters in foreign countries, we used the Stata 14 program as an analysis tool after data processing. In the data processing, after excluding data with missing values of the home country or selecting China as the home country, 868 items remained. We identified multiple business-investment cases within one company, leaving 676 items. We then removed all except the largest subsidiaries, leaving 636 items after correcting errors in the original materials. Finally, we removed every observation with a home country of Labuan, Mauritius, Bahamas, Cayman Islands, International Finance Corporation, Virgin Islands, Cyprus, and Malta, which are known as paper-company countries, and then selected 570 items (205 companies by each home country) as analysis subjects. As these constituted unbalanced panel data that do not have every object (i) depending on time (t), removing items with missing values or multicollinearity in the panel data analysis process left 520 items as analysis subjects and 186 panel groups (subsidiaries). After data preprocessing, we revised the observation years to the period between 2006 to 2010. The minimum observation value of each year per group was 1 year, and the maximum observation value was 5 years. The average observation value was 2.7 years.

3.2. Measurement

3.2.1. Dependent Variable

This paper calculated the proportion of local managers of total managers by using the number of local managers and the number of Korean managers suggested in the survey.

3.2.2. Explanatory Variables

By using the four cultural dimensions developed by Hofstede et al. [43] and Kogut and Singh [1] of power distance (the solidity of social class; PDI), individualism-collectivism (IDV), masculinity-femininity (task orientation-human orientation, MAS), and uncertainty avoidance (UAI), we determined cultural distances for each country. The cultural distance between home and host and cultural distance between home and intermediate country are included in the analysis. The cultural distance calculation formula was derived using formula (1). For example, China's PDI, IDV, MAS, and UAI values were 80, 20, 66, and 30, respectively, and Korea's values were 60, 18, 39, and 85, respectively. The cultural distance between two countries is calculated as

$$Cultural\ Distance_j = \sum_{i=1}^{4} \sqrt{\left(I_{ij} - I_{iu}\right)^2} \tag{1}$$

where I_{ij} and I_{iu} are the values of the standardized characteristic i corresponding to countries j and u, respectively.

We established an investment period, which is a substitute for the experience capability of a subsidiary. We then calculated the investment period with investment age using the initial year when the subsidiary of the intermediating country invested in the local subsidiary. The intensity of competition considered a liability of foreignness at the industrial level utilized a survey item to describe competitive relationships with local companies. The answer sheet consisted of a 5-point scale of very poor, poor, neutral, good, and very good, with very good assigned a value of 1 point and very poor 5 points. The larger the observation value, the stronger the competition.

3.2.3. Control Variables

This paper measured control variables of subsidiaries in the mediating country (Korea), such as listed corporations, company age, sales, and whether they engage in manufacturing. Listed corporations were divided into listed corporations, designated listed corporations, externally audited corporations, generally listed corporations, designated KOSDAQ corporations, listed KOSDAQ corporations, closure corporations, and merged corporations, with a value of 1 given to listed corporations, designated listed corporations, designated KOSDAQ corporations, and listed KOSDAQ corporations, and 0 assigned to the others. We used the year of establishment of the Korean corporation, and natural-log values were used for sales. In the case of manufacturing companies, because most categories were divided into manufacturing and service from the survey items, we coded the manufacturing industry as 1 and the service industry as 0.

For control variables of the local-country (China) subsidiaries, we selected an asset scale, whether the manufacturing industry exists, and whether independent investment exists. We utilized a survey item related to the total assets of a local subsidiary for the asset scale and used an industry code for the local corporations to determine whether a manufacturing industry exists. Both control variables of the intermediating and local countries were used after referencing prior research.

The controlling factors of local experience of local companies take advantage of the number of business years and the reverse causality in the basic research model. Converting the business period into the empirical competency according to entering time is problematic because the amount of experience over time and its quality can differ among companies. Local experience and knowledge tend to increase over time, but the amount of the increase depends on the subsidiary's ability to adapt to local conditions. For example, when investing in local companies, if a company enters a market through a joint venture or syndicated investment with local companies, the entering company can adapt more rapidly because it can learn the capabilities of the local company. However, in the case of a single investment, it is difficult to assume that the entering company can accumulate a comparable amount of experience during the same 1-year period because the company does not immediately recognize the local environment and practices. We, therefore, controlled for whether a single investment exists and applied the experience of subsidiaries as a controlling variable. For whether a single investment exists, we coded a single investment as 1 and the others as 0, out of each observation value of a single investment, joint venture, and syndicated investment, using the survey items related to the investment types.

3.3. *Methodology*

We conducted a panel analysis on 520 observations using Stata 14, a statistical software package. Our analysis involved 186 headquarters-intermediating subsidiaries and local subsidiaries out of the Export-Import Bank of Korea. After conducting a model test to determine the panel data, we conducted correlation analysis in Table 1 and panel data analysis in Table 2.

Table 1. Illustration of "Home-Subsidiary-Subsidiary" Investment.

		Mean	SD	1	2	3	4	5	6	7	8	9	10	11
1	LOCAL	0.74	0.34	1.00										
2	LISTED (IM)	0.3	0.46	0.00	1.00									
3	AGE (IM)	25.76	12.98	0.16 ***	0.34 ***	1.00								
4	SIZE (IM)	25.7	1.61	0.03	0.51 ***	0.28 ***	1.00							
5	MNF (IM)	0.87	0.34	0.07 *	−0.07 *	−0.02	−0.20 ***	1.00						
6	SIZE (HS)	16.64	1.34	−0.01	0.23 ***	0.16 ***	0.54 ***	0.06	1.00					
7	MNF (HS)	0.89	0.32	0.11 **	−0.14 ***	0.05	−0.36 ***	0.45 ***	0.09 *	1.00				
8	WOS (HS)	0.65	0.48	−0.11 ***	0.00	−0.22 ***	−0.13 ***	−0.12 ***	−0.33 ***	−0.07	1.00			
9	CD (HM-IM)	68.33	14.17	0.01	0.01	−0.18 ***	−0.05	−0.08 *	−0.12 ***	−0.04	0.09 *	1.00		
10	CD (HM-HS)	75.51	14.67	0.14 ***	0.11 **	0.03	0.07	−0.08 *	−0.16 ***	−0.03	−0.04	0.31 ***	1.00	
11	LOCEXP	6.78	4.1	0.05	0.15 ***	0.26 ***	0.14 ***	0.02	0.21 ***	−0.01	−0.10 **	−0.03	−0.20 ***	1.00
12	CMPTN	2.74	0.76	0.07 *	0.04	0.23 ***	−0.08 *	0.04	−0.14 ***	0.01	0.01	−0.12 ***	−0.03	0.13 ***

* $p < 0.1$, ** $p < 0.05$, *** $p < 0.01$; (HM): Home, (IM): Intermediary, (HS): Host; LOCAL: Staff Localization; CD: Cultural distance; LOCEXP: Local experience; CMPTN: Competition intensity; LISTED: Listed firm; AGE: Firm age; SIZE: Firm size (Firm asset); MNF: Manufacturing; WOS: Wholly owned subsidiary.

Table 2. Results of the GLS Regression Analysis.

DV: LOCAL	Model 1	Model 2	Model 3	Model 4	Model 5
LISTED (IM)	−0.043 (0.061)	−0.048 (0.060)	−0.054 (0.059)	−0.044 (0.060)	−0.050 (0.059)
AGE (IM)	0.004 ** (0.002)	0.004 ** (0.002)	0.004 * (0.002)	0.004 ** (0.002)	0.004 ** (0.002)
SIZE (IM)	0.030 (0.020)	0.027 (0.020)	0.028 (0.020)	0.025 (0.020)	0.026 (0.020)
MNF (IM)	0.041 (0.071)	0.043 (0.071)	0.033 (0.070)	0.042 (0.071)	0.031 (0.069)
SIZE (HS)	−0.031 * (0.019)	−0.026 (0.019)	−0.029 (0.019)	−0.024 (0.019)	−0.027 (0.019)
MNF (HS)	0.226 *** (0.075)	0.215 *** (0.075)	0.236 *** (0.075)	0.213 *** (0.075)	0.236 *** (0.074)
WOS (HS)	−0.077 (0.050)	−0.069 (0.050)	−0.071 (0.049)	−0.071 (0.050)	−0.073 (0.049)
CD (HM-IM)	0.001 (0.002)	0.000 (0.002)	0.001 (0.002)	−0.000 (0.002)	0.000 (0.002)
CD (HM-HS)		0.002 (0.001)	0.001 (0.002)	0.002 (0.002)	0.001 (0.002)
LOCEXP			0.010 * (0.005)		0.010 * (0.005)
CD (HM-HS) * LOCEXP			0.037 ** (0.015)		0.042 *** (0.015)
CMPTN				−0.002 (0.020)	−0.003 (0.020)
CD (HM-HS) * CMPTN				−0.036 ** (0.017)	−0.042 ** (0.017)
Constant	0.128 (0.475)	0.046 (0.478)	0.045 (0.470)	0.062 (0.489)	0.065 (0.479)
N	520	520	520	520	520
Chi2	23.39861	24.96160	34.43298	29.64265	41.08551

* $p < 0.1$, ** $p < 0.05$, *** $p < 0.01$; Standard error in parentheses.

Panel data for various objects have been researched at several time points using variables of the object (i) over time (t). Independent variables and error of basic assumptions of ordinary least squares (OLS) regression analysis violate a condition that the problem of omitted variable bias is not severe. It was, therefore, necessary to control unit-specific unobserved heterogeneity. To resolve the heterogeneity problem, fixed effects and the possibility of random effects should be determined. The fixed effect is such that the original characteristics of an object are assumed as a fixed parameter with independent variables; it then controls the variable by estimating or removing it. Because this parameter is estimated and a characteristic of an object that cannot change with time, individual property effects should be eliminated through assumptions such as within transformation, first deviation, and least squares dummy variables. However, the possibility of random effects assumes that an individual original characteristic is given randomly, meaning it is not related to the independent variable but is regarded as a random variable. Although the fixed effects focus on the variance in the panel object (i), the random effects estimate the weighted average of the between effect and the fixed effect. The weight will be determined depending on the relative size of the error term between effects and the fixed effects and on the number of observation values for each object.

Hypothesis testing to determine the model to provide estimates includes F, Hausman, and Breusch-Pegan tests. F tests determine the model between the fixed effects and the joint OLS. The Hausman test determines the fixed effects and the random effects. The Breusch-Pegan test determines the random effects and the joint OLS. We selected an appropriate model between the fixed and random models through the Hausman test, considered the degree of appropriateness between this model and the joint OLS, and then determined a final model.

The Hausman test produced a p-value of 0.8313, which means we could not reject the null hypothesis that there is no significant difference between the two regression coefficients and that there is no difference between the two regression coefficients. Because estimates of the random model do not differ from the estimates of the unbiased fixed model, both models were deemed unbiased, but the random model was selected because it was more efficient [8]. In the case of the Breush-Pegan test, we rejected the null hypothesis because the p-value was 0.0000. The heterogeneity between individuals was 0, and the random model was again selected because the random model results were significant.

Since the panel data include characteristics of time series data, autocorrelation was possible. In the random-effects model determined through model tests, a generalized least squares estimation was utilized if autocorrelation occurred.

4. Results

Model 1–5 in Table 2 report the relevant regression results of the relationship between cultural distance and localization level. We tested for the presence of multicollinearity in our analyses by examining variance inflation factors (VIF). All VIFs (max: 2.50; mean: 1.47) were below 10, confirming that multicollinearity is not a severe problem in our study. The coefficient of cultural distance (Home-Host) in model 5, the overall model is not statistically significant ($p = 0.05$). Therefore, Hypothesis 1 is not supported. However, we considered Hypothesis 1 as supported because it was marginally significant. Because the estimated coefficient for the localization level of cultural distance (Home-Intermediary) is not statistically significant either in model 2 or model 5, Hypothesis 2 is not supported. Because the cultural distance is fixed as the difference value between countries, we expect to find no variance for each year on panel data with time-series data. The overall estimated coefficient in the model could have less statistical significance compared with cross-sectional data. In addition, because this study fixed the intermediating and local countries like Korea and China, respectively, the variance with the home countries also represented a certain value, and the coefficient in the model had less statistical significance.

Next, model 3 shows the moderating effects of the local subsidiary's experience, as measured by the investment period, are statistically significant at a 0.05 level, with an estimated coefficient of 0.037. This influences the relationship between cultural distance (Home-Host) and localization level and supports the moderating effect of hypothesis 3: when the cultural distance between home and the local country is long, the level of localization will increase. Subsidiaries in the mediating country can control this relationship depending on their experience operating in the local country. As it mediates the control to a positive direction, the longer cultural distance becomes and the more experience subsidiaries have, the greater the localization level becomes.

In model 4, the intensity of competition is statistically significant since its mediating effect on the localization level has a mediated coefficient value of −0.036 at the 0.05 level. Therefore, Hypothesis 4 was supported. This means that the basic model—the longer the cultural distance between home and local countries, the greater the localization level—would change depending on competitive intensity. Therefore, the mediating effects were controlled in a negative direction: if the cultural distance is great, the localization level increases, but if competition intensifies, the level of localization decreases.

Figure 3 suggests that the joint effect between longer cultural distance (Home–Host) and local subsidiary's experience makes a firm more likely to be localized. This result supports Hypothesis 3. Similarly, Figure 4 demonstrates that in a local country with a long cultural distance (Home-Host), the more intense the competition, the lower the localization level of firms. This result supports Hypothesis 4.

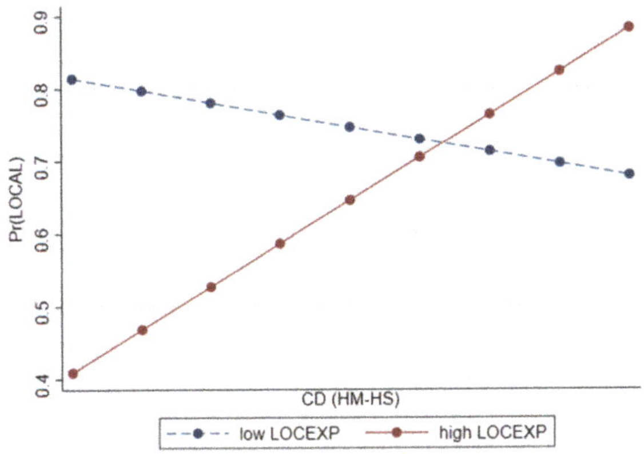

Figure 3. Interaction between CD (HM-HS) and LOCEXP.

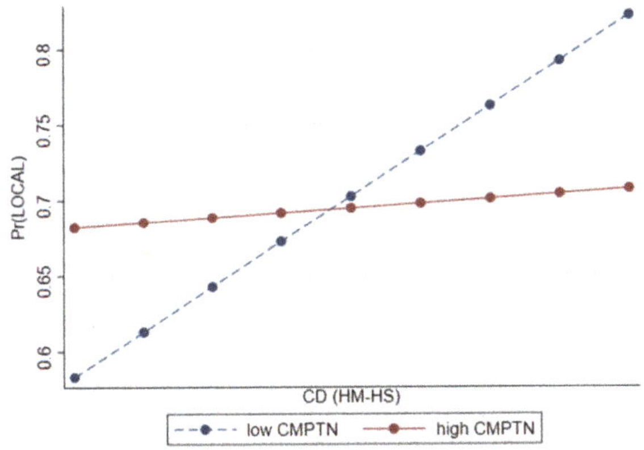

Figure 4. Interaction between CD (HM-HS) and CMPTN.

5. Discussion

5.1. Implications

Based on prior research, the more heterogeneous two countries become due to long cultural distances, the greater the localization level. We reviewed existing theories on headquarters-subsidiary-subsidiary investment structure and determined that this theory requires revision. Although we did not verify new determinants of localization, this paper is the first to develop and explain a new and expanded investment structure for headquarters-subsidiary-subsidiary relationships by utilizing variables that prior studies on multinational companies had used. We provide a theoretical contribution that expands our understanding of the effects of cultural distance on multinational companies by applying a new investment structure. In addition, we suggest the relationship between an organization and its environment differs according to local conditions [64]. By integrating international management strategies [20–23] and organizational learning [65], we provide an explanation for behavior associated with dual pressures involved in headquarters-subsidiary-subsidiary investment structures.

Our research of the behavior of multinational companies concerning actual headquarters-subsidiary-subsidiary investment structures suggests practical implications. Whether the investment structure covered in this study involved independent subsidiaries or bypass-investment strategies made at headquarters remains unknown, the cultural distance between home and local countries still affected the localization in the headquarters-subsidiary-

subsidiary investment structure. Regardless of whether a subsidiary in the intermediating country entered a foreign nation or headquarters used a bypass investment strategy through a subsidiary in the mediating country, the effects of headquarters were at least partially maintained.

We verified the effects of a local subsidiary's experiences by controlling investment types. Prior research considered entry mode as a determinant of localization. Still, we regarded it as a control variable because a joint venture or syndicated investment allows a foreign company to adapt more rapidly to local conditions and acquire different qualitative and quantitative local experiences over the same business period (1 year), compared with the single-investment strategy. We found that the subsidiary's experience further expanded localization despite this control, contrary to prior findings. This means that, when entering a foreign market with a considerable cultural distance, it is important to hire local managerial staff and ensure local autonomy, rather than embrace a global integration strategy over time and encourage subsidiaries to have independent competency. MNEs should design localization strategies by taking cultural differences that characterize subsidiaries located in different contexts into account. Our results further support the role of staff management in reducing internal barriers concerning the nature of work within MNEs. Taking MNEs entering the Asian market as an example, the performance of American companies is generally better than that of European companies, which is directly proportional to the number of local talents. For instance, VIACOM, one of the three big media giants in the world, has introduced MTV programs and consumption patterns to China successfully because of its employment of Li Yifei, who is familiar with China's market environment, policies and regulations, and is well versed in western thinking and corporate culture.

Finally, considering the aspect of local competition, we verified endogenous characteristics that originate in specific companies based on national factors because the cultural distance is a variable at the national level. However, it has a structure that companies could not know about the external industrious environment where companies operate the business. Because it is necessary to consider the liability of foreignness (in the form of cultural distance) and the liability of foreignness at the industrial level, there is room to determine if localization can increase when the liability of foreignness increases considering competition intensity. According to prior research, the liability of foreignness increases because of the lack of local competence, indicating that localization should increase because local competition becomes more critical as it intensifies. However, local competition can lead to price competition and increase marketing and promotional costs. From the perspective of the competitive superiority of a company, MNEs that lack local capabilities may have successful business models and other advantages, such as advanced management systems and extensive human resources, compared with local companies. Therefore, multinationals can introduce new competitive methods that utilize the management system of headquarters, including innovative marketing strategies, efficient production management, and the dispatching of skilled expatriates familiar with strategies of headquarters to create differentiated competitive structures.

5.2. Limitations

This study has several limitations. First, the measurement of cultural distance can be problematic. The effects of cultural distance on business operations or performance can differ depending on the local situation, and cultural differences may act as a liability of foreignness. As the world becomes globalized and information technology spreads, people experience reduced levels of heterogeneity, reducing the value of time-invariant variables according to scoring at the national level. Because cultural distance is a time-invariant variable, examining only two cultural distances acquires a high priority. Because this study dealt with relationships between three countries, three variables on cultural distance should have been derived. Still, the differences between intermediating and local countries were excluded due to multicollinearity problems with the other variables. Further research on panel data analysis that considers all three cultural distances using variables that change every year is necessary.

Second, whether the empirical capability of subsidiaries is based on the competence of headquarters or established by subsidiaries, which headquarters cannot have, remains unknown. Although we controlled for a single investment type to calculate the ability of subsidiaries from the time of investment, further research is needed to reveal when the knowledge transfer occurs from headquarters or subsidiaries with independent capabilities. This could be applied to all empirical research on the abilities of subsidiaries of MNEs. The international management strategies and organizational learning of multinational companies also warrant further study.

Third, because this study treated the localization level as a dependent variable, we only observed behaviors of multinational companies at the system level. We did not research performance and therefore could not determine how the localization level can affect the survival of actual companies. Because we utilized panel rather than cross-sectional data, reverse causality cannot be ruled out. Because a company's performance through localization is the final concern of multinational companies, further empirical analysis on the effects of localization on the performance of a company in the headquarters-subsidiary-subsidiary structure would have theoretical value.

Fourth, considering every intermediating country in our study was Korea, and every local country was China, some potentially influential factors in the research model may have been overestimated or underestimated. However, this limitation is inherent to any study of theoretical and practical issues in the investment structure of headquarters-subsidiary-subsidiary relationships.

5.3. Future Research

Future studies may identify other factors and conditions to advance research on the relationship between MNEs' localization strategy and cultural distance. First, since the structure of MNE investment (i.e., the percentage of the parent MNE's ownership in the focal investment) affects MNE expatriate staffing strategy, future studies are encouraged to collect and test parent MNE ownership. Second, our sample includes Chinese (i.e., host) and Korean (i.e., intermediary) subsidiaries headquartered in other countries, such as Japan. However, it is still unclear whether this model can be applied to the influence of the cultural distance between host and intermediary countries on staffing localization. Thus, we call for future studies to include the cultural distance between host and intermediary countries. Third, other mechanisms in addition to cultural distance may correspond to the staffing localization. Future research should consider whether different types of distance, such as institutional distance, influence MNE staffing localization.

Author Contributions: Conceptualization, C.B.K. and S.-J.C.; methodology, C.B.K. and S.-J.C.; formal analysis, C.B.K.; investigation, L.Z. and resources, C.B.K.; writing—original draft preparation, C.B.K.; writing—review and editing, C.B.K. and S.-J.C.; supervision, S.-J.C. and L.Z.; project administration, L.Z. and S.-J.C.; funding acquisition, S.-J.C. and C.B.K. All authors have read and agreed to the published version of the manuscript.

Funding: This research received no external funding.

Institutional Review Board Statement: Not applicable.

Informed Consent Statement: Not applicable.

Data Availability Statement: Not applicable.

Conflicts of Interest: The authors declare no conflict of interest.

References

1. Kogut, B.; Singh, H. The effect of national culture on the choice of entry mode. *J. Int. Mark.* **1988**, *19*, 411–432. Available online: https://www.jstor.org/stable/155133 (accessed on 1 October 2021). [CrossRef]
2. Xu, D.; Shenkar, O. Institutional Distance and the Multinational Enterprise. *Acad. Manag. Rev.* **2002**, *27*, 608–618. Available online: https://www.jstor.org/stable/4134406 (accessed on 1 October 2021). [CrossRef]
3. Beugelsdijk, S.; Kostova, T.; Kunst, V.E.; Spadafora, E.; van Essen, M. Cultural Distance and Firm Internationalization: A Meta-Analytical Review and Theoretical Implications. *J. Manag.* **2018**, *44*, 89–130. [CrossRef] [PubMed]
4. Belderbos, R.; Du, H.S.; Goerzen, A. Global cities, connectivity, and the location choice of MNE regional headquarters. *J. Manag. Stud.* **2017**, *54*, 1271–1302. [CrossRef]
5. James, B.E.; Sawant, R.J.; Bendickson, J.S. Emerging market multinationals' firm-specific advantages, institutional distance, and foreign acquisition location choice. *Int. Bus. Rev.* **2020**, *29*, 101702. [CrossRef]
6. Brouthers, K.D. Institutional, cultural and transaction cost influences on entry mode choice and performance. *J. Int. Bus. Stud.* **2002**, *33*, 203–221. Available online: https://www.jstor.org/stable/3069541 (accessed on 1 October 2021). [CrossRef]
7. Quer, D.; Claver, E.; Rienda, L. Political risk, cultural distance, and outward foreign direct investment: Empirical evidence from large Chinese firms. *Asia Pac. J. Manag.* **2012**, *29*, 1089–1104. [CrossRef]
8. Busse, M.; Hefeker, C. Political risk, institutions and foreign direct investment. *Eur. J. Political Econ.* **2007**, *23*, 397–415. [CrossRef]
9. Ambos, T.C.; Fuchs, S.H.; Zimmermann, A. Managing interrelated tensions in headquarters–subsidiary relationships: The case of a multinational hybrid organization. *J. Int. Bus. Stud.* **2020**, *51*, 906–932. [CrossRef]
10. Slangen, A.H. A communication-based theory of the choice between greenfield and acquisition entry. *J. Manag. Stud.* **2011**, *48*, 1699–1726. [CrossRef]
11. Chang, Y.C.; Kao, M.S.; Kuo, A.; Chiu, C.F. How cultural distance influences entry mode choice: The contingent role of host country's governance quality. *J. Bus. Res.* **2012**, *65*, 1160–1170. [CrossRef]
12. Beugelsdijk, S.; Slangen, A.; Maseland, R.; Onrust, M. The impact of home–host cultural distance on foreign affiliate sales: The moderating role of cultural variation within host countries. *J. Bus. Res.* **2014**, *67*, 1638–1646. [CrossRef]
13. Franco, S. The influence of the external and internal environments of multinational enterprises on the sustainability commitment of their subsidiaries: A cluster analysis. *J. Clean. Prod.* **2021**, *297*, 126654. [CrossRef]
14. Almond, P.; Edwards, T.; Kern, P.; Kim, K.; Tregaskis, O. Global norm-making processes in contemporary multinationals. *Hum. Resour. Manag. J.* **2021**. [CrossRef]
15. Eden, L.; Miller, S.R. Distance matters: Liability of foreignness, institutional distance and ownership strategy. *Adv. Int. Manag.* **2004**, *16*, 187–221. [CrossRef]
16. Meyer, K.E.; Li, C.; Schotter, A.P. Managing the MNE subsidiary: Advancing a multi-level and dynamic research agenda. *J. Int. Bus.* **2020**, *51*, 1–39. [CrossRef]
17. Gaur, A.S.; Lu, J.W. Ownership strategies and survival of foreign subsidiaries: Impacts of institutional distance and experience. *J. Manag. Stud.* **2007**, *33*, 84–110. [CrossRef]
18. Fang, Y.; Jiang, G.L.F.; Makino, S.; Beamish, P.W. Multinational firm knowledge, use of expatriates, and foreign subsidiary performance. *J. Manag. Stud.* **2010**, *47*, 27–54. [CrossRef]
19. Doz, Y.L.; Bartlett, C.A.; Prahalad, C.K. Global competitive pressures and host country demands managing tensions in MNEs. *Calif. Manag. Rev.* **1981**, *23*, 63–74. [CrossRef]
20. Doz, Y.; Prahalad, C.K. Patterns of strategic control within multinational corporations. *J. Int. Bus. Stud.* **1984**, *15*, 55–72. Available online: https://www.jstor.org/stable/154232 (accessed on 1 October 2021). [CrossRef]
21. Ghoshal, S.; Bartlett, C.A. The multinational corporation as an interorganizational network. *Acad Manag. Rev.* **1990**, *15*, 603–626. [CrossRef]
22. Ghoshal, S.; Nohria, N. Internal differentiation within multinational corporations. *Strateg. Manag. J.* **1989**, *10*, 323–337. [CrossRef]
23. Edwards, R.; Ahmad, A.; Moss, S. Subsidiary autonomy: The case of multinational subsidiaries in Malaysia. *J. Int. Bus. Stud.* **2002**, *33*, 183–191. Available online: https://www.jstor.org/stable/3069580 (accessed on 1 October 2021). [CrossRef]
24. Prahalad, C.K.; Doz, Y.L. *The Multinational Mission: Balancing Global Integration with Local Responsiveness*; Free Press: New York, NY, USA, 1987; pp. 154–196.
25. Spender, J.C.; Grevesen, W. The multinational enterprise as a loosely coupled system: The global integration–local responsiveness dilemma. *Manag. Financ.* **1999**, *25*, 63–84. [CrossRef]
26. Kobrin, S.J. An empirical analysis of the determinants of global integration. *Strateg. Manag. J.* **1991**, *12*, 17–31. [CrossRef]
27. Birkinshaw, J.; Morrison, A.; Hulland, J. Structural and competitive determinants of a global integration strategy. *Strateg. Manag. J.* **1995**, *16*, 637–655. [CrossRef]
28. Johnston, S.; Menguc, B. Subsidiary size and the level of subsidiary autonomy in multinational corporations: A quadratic model investigation of Australian subsidiaries. *J. Int. Bus. Stud.* **2007**, *38*, 787–801. Available online: https://www.jstor.org/stable/4540457 (accessed on 1 October 2021). [CrossRef]
29. Slangen, A.H.; Hennart, J.F. Do multinationals really prefer to enter culturally distant countries through greenfields rather than through acquisitions? The role of parent experience and subsidiary autonomy. *J. Int. Bus. Stud.* **2008**, *39*, 472–490. [CrossRef]
30. Wang, S.L.; Luo, Y.; Lu, X.; Sun, J.; Maksimov, V. Autonomy delegation to foreign subsidiaries: An enabling mechanism for emerging-market multinationals. *J. Int. Bus. Stud.* **2014**, *45*, 111–130. [CrossRef]

31. Beugelsdijk, S.; Jindra, B. Product innovation and decision-making autonomy in subsidiaries of multinational companies. *J. World Bus.* **2018**, *53*, 529–539. [CrossRef]
32. Dowling, P.J. Completing the Puzzle: Issues in the development of the field of international human resource management. *Manag. Int. Rev.* **1999**, *15*, 27. Available online: https://www.jstor.org/stable/40835829 (accessed on 1 October 2021).
33. Delios, A.; Beamish, P.W. Survival and profitability: The roles of experience and intangible assets in foreign subsidiary performance. *Acad. Manag. J.* **2001**, *44*, 1028–1038. Available online: https://www.jstor.org/stable/3069446 (accessed on 1 October 2021).
34. Luo, Y.; Peng, M.W. Learning to compete in a transition economy: Experience, environment, and performance. *J. Int. Bus. Stud.* **1999**, *30*, 269–295. Available online: https://www.jstor.org/stable/155313 (accessed on 1 October 2021). [CrossRef]
35. Hennart, J.F. A transaction costs theory of equity joint ventures. *Strateg. Manag. J.* **1998**, *9*, 361–374. [CrossRef]
36. Berry, H.; Sakakibara, M. Resource accumulation and overseas expansion by Japanese multinationals. *J. Econ. Behav. Organ.* **2008**, *65*, 277–302. [CrossRef]
37. Hartmann, E.; Feisel, E.; Schober, H. Talent management of western MNCs in China: Balancing global integration and local responsiveness. *J. World Bus.* **2010**, *45*, 169–178. [CrossRef]
38. Lasserre, P.P.S.P.; Ching, P.S. Human resources management in China and the localization challenge. *J. Asia Bus.* **1997**, *13*, 85–100.
39. Rosenzweig, P.M.; Singh, J.V. Organizational environments and the multinational enterprise. *Acad. Manag. Rev.* **1991**, *16*, 340–361. [CrossRef]
40. Chen, N.Y.F.; Tjosvold, D. Guanxi and leader member relationships between American managers and Chinese employees: Open-minded dialogue as mediator. *Asia Pac. J. Manag.* **2007**, *24*, 171–189. [CrossRef]
41. Gong, Y. Subsidiary staffing in multinational enterprises: Agency, resources, and performance. *Acad. Manag. J.* **2003**, *46*, 728–739. [CrossRef]
42. Gaur, A.S.; Delios, A.; Singh, K. Institutional environments, staffing strategies, and subsidiary performance. *J. Manag.* **2007**, *33*, 611–636. [CrossRef]
43. Hofstede, G.; Van Deusen, C.A.; Mueller, C.B.; Charles, T.A.; The Business Goals Network. What goals do business leaders pursue? A Study in fifteen countries. *J. Int. Bus. Stud.* **2002**, *33*, 785–803. Available online: https://www.jstor.org/stable/3069594 (accessed on 1 October 2021). [CrossRef]
44. Stöttinger, B.; Schlegelmilch, B.B. Explaining export development through psychic distance: Enlightening or elusive? *Int. Mark. Rev.* **1998**, *15*, 357–372. [CrossRef]
45. Peng, M.W.; Wang, D.Y.L.; Jiang, Y. An institution-based view of international business strategy: A focus on emerging economies. *J. Int. Bus. Stud.* **2008**, *39*, 920–936. [CrossRef]
46. Cui, G.; Chan, T.S.; Huang, S. Global Firms Competing Locally: Management Localization and Subsidiary Performance in China. In *Multinationals and Global Consumers*; The AIB Southeast Asia Series; Chan, T.S., Cui, G., Eds.; Palgrave Macmillan: London, UK, 2013. [CrossRef]
47. Kang, Y.; Jiang, F. FDI Location Choice of Chinese Multinationals in East and Southeast Asia: Traditional Economic Factors and Institutional Perspective. *J. World Bus.* **2008**, *47*, 45–53. [CrossRef]
48. Dunning, J.H.; Lundan, S.M. Institutions and the OLI paradigm of the multinational enterprise. *Asia Pac. J. Manag.* **2008**, *25*, 573–593. [CrossRef]
49. Chan, C.M.; Makino, S. Legitimacy and multi-level institutional environments: Implications for foreign subsidiary ownership structure. *J. Int. Bus. Stud.* **2007**, *38*, 621–638. Available online: https://www.jstor.org/stable/4540446 (accessed on 1 October 2021). [CrossRef]
50. Ahuja, G.; Katila, R. Technological acquisitions and the innovation performance of acquiring firms: A longitudinal study. *Strateg. Manag. J.* **2001**, *22*, 197–220. Available online: https://www.jstor.org/stable/3094458 (accessed on 1 October 2021). [CrossRef]
51. Barkema, H.G.; Bell, J.H.; Pennings, J.M. Foreign entry, cultural barriers, and learning. *Strateg. Manag. J.* **1996**, *17*, 151–166. Available online: https://www.jstor.org/stable/2486854 (accessed on 1 October 2021). [CrossRef]
52. Baik, Y.; Kim, H.; Park, Y.-R. Environmental Multi-dimensionality and Staff Localization in Multinational Enterprises: The Case of Korean Firms. *Can. J. Adm. Sci.* **2021**, *38*, 68–79. [CrossRef]
53. Boyacigiller, N. The role of expatriates in the management of interdependence complexity and risk in multinational corporations. *J. Int. Bus. Stud.* **1990**, *21*, 357–381. Available online: https://www.jstor.org/stable/154951 (accessed on 1 October 2021). [CrossRef]
54. Harzing, A.W.; Pudelko, M. Do We Need to Distance Ourselves from the Distance Concept? *Why Home and Host Country Context Might Matter More Than (Cultural) Distance. Manag. Int. Rev.* **2016**, *56*, 1–34. [CrossRef]
55. Petersen, B.; Pedersen, T. Coping with liability of foreignness: Different learning engagements of entrant firms. *J. Int. Manag.* **2002**, *8*, 339–350. [CrossRef]
56. Singh, D.; Pattnaik, C.; Lee, J.Y.; Gaur, A.S. Subsidiary staffing, cultural friction, and subsidiary performance: Evidence from Korean subsidiaries in 63 countries. *Hum. Resour. Manag.* **2019**, *58*, 219–234. [CrossRef]
57. Hitt, M.A.; Hoskisson, R.A.; Kim, H. International diversification: Effects on innovation and firm performance in product-diversified firms. *Acad. Manag. J.* **1997**, *40*, 767–798. Available online: https://www.jstor.org/stable/256948 (accessed on 1 October 2021).
58. Chen, M.J.; Miller, D. West meets East: Toward an ambicultural approach to management. *Acad. Manag. Perspect.* **2010**, *24*, 17–24. [CrossRef]

59. Gates, S.R.; Egelhoff, W.G. Centralization in headquarters–subsidiary relationships. *J. Int. Bus. Stud.* **1986**, *17*, 71–92. Available online: https://www.jstor.org/stable/154584 (accessed on 1 October 2021). [CrossRef]
60. Song, J. Firm capabilities and technology ladders: Sequential foreign direct investments of Japanese electronics firms in East Asia. *Strateg. Manag. J.* **2002**, *23*, 191–210. Available online: https://www.jstor.org/stable/3094361 (accessed on 1 October 2021). [CrossRef]
61. Miller, S.R.; Parkhe, A. Is there a liability of foreignness in global banking? An empirical test of banks' X-efficiency. *Strateg. Manag. J.* **2002**, *23*, 55–75. Available online: https://www.jstor.org/stable/3094274 (accessed on 1 October 2021). [CrossRef]
62. Cavusgil, S.T.; Zou, S. Marketing strategy-performance relationship: An investigation of the empirical link in export market ventures. *J. Mark.* **1994**, *58*, 1–21. [CrossRef]
63. Edström, A.; Galbraith, J.R. Transfer of managers as a coordination and control strategy in multinational organizations. *Adm. Sci. Q.* **1977**, *22*, 248–263. [CrossRef]
64. Child, J. A configurational analysis of international joint ventures. *Organ. Stud.* **2002**, *23*, 781–815. [CrossRef]
65. He, Z.L.; Wong, P.K. Exploration vs. exploitation: An empirical test of the ambidexterity hypothesis. *Organ. Sci.* **2004**, *15*, 481–494. [CrossRef]

MDPI
St. Alban-Anlage 66
4052 Basel
Switzerland
Tel. +41 61 683 77 34
Fax +41 61 302 89 18
www.mdpi.com

Sustainability Editorial Office
E-mail: sustainability@mdpi.com
www.mdpi.com/journal/sustainability

www.ingramcontent.com/pod-product-compliance
Lightning Source LLC
Chambersburg PA
CBHW040807250926
51850CB00007BA/1105